The Talking Drums of Congo

The Story of
Two Trailblazers for God

Kim A. Halberg

Melvin and Eleanor Jorgenson
with Kim Halberg

ExulonELITE

The Talking Drums of Congo
The Story of Two Trailblazers for God
by Melvin and Eleanor Jorgenson with Kim Halberg

Edited by Xulon Press.

Printed in the United States of America

ISBN 9781498466752

Unless otherwise indicated, scripture quotations are taken from The King James Version (KJV). Used by permission. All rights reserved.

Maps illustrated by Karen Richardson.

All photographs from the Jorgenson family collection.

www.xulonpress.com

Dedication

W e would like to acknowledge with gratitude our Christian parents who trained us in the ways of the Lord.

Our son, Richard, and our daughter, Aldene, who have been a great blessing to us and who have shared wonderful and happy days with us as well as difficult, dangerous, and life-threatening times. Also, sharing their memories and personal stories to help complete the story.

We want to further acknowledge Kim Halberg, the co-author of this book, for her devoted heart for missions, and her dedication to mission work. It has been a joy to work with Kim as we shared our story, often with great emotions and tears. Without her, our story would have never been written.

Thank you Kim!

Without the prayers of family and our many friends who continually prayed for us during times when prayer was most needed, we truly believe we would not have survived.

Melvin and Eleanor Jorgenson retired from active mission work in July 1999. They currently reside in Burnsville, Minnesota, while staying in Lake Havasu City, Arizona during the harsh winter months.

Melvin, after retirement, taught an adult Bible class every Sunday morning for ten years and was awarded Teacher of the Year in 2005 by the General Council of the Assemblies of God.

Acknowledgments
from Kim Halberg

For my three sons, Carl, Peter and Jordan.
With thanksgiving to my Heavenly Father.

Kim Halberg splits her time between Minnesota, Florida, and Vieques, Puerto Rico. Numerous international trips working with missionaries and non-profit organizations have impacted her world view and given her insights for *The Talking Drums of Congo: The Story of Two Trailblazers for God.* Kim would like to offer her heartfelt appreciation to those friends and family (husband included) who supported, encouraged, and prayed for her during the past three years writing The Talking Drums of Congo. A special thank you to her diligent team of content readers: Stacy Bellward, Dan Erickson, Dale and Shirley Halberg, Joleen Kubiszewski, Kim Stariha, and Mike Tharp.

A final acknowledgement to the Jorgenson family—your family story is a gift to the world and honors God. Thank you for sharing your hearts and souls with me.

Melvin and Eleanor Jorgenson
December 2015

Table of Contents

❧

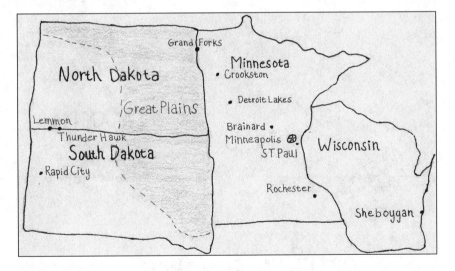

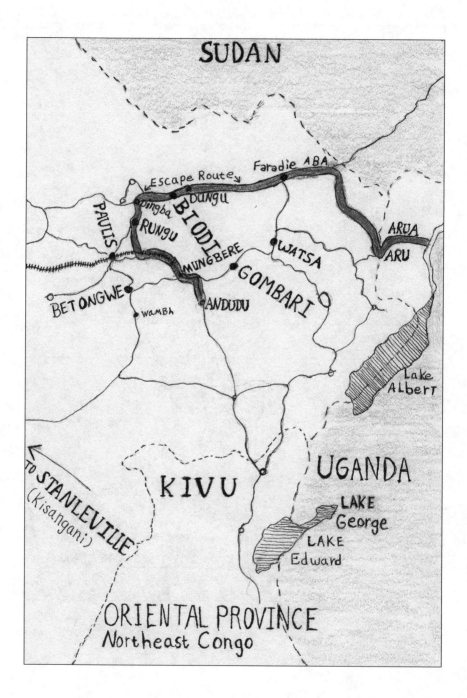

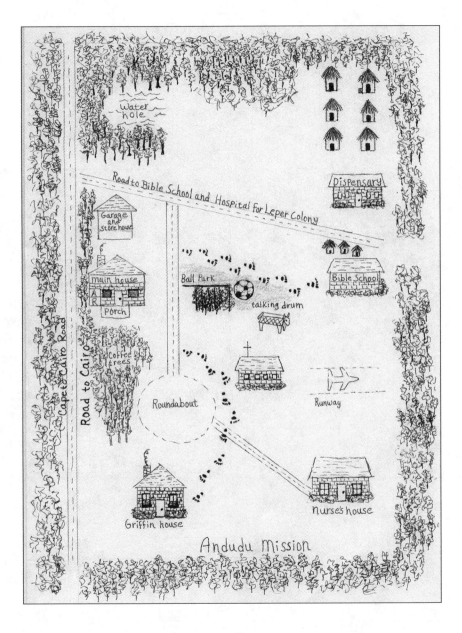

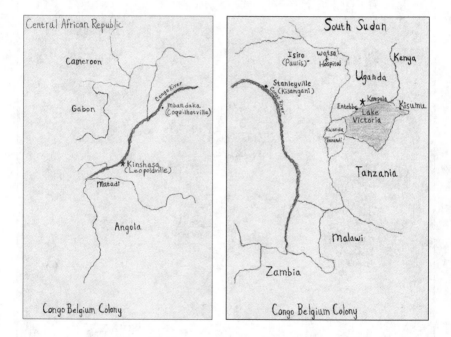

Remember...............THE JORGENSONS

Prologue

Africa, 1996

M elvin and Eleanor Jorgenson waited at the small airport in Isiro while the tropical rainstorm pelted the metal roof of the hanger. They were the older kind of couple that young people dream of growing into on their wedding day. Their fifty-one-year-old son Richard had taken time off from his job of international exports to join them for ten days of their month-long trip back to Congo. In 1971 the country was renamed Zaire when Mobutu sought to return the people to their African heritage after being a colony of Belgium.

"I guess if we have waited over thirty years, we can wait a few more hours," Melvin mused to his wife.

Next month they would be wed for fifty-three years. He smiled down at her face with glasses over his jaybird blue orbs. His aging frame of seventy-seven years stood tall, energized by the thought of returning to their former mission station in Andudu, nestled in the Ituri Rain Forest in northeast Zaire. "The last time we were here, Isiro was called 'Paulis'."

Eleanor returned his smile. Her hazel eyes shone brightly through her glasses, framed with softly curled sandy brown short hair, cropped short, "Yes, and the first time we came to Congo, we came through Leopoldville from the mouth of the Congo River." She let out a laugh, touching the arm of her husband. Her diminutive shoulders just reached his broad chest. "Then it was feasting on worm soup while riding the riverboat to Stanleyville for two weeks."

"I barely survived that trip," Melvin said, "but the Lord saw us through and a lot more after that."

"Yes, He certainly did," Eleanor returned. Then she commented, "It was a hard life living here, but it was a good life, wasn't it?"

"Yes, it was."

Richard made small talk with the other passengers waiting to embark on the small Cessna 206 operated by Missionary Aviation Fellowship. Gail Winters and Phil Cochrane, former colleagues of Melvin and Eleanor, were bonded to Richard and his parents in a way that only those who survive the crucible of a civil war together can be. Switching back and forth in conversation from Bangala to English and sometimes a bit of French, the tiny group quieted down when the pattering on the roof grew silent and the sun pierced through the sky to cook the red African dirt. By the time they flew into Andudu, the temperature would be stretching toward a humid ninety-two degrees.

After takeoff, the hum of the plane engine buzzed in their ears like a gargantuan mosquito. From Isiro to Andudu, it took a mere forty minutes, a trip that otherwise would be a four-hour drive on one hundred kilometers of bumpy dusty roads through the Ituri Rain Forest. As the red-striped plane made the journey southeast across grasslands, melting into rolling hills of forest veined with rivers, the pages of their lives turned back to gentler days when Melvin and Eleanor were young, and a call started sounding in their spirits for missionary work. Minutes ticked by and so did the memories.

In the back of their minds, and deep in the recesses of their hearts, their joyful days of living among the Congolese in the harsh conditions of the jungle mingled with the horrors of the evacuation when blood flowed and bodies were often tossed into watery crocodile-infested graves.

Flying among the clouds over a lush green canopy of foliage, everything came rushing back crystal clear for Melvin and Eleanor. Their last day in Andudu. The drive out. The rebel soldiers. . .the massacres. . .the screaming and wailing. . .the shooting. . .and the chopping of machetes against human flesh. Was it really February 1996 or was it August 1964?

Part One: The Call
1918-1950

Chapter One

Melvin Ernest Jorgenson

"It's a boy!" His parents, John Jorgenson and Anna Elizabeth Vick Jorgenson, discussed possible names while getting acquainted with their new son, born on April 8, 1918. Both immigrants from Norway, John had come from the town of Gyland, and Anna from Homvikia Sandnessjoen, an island accessed only by ship, in the northern part of Norway, close to Lapland, "Land of the Midnight Sun." Employed at Crookston Lumber Co., John Jorgenson made an adequate wage providing a comfortable living for his family.

All their children had been born in the white two-story house on 605 Pleasant Avenue that John built in the early 1900s, when the population of Crookston, Minnesota was eight thousand. The sturdy white clapboard sided house contrasted proudly with the black-pitched roof. Setting off the white eaves, a black triangle crowned the two upstairs bedroom windows seen from the street. On the right side of the house, a bay window to the dining room presided between the front and back of the house. The front porch had white walls the height of a table with three white pillars supporting its roof. Three steps down the porch to a sidewalk led to five cement steps fanned out to Pleasant Avenue. A black front door stood bravely on the right side of the porch, which opened to the hallway and stairs. Light filtered in from the front window. A davenport and several chairs assembled themselves on a thick area rug with cream tassels. The family piano rested along the interior wall to the living room.

Located in the Red River Valley region of northwest Minnesota, Crookston attracted many immigrants who plowed the rich fertile landscape of the prairies into farmlands. After the oxcart trails to St. Paul became the Pembia Trail pioneered by Joe Rolette, along came the railroads. Steamboats navigated the Red Lake River that coursed through Crookston like a finger-painted blue line winding up and down its neighborhoods and streets of shops, county courthouse, jail, churches, hotels, hospitals and one school. Flour and lumber mills, along with brickyards, a cigar factory, and foundry clustered around the river and railroad.

The Great Northern Railway and the North Western Railroad took travelers two hundred and ninety miles to Minneapolis every day except for Sundays. On July 29, 1895, one such train brought the Great American Humorist, Mark

Twain, for a lecture at the Grand Opera House, which was a part of the Crookston Hotel.

Married on the dawn of a new era on December 19, 1899, John and Anna's family had grown. Still, times were difficult for childbirth. Four of their ten children had died at birth or infancy, with dear Gladys, their fifth child, from scarlet fever at age three years and two days.

In light of those past sorrows, their son's safe arrival into the world was celebrated with joy and thanksgiving. Eventually, the proud parents were ready to announce his name to the rest of their five children. Myrtle, Josephine, Clarence, Julia, and four-year-old Lloyd waited in the living room. Finally, they heard the padding of their father's feet from the main floor bedroom. "Come and see your new brother, Melvin Ernest Jorgenson."

Resting in bed after her tenth delivery, Anna cradled the baby in her arms. The children called to their mother as they circled the bed. Lloyd's eyes widened as he inspected the bundled up creature. Anna reached out a gentle hand to him, "Come here, Lloyd." She smoothed his soft brown hair across his forehead and his shyness faded, "You're a big brother now. What do you think about that? Do you think you can help me look after Melvin Ernest?"

What it meant to be a big brother, Lloyd wasn't sure at this point. All he could manage was a nod, but it was a serious nod, and he was determined to do a good job. The three older children – Myrtle, Josephine and Clarence – wondered the obvious, *why Melvin Ernest?* John's patriotic answer satisfied their question, "Melvin and Ernest are names of two fallen soldiers who bravely fought in the Great War."

"We want to honor their memory and their families by having their names live on in our family," added Anna.

When Melvin Ernest was six months old, the war ended. Former enemies signed papers in a railroad car in France on November 11, 1918, Armistice Day.

A few years later, in 1921, along came baby Leona. Soon Anna settled back into her usual routine of cleaning, laundry and making the family meals. Her singsong voice could be heard throughout the home, "Josephine, Josephine you are so fine." Melvin toddled after Lloyd and in turn, after baby sister Leona found her legs, she was Melvin's shadow. This last trio of siblings would remain closely knit together for the rest of their lives no matter the distance.

Winters in Crookston could shrink the mercury down to an average of seventeen degrees to zero degrees Fahrenheit making the coal-fed heating stove work hard in the dining room. The stove radiated its warmth around the table and bay windows adorned with lush green roller curtains accented by Anna's treasured flowering plants. The chimney itself came up into the upstairs hallway to the second floor, heating the two bedrooms for Melvin and his sisters. The coal was loaded in the stove from the connected storage compartment with the main supply stored in the garage. On the side of the garage, a cord of split wood was neatly stacked for the cooking stove Anna used in the kitchen.

The backyard consisted of the garage and a small building with the chicken coop next to that, and an outhouse. An alley ran across the width of their city lot. Anna mainly took care of the chickens. However, John was the executioner. One night for dinner, he chopped the head off one robust chicken for dinner and it flip-flopped the length of the backyard, down alongside the house to the front yard. John came into the house triumphantly, "Our dinner almost ran to the neighbors before I tracked it down!"

Later after giving thanks for the meal, John retold the story to his children, "Anyone interested in eating the legs before they hop off the plate?"

Lloyd and Melvin looked the chicken legs over before they took their first bite. Anna and the older children laughed at their anxious faces. John had a twinkle in his eye that hid his uneasiness about the possibility of moving to look for better employment.

Melvin sat on the steps of the front porch that had a two-person swing suspended with chains. "One potato, two potato, three potato, four; five potato, six potato, seven potato more!"

Leona echoed him like a parrot counting on her chubby fingers. His mother came to the front door, "Look what I have for you, Melvin!" She held up a blue sailor styled shirt with white trim.

A few minutes later Melvin stood as best as he could for a five-year old, next to Leona who would not be still for long. Her soft white dress and dark shoes contrasted with Melvin's crisp sailor outfit, complete with the sailor hat. Melvin instinctively put a protective arm around Leona's tiny shoulder and kept her close. Their mother looked down the viewfinder finding the two figures in front of the dining room bay window.

Anna coaxed, "Now hold still, I want to get a snap of the two of you before you both get any bigger." Satisfied with the pose, she pressed the button on the Eastman Kodak camera.

Melvin didn't know where babies came from, but he knew his mother was going to have another one. However, for some reason the decision had been made to deliver at one of the local hospitals.

"It's another girl!" John announced to everyone after getting home from the hospital. He scooped up Leona in his arms, "You have a new little baby sister, Leona. What do you think about that?" He tickled her before he let her escape with a giggle.

The next day, John came home from the hospital with a look on his face Melvin had not seen before. It was ashen, twisted with pain, and a deep sadness filled his eyes. His father and the older children talked in hushed voices in the living room. No one was sitting on the davenport or chairs. Myrtle and Josephine began to cry openly. Julia ran upstairs to her room. Clarence's back stiffened as he took in the news. Something had happened at the hospital.

There was talk that the child was dropped. Melvin watched as his father and Lloyd left the house and went down the cement sidewalk to the steps that fanned outward to the street. In his left hand, John held a black nondescript suitcase. Later, there was a service for baby Irene. After the funeral, Melvin sat on the front porch in silence. Lloyd came through the black front door and sat by him.

"Why did Dad take that suitcase?"

"It was to carry the baby from the hospital to the funeral parlor." Lloyd picked at his shoelace for a moment. "They had wrapped her in a blanket. Dad kept saying how pretty she was and delicate like a china cup. He said he should have never let her be born there."

Slowly the Jorgenson family maneuvered through days filled with grief. The days turned into weeks, and then into months. Anna kept watering her plants in the dining room and making delicious meals. John split another cord of wood with the help of Clarence. The older girls, Myrtle and Josephine, chattered about the latest fashions and how much they cost. There was school for the older kids and John went to work. There was also sadness.

* * * * *

Lloyd liked chickens, but Melvin couldn't really tell by the way he treated them. One day, Lloyd got a stick and tried to get two roosters fighting, enjoying himself while the roosters were squawking. After he got tired of that, he singled out a rooster, poking it with a stick that had a nail on the end of it, which punctured the vital organs of the panic-stricken fowl. There was one last blood-curdling SQUAK! Then it gave up the ghost.

Suddenly, his father showed up with a spanking right on the spot. Melvin looked on with wide eyes and wisely decided not to follow in Lloyd's footsteps of persecuting the chickens. Despondent, Lloyd ran to the house with tears rolling down his face.

Working in the kitchen, Anna asked, "What are you crying for?"

"Dad spanked me!"

"Why?"

"Because I killed a rooster with a stick!"

Next thing Lloyd knew, he was getting a spanking from his mother. Right after this, John walked into the kitchen and was still so angry with Lloyd killing the rooster that he spanked his son a second time.

"This is enough. I'm leaving home," Lloyd pouted all the way to the alley for a bit. Then he came back.

Melvin watched the whole affair unfold and quietly went to the front porch, his favorite place to sit, play, or sway in the swing. Through the open window to the living room, he could hear his parents talking. At first, it was about Lloyd and his follies with the chickens. Then their voices turned somber as they talked about how much they would miss the house John built if they ever had to move. Melvin turned toward the shouting in the street. His parents came to the front door to hear their neighbors passing the tragic news, "The President is dead!"

After two years in office, President Warren G. Harding died suddenly from illness on August 2, 1923. He was the first president voted in by women. It was also a time when prohibition was in full swing, with flappers and the Charleston dance craze.

Chapter Two

Eleanor Aldene Groat

With the hope of spring, a daughter was born on March 4, 1919 in the windy prairie town of Lemmon, tucked just under the North Dakota border. Her parents, Edward and Hazel, were smitten with their firstborn child, Eleanor Aldene Groat.

"Just look at her." Edward James Groat told his wife, "A beautiful mix of English, Irish, and French."

A contented smile crossed Hazel's face, "Yes, she is that for sure, and healthy too. What a blessing from God."

At age twenty-three, Edward was also feeling the responsibility of providing for his family. He had married Miss

Hazel Bell Munyon on July 31, 1917, and now they were parents. Every so often, he felt it his duty to remind her that he had married an older woman. Born in Randolf, Nebraska, on June 3, 1895, Hazel had been born seven months before him in Decatur, Iowa, on October 31, 1894. They were midwestern folks of deep faith, practical values, and willing to work hard at carving out a life together in northwest South Dakota.

It had been the idea of the vice president of the railroad company to name the "Tent Town" after cattle rancher George Edward Lemmon, who had a significant range just east of there. After surveying the plentiful land available for ranching in 1902, Lemmon had set his mind to fencing in 865,000 acres of leased land on the Standing Rock Reservation. The three-wire fencing encompassed the largest pasture in the world at the time. The Chicago, Milwaukee, St. Paul, and Pacific Railroad mainline had begun operating in Thunder Hawk beginning in 1908 and the sleepy village woke up. In the fall of 1919, six months after Eleanor's birth, Edward purchased a general store in nearby Thunder Hawk and moved his family ten miles east.

A dirt street split the town into two boarded sidewalks like a row of piano keys on either side. Up and down boots and shoes would clomp out percussion beats to the bakery, feed store, two churches, black smith shop, and train depot. The one school was set back from the rest of the town's buildings. At the time, Thunder Hawk didn't have street names. The Groat family owned and operated a business simply known as "The General Store" that was easy to find on the main street. Their practical two-story two-bedroom house sat conveniently behind the store.

In 1920, Edward Groat received a government appointment as postmaster serving the outlying community in Corson

County. Rushing to make the deadline every day to the train depot with the outgoing mail, Edward would hang the mailbag on the metal hook that extended like a long bony finger. The passing train automatically collected the bag without stopping. That same year Edward added a meat market. He bought the cattle from a farmer and butchered it. He was pleased with the progress of his store and his family. Another girl, Esther, born a year after Eleanor, made them a family of four.

Their joy was short lived. Like other church folk, Eleanor's parents would take in people that were travelers in the ministry doing the Lord's work. These travelers might be evangelists or sometimes missionaries on furlough. One such evangelist came to stay in their home with his family. A few days after the family left, Hazel noticed a mucus discharge coming from Esther's nose. Soon Eleanor's nose looked the same. Hazel felt their foreheads, "You both feel warmer than usual. Let Mama cool your face with this cool rag."

Then came the coughing spasms, followed by a whooping gasp for air and vomiting. Hazel and Edward spent long nights walking the floor, soothing their children in their arms. Eleanor's parents didn't realize it, but the children of the travelers had been infected with pertussis, a respiratory infection commonly known as whooping cough. At eighteen months old, Eleanor was old enough to survive. Esther did not.

In the living room, Edward gently rocked his lifeless six-month-old daughter committing her into the hands of the Lord. Hazel cried softly. She kept glancing over at Eleanor in the bed they had made up in the living room to tend to her needs. Friends and relatives were in shock. The two girls had been so healthy and robust.

After the funeral, Edward sat in his chair looking out the kitchen window at nothing. "They must have known that their children were infected with the whooping cough when they stayed with us. It was right after they left when the babies got sick. No other family in Thunder Hawk was infected. How could they take advantage of our hospitality like that?"

Hazel could see her husband was wrestling with anger and forgiveness. She had no words to offer him. Everything was flat right now. She felt sucked into a tunnel of grief with no way out.

Eleanor slowly recovered and began filling out again. She bounded around the house and yard with the endless energy of a two-year-old. Her thoughtful hazel eyes captured everything around her while brown curls danced around her face. Edward focused on The General Store and running the mail to the train depot every day except on Sunday

"Come on, Eleanor," her mother called to her from the kitchen, "It's time to go help Daddy at the store."

Together they walked the few feet from their house to the back door of the store. People were shopping for general goods, while others were exchanging tidbits of news and gossip.

* * * * *

When Eleanor was three years old, both mother and daughter were sick in bed with the mumps. Every time Eleanor chewed or swallowed, her throat hurt. After a few days, little Eleanor decided she had enough of being sick.

"Why should I lay here with this pain," she said to her mother, "when Jesus can make me well?"

After that, Eleanor got up and her mumps disappeared. However, poor Mother continued in her affliction for the normal course due that illness.

Eleanor's parents had taught her at an early age about Jesus and healing power. Long before Eleanor's parents were married, a revival had swept through the Midwest prairies that changed people's lives. Many people became Christians who believed the biblical stories of healings, and the filling of the Holy Spirit, were more than historical information. Because there were no church buildings for the Pentecostal believers, people met in their homes for prayer meetings, much like the early disciples of Jesus.

The arrival of Lorraine on June 25, 1923 made Eleanor a big sister. Posing for a family portrait, Eleanor sat between her parents on the living room couch holding Lorraine. Eleanor's dark hair was gathered into a white bow on the crown of her head with short bangs hung across her brow several inches above hazel eyes identical to her mother. Her dress had a nautical style with a white-trimmed collar and sailor tie. Edward smiled at her attentiveness to Lorraine. His thick hairline crept back a bit each year, but he still was a handsome match for his beautiful Hazel. Her dark long-sleeved dress fell below her knees, with woven stockings and black boots with tiny buttons on each side. Her chocolate-brown hair curved softly around her oval face. Four-year-old Eleanor leaned in slightly toward her mother never taking her eyes off her new little sister.

During this time, a missionary from India would stay at their home when she was on furlough. If Edward had any reservations about having visitors stay in his home again, Eleanor didn't hear him voice them. She found herself slipping into the welcoming arms of this kind woman wearing a simple print dress. She situated herself comfortably on the missionary's lap. Then, the stories about the children in India would begin. In her mind, Eleanor could picture everything Miss Eunice Lee was telling her.

When people would ask the classic question, "What do you want to be when you grow up?" Eleanor's immediate reply would be, "I want to be a missionary."

"Where are you going to be a missionary?"

"I don't know. All I know is I am going to be a missionary one day."

Another aspect of Eleanor's faith shining bright for all to see was singing sacred melodies. Wherever they would go, Eleanor would stand on a chair or stool and sing songs such as, "I remember when my burdens rolled away, I had carried them for years night and day. . .and at last all my burdens rolled away."

Tent meetings were also part of young Eleanor's life. After men hammered stakes into the ground and thick ropes were in place, the tent reached slowly toward the sun. Chairs, placed in neat rows, waited for people from Thunder Hawk and nearby Lemmon. A piano was moved in place for Eleanor's mother to play. Even at her tender age, Eleanor grasped what was going on at these meetings. After the music came the preaching. After that came the altar calls for souls to come forward to pray for salvation through Jesus Christ. A friend of Hazel's would hold Eleanor's hand as they walked to the tent meeting. One night on the way to a meeting Eleanor exclaimed to her mother's friend, "I hope a lot of Catholics get saved tonight."

That August of 1923, Eleanor's parents listened intently to the radio in the living room as the news crackled over the speaker. Vice President Calvin Coolidge was sworn in as President at 2:34 a.m., after President Harding's sudden death the day before. Eleanor sat on the area rug playing with her dolls, while baby sister Lorraine slept, cradled in Hazel's arms.

Chapter Three

Sheboygan

❦

"We're moving," Melvin's father announced at the family dinner table in Crookston. All eyes fastened on him. Questions peppered from Myrtle, Josephine, Clarence, Julia and Lloyd. Melvin listened quietly, while Anna attended to Leona in her wooden high chair.

"Where?"

"Sheboygan. It's about six hundred and forty miles east of here along the shores of Lake Michigan, north of Milwaukee."

Several of the older children snuck a look at Anna.

"I was offered a job with Kohler." John continued, "They make enameled bathtubs and fixtures for indoor plumbing."

Melvin chewed on this information a bit. His family didn't have an indoor bathroom.

The next few weeks, the Jorgenson home was a beehive of sorting, packing, and cleaning. The long dining room table had a hollow center pedestal with claw feet. Anna wrapped items in cloth rags to pack in the pedestal. Melvin sat on the porch, hoping to return to Crookston one day. Maybe they could find renters for their beloved white home with the friendly porch swing while they lived in Sheboygan.

Finally, the day came when the Jorgenson family took the train from Crookston to Duluth, the halfway point. The vast waters of Lake Superior greeted them as they pulled into the depot. The whistle blew, and they were on their way again.

Melvin watched the Wisconsin scenery fly past the window, his lean frame acquiesced to the rhythm as the train swayed back and forth on the tracks to Sheboygan, a city split in half by the Sheboygan River. Upstream at the falls, close to inflowing Muller River, was the birthplace of Sheboygan's first sawmill. The Potawatomi referred to the falls and its tumble down to the lake as "great noise underground," the Chippewa calling it, "Schwab-we-way-kum".

After arriving in Sheboygan, the Jorgenson family of nine settled into unpacking and organizing their lives. Anna began sorting out her kitchen, and the next day John began his new job at Kohler Company at the melting pit. As Anna walked the streets named after various trees, she noticed all the furniture stores. On the corner of Chestnut and Indian Avenue was Northern Furniture Co. On the outskirts of town, a smoke stack like a mast on a ship rose high above the Sheboygan Chair Co., billowing out black clouds. Men built the furniture and the furniture built the local economy. At one time, people called Sheboygan the "city of cheese, chairs, churches, and children - the four C's."

Mr. and Mrs. Jorgenson found a church to attend and enrolled their children in school. Melvin's first day of kindergarten at Pigeon River School didn't go so well. He felt alone in the new school and couldn't find the bathrooms. He soon became Mrs. Bonesack's favored teacher's pet. Whenever anyone would ask Melvin how old he was, he would reply, "I am five-and-a-half years old."

Melvin enjoyed playing outside, doing all the usual things winter brings for the young living in northern climates. With the lake effect, the depth of snow in the banks of the roads in Sheboygan could be daunting. One snowstorm dumped enough white powder to block the highway with banks ten feet deep in front of Melvin's home. His father, Clarence, and Lloyd shoveled paths through the towering drifts swirled across the neighborhood like meringue on a giant cream pie. Meanwhile, Melvin and some neighbor boys had created trenches for fortification of their domain. As Melvin was making snowballs, a boy across the trench from Melvin asked in a quavering voice, "You're making so many snowballs and you're throwing them at me?"

Melvin's eyes twinkled with mischief, "Yeah!"

* * * * *

One day Melvin came home from school to find his father in bed. John worked along the cart tracks on the edge of the melting pit used to refine the ore brought into the factory. It was the first step in manufacturing Kohler Co. products. A cart filled with the raw ore ran into him and he lost his balance. One leg caught on the edge of the pit. He steadied himself above a sea of pulsating coals of blistering heat, one step away from a sulfuric death. John limped around home for a couple weeks before returning to work.

In 1929, common stock prices rose to record highs and sixty percent of Americans were making less than $2,000 per year, barely enough to survive. On Tuesday, October 29, 1929, the stock market crashed. The depression hit nation-wide. It hit hard. Melvin's father came home from work to tell his family he had lost his job.

After the train ride back to Crookston, ten-year-old Melvin sat on the porch at 605 Pleasant Avenue. It was a big change to leave a third of the family behind in Wisconsin.

Myrtle, Josephine, and Clarence were married and would remain in Sheboygan with their spouses.

It was during this time that John Jorgenson began a home improvement project to turn the cellar into a basement, which would allow room for a potential boarder. With the downturn of the economy, people had to be creative in generating income. Melvin stood ready with the shovel in his hands. Dirt flew up from the cellar through a small window in the block foundation. Once the pile was a decent mound, young Melvin would shovel the dirt into the wheelbarrow for his father to roll it across their street to the riverbank a half-block away. After hand-excavating the cellar, a cement floor poured and stud walls built, Lloyd and Melvin moved down to their new room, and a renter was found.

Life got into a routine going to the Norwegian Lutheran Church in town on Sunday and John going to work as a carpenter for Great Northern Railway yard. Anna kept the house running smoothly and began sewing clothes for the winter.

The long summer days grew shorter until September brought the beginning of school for Julia, Lloyd, Melvin and Leona. After school, Melvin practiced his piano lessons before going outside to play marbles. He had started taking lessons from a piano teacher who boarded with their family. While having a boarder stretched the family budget, it also meant Melvin's piano teacher knew how much he practiced. In the living room, Melvin sat at the Marlboro upright piano from Chicago and practiced his scales. He began singing as his young fingers marched up the ivory keys, "do-re-mi-fa-so-la-ti-do."

His mother came in with a smile from the kitchen, "I'm making biscuits for dinner tonight. Would you please go to the dairy, Melvin, and pick up a gallon of buttermilk for me?"

"Yeah, sure, Mom."

After Melvin got to the dairy, he grabbed the wire handle for the covered metal pail. By the time he got home, a few blocks away, his arms were feeling a bit longer. He soon recovered after delivering the buttermilk to his mother. Now it was time to play marbles with Armand Gammy who lived across the street. First, they drew a circle on the sidewalk. With tongues set in one corner of their mouth and eyes squinted, they began aiming the prized agate at the marbles. *Click* went the sound of glass marbles colliding. The trick was to get one out of the circle without losing your agate.

"Let's play the Sheboygan way," Melvin suggested.

"I thought we already were," Armand said.

"That was how to shoot the agate with your thumb at the other marbles," Melvin explained.

Both boys sat on the sidewalk spreading their legs as far apart as possible. They were in the midst of a hot battle when suddenly hands scooped up their marbles. Dismayed, Melvin and Armand watched the bigger kids walk away laughing.

That fall, Melvin's mother finished the sewing project she had in mind for Melvin. She held up the brown jacket with buttons, in front of Melvin to make sure it would fit properly at waist length, "This should keep you warm walking to and from school."

"Thank you, Mom," Melvin beamed his appreciation, "It looks swell."

The next day Melvin buttoned up his new brown jacket and smoothed it down to his waist. It looked so nice with his pants. Melvin didn't wear knickers anymore like he did when he first started school in Sheboygan. On his way to school, Melvin saw his shadow and stood up straighter and taller feeling proud of the jacket his mother had made for him.

That summer, Melvin's mother bought him his first swimsuit for seventy-five cents. It was a cardinal red one-piece with a scooped front that came all the way over the shoulders. Melvin felt proud of that suit when he went to the downtown city pool. He would throw a stone into the deep end of the pool and dive in after it. Beyond the city pool was Central Park, which had a few baseball diamonds for adult leagues and an organized city league for kid's softball. Melvin joined, and his coach played him at second base.

The cool fall days drifted into winter frost and frozen lakes. Melvin opened up the front door to check the milk bottles the milkman had delivered. The caps had popped up a bit from the glass bottles stored in the wire crate, but the milk wasn't entirely frozen. Melvin carried the milk past the fully adorned Christmas tree in the living room with brightly wrapped gifts tucked under its pine canopy. Wonderful smells of Christmas greeted him in the kitchen. Beside pies, there were other baked pastries filling every space available including the dining room. For Christmas Eve, there would be lutefisk (codfish soaked in lye) topped with melting butter, salt and pepper. Steaming mashed potatoes and vegetables rounded out their plates. On Christmas Day, the meal consisted of meatballs, potato lefsa, and all the pastries a person could fill themselves with. Sometimes a few of Melvin's older siblings and their growing families would take the train from Sheboygan and stay overnight.

With Christmas past and April spring flowers starting to break bravely from winter's sleep, a lanky Melvin turned thirteen. Usually he spent Saturday mornings at confirmation classes. After baptism as a baby, the next important event was confirmation into the Norwegian Lutheran Church. During the past year, Melvin began reading for the minister Saturday mornings. Not only did Melvin learn a lot about the Christian faith in the classes, he also grew in his ability to speak confidently in front of a group of people. He would always say in the future, "Lutherans are good teachers."

At the time, Melvin didn't know that in a few months the compass of his soul and destiny would be set. Christian Hild would walk into Crookston with the Holy Ghost fire of revival and the ordinary life of this confirmed Lutheran would be turned upside down. Until then, life moved along filled with all the adventures young boys enjoy growing up in a small town set between the twists and turns of the Red Lake River.

Chapter Four

Dakota Prairie

"Eleanor, time for your bath." Hazel filled the washtub in the kitchen with warm water from the reservoir on the stove. "We have to get you all cleaned up for your first day of school."

Soapsuds foamed in Eleanor's brown hair while Hazel sang a hymn. After slipping into her nightclothes, Eleanor took one more look at her outfit for school. Her new dress would have to be changed for play clothes when she got home. Black shoes with a strap coming across the middle fastened by a round button sat on the floor.

Miss Montgomery taught grades one and two. "Good Morning, Eleanor! Welcome to first grade. You may sit over there in the row by the window."

Eleanor shyly sat down in the wooden desk. She surveyed the room of books, maps, black boards, and a picture of President Calvin Coolidge. A boy sat behind her. After the school bell rang, Miss Montgomery took attendance and explained the rules of the classroom.

"Now, when the Catholic Priest comes in, stand and say 'Good morning, Father'."

Miss Montgomery, a Catholic herself, was quite pleased to have the priest come to her classroom. A puzzlement filled Eleanor's eyes. She wondered what her mother would think. Eleanor didn't know much about Catholics, but she knew that she was a Pentecostal Protestant and that Catholics and Protestants were different. Then she remembered her Grandma Groat was an Irish Catholic. She died the year before Eleanor started going to school. Her mom told her she was a beautiful Christian lady. After that Grandpa Groat would come and live with them for a period of time. He didn't have a preference of faith. Eleanor's father would talk about Nebraska and growing up there, but they never went back to visit anyone.

Winter came and melted into March. It was Eleanor's birthday and she knew that Dad would make homemade ice cream. Eleanor watched him drop ice and salt in between the wooden bucket and the metal container filled with cream and sugar. Eleanor and Lorraine swarmed their father like flies on honey watching him crank the turning wheel paddle on the bucket, "Is it getting done yet?"

"Just a little longer," Edward's eyes danced brightly at the impatience of his two daughters, "go ahead and get out the spoons."

He laughed as Eleanor and Lorraine ran and reappeared, "You two remind me of prairie dogs popping in and out of their holes."

"M-m-m, you make the best ice cream, Daddy." Eleanor enjoyed the cold creamy vanilla taste in her mouth for a moment before swallowing and dipping her spoon back into her bowl.

Later that fall, after Eleanor started second grade with Miss Montgomery, Wayne was born on a crisp November day in 1926. Seven-year-old Eleanor proudly held her baby brother while Lorraine talked to him about Christmas coming soon. Christmas was a wonderful occasion in the Groat home. The house was decorated and Hazel made oyster stew, Edward's favorite, for Christmas Eve dinner. Later, they would gather around the piano and sing Christmas carols together as the stove in the living room kept the cold South Dakota winters at bay.

Instead of looking for wrapped gifts under the tree, Eleanor had to find her gifts hidden in the pine-scented boughs. Her parents sat late into the night waiting to secretly slip a gift in the tree for each other. Then, waking between four and five o'clock, the Groat family drove out to farms to sing carols. To keep warm they loaded up robes and blankets, and placed heated red bricks at their feet. One of Hazel's friends, Hilda Jackson, joined them in their quest to wake up people with some Christmas cheer singing by bedroom windows. Hazel and Hilda also sang duets, as Hazel played the piano for church and for funerals in the community.

The Christmas of 1928 was a memorable one because of the birth of Lois. However, the next Christmas was very different. Herbert Hoover became president two months before Eleanor turned ten years old. In October, when the stock market crashed on Black Tuesday, Lorraine was six and Wayne was on his way to turning three. By the time Lois reached her first birthday, it would be a different world.

In their room upstairs, Eleanor and Lorraine lay on their stomachs, looking through the floor vent. The two sisters peered into the living room. Mother and Hilda Jackson were practicing duets, while Mother played the piano. Eleanor felt content in their home. She shared a bed with Lorraine and had nice clothes to wear to school and church. Every time she slipped into her Sunday shoes and fastened the strap across with a button, she would turn her feet a bit admiring the hard glossy black patent leather. One time, Lorraine tried to get her Sunday clothes on and go somewhere and her folks wouldn't allow it.

Eleanor leaned toward the floor vent trying to catch her mother's soft voice, "I'm so looking forward to seeing Grandpa George and Grandma Bell this Sunday after morning prayer meeting. It's nice to get away from town and the store for a visit with them. Their sod house is so cool in the summer."

"Did you hear that?" Eleanor elbowed her sister, "We're going to Great-Gramps and Great-Grams for dinner this Sunday!"

Everyone in the family knew Grandma Bell made the best biscuits and gravy in the county. Hazel's parents had also been "sod busters" when they first came to South Dakota in a covered wagon from Iowa. Grandpa Munyon's health was not good, and they heard the South Dakota air was healthy compared to hot and muggy Iowa.

When Hazel was twelve years old, she was already an accomplished pianist. In light of this, Grandpa Munyon placed an order for the piano to be shipped to South Dakota. A lot of musicians and schoolteachers came along, with people from all walks of life to remain there a while to claim the land. Someone organized a band for entertainment and dances were held at a schoolhouse or town hall in the larger towns of Meadow and Coldsprings.

Years later, Hazel shared the memory with her children: "I would play the piano for the dances and concerts. They had people from Chicago who brought their musical talents as well. We were out there just having a good time together until they homesteaded, and then they could go back home."

During this time of homesteading, someone brought the message of Pentecost to Uncle Lute Brown. He was a

Baptist minister from Iowa. Someone explained to him about the second birth, a spiritual birth known as "getting saved." After believing in Jesus Christ for the forgiveness of sins, an internal transformation began. A second experience, known as "filled with the Holy Spirit," gave the believer empowerment to live the Christian life. This second experience, also called the Baptism of the Holy Spirit, was often accompanied by "speaking in tongues" as the disciples of Jesus did at Pentecost. Uncle Lute eagerly wanted to share what the Lord had done for him, so he came to South Dakota and held meetings in various schoolhouses.

He also brought the message of Pentecost to his relatives. They would tarry, waiting on the Holy Spirit to come with power in their midst as recorded in the book of Acts. Besides preaching, Lute Brown decided he needed someone to play the piano and sing: "Hazel, would you be willing to give up playing at the dances and play for the Lord instead?"

A young woman now, Hazel answered, "Uncle Lute, my days of playing for the dances are over!" The decision was firmly etched in her soul, "If I'm going to live for the Lord I'm going to be 'all hog or none.'"

During the Prairie Revival of the early 1900's, Hazel traveled with Uncle Lute Brown bringing the message of Pentecost to whoever would listen. Some of her musician friends couldn't believe the news when they heard it – "Oh, come now, Hazel, can't you still play for our dances? What's the harm in that?"

Hazel stood true to her convictions and prayed for a husband that would do the same. Saved, and filled with the Holy Spirit, Edward Groat was the answer to that prayer. Together they would raise their children to know the love and forgiveness of Jesus Christ and the riches of His resurrection power for their daily lives.

That Sunday, after the morning prayer meeting, Edward and Hazel loaded up the Chevrolet with their four children. The car jostled across the prairie for an hour or so for a visit with George and Bell Miller, Eleanor's great-grandparents. Eleanor sat in the back with Lorraine and Wayne, while Lois rode up front with their parents. The wooden-spoke tires rolled along the dirt roads winding through the sea of undulating grasses. There was always wind on the Great Plains and today Eleanor was grateful for the breeze on her face on a warm summer day.

As long as she could remember, her father had always had a car. He also had a "puddle-jumper," as they called it. The puddle-jumper was a combination of a wooden wagon with an engine on the front instead of a horse. Edward used it daily for going to get beef and other things for the store. Fritz, their brindle-coated Boston Bull Terrier, would bark up a storm unless allowed a spot on the front seat. Usually a quiet, well-mannered dog for living in town, Fritz got a bit stubborn about the puddle-jumper.

A startled ringed neck pheasant spread its multicolored wings to escape the iron predator. Rust and black tail feathers made for a graceful flight away from them. An abundance of prairie dogs poked in and out of holes much to the children's amusement. A flat, treeless landscape floated by with cattle ranches and farms.

Soon the fences to keep George and Bell's cattle in stretched across the horizon. At the gate, Eleanor's father stopped the car, unhitched the gate, drove through, and then hitched the gate back up again.

"There goes a chicken's neck," Wayne exclaimed, "I can't wait for those biscuits and gravy."

"Me either," agreed Eleanor.

There was no phone at the sod house to call about their coming, but great-grandma Bell heard the gate swing and by the time the car got to the sod house, a chicken's neck would be wrung and she was plucking the feathers off the limp bird. Soon after exchanging greetings, chicken and gravy and biscuits were being prepared for a meal.

"Look at the roof. There are flowers growing in with the grass," Hazel pointed out.

With trees being scarce, the sturdy sod house had been carved out from the thick carpet of prairie grass. The tightly knitted grass roots enabled cut blocks of sod to be put together just like a brick house. Not only was a sod house cool in the summer it was equally warm in the winter with no need to worry about it burning down. Only the out buildings for storage and the outhouse were built with wood. A water bucket by the well completed the quaint picture of prairie living.

Inside, the sod house was decorated with wallpaper and wall-to-wall woven rugs nailed to the floor. When it was time to wash the rugs, Bell would take the rug floor apart, wash it, and reassemble it again. In the kitchen, there was a cast iron stove and oven, which was the main source of heat. There was no fireplace. During the summer and fall, they would gather dried cow dung, and store it in a shed next to the outhouse to burn as fuel in the winter.

A few windows let in light throughout the house. In the corner of the living room, George sat in his rocking chair, smoking his pipe. After dinner, talk turned to the economic depression, the drought and Mt. Rushmore.

"We haven't seen a lick of rain all summer." Grandpa George's pipe smoke circled above him while the rocker creaked in rhythm, "Usually we get around nineteen inches a year."

"That'll mean hard times for the ranchers and farmers," Edward said. "Hopefully they can hold on till next year."

"Times are bad enough with the depression and all," George kept puffing and rocking, "You still planning on going to the Black Hills?"

"Yes, sir," Edward beamed, "I'm hoping to get a string of trout. Nothing better for breakfast than fried fish and potatoes cooked over an open fire." Then he thought for a moment, "Except for hunting of course."

"That sculptor is blasting away on Mt. Rushmore, so be careful a rock doesn't fall on your head," Grandma Bell teased.

Hazel had been reading the newspapers about the new monument project. "Eleanor will probably be a married woman by the time Gutzon Borglum gets all those Presidents carved out of that mountain side."

"What an undertaking," Edward said. "I'll stick to running the General Store."

Chapter Five

Sufficient Grace

Thirteen-year-old Eleanor walked home from school for the noon meal. Tumbleweeds blew between her legs. Dirt stung her eyes. The wind picked at the scarf protecting her nose and mouth. She turned a couple times to make sure Lorraine was still coming. It was a bad time for the Dakotas and the Great Plains of America. In Thunder Hawk, and most of South Dakota, there were few trees to break the wind. The farmers had stripped off the prairie taking with it the tightly knotted roots that kept the precious fertile topsoil intact. Cattle ate whatever they could find, which wasn't much after the drought began in 1931. Often a rancher would find dirt inside a dead cow's stomach.

Eleanor shook the dirt off her scarf and outer coat just outside the door of their house. Lorraine did the same and they slipped into the oasis of the kitchen. Fritz met them at the door wiggling his compact brindle body down to his short tail. The dog's intelligent eyes and erect ears took in everything.

"I feel like we're dressed for a blizzard out there, but it is dirt instead of snow."

"I miss the snow and sledding on Pumpkin Butte. Wouldn't it be fun to pull out the sled and take a run down the hill?"

"Hello girls," Mother greeted them. "Get washed up. Dinner is ready."

All six heads of the Groat family bowed in prayer before they partook in the main meal of the day. Fritz sat in the kitchen with his white chest and muzzle like a butler in formal wear. He did not beg.

Because Mother spent the afternoon at the store helping Dad, dishes were left in the sink for Eleanor to wash and dry later. After school was done for the day, Eleanor had to go directly home. Her other friends could do whatever and go wherever after school, but not Eleanor. She helped with meals and watched the other children. Eleanor dreaded the sink full of dirty dishes when she got home from school. It was the largest meal of the day, so it was no small matter cleaning up the kitchen. She began filling the wash pan with water from the reservoir on the stove. Eleanor knew Lorraine was old enough to help her. For some reason Lorraine's stomach got upset when it came time for washing dishes, and she excused herself for a visit to the outdoor biffy. The only time Eleanor got a break from the mountain of plates, cups, pots, pans, and utensils was when Grandma Munyon would come and stay. A gifted seamstress, Grandma Munyon made clothes out of old suits in between cleaning the kitchen and attending the younger children.

* * * * *

As Eleanor matured she helped with customers at the General Store, but mostly she did work at home, so Mother could help Dad. Now that she was a teenager, she knew how to prepare dinner for a family of six, cooking whatever Mother set out for the next meal. Eleanor worked on the coals in the blue porcelain iron range. It had two warmers up above, a reservoir for water connected to the stove on the right, and an oven for baking cakes. Sometimes Eleanor would put a roast in the oven or she would make fried chicken. She learned the art of banking the coals in the stove to get the heat just right.

One morning, Grandma and Grandpa Munyon gathered around the table with their daughter's family. Edward finished his breakfast with one last sip of coffee. "Eleanor, can you help your mother with the customers? Fritz and I are heading to the butcher's shop. I picked up a cow yesterday. It's been hanging overnight to cool, and I think it's ready to cut up."

Curled up on the kitchen floor for a morning snooze, the Boston Bull Terrier snapped to attention ready for the puddle-jumper. "Come along my American Gentleman!" Edward called to his side-kick.

"I'll see to the dishes," Grandma Munyon offered as she cleared off the table stacking dishes next to the sink with the attached water pump.

Lorraine and Wayne ran off to play, while Lois stayed close to Grandma. Eleanor walked past the icehouse to the back door of the store. In the winter, her father cut big blocks of ice from the Cedar River and hauled them to the icehouse. Then he took bales of straw to put around the ice to keep it frozen all summer long.

During the Great Depression years, when President Roosevelt was working out his New Deal programs, the government sent welfare help to the store in Thunder Hawk. Eleanor's father gave instructions to Eleanor and her mother, "Each family gets one case of grapefruit."

Eleanor looked at the fresh grapefruit almost tasting the pinkish-orange flesh, "Do we get a case?" she hoped.

"No. I'm sorry; it's only for those on welfare."

Eleanor handed out the cases of fruit with as much kindness as she could muster. Dad would give groceries away to people in need, but he didn't get much back in return. She would always remember her father as a good businessman with a big heart.

That December, on Christmas morning at six o'clock, Eleanor nudged her sleeping sister.

"Loraine," she prodded the lump next to her again, "Wake up! It's time to find our gifts."

Eleanor searched through the pine boughs. The scent reminded her of family vacations in the Black Hills. There were hardly any trees on the prairie where she lived, so it was such a pleasure to surround herself with Black Hills Spruce and Ponderosa Pine sprinkled in with aspen, bur oak, and birch. Ornaments tinkled and shimmered as Eleanor kept searching for her gift. She had come across everyone else's nametag but her own.

"Oh, there it is!" She slipped the silver watch with a white face onto her wrist. It was as beautiful as the ring made from Black Hills gold she had gotten a few years before that.

* * * * *

Another year passed by at Thunder Hawk School for Eleanor as she blossomed into a young woman. At the General Store she picked up the earpiece from the side hook of the crank phone on the wall and turned the crank two longs and one short on the ringer. She could hear receivers going down the line while she waited for the call to go through to her cousins Margret and Anna. There were no secrets in this town.

One of her cousins answered the phone, "Hello?"

"Hello. It's Eleanor. When can Uncle bring you girls into town again?"

"I'm not sure. Maybe you can come out here. I'll talk to Mother."

During the winter, Uncle Dick brought his daughters into town for school using the horse and sleigh. However, once school let out for the summer, the girls usually had to wait for a visit with the folks, or an errand of some type, to bring them into town. Margret and Anna, who were on Grandma Munyon's side of the family, felt more like sisters to Eleanor than cousins, and were her closest friends.

Eleanor hung the earpiece back in the side hook and waited for her father to finish up with a customer. "Dad, when do you think we can go out to Uncle Dick and Aunt Edith's again? I would like to try out my Brownie camera in the Petrified Wood Park."

"Talk to your mother. I think she and Aunt Edith were making some kind of plans. Otherwise, I might need to run an errand in that direction this week. I could drop you off."

Besides running the store, butchering his own meat, managing the icehouse, and postal duties, Edward ran a delivery service for people.

After Sunday dinner at Uncle Dick and Aunt Edith's home in the country, Eleanor and her cousins went to the Lemmon Petrified Wood Park to take snaps with the Brownie camera. There wasn't much else for the young women to do with their free time, so the new attraction seemed an interesting destination for them. Local town men under the supervision of an amateur geologist had built it. The three girls wandered through the city block of piled sculptures made from petrified wood, fossil bones, and stones looking for the right place for a snapshot. The cardboard box camera made by Eastman Kodak cost one dollar when first introduced in the early 1900's and was easy enough for amateur photographers to use.

* * * * *

Another uncle, Edward's brother, lived on a farm near Thunder Hawk. Uncle Roy and Kitty didn't have any children, but Eleanor and Wayne were often invited to come for a stay. They would go out there for a week or so spending their time riding over the prairie or trying to hit targets. Aunty Kitty had been a cowgirl, so teaching Eleanor to ride and shoot seemed a normal activity for a girl.

Uncle Roy had his favorite horse that was trustworthy enough for Eleanor to ride. After cinching the western saddle on the palomino, and checking the bridle, Uncle Roy handed over the reins to Eleanor, "Here you go."

"Thanks, Uncle Roy," Eleanor said as she slipped her left foot into the stirrup and deftly mounted the horse.

The vast prairie spread out before them like an ocean. They picked their way along the trail through sagebrush while leather saddles creaked on the horses' muscular frames. Suddenly, there was a rattle and Eleanor's horse spooked. Before she realized what had happened Eleanor sailed off to a hard landing on the sand.

When Eleanor got home, Aunt Kitty made a fuss over her, "What happened?"

Uncle Roy relayed the story while Aunt Kitty checked Eleanor over for injuries.

"I'm fine really. Look, no broken bones, just a few bruises," Eleanor tried to brush off the incident.

After dinner, Uncle Roy sat down with Wayne and taught him how to roll cigarettes. Eleanor knew her mother would not be happy. Uncle Roy rolled his own cigarettes and now he had Wayne rolling cigarettes for him. Unlike Uncle Dick and Aunt Edith, they were not of the Pentecostal tradition. In fact, they never went to church. Period. When Hazel got saved during the prairie revival and quit playing at the dance band, Uncle Roy wasn't happy with his sister-in-law.

Hazel had responded boldly, "I quit. If I'm going to live for the Lord I'm going to be 'all hog or none'."

Eleanor thought of this story often. There was a cost in following Jesus. Not just believing He came at Christmas, died on Good Friday, and rose victoriously Easter morning as many fine Christians believed. Raised in a family of strong faith and Christian practices, Eleanor could not remember not knowing Jesus as her Lord and Savior. Yet, there came a day that marked a spiritual experience for Eleanor that she would recall the rest of her life, as if it had happened the day before.

On Sunday, town and country families gathered for church services held in homes. Eleanor's mother was always at the piano singing. After reading and discussing the word of God, long sessions of prayer followed. At home, it was the same, reading the Bible with Edward and Hazel praying with their children for various needs. Eleanor was thankful for her Christian upbringing. She enjoyed singing hymns and playing the piano. She read her Bible out of desire and not duty. Her faith kept growing like a tiny mustard seed Jesus had talked about in the Gospel of Matthew. Nevertheless, there was a turmoil churning inside of her. Eleanor knew her parents were strict. She was not allowed to go to dances or movies. She really had no Christian young people to be with, only her two cousins, Margret and Anna. During summer, when school was out, she didn't see them as much. It seemed loneliness followed her wherever she went. She just could not shake it.

One summer before she turned sweet sixteen, Eleanor came home from one of the church meetings feeling lonely again. She helped with dinner and dishes. Then she strolled along the boardwalks along the quiet main street. Dust swirled around, never finding a place to rest. The break from schoolwork was delightful. It was also pleasant not listening to her classmates talk about the latest movie or dance they had gone to. Honestly, sometimes she didn't see the harm in it. Something deep inside of her started churning again.

Eleanor walked home and closed herself in her room.

She fell to her knees, "Oh Lord, I don't know what to do. I love you and I want to follow you, but I am so lonely. I have no real friends except Margret and Anna, and they don't live in town."

Tears began to flow out of Eleanor's tender heart, "I know my parents mean well, and I want to obey them. . .but sometimes it just isn't fair." Eleanor began crying out to the Lord in earnest, "Lord, you've got to help me with this burden. I can't do it on my own. Without your help I can't continue to stand true to you."

That night, as Eleanor sought the Lord, she was filled with the Holy Spirit just as Jesus foretold in the book of Acts, "But you will receive power when the Holy Spirit comes on you and you will be my witnesses."

Eleanor began praying in a language she had never learned. Soon she was singing in a language that she had never learned. Out of the depths of her soul flowed living waters that she had never tasted before. It was as if her deepest longings and desires were satisfied. She also felt a power and strength not her own, that would carry her through the years.

Eleanor stayed up until three o'clock in the morning singing heavenly words of worship and praise to the Lord. The next morning when she woke up and went outside the air seemed fresher and the few trees they had around them were brighter. The world pulsated with life and joy. That spiritual experience never left Eleanor. It would take her through many hard trials and difficult times. No matter her age, it would remain as real to her as it was on that summer day when she was a teenager living in South Dakota in the midst of the Great Depression and the Dust Bowl. The testimony of her entire life would echo the Apostle Paul's words, "His grace is sufficient."

Eleanor turned the pages of her Bible to the book of Romans. Her finger ran down the print to Romans 11:33, "O the depth of the riches both of the wisdom and knowledge of God. How unsearchable are his judgments, and his ways past finding out" (Rom. 11:33, KJV).

Chapter Six

Christian Hild

"We're going to church tonight," Anna Jorgenson announced to her family during the evening meal in the dining room.

"But, Mom, we don't have church tonight," Melvin pointed out.

"Yes, but we are going to a different church."

Julia, Lloyd and Leona snuck a look at Dad. He seemed in on the idea. At age thirteen, Melvin's family began going to evening church services held at the Methodist church building affectionately called, "the Little Brown Church in the Vale".

Melvin lived in the Sampson Addition, so on Sunday mornings his family would walk to the cluster of churches across town to the Norwegian Lutheran church. Then in the evenings, they walked to the Pentecostal meetings. At the corner of a street near the churches, the Lutheran Pastor sat in a chair on his front porch and watched the Jorgenson family turn right and walk the almost two blocks to "the Little Brown Church in the Vale".

That spring, Melvin wore a new dark colored suit and tie to his confirmation ceremony. His freshly cut dark hair was parted on the left and smoothly combed down to scrubbed ears. His oval face held a youthful appearance of hope in his blue eyes. He proudly stood where his mother usually took pictures, on the narrow sidewalk along the side of their house in front of the dining room window where she hung her favorite plants. A new Bible was tucked under Melvin's left arm. On his lapel gleamed two pins of accomplishment and recognition for Christian service. This would mark the beginning of a new journey of faith for Melvin. Only, it wouldn't be with the Norwegian Lutheran Church.

The first time he saw Christian Hild, Melvin was walking to school in the morning. The young evangelist was in a parking area just off the street handing out pamphlets after speaking to the crowd. Melvin read over the invitation to a meeting and then looked the young man over. He was clean-cut, wore a dark suit and carried a Bible. After school, Melvin brought the pamphlet home to his mother, "Maybe we should go there."

Mr. Hild walked down main street Crookston, and around the town greeting folks of all ages, "Hello, I'm Christian Hild, and I would like to invite you and your family to attend a meeting tonight."

That night at the Little Brown Church in the Vale, in filed John and Anna with Julia, Lloyd, Melvin, and Leona all wearing their church clothes. The Jorgenson family found a middle pew to sit in for the meeting. They had never been to another church in town except for a funeral or wedding. Mr. Hild greeted the small crowd and opened the service with prayer. He was an average-built man with attractive features and well-groomed dark wavy hair.

He then introduced the three Olson sisters from the little town of Walton, near Fargo, who sang beautifully, with blended harmonies. One of the sisters played the piano. Melvin thought the young trio was inspirational and easy on the eyes. Their dresses, modest in fashion, seemed coordinated in color and style. When they finished, Mr. Hild walked to the podium and gave his testimony of coming twenty miles from Fargo, North Dakota, to bring them the message of what the Lord had done for him. He had been in trouble with the law for stealing, even spending time in youth corrections. His life was going downhill and fast. Then he heard the message of God's love and redemptive power for sinners, "It was the goodness and kindness of God that led me to repentance. And I knew I wanted to be an evangelist for the Lord, and that's why I'm here tonight."

Even at the age of eighteen, Mr. Hild was well spoken. Melvin felt great respect for anyone willing to go out and preach at that age. At the end of his talk, Mr. Hild gave an invitation for those who wanted to make Jesus their Lord and Savior to come forward to the altar to pray. The Olson sisters began to sing accompanied by one of them at the piano. Prayer was offered for any needs anyone had: healing, financial, family issues, or anything else. The Lord was there to help them.

Melvin had never seen anything like it. His church, while reverent, and based on the teachings of the Bible, was scripted with liturgical repetition like a shirt ironed with so much starch that there was no softness or freedom of God's Spirit. Here, it was different. It was hard to describe. He couldn't wait to go to the next meeting.

As the meetings continued, one by one, Melvin's family began going forward to the altar for prayer. When Melvin went forward, he stood on the music platform praying for salvation as the Olson sisters ministered in music. Then one night, he heard about the second experience: the infilling of the Holy Spirit. Melvin went to the altar to ask the Lord

Jesus to baptize him with fire as foretold by John the Baptist. After the ascension of Jesus into heaven, John's prophecy was confirmed with the tongues of fire that separated and rested on each head of the believers at Pentecost. (Gospels of Matthew 3:11; Luke 3:16; and Acts 2:3)

A great revival swept through Crookston and the region, but it was not accepted by everyone. At times, there was a crowd opposing the services and the seekers. Who did this eighteen-year-old-kid from Fargo think he was showing up in their town? Why, he is turning Crookston upside down.

In response to this persecution, Christian Hild and his comrades would stand on the front three steps of the church and preach another sermon to them. This young evangelist roused up the town so much, they wanted to run him out on a rail and tar him with feathers. Mr. Hild lifted his hand. He calmly asked them to quiet down so he could talk to them, and he did.

The meetings continued, and soon home prayer meetings sprung up around town. It was at one of these house meetings close to the Little Brown Church in the Vale that Melvin received his call into the ministry. He began to read his Bible and seek the Lord privately on his own. One day while in prayer in his room, he began seeing in his mind's eye a map of the world. The edges became darker until only the continent of Africa stood out. Then a light concentrated on central Africa in the Congo River region. After that, details of the rain forest came into view. Melvin saw huts with Congolese families and also groups of nomadic pygmies. Lastly, he saw himself standing in the middle of a crowd of Africans. He was preaching the Good News of following Jesus. People at the edge of the crowd were clutching machete type knives. Melvin wondered about the men and felt danger. However, a thought came to him and he knew it was the Lord speaking to him that there would be people trying to harm him. *I will be between you and them.* Melvin knew, without a doubt, he was going to be a missionary to Congo, Africa one day. He didn't exactly know how or when. Nevertheless, he knew and it was sealed in his mind, will, and emotions from that day forward.

Now a soldier in the Lord's Army, Melvin started going door to door handing Gospel literature pamphlets about salvation through Jesus Christ. They would cover different sections of the town going two-by-two or sometimes in groups. Some people were receptive, while others would become quite upset about it, saying, "Hey, I don't want that."

It was during this time that Mr. Hild announced there would be a special healing service. The timing could not have been better for Melvin's father. Recently John's lower back bothered him to the point that it began to be painful for him to walk. Then, sitting too long bothered him. Eventually, his back was so bad he could not stand up straight. Nonetheless, he hobbled across town to the church.

After music and the message, he went forward for prayer, and soon he was walking back and forth at the front of the church. He kept pacing back and forth past the preacher's pulpit with a straight back giving thanks to his healer, Jehovah Rapha, the God who heals. On the way home, Melvin watched his father jumping and bouncing like a ball all the way to 605 Pleasant Avenue.

Later, at one of the meetings, John gave his testimony beaming with joy, "I felt so happy; I felt like I was jumping inside."

He had suffered in terrible pain for at least a month. Now he was giving thanks to Jesus Christ who had not stopped healing people of their ailments and afflictions for over two thousand years.

Meanwhile, at the Jorgenson home, music was woven into the fabric of everyday life. The Marlboro upright piano nestled against an inside wall of the wallpapered living room was played by all four children, including Anna. Melvin's father was supportive of his children being involved in music. Before moving to America, John learned to play the violin becoming proficient enough to earn the title of a "Fiddler." At Christmas, the family gathered around the piano to sing Christmas carols and hymns. Lloyd and Julia would sing duets, and then they would switch with Melvin.

Melvin continued piano lessons with a nun at a Catholic Convent every Saturday morning for one hour. He would walk to the other side of town to take lessons from Sister, as they all called her. Clad in the classic black and white habit, Sister would invite other people over to listen to Melvin play so he could gain confidence in performing.

Step by step, Melvin grew in the music ministry at church humbly beginning with a triangle. Next, he was playing the guitar. Soon after this, Melvin's rich tenor voice was ringing out praises to God. Eventually, he was playing the piano and leading different aspects of the music ministry.

Mr. Hild spent a year sowing spiritual seeds and harvesting souls in Crookston. As the revival continued, Melvin enjoyed meeting the cross-section of people that would come together to meet in the homes for prayer.

"Hello, my name is Carl Cornelius." He was six years older than Melvin. His hair cut short around his ears swirled on the top of his head in dark waves on his tall frame, "My family attends the Swedish Covenant Church, but I got invited to one of Brother Hild's meetings and I haven't stopped going."

Carl's broad smile came easy and they became fast friends. They also got to know each other through working in the sugar beet fields.

A pickup truck would swing into town at six o'clock in the morning to load up ten to twenty boys for the sugar beet fields. The group jostled around in the open truck bed for a couple miles on dirt roads. Then, the thinning of beet plants and the wearing out of trouser pants lasted for six to eight hours. Hearing of Melvin's plight, his mother made padded knee patches and sewed them on his work pants.

Melvin crawled on his knees between two rows working each row from beginning to end. The object was to weed out the seedlings so the remaining beets would mature to the appropriate size. If the seedlings were too close both plants would remain stunted. Every row had to be evenly spaced.

A man overseeing the workers barked at one of the boys, "Hey, you are leaving too many plants in the ground. Look at Melvin's row. He is doing it the right way, with the right spacing."

"Oh, he does it the way we do it sometimes," grumbled another boy.

Melvin did not. He had attention to detail. Diligent in little things, even toilsome things like picking beets, he tried to do his best. Unlike some people waiting for the grand things in life to try to shine, Melvin was quietly polishing his character a little bit every day in the mundane.

The boys were allowed a mid-day lunch break. Melvin and Carl sought out the shade of a small shed and sat on the threshold. Carl had brought his guitar. After a few songs he handed it to Melvin, "Here, you give it a strum."

As Carl talked about going to Bible college and saving his money, Melvin listened with interest, knowing he needed to go to Bible college to be a missionary, "So, where are you going?"

"I'm not sure yet," Carl answered, taking a drink of water from his metal cup after finishing his lunch stored in a pail.

"Someone told me about a college in Minneapolis. North Central I think it's called. Anyway, I'm going to send for some information about it."

At the end of the day, the same pickup truck brought the tired boys back to town. Melvin felt the money in his pocket. After getting home, he gave it to his mother to hang on to it for him. "Here's sugar beet money for Bible college."

Toward the middle of the summer, when the afternoon sun grew hot, their days were shortened to noon. After that, the hours dwindled down and Melvin had the rest of the summer off.

* * * * *

When Melvin turned fifteen, he got a summer job at the grocery store up town as a store clerk. His duties included placing orders for customers by taking inventory off the shelves to place on the counter for purchase. Sometimes he was asked to add up the bill for the goods. He also had to carry out the purchased goods for the customers. Big burly men would buy eighty pound flour sacks and watch slender Melvin lug the sack to their truck and placed it in the back with no tips for all his work. He took home his hourly wage from the store.

"Here Mom," Melvin dropped the coins in her hand, "put this in my fund for Bible college."

In addition to working in the store, Melvin began helping his father at home with the heavier tasks. When a cord of wood was ordered, Melvin would have to saw the logs into the right lengths and then chop it with an axe to split it for burning in the kitchen stove.

Although his savings kept growing, Melvin did keep a little of his paychecks to contribute to his own needs of clothing and other things. He enjoyed wearing suspenders with his pants and a pin or clip for his tie that he purposely bowed out a bit according to the fashion trend. One day he went to the corner store, Routell, looking for shoes. That's where he spotted a pair of men's white dress shoes.

Melvin tried them on and they fit like a glove, "I'll take them."

The store clerk took his money and Melvin took his prized white shoes home.

They now had indoor plumbing in the second floor bathroom where Melvin used the mirror to adjust his tie. Assembling his new outfit of dark pants, matching dark suspenders over a white shirt, yellow tie with clip and white shoes, he was satisfied with his appearance except for one thing: his glasses. His last eye examination revealed he needed glasses to see distance. Melvin took his glasses off and left them at home. He placed them on the stand next to the newly acquired ringer telephone hung in the hallway on his way out the front door.

With a group of friends, Melvin made the twenty-mile trip to Grand Forks to hear a young woman, Deloris Dudley, preach. He had never seen a woman preach before let alone a girl only sixteen or seventeen years old. Nonetheless, revival was pouring out on sons and daughters just like it said in the Book of Joel. Even Melvin got the opportunity to try his hand at Bible-teaching at the home meetings.

One day, Carl Cornelius showed up on Melvin's doorstep. Carl's parents were members of the Swedish Covenant Church, and Carl's conversion did not sit well with his parents. They had put a suitcase on their porch for him to take. Consequently, Carl went to live with the Jorgenson family for several weeks until Carl set off for North Central Bible Institute in Minneapolis in 1934. The Bible college was affiliated with the Assemblies of God, part of the Pentecostal stream of Christian faith. Julia and Lloyd began attending the Bible college as well.

By the time Melvin graduated from high school in 1936, he was proficient at piano and vocals. He had participated in choir recitals, including the high school quartet, which took state in that category his senior year. Later on, Melvin would credit most of his musical training and knowledge of music theory to his high school music teacher, Mr. T.W. Thorsen.

In the midst of all this was the call to Africa. It was like a steady beat of the African "talking drums" used in the grasslands, forests and mountains to communicate back and forth. Deep in the recess of Melvin's soul, Africa was calling to him, prodding him forward to his destiny.

Perhaps if the beating of the drums could be translated into words it would sound out, "Come. There are souls for the harvest of my kingdom. Come. Bring my light to the darkness. Come."

Chapter Seven

Rapid City

S tuck in a drought since 1931, Thunder Hawk and the Great Plains suffered through the black blizzards. In May of 1934, one dirt storm blew dust from the Great Plaines to the East Coast affecting three-fourths of the country. Black gritty drifts swirled over houses and barns leaving only the roofs exposed.

Right after Eleanor turned sixteen years old, another black blizzard screamed across the Great Plains, reaching sixty miles per hour on Sunday, April 14, 1935. In response to Black Sunday, soil conservation came to the forefront of Roosevelt's administration under the guidance of Hugh Bennett. Agencies were created to save family farms and introduce new farming methods. Farmers began to protect the precious topsoil by terrace, contour, and strip farming. Rows of tree belts began to rise on farmland and roads.

In Thunder Hawk, and across the nation, rain and the economy were constant topics of conversation and prayer. Dirt got into every nook and cranny of the Groat home. Inside cupboards, dishes were dirty and everything in the house was constantly dusty. Everyone was cleaning or coughing. Washing clothes seemed impossible. The General

Store wasn't much better. Sometimes they used a shovel instead of a broom to clear off the boardwalks and walking path between the store and their house. Normal life came to a standstill. The redbrick school closed, motors in cars and tractors failed, there was dirt in food and water. People wore wet cloths over their faces; the young and old succumbed to something doctors called "dust pneumonia."

It was during this time of dust and depression that the Groat family had to part with their faithful Fritz.

"Poor thing was run over by a car," Hazel explained to the children.

Eleanor, Lorraine, Wayne, and Lois gathered around the burial site with red eyes, trying to hold back tears or openly crying. Their father gently laid the home made wooden box into the freshly dug grave in their yard. A few words were said and a prayer. A little marker was placed over the mound of South Dakota dirt to commemorate their faithful friend. When Eleanor came home from school she would expect his bark of greeting as she opened the door to kitchen. There was only silence.

Time kept marching on toward Eleanor's graduation from Thunder Hawk High School in the northeast corner of Corson County. She had attended the brick schoolhouse since first grade. The Class of 1936 consisted of five girls and three boys. Eleanor looked the classroom over for one last time. One of the boys had started first grade with Eleanor and they had been classmates the entire twelve years.

Margret, Eleanor's cousin, interrupted her thoughts, "Eleanor, did you pick out your dress yet for the ceremony and picture?"

"I ordered a light blue dress with a two inch ruffled collar," replied Eleanor. "It has a seam going across the top with full shoulders. The hemline is cut between the knees and calves. What about you?"

"Mine has cloth-covered buttons all the way down the front that match the dress with a matching cloth belt at the waist. The collar is flat with rounded corners, a Peter Pan collar I think they call it. I can't wait to wear it."

For their graduation ceremony, Eleanor and Margret wore their hair cut in a bob, parted on the side and waved. The finger waves known as a "C-curl" were made by pushing a comb back and forth on wet hair lathered in styling lotion. One-inch rows were formed using a finger to hold the hair down between the ridges and waves starting at the crown and working down. Eleanor's C-curls were more distinct than her cousins with brunette crisp ridges. Margret's blonde waves were a softer version of finger waves with more volume. Her lighter features stood out well under wire rim glasses. Eleanor's darker features contrasted beautifully with the striking sapphire dress accented with a round corsage of cloth flowers. Her hazel eyes shone with a new future, while her soft curved lips held contentment. The boys wore new three-piece suits with ties. They all had a generous amount of hair, cropped short around the ears. However, one young man was starting to show a higher forehead.

By the time Eleanor graduated from high school, the town of Thunder Hawk consisted of two general stores, a hotel, hardware store, pool hall, lumberyard, restaurant, bakery, feed store, gas station, library, garage, train depot, three grain elevators, blacksmith shop, State Bank, community hall, and school house. The only two churches in town were Catholic and Presbyterian. The population of Corson County peaked at 9,535 in 1930. However, since then, people were leaving and numbers dwindled every year.

Eleanor knew what she wanted to do after graduation. She had thought and prayed about it often. Deep in her heart was the desire to become a missionary. However, in the fall of 1936, Eleanor attended Rapid City Business College for one year. Her parents drove her two hundred miles to Rapid City to make sure she got settled in with Aunt Francis and her family.

Ten years prior, Aunt Francis had been married to Raymond Munyon, Hazel's only brother, when he was in his early twenties. The young couple lived in the Black Hills with their six-month-old son. Raymond worked in a sugar beet factory on the night shift. One night as he was getting ready to leave, he put on his sweater and then decided to check on a machine. He leaned over the machine and it grabbed him and crushed him to death. After the accident, Francis and her little son, Raymond Laverne Jr., stayed with Grandpa and Grandma Munyon. Eventually, Francis married again, to Elmer Dutton, a wonderful Christian man.

Despite her longing to go to Bible School, Eleanor found herself captivated by the scenery of the Black Hills. Fresh scents of trees and streams greeted her with every twist and turn of the road. Her father clearly enjoyed the drive as well as her mother.

Hazel smiled under the brim of her hat, "That sculptor, Borglum, figures he's got another five years until the project is finished."

Eleanor had been watching the construction on Mt. Rushmore since she was eight years old. There was always the rumbling of blasting dynamite as the sixty-foot tall faces of Washington, Jefferson, Roosevelt, and Lincoln emerged from the rock a little bit more each year. Now the faces of the four presidents firmly jutted out from the side of the mountain.

Edward commented, "Just think, Eleanor, you'll be twenty-two, when the project is done."

Hazel glanced at her daughter in the back seat, then at her husband, "Oh dear, please let her be seventeen for now. This is hard enough for me."

Eleanor knew Aunt Francis from their many visits to the Black Hills for hunting, fishing, and camping. Recalling the memories, Eleanor could almost taste the trout her father cooked for breakfast with fried potatoes. Finally, their car rolled into Aunt Francis and Uncle Elmer's place. Everyone unloaded the luggage, and after a few days, Edward and Hazel left their oldest daughter in Rapid City. Eleanor settled into her new routine of going to the business school and helping her aunt at home, to whom Eleanor would become close in the coming months.

An unexpected pleasure for Eleanor was to attend an Assemblies of God (AG) Church. She found good friends in the AG church and it was a time of rich Christian fellowship. Eleanor became close the Zink family, which included Beatrice, Mildred, and Dale. After Sunday services ended, Eleanor gathered with her new friends to make social plans for the week. How much she enjoyed being in a real church building with a group of people her own age. This was something she had never had in Thunder Hawk. She wrote letters to her sisters and cousins about everything: "They are such a nice group of young people. This is like heaven for me."

Eleanor listened as Dale Zink announced to their group of friends that he was going to North Central Bible Institute. The news pricked her heart to the point of praying about following her desire to become a missionary, but for now her place was in Rapid City. She would just have to trust the guiding hand of God.

Chapter Eight

Pockets of Straw

That September, after Melvin walked down the front steps of the two-story white house on 605 Pleasant Avenue he took one last glance at his childhood home. At the Greyhound Bus Line stop in Crookston, he said good-bye to his folks as the metal covered bus with the racing dog logo on its side pulled into the parking lot. Melvin picked up his suitcase. It was an old brown suitcase and Melvin thought about how he had never used a suitcase before.

Along the three hundred miles to Minneapolis, the Greyhound stopped at every corner, in every town. Melvin impatiently rode the bus mixed with dreams of his future until he finally arrived in Minneapolis. Then he had to find the right streetcar according to the written instructions sent from Carl Cornelius. Melvin dug a dime out of his pants pocket and paid the fair. Nervous and tired, Melvin had reached the end of the road in many different ways.

Stepping off the streetcar, Melvin stood on the corner. His eyes scanned his new environment. Suddenly he recognized a tall, slim form, and familiar face, walking toward him.

Carl's dark eyes smiled through his wire rimmed glasses, "Hello, Melvin, you made it."

Relief washed over Melvin as they shook hands. They strode one block to the Minneapolis Gospel Tabernacle on 3015 Thirteenth Avenue South. Then they walked up the steps of the church and through the double doors, to Melvin's new world.

Once inside the three-story brick building, Carl introduced Melvin to several students including one of his new roommates, George Erickson, "Welcome to Mill City my fellow Crookstonian."

George shook Melvin's hand. They had attended high school together, both graduating in May. George was average height and build, with the typical features of a Scandinavian. Round wire frames sat over blue eyes.

"So we meet again George, only now in the big city," returned Melvin.

"It's nothing like Crookston, but once you get to know the street names and landmarks it's not bad for getting around town."

Carl offered, "Speaking of landmarks, we can go see the Foshay Tower sometime. The thirty-floor observation deck is swell. You can view the entire city with all the lakes, parks, and the flourmills at St. Anthony Falls."

The three from Crookston walked to Melvin's first place to live away from home, on 34th and Portland.

"Here's our room," Carl announced.

Melvin set down his suitcase and looked it over. Three beds and a window with an orange-crate box attached to the outside of it that served as a refrigerator in the cooler months.

"The bathroom's down the hall, "explained George tipping his head in the general direction.

Next on the list was registration and payment of fees. Melvin knew from the 1936-1937 catalog that estimated expenses for books and notes was $10.00; registration fee, $15.00; tuition, $25.00; library fee, $1.00; and personal service, $2.00. He needed to pay $30.00 for the down payment of the $53.00 total due for the three-term school year. Generous donations from "consecrated Christians" helped offset the tuition in order to promote training of young men and woman for service in God's kingdom, and for the goodwill of humanity.

On September 22, 1936, Melvin dove into student life with nine subjects his freshman year. One credit was given for Practical Work—student-led services held at old folks homes, mental health facilities, and churches—making the final tally of twenty credits.

Looking over the almost eighty freshmen students, college President Lindquist made the observation to a couple of faculty members, "Well, it looks like we are getting more students this year, but a lot of them still have straw in their pockets."

Brother Lindquist, as he was called, was a tall man of average build with dark, sharply defined features. The two Miller brothers, who flanked Brother Lindquist, smiled in agreement. Both brothers had broad sturdy frames, with slightly rounded faces of lighter, less chiseled features than Lindquist. The trio worked well as the team of President, Dean and Secretary.

Brother Lindquist continued, "Their small-town churches served them well in many ways. However, much more needs to be done in order to groom these men and women for the call into the ministry."

The men wore suits of various colors, while the women's dress code featured black dresses with white collars. As Supervisor of Women, Miss Anne E. Froland measured each dress from the hem down to the floor to make sure it was the proper length. In addition to grooming for preaching and teaching, "Etiquette," taught by Sister Froland, would also help students lose some of the straw in their pockets.

Every day of instruction began with a chapel service in the sanctuary. The freshman classes and prayer room were downstairs, with other classes held in the chapel or balcony. At the close of the day, a half hour was spent praying for workers around the world.

As the weeks passed by, Melvin enjoyed getting to know the faculty members. At the helm was Brother Frank J. Lindquist, President, District Supervisor, and Pastor of Minneapolis Gospel Tabernacle. He taught Doctrine, Divine Healing, Pneumatics, and Methods in Evangelism. In addition to classroom responsibilities he often invited students to his home for dinner.

Ivan O. Miller was Dean, as well as teaching several classes. He was known for "tarrying," or waiting in prayer for the falling of the Holy Spirit, in chapel and in his classes. His brother, Marvin Miller, was Secretary of the college and AG District. Melvin thought he had a fine way of teaching Old Testament; and appreciated the times when Brother Miller would go out and shoot baskets.

W.H. Boyles, Pastor of St. Paul Gospel Tabernacle, taught Personal Evangelism and Church History. Then there was Emil Balliet, who rounded out the training experience with Music and Public Speaking. He also gave the students the hands-on experience they needed to become "instant in season, and out of season" by overseeing Chapel, and Practical Work ministry.

The advertisement of the college at the time was "Earn while you learn." With the downtown location of North Central, students could walk to their jobs instead of paying a nickel or dime on the streetcars. Some students worked in restaurants or performed maintenance in buildings. Women students generally worked for the homes they stayed in, earning a dollar or two a week. Seated alphabetically, Melvin became friends with Orrin Kingsriter, who came from a large family in Paynesville, Minnesota. Many of his older siblings were alumni of North Central. Orrin "earned while he learned" by working early paper routes in the morning.

Melvin found employment at North Central in the general office department with various duties as required, at twenty-five cents per hour, applied toward his tuition. He continued to work in the office the entire three years of his studies. As his duties and responsibilities increased every year, so did his wage, to thirty-five cents an hour applied to tuition.

He began as a stenographer. In high school, Melvin had learned to take and transcribe dictation. Working in the office gave Melvin many opportunities to interact with Lindquist and the two Miller brothers. They were open about the financial needs of the college and Melvin was privy to many of their conversations.

"Well, we started North Central with one hundred dollars and the Lord came through then, so we can trust him now that we are needing a lot more than that to get into a new building," began Lindquist.

Melvin could hear another one of those conversations drifting toward his ears as he worked at his desk. One of the Miller brothers spoke, "And we only had nineteen students in our first graduating class. By the time spring rolls around, there will be thirty-nine graduates. This year's freshman class is twice that size. The church building is bursting at the seams with more applications coming in every year."

The other brother added his thoughts, "Not to mention adding the business school. We need something that could accommodate housing and classes for three hundred to four hundred students."

Lindquist wrapped things up, "Let's keep waiting on the Lord for wisdom and guidance."

Melvin heard the three men end their conversation in prayer. In addition to the college, Brother Lindquist would accept speaking engagements in the evenings. Riding the train to these places, back and forth to the school to teach in the morning, Lindquist would correct papers and work on other details of the college. He also drove students to musical performances. Melvin would sing solos, or with the quartet, so he was able to ride with him on occasion. Melvin would hear the men talk about ordinary things and think, *why, they are just like the rest of us,* and then they would discuss subjects that were above the rest of the students, such as district affairs. Melvin listened with interest, taking mental notes.

During Melvin's first year at North Central, the three from Crookston spent the last half of the school year with a family of four. The family lived on 10th Street, across from the towering Sears Roebuck building dominating the block on 900 East Lake Street. The lady of the house was a God-fearing woman, and devoted mother of two children. But her husband was not saved. She had arranged three beds in the living room for the young men. Every Saturday she set out to grocery shop, starting on foot, and returning by streetcar with bags of food. Then on Sunday, she prepared a special dinner for Melvin, Carl, and George. All week long, those young men's hearty appetites would grow in anticipation of that meal.

Her husband smoked, and one day his wife said, "You better get rid of that, that's not healthy. It's not honoring to the Lord to do that to your body."

He had hidden his tobacco can and pipe in the house somewhere. However, the Lord told her where he had hidden it, so one day she told her husband, "Watch this," and she opened the door to the basement steps, took two steps down, turned around and there above the doorway was a small shelf. She deftly reached up to that shelf and out came the hidden can of tobacco and the pipe. "The Lord told me where this is because he wants you to quit smoking."

The husband was so astonished that he quit smoking and gave his life to the Lord. Sometime later, the family moved to California where they had a small hotel business.

That winter, Melvin walked down to Powderhorn Lake to watch some of the students ice skate. Then he headed back to the Gospel Tabernacle, shortened to just "the Tab" by the students, for office work.

Another stop on his many brisk walks in the winter was the Glad Tidings Chapel, two miles west of the college, a half-block south of Lake Street and Second Street. Run by the students, every evening and twice on Sunday, Glad Tidings Chapel became "a soul saving station." Neighbors and strangers off the streets would come to listen to the students sing and preach. Seniors were of course, given the first opportunity to practice their preaching skills. One student had an accent, so when he preached his words came out, "The devil is the father of all lice" instead of "the father of all lies." Nonetheless, Melvin thought him to be a fine fellow and he turned out to be a good pastor in Wisconsin. Melvin contributed often with vocals and as a pianist. There was also the Gospel Mission, a place where they had meals for the needy. Melvin sang tenor in an impromptu quartet at dinnertime, receiving a delicious meal afterward.

Other activities in which Melvin became involved were the missionary society, and participating in the 1937 ARCHIVE Contest for subscriptions of the annual college yearbook. Melvin's group came in second place with one hundred and eighty-three points, after the winning group's one hundred and eighty-eight points. He also participated in the large college choir, mixing in easily with everyone. Because Melvin was cordial with all the students he met, sometimes his charming personality led female students to invite him to outings. One time, an attractive woman asked him to go canoeing with a group of fellow students, but Melvin declined her invitation. Something inside of him didn't want to chance creating a closer friendship with her.

Melvin later confessed to Carl, "She's a very nice girl, but I didn't want to tangle up anything I would have to detangle later. I guess I just have it in my mind that when I start going with a girl, it will be the one I intend to marry."

Carl heard his friend out. He knew that although Melvin was friendly in groups, he intentionally did nothing one-on-one with girls. But that didn't stop people trying their hand at matchmaking for Melvin.

On Tuesday, May 11, 1937, Melvin watched Class President Carl Cornelius receive his diploma from Rev. F.J. Lindquist. Then Rev. Ivan O. Miller closed the commencement ceremony with the benediction. In keeping with the times, Melvin's tie lifted out slightly with the tails tucked neatly into his double-breasted three-piece suit. He now parted his hair toward the middle combing it smoothly back. His sky-blue eyes, and clean-shaven triangular chin made him a handsome young man. Growing in stature, wisdom, and favor with faculty and students, Melvin had lost some of the straw in his pockets over the course of his freshman year.

At the bottom of the program Melvin read, "CLASS MOTTO: 'We Have Heard Thy Call. . .We Will Arise And Go.'" In the 1937 ARCHIVE, Carl's picture came first in the Seniors' section. Under his name, designation of Class President, and hometown of Crookston, Minnesota, Carl had chosen the scripture verse from Philippians 3:10: "That I may know him, and the power of his resurrection, and the fellowship of his sufferings."

* * * * *

That summer, Melvin performed janitorial duties in exchange for a room at the Tab. Carl was staying at the church too, traveling back and forth to speak at churches in Wisconsin. In the sanctuary of the Tab, behind the curtain-skirted platform, an elevated choir section held three rows of seats. On either side rose white walls with arched hallways leading toward office and storage rooms. One storage closet became Melvin's room. On Sunday mornings, the bellows of the organ roused him from his sleep. Brother Lindquist would check the furniture on the platform and run his hand over the pews to see if they were dusty. He would be very plain about saying something if it was not clean enough, and Melvin would be sure to fix it.

Carl gave Melvin one of the loneliest days of his life when he accepted a church and became a full-time minister. Melvin walked the streets by Sears Roebuck, thinking of the room they had shared with George. Then he walked down Lake Street, past the first home they had lived in and the Glad Tidings Chapel. He really could not remember ever being so lonely. The initial homesickness he felt in the beginning of the year had evaporated from the bonds of friendship with Carl and the other seniors.

Melvin let out a sigh, walking up the front steps of the Tab, "I guess I'll just have to make new friends."

Chapter Nine

Keeping Along the King's Highway

❧

I n the summer of 1937, North Central Bible Institute purchased its first building for $75,000. Two miles north of the Minneapolis Gospel Tabernacle, the five-story stone structure on 910 Elliot Avenue ran the length of a city block. The main entrance faced Elliot Park, with the Swedish Hospital to the north and Asbury Hospital to the south. The Elliot Park neighborhood, east of downtown Minneapolis, had once been a sought-after area for the city's founding fathers building their mansions in the late 1800s and early 1900s. Brownstone row houses were built for businessmen and their families, while the working-class found sufficient housing as well.

The former hospital building was ideal for the needs of a growing college. The five floors could accommodate offices, classrooms, student dorm rooms, and a larger chapel space. However, the building had been not operational since the World War had ended. Nineteen years of abandonment created a massive renovation project that needed to be completed before fall classes started that September, with two hundred students registered.

Many students were tearing things down, hauling away debris, and cleaning, while others were rebuilding and painting, but Melvin was mostly working in the office. He worked four hours a day making a dollar a day toward his tuition. His desk was in the main office, off the front door and lobby. From the lobby, a short hallway led to Brother Lindquist and the Miller brothers' offices clustered together on either side of the central elevator and steps. A long hallway leading in both directions away from their offices split the first floor in two halves. Additional offices and classrooms filled either side of the hallway with the cafeteria on the very north end of the floor. Behind the elevators and the stairs was a large, open space reserved for the future chapel. Nineteen-year-old Melvin poked his head in the door to survey the empty room. The second-hand opera chairs purchased for the chapel would soon be fastened to the floor.

One of the things Melvin enjoyed was standing on top of the building and overlooking the Minneapolis cityscape. To the east, he could pick out the Gold Medal and Pillsbury Flour signs along the Mississippi River. There was also the North Star Woolen Mill on 109 Portland Avenue South. To the west of North Central's new building, Melvin could easily pick out the Foshay Tower on 821 Marquette Avenue South. It was the paramount tourist destination of anyone coming to Minneapolis. Fashioned after the Washington Monument, each of the thirty-three floors were built smaller as it rose from its massive first base floor. The four hundred and forty-seven-foot tower, built in 1926, with an exterior of Indiana limestone was the tallest skyscraper in the city. With the added antenna, it stood a staggering six hundred feet. The ten-foot letters on all four sides just below the top of the tower spelling out "FOSHAY" dominated the area for miles. The lavish interior was in keeping with the Art Deco design.

Back at his desk, Melvin heard the sounds of renovation. Students and workers streamed in and out of the front doors of 910 Elliot Avenue. All the electricity, plumbing, furnace, and heating systems needed a complete overhaul. The depression was still lingering on, despite the work programs created by the Roosevelt administration. Unemployment rates had hit twenty-nine percent with twice that percentage for iron ore miners. Farmers had suffered as well. Governor Floyd Olson and his Farmer-Labor Party were taking measures to protect people from losing their homes and land to the banks, as well as legislate a minimum wage of forty-five cents an hour. Still, times were hard and everyone was looking for work. The local unions began investigating North Central's work force. Telephone calls in threatening tones concerning the use of students and non-union men for laborers increased until one day a few labor union leaders decided to pay the college a visit to spell things out clearly face-to-face.

It was another routine day for Melvin performing his regular office duties, which included operating the switchboard for phone calls. People came and went through the lobby. He could hear Brothers Ivan and Marvin Miller in their offices working along with college treasurer, Hubert R. Schneider. Suddenly three visitors barged through the front door without stopping at the reception desk. An unfriendly confrontation began. Melvin found himself drawn to the door of his office like a moth to light. To his astonishment Hubert, Ivan, and Marvin were embroiled in a heated discussion with three men representing the union. The six men bunched into a group in front of the elevators.

After the representatives of the union started making threats, one of the college staff members told them, "Let's not talk here. Can we discuss this outside in a calm manner like gentlemen?"

The union leaders stood their ground in front of the elevators. Melvin could see from his perch between the office threshold and the front lobby that Brother Marvin Miller had had enough of the bully tough talk, "Look, you men can't tell us what to do."

Brother Miller's voice grew stronger with every sentence. "We don't want you here. And this is our property."

Then in a deep authoritative voice, Brother Miller commanded like Moses parting the Red Sea, *"You men get out of here."*

Melvin's attention was now riveted on the situation. Seeing the reluctance of the union leaders to move, Brother Miller decided they needed a little help. He took the arm of one of the intruders and shoved him out the front door with Brother Ivan Miller, and Brother Schneider assisting.

With snarling faces, the remaining two union men planted their feet to the floor. Brother Marvin simply walked over and escorted the second one out of the lobby with his brother and college treasurer for back up. The third man was a big fellow. From the safety of his office, Melvin wondered how this larger man would react. This could mean trouble. Brother Miller was still keyed up. He grabbed the last visitor by his arm and marched him out of the building to the sidewalk. Flanked by his brother and staff treasurer, Brother Miller completed the job.

Out on the sidewalk he barked, "You're still on our property; now get off our sidewalk."

The men stepped into the street, never to be seen again. Melvin went back to his office work, but it was hard to concentrate on his duties for a bit. After that, some students stashed two-foot lead pipes under their beds at night and kept the pipes handy during the day. They talked about rigging up ropes or wires across the steps going to the second level where the living quarters began for male students. Even though Melvin had witnessed the confrontation, he didn't feel the need to take such measures of protection, and kept working in the office waiting for the routine of classes to settle everything down into a pleasant environment of peace and order.

New and returning students began trickling in through the front doors of the newly renovated building, each one walking under a round emblem etched in stone over the main entrance that read on an S-curved ribbon: *"Not to be Ministered unto, but to Minister."* During the inaugural year in the 910 Elliot Avenue location, the Bible Institute relied on special Sunday afternoon services for offerings designated to the building budget. The enthusiasm over the new building drew people from all over Minnesota.

Melvin greeted a man from a small town south of Minneapolis who had a typical Scandinavian accent, "Yah, I come from Jordan."

Every Thursday an all-student dinner was prepared and served. The menu consisted of generous donations from farmers including carrots and potatoes. Melvin would always remember the farmers that dedicated a cow or a calf on behalf of the Lord to bless the college.

"Melvin," Dale Zink smiled with handsome features and chestnut brown hair, "can you come out of the office for a moment to meet my sister? She's come all the way from Rapid City."

Dale came in as a junior and had a knack for woodworking, spending his free time in the tool shop. Melvin obliged and stepped through the doors onto the sidewalk.

"Melvin this is Beatrice. We call her Bee." He was obviously proud of his sister and thought her to be a quality girl for Melvin. Melvin could see the family resemblance down to sparkling hazel eyes. "Bee this is Melvin. You should hear him play the piano. He sings tenor real good too."

The threesome chatted for a few minutes until Melvin excused himself, "Well, I must be getting back to my duties, but it was a pleasure to meet you Bee."

Dale gave him the sly look of *what do you think?* Melvin assured Dale that he she was a sister to be proud of, but as a future prospect Melvin thought to himself, *nothing*. So, Melvin kept waiting. He was looking for the Lord to show him. He would know it, when he knew it, all right. However, that didn't stop the speculation of others on his behalf.

Before the school term began, Melvin moved into room 410 on the men's floor with George Erickson, "Melvin, I'll take the top bunk. Don't want you to get nosebleeds."

The room was a small simple space that accommodated two small desks, the beds, a few lamps, and storage for a limited wardrobe. One tall, rectangular window overlooked Elliot Park. One night George plunked into his top bunk with a sigh, "The end of a perfect day."

Melvin heard a crash as George's glasses hit the floor next to Melvin's lower bunk. Somehow, George thought he was placing his glasses on a nightstand that only existed in his mind.

Melvin's second year moved along with classes and activities. He once again sang tenor in the full size choir, Men's Quartet and featured solos. The choir performed songs such as *Keep Along the Middle of the King's Highway* with the male quartet adding special numbers. Melvin arranged a light-hearted rendition of *Blow Ye Winds of the Sea,* starting with the bass line and adding harmonies from the two tenors and baritone until the group created a voice chord. For added entertainment, a loose handkerchief was stowed in a back pocket and pulled out to blow into it with ruffled sounds on cue of the line: "Blow ye winds of the sea." The bass singer and one tenor held their harmonious notes while the other two blew their noses. Later someone asked Melvin, "Was that blow you winds of the sneeze?"

Practical Work locations included churches, and out-stations throughout the city such as homes for the elderly, Children's Mission, and Gospel Halls. The students would also travel to Fort Snelling, Ramsey County Correctional facility, and the Anoka State Hospital. One particular evangelistic outreach was visiting beer parlors, also known as saloons, where the students were never to go alone, but always in a group. Times changed during the depression and people moved away from the once fashionable neighborhood of Elliot Park. Bums would hang out in Elliot Park and things would happen that shouldn't be happening. There were apartments that some students rented, mixed in with undesirable tenants. But the presence of the students helped to sanctify and change the neighborhood. On 14th and Chicago, there was a beer parlor.

One morning during chapel, Brother Ivan Miller declared to the assembled students, "This saloon is an unsavory business."

He then led the charge to storm the place with prayer, "Let's just pray and smoke them out of there. We don't want that saloon here."

After a while, a furniture store replaced the beer parlor.

At the close of the day, students continued in the tradition of a half hour praying for workers around the world. Sometimes the Holy Spirit would come in a unique way. Planned studies for the day would be set aside as they collectively gave room for God to do his work and his agenda. Staff and students would wait on the Lord as Brother Ivan Miller encouraged the students to tarry for the Holy Spirit. Then times of spiritual refreshment would follow. Melvin took pleasure in these times of outpouring of the Spirit, delighting himself in the Lord.

Melvin felt comfortable as a pianist or vocalist during the daily chapels. However, public speaking was a different matter; and today he was scheduled to speak at the chapel service. As he sat in his chair waiting to speak, Melvin surveyed the large crowd of fellow students and teachers. He had experience participating in services at the old folks homes and other places, which seemed easier than to speak to his own peers. The more he thought about it, the worse his anxiety got. He began to imagine the kind of comments people think to themselves when they are listening to a speaker. *Oh, he's not doing very well. Why did he say that? He'll never make a good preacher.* Melvin didn't have the anointing that morning and he knew it. Time dragged on and suddenly it was time for the closing hymn and prayer. Melvin left the chapel room light as a feather. The Lord had delivered him out of the lion's den.

Spring came and with it, the annual picnic at Powderhorn Lake Park. The dress code was lifted as men shed their suit coats and the ladies donned a variety of colorful dresses and accessories, which added to the festive occasion. The ARCHIVE staff was on hand to record the event with cameras. Tables were laden with a variety of picnic fare. Groups gathered on the grass to eat or participate in relay games.

While eating, Melvin overheard Avis Opsal, one of the associate editors, discuss the 1938 ARCHIVE.

Gerald Houk, a graduating senior, came over to the group, "Melvin, I'm heading out this summer to southern Minnesota, places like Rochester. Would you care to work with me when you can?"

"Rochester sounds good to me," replied Melvin.

Ann Strauman and a young woman on her way for a stroll along the lake paused to chat.

"It's an exceptional day for the picnic isn't it?" Ann said to Melvin and Gerald.

"Yes," Melvin agreed, "no suit jackets or coats."

Ann Straumen, from Superior, Wisconsin had dark hair, styled in the fashionable finger waved bob. Her dark eyes and warm smile had won Carl Cornelius over and they were making plans for their future together. Avis Opsal's eyes sparkled through her round wire glasses.

"Melvin, I saw the pictures of the Missionary Society for the ARCHIVE. There's one of you and the executive committee with your finger pointed to someplace on the globe. The art editors are framing the snap into a circle. In fact, I think they did the same with the Men's Quartet snap."

"Didn't you serve as treasurer for the committee this year?" Gerald asked Melvin.

"Yes, I did. You know we had a good year for contributions toward projects, considering we are all poor Bible students."

It had been a good year in many ways for Melvin at North Central. In the future, he would rely on the lessons he learned in the classroom, chapel, and Practical Works. He would also remember the daily examples of the faculty, some who stood their ground with courage when threatened by the union. His third and final year lay ahead of him and then it was on to Africa. Always Africa.

Chapter Ten

I Have Set My Face Like Flint

❧

In the summer of 1938, when Eleanor learned that North Central added a business college, she jumped at the opportunity to present her case to her father. In Eleanor's mind, that meant going to Bible college, which was in keeping with her heart's desire to become a missionary. In her father's mind, it meant his daughter would be prepared for the responsibilities of life. How could either of them know how that one year of business college would accomplish both goals, and more?

Eleanor wrote North Central requesting an application. Every day she checked the mail or asked her father if the train had brought the postal bag. Finally, an envelope marked with a return address from the Bible college in Minneapolis arrived. Sitting at the kitchen table, Eleanor wasted no time in filling out the application, attaching a recent square black and white photo of herself, and sealing the back of the envelope. Her father made his daily run to the depot, set the bag on the mail hook, and Eleanor waited for a reply of acceptance.

Meanwhile, Melvin traveled with Gerald Houk to southeast Minnesota. A pastor from Rochester, who requested help with the nearby town of Harmony, gave them the address of the home for their stay. A small but adequate building with a piano, pulpit, and chairs had been rented for services there. Neither of the young men had a watch to keep track of time for the meetings. However, there was an alarm clock in their bedroom, so they asked the lady of the house if they could bring it to the hall.

Rev. Houk opened the meeting with prayer and introduced himself and Melvin. As Melvin began to play the opening hymn, he noticed the crowd was not too bad for this size of town. He switched tempo for his next selection singing with as much enthusiasm appropriate for the occasion. Gerald preached a powerful sermon and people responded favorably. The next evening things were going well for the team of two. Gerald was behind the pulpit leading the church service in song and Melvin was playing away, when all of a sudden, *b-r-i-n-g-g-g*. The clamorous ringing of the alarm clock startled everyone in the hall. Melvin sprinted to the back of the piano where the clock vibrated its alarm. He pushed the off switch and the brash intrusion ended. Satisfied, Melvin hurried back to the piano bench and moved his hands along the ivory and ebony keys to continue the song.

Between traveling with Gerald, and working in the college office, the summer passed pleasantly by. Sometimes, Melvin would find a newspaper around the reception area and glance over the headlines. Since Melvin had graduated from high school in 1936, Germany, Italy, and Japan created a new world order calling themselves the "Axis Alliance". President Roosevelt kept pressing the idea of repealing the Neutrality Act, but many isolationists supported it. No one liked the idea of going to war again.

"The mail is in," a fellow office worker delivered the stack to Melvin's desk.

Melvin folded up the newspaper and began another four-hour, one-dollar shift in the office. One of his responsibilities was to open the envelopes for the application forms. He had nothing to do with the decisions of accepting or denying the application. Ivan Miller always took them and discussed them with Lindquist or other staff leaders. Melvin would unfold them and place them in a pile as they came in. He could not help but see the pictures as he laid them in the pile. Well, he thought, it was free for him to read, as no one had told him not to read them.

That day, a certain application came in from Thunder Hawk, South Dakota. Melvin opened the envelope. As he slipped out the paper and unfolded it, his eye caught the snapshot attached to the far right corner. He found himself attracted to the young woman's face in the black and white photograph. Her dark hair framed eyes that seemed thoughtful and sincere. Melvin looked at the photo a little longer. A whisper escaped his lips, "Oh, my." Melvin carefully read the neatly filled-out application for the business college. A thought passed through his mind—*I'm going to wait for her to come.*

When the letter of acceptance into North Central Business College came, Eleanor raced her eyes over every detail. She needed to order a modest, long-sleeved black dress. Once it arrived, she got it fitted and added the white collar that was also required. Her parents ordered a brown wool coat with a raccoon collar to fend off the Minneapolis winters in style. For a hat, Eleanor chose one typical of late 1930's fashions. Its dark felt design featured a smaller brim smoothly cresting up accented by a bit of tulle held down with an ornate pin. Adding the leather gloves and shoes, Eleanor struck a classic picture of a young beautiful woman, poised, elegant, and charming.

Eleanor's father drove her five hundred and fifty miles from Thunder Hawk to her destiny. When they arrived in Minneapolis, Eleanor's attention was drawn to the Foshay Tower, Elliot Park, the five-story stone college building, and all the students her age. After getting out of the car, Eleanor adjusted her traveling hat, making sure it was sitting diagonally across her forehead, and slipped on her day gloves and purse. Father and daughter approached the thick oak doors with glass paned windows. Eleanor briefly glanced at the school motto etched in stone over the doors.

After checking in at the office, a young woman offered to help, "Miss Groat, I can take you to your room on the women's floor, number 210."

She was excited and distracted by all she saw, but a young man, who had carefully read over her application, noticed her. *How interesting,* thought Melvin, that they both had the same room number with only a floor separating them.

By the time Melvin started his final year at NCBI he was leading and organizing the chapels, including the Welcome Chapel for the freshmen, and inaugural-year business students. He watched as the secondhand brown opera chairs began to fill up with students wearing suites or black dresses.

After the opening prayer and song, Melvin announced in his clear tenor voice, "Well, to start things off, I will ask some of the incoming freshmen to share where they are from, and perhaps a word, testimony, or a scripture."

After a few students responded, Melvin surprised Eleanor by calling her name. Without missing a beat, Eleanor stood and recited Romans 11:33, "O the depth of the riches both of the wisdom and knowledge of God! How unsearchable are his judgments, and his ways past finding out!"

She calmly sat down and smoothed out her black dress. She felt something different stirring in her heart for the young man leading chapel that she had never before experienced.

After the Welcome Chapel, Eleanor found her way to her classes. Miss Leora Wead, who wore a large silk bow at her neck, taught most of the subjects including Gregg Shorthand, Court Reporting, Filing, Penmanship, and Secretarial Practice. At the end of the day, Eleanor walked the hallway back to the chapel service for prayer. In the coming year, she would experience "an atmosphere of friendliness charged with the presence of the Holy Ghost" as described by the college in the brochures.

As each day progressed, Eleanor began forming friendships with students through her classes and mock-up business settings. That Thursday night, sisters Pearl and Ruth Helgren from Moorhead, Minnesota, who both had Shirley Temple hair and dimple smiles, sat with Eleanor during the weekly student dinner. Esther Lien from Westby, Montana filled the fourth chair. Farmers had donated carrots and potatoes, and enough chickens to feed the student body of three hundred and seventy-six. The freshmen roster alone was three times the size of the exiting seniors. Sitting on wooden chairs, Eleanor and the girls clustered around one of the square tables topped with crisp white cloths and linens. Milk glass dome lights hung on brass chains, several feet from the smoothly painted cream ceiling. The wood floor creaked as students moved in and out of the cafeteria.

Across the room at another table sat Melvin with his new roommate Dale Zink, former roommate, George Erickson, and his usual alphabetically arranged classmate Orrin Kingsriter. At the next table sat Tom Griffith, Bill Shaw, and George Oxentenko. This last trio included some of the few students who owned cars.

One of the young bucks asked Oxentenko about his new barbershop in the building. "How much are you going to charge per head?"

Oxentenko smiled, "Twenty-five cents, which includes a shave right down the Adam's apple."

Talk turned to the new classes and Brother C.M. Ward, who taught The Book of Revelation. Brother Ward had told all of the male students, "Wear cleats on your heels so when you walk down the hall people will hear you coming; and wear a red tie."

Melvin noticed Eleanor every day during chapel, and between classes. When they met in the hallway, he would greet her with a gentle, "Hello." According to school etiquette, he could say hello to a girl, as he walked down the hallway, but needed to watch the inflection of his voice. In the meantime, the other fellows had noticed her too.

"Melvin," George Erickson prodded him with his elbow, "are you even in this conversation?"

Melvin smiled and glanced away from Eleanor and her group of lady friends. "She seems real nice."

"Who is she?" Orrin asked.

Dale Zink offered the information, "Her name is Eleanor Groat. She's from Thunder Hawk, South Dakota. I met her in Rapid City when she was attending business school there."

Melvin raised his eyebrows and before he knew it he blurted out, "Her last name 'Groat' is an old English term for coin." Then he added for all to hear, "You can't get my groat. I've been waiting for her since I first saw her application."

George eyed his former roommate with admiration, "Well, Melvin, I believe you've been waiting long enough. So if Miss Groat is the one, then she's the one."

After the word got out about "Melvin's groat" the male student population respected Melvin's request, and waited for the first official date.

It wasn't easy dating at North Central. Group activities were fine, but there could not be any one-to-one male-female interaction unless permission was granted. And then only one date every two weeks. First Melvin needed to ask Eleanor if she would consider going on a date with him. She seemed interested he thought, but a little reserved at times. Working on activities such as the mission bands and ARCHIVE gave him plenty of reasons to talk to Eleanor about things. He often went to the business school with the ARCHIVE photographer, documenting the inaugural year of the business college. One snap of Eleanor working with an associate and the touch typewriting would make it to the first page of the business division. Her brunette hair had grown longer, and she arranged it stylishly off her collar during school hours. Melvin also looked forward to seeing her Sunday mornings at the Tab.

One evening, in room 210, Eleanor relaxed after finishing her studies for the day. Her roommate Elsie Fink from Bismarck, North Dakota, washed her boyfriend's socks and ironed his shirts.

"You're crazy," opined Eleanor.

Elsie spouted back, "Oh, just wait until you get a boyfriend," her curls, parted down the middle, bounced with a shrug of her shoulders. "Haven't you spotted anyone you'd be willing to wash clothes for yet?"

Eleanor combed her smooth brunette hair before going to bed for the night. Her thoughts turned to Melvin. She knew she wasn't the only one interested in him. Some of the girls dropped hints of letting him know their interest in missions, just to get his attention a bit. She knew she felt attracted to him, but she wasn't willing to show him her full hand yet. What if he was merely interested in any able-bodied woman willing to go to Africa with him, as long as she wasn't too hard to look at or deal with?

Finally, Melvin took the plunge and formally asked "his groat" for a date. Up and down the men's floor bets were on, as much as Bible students are allowed to bet. It was getting close to Thanksgiving when Melvin got permission from North Central to take Eleanor out for a date. They took the streetcar to a restaurant for lunch. Neither one would ever be able to remember what they ate or said. Melvin needed to get back for the afternoon chapel service to play the piano and accompany Dale on the saxophone solo. In order to save time Melvin pulled out his last dime to take a taxi back to the college. As Melvin played the piano that afternoon, he thought Dale played beautifully. In fact, the entire chapel service seemed especially anointed.

Since only one date every two weeks was allowed, Eleanor and Melvin decided to visit a Baptist Church away from the usual crowds at the Tab and other AG churches in Minneapolis. Pastor A.W. Riley presided over his Baptist flock every Sunday morning, while a certain Pentecostal couple sat together enjoying his preaching immensely. It was good-sized church, built of brick, providing a nice long stroll from North Central.

The only other way to see each other was passing in the hallway or, according to the dating code of North Central, a couple could sit together in the cafeteria once a week. As Melvin and Eleanor forgot about the room full of students surrounding them, he knew they couldn't hold hands so he squeezed Eleanor's feet with his rust toned wingtip shoes. One observant young woman made it a point to follow

Eleanor out of the cafeteria, "I saw Melvin squeezing your feet with his shoes. You better watch yourselves."

For their next date, Melvin decided they needed some privacy. He sought out one of his fellow students who owned a car.

George Oxentenko, who was frequently open with his schedule, handed Melvin the keys, "Anything to help you out with 'your coin' of great price Melvin."

George's good-natured ways were popular with the students. The 1939 ARCHIVE featured a snap of him behind the barber chair, his tools of the trade in hand, with the caption: "Mr. George Oxentenko, School 'tonsorialist'; operates on a member of the faculty."

Melvin sped away with "his groat" in their carriage to a destination less traveled by faculty and students. Eleanor moved a little closer to Melvin. Her raccoon collar almost touched his dark winter coat. Small drifts of snow lined the city sidewalks. The setting sun created bright hues in the sky and long shadows on the streets.

After parking the car near Minnehaha Falls, Melvin gallantly opened the door for Eleanor and she gracefully took his hand in hers. The one hundred and fifty-acre park was located along the west bank of the Mississippi River where Minnehaha Creek ended its journey, flowing into the Mighty Mississippi. Filled with an abundance of pines in the winter, and flourishing elm, oak, and silver maples in the summer, the park was a haven of pleasure to the senses and an incubator for romance. As they wandered past leafless trees toward the thunderous falls, Melvin stopped under the canopy of the petite train depot affectionately called "the Princess" by the Milwaukee line workers because of its ornate Victorian architectural style. The fifty-three-foot falls, not frozen into their winter ice sculpture yet, pounded with the intensity of two people falling deeply in love. Melvin drew Eleanor into his arms. He momentarily studied her hazel eyes. Eleanor's lips parted. The crisp December air captured her breath into a mist. He knew she was the one, and he kissed her passionately.

After that date, Melvin and Eleanor desperately wanted to spend more time together. There weren't too many options for them for dates besides restaurants and sightseeing. Movies and dancing were a sin. On occasion, the lovebirds took in the observation deck of the Foshay Tower overlooking the cityscape, "Look, there's the Dayton's store."

Eleanor marveled at how much she could see, not to mention the thirty-three-floor elevator ride. "The first time I rode that elevator, I thought my stomach was going to bounce down to my shoes," she confided to Melvin.

"I tossed a penny from here one time," Melvin reached for her hand, "and never found it in the street."

On the way back to North Central they passed the marquee of a lavishly decorated cinema touting upcoming Hollywood films featuring the musical fantasy, *The Wizard of Oz*, starring Judy Garland and the Civil War drama, *Gone With Wind*, with Clark Gable and Vivien Leigh. Ordinary people looking for a way to escape the decade-long depression and rumors of another world war, swarmed to the movies. Snug in her wool coat and raccoon collar, Eleanor smiled up at Melvin on their walk home. The young couple talked about their future and leaning on the Lord for guidance and strength for whatever life brought their way.

After passing through the front doors of the college, Melvin walked Eleanor as far as the second floor landing in the stairway to say good night to her. Although there was a back stairway known as a "kissing area," Melvin and Eleanor never took advantage of it. He knew that if he paused too long at the landing, someone might write him up, and he didn't want that to happen again. Not long ago, Melvin presented Eleanor a bouquet of red roses while standing in this very spot, and they lost themselves in a kiss. Abruptly, the spell of love was broken by a distinct clearing of a throat. C.M. Ward had been passing by. Obviously, the cleats on his heels did not alert the young couple of his presence, and Melvin didn't bother to see if he was wearing a red tie.

However, it was not long until another infraction of the dating code would occur. Walking from the college to the Tab for a Sunday morning service, Melvin and Eleanor took a slight detour through Powderhorn Park and discreetly kissed. The next day, Eleanor was called into Miss Froland's office. The Dean of Women asked her to please sit down. Eleanor nervously smoothed out her black dress and folded her hands in her lap.

"Miss Groat, do you know why you are here?"

"No, Miss Froland."

"Someone saw you and Melvin in Powderhorn Park yesterday, kissing."

Miss Froland could tell by Eleanor's face that the report was accurate. Eleanor didn't know what to say. The last time they were reported, their punishment was losing one of their biweekly dates including their once a week table date at the cafeteria.

Miss Froland's voice softened, "I am not going to write you up for your indiscretion." Then she gently advised, "Eleanor, you have to be careful. People are watching you and Melvin. Spring will come eventually, and with it, commencement and the freedom to see each other as much as you want."

After spending Christmas break in Crookston, Melvin anxiously waited to get back to North Central to spend time with Eleanor. He envisioned her walking by his side through the streets of Minneapolis, wrapping his arm around her small waist. However, once he arrived he spent his time in his dorm room sick in bed with the flu.

"Here, Melvin," Dale handed him a brown-paper-wrapped gift the size and feel of a book, "It's from your not-so-secret admirer."

Melvin unwrapped the paper and looked over the title, *Lady of the Parsonage.* "I hope she will be my lady of the parsonage someday," Melvin crooned.

After reading a couple of chapters, he slid his glasses off and ran a hand across his hair. Before falling asleep that night, he stared at the baseball pennants on the dorm walls. His thoughts turned to Eleanor and perhaps slipping a ring on her finger and setting a date for their wedding.

Once Melvin was back on his feet, there was homework to catch up on, Practical Work outreaches, chapels, choir and Male Quartet. Mixed in with these activities he continued his office duties and the ARCHIVE. One winter night he assisted the photographer for a special snapshot of the building. Melvin's job was to make sure only the lights in the center above the main entrance would be turned on and a few rooms on the fourth floor on each side to form a lit cross in the darkness.

Commencement on Tuesday May 9, 1939, was held in a rented theater space large enough to accommodate the seniors, remaining student body, faculty and invited guests. Melvin sat in his alphabetically designated seat to the left of Orrin Kingsriter. He glanced around, looking for Eleanor. After the organ prelude, the college orchestra played Mozart's *Minuetto,* followed by the invocation. Melvin sat placidly listening to the music and eloquent words, reminiscing his past three years at North Central. He hoped most of the straw was out of his pockets by now, but perhaps he would fill them up with fresh straw when he got to Africa. Class President, Dale Zink performed a saxophone solo *From the Garden to the Cross Alone* by Phillips.

Finally, with his diploma in his hand, Melvin listened with one ear to Rev. I.O. Miller give the benediction while the call to Africa sounded louder than ever. He reflected on the class theme: the Call of Calvary; and class motto: "Calvary for All". Melvin had served as the president of the Executive Missionary Society, and now he wanted to *become* one of those missionaries. His senior picture in the 1939 ARCHIVE showed a young man dedicated to following the scripture printed under his name: "For the Lord God will help me; therefore shall I not be confounded: therefore have I set my face like a flint, and I know that I shall not be ashamed" (Isaiah 50:7 KJV).

Chapter Eleven

March 18, 1942

After Melvin graduated from NCBI in 1939, he worked at the catalog and order desk at Sears and Roebuck on Lake Street earning thirty-nine cents an hour until he paid off his remaining tuition. His brother, Lloyd, came to Minneapolis and they found a room to rent. During this time, Melvin traveled with Lloyd, holding evangelistic meetings in North Dakota, Wisconsin and Minnesota sleeping in their car or staying in homes. At each location they started with a two-week campaign, and at times stayed as long as six weeks. This continued until they went to Jackson, a small town one hundred and eighty miles southwest of Minneapolis, close to the Iowa border. Lloyd was planning to stay on as pastor, with Melvin assisting him for several months. However, that winter, a twist in the plan changed everything.

"Well, you rest up Lloyd and we'll see you in three weeks after you recuperate," Melvin stood on the curb as the Greyhound bus arrived in Jackson.

"Sorry to put you in charge of the new work here, Melvin," Lloyd said, "but I have confidence that you will do a fine job until I get back."

Suddenly, Lloyd turned and hurled the contents of his stomach onto the nearby snow bank. Red blood melted into the snow. Lloyd pulled out a handkerchief to wipe his mouth. Neither said a word as Melvin shook hands with his brother and watched him slowly step into the Greyhound bus bound for Crookston. For now, Melvin would have to postpone his intentions to travel to Wisconsin for evangelistic meetings.

After three weeks, a letter from Crookston arrived at the church. Sitting at his desk strewn with books and papers, Melvin read his brother's strained handwriting, "The doctors say I have a bleeding ulcer. It looks like it will be three months until I am ready to come back to Jackson."

Melvin kept up the work in Jackson doing everything he had been trained for, not only at North Central, but also from his days as a teenager during the revival in Crookston with Christian Hild. After three months, another letter came from Crookston. This time Lloyd wrote, "I don't understand why it is taking so long to heal from these ulcers. I am truly sorry, Melvin. I don't think I will ever be coming back."

In addition to his pastoral duties, Melvin feverishly embarked on a renovation project, completing a second-floor apartment over the front entrance of the curved roof church for his bride to be. He was now making ten dollars a week. However, the AG paid for all expenses concerning the church and parsonage, including maintenance. A favorable bond formed between the shepherd and his flock, and a small contingent from the Jackson Gospel Tabernacle joyfully anticipated attending the future wedding in Minneapolis.

Meanwhile, Eleanor worked in the bookkeeping department at National Battery Co. housed in the First National Bank building in St. Paul. After renting an efficiency apartment with former North Central students for one year, Eleanor found a room available with a family and boarded there for her remaining two years as a single woman. It was a charming older brick home located on 3115 Edmund Boulevard in Minneapolis, close to the west bank of the Mississippi River. The main floor had a formal dining room with a generous bay window facing the street. From the sidewalk, a heartwarming scene of the family eating at the table could be seen. The owners, Mr. and Mrs. Lakeman, had one daughter, Delphine, who was ten years old. The kind couple took Eleanor in like she was part of their family.

Melvin ate there only one time during their courtship. While Melvin enjoyed the delicious meal prepared by Mrs. Lakeman, Mr. Lakeman stirred the conversation to the topic of Melvin dating Eleanor. Gradually, he began elevating Eleanor above Melvin, who had no problem agreeing with Mr. Lakeman's assessment of Eleanor as the winning prize of the two of them. Nonetheless, Melvin felt the protective stares of the entire family sizing him up. They were clearly giving him the once over wondering if he was good enough for their Eleanor. After dinner and the interrogation, the young couple escaped to the tree-lined sidewalk along Edmund Boulevard.

* * * *

That winter, Eleanor spent one last Christmas at her childhood home in Thunderhawk. Her parents were making plans to sell the General Store and move to Lemmon. She visited with her cousins, Margaret and Ann, discussing all the changes in their lives since high school. When Roy and Kitty found out Eleanor was going to marry a minister, Uncle Roy was upset, "I was going to put you in my will, but if you marry a minister I won't put you in my will."

Aunt Kitty added her displeasure and said, "I can't imagine you wearing all those hand-me -downs, being a poor minister's wife."

On March 18, 1942, Melvin Ernest Jorgenson and Eleanor Aldene Groat stood before Rev. Frank J. Lindquist, their parents and wedding guests at the Minneapolis Gospel Tabernacle on 3015 Thirteenth Avenue South. Melvin's brother-in law Rev. Kenneth Olson, Julia's husband, assisted in the double ring ceremony. It began at seven o'clock with several selections on the organ preceding the entrance of the matron of honor Mrs. Carl Cornelius.

Ann wore a daffodil gown of marquisette netting over nylon and carried a bouquet of Talisman roses. Acting as best man, Rev. Lloyd Jorgenson wore a dark suit, white shirt, and black bow tie similar to the groom's attire. Eleanor glided down the white bridal carpet toward her groom on the arm of her father. Her fingertip veil fell over her eyes, down across her shoulders to her back, as her pure white marquisette and lace short-sleeved gown flowed gently with each step. White, formal-length gloved hands held a bouquet of white narcissus, gardenias and roses. The enchanting floral aroma lingered as she passed each row of guests toward the altar adorned with palms and candelabra. Melvin waited for "his groat" to take his hand for today, and forever, until death do they part. The rest of the "Crookston three," Rev. Carl Cornelius and George Erickson served as ushers.

The wedding reception was held in the Lakeman's family room downstairs. It was a direct drive five miles east of the church on Lake Street, filled with passing automobiles and streetcars. Pedestrians bundled up against the lingering winter chill in the breezes blustering through downtown Minneapolis. In the kitchen, Mrs. Lakeman bustled about with the finishing touches of the food as Melvin and Eleanor made their way to their places at the white linen setting. A toast was raised to the new couple, seated at their table that held a three-tier white frosted cake. Lloyd sat on the newly-wed's left and Ann to the right. As people mingled, Melvin's parents were remarking to their sons about how fast the last forty-two years had gone since they were married, while Eleanor was asking her parents how they liked living back in Lemmon after her father sold the General Store.

"I'm still keeping busy with a rural postal route." He was obviously smitten with his beautiful daughter, "I can't believe my oldest is all grown up and married."

Ken Olson stuck out his hand to Melvin and nodded a smile at his new sister-in-law, "Congratulations Mr. and Mrs. Jorgenson! I'm sorry Julia couldn't make the wedding. With the baby coming soon she just couldn't risk it."

"At least we got to see Julia at your place for Christmas when we made the announcement of our wedding date," Melvin said squeezing Eleanor's hand.

"I'm so thankful she's feeling well and things are going better for her this time around," Eleanor added.

Julia and Ken lived at the parsonage in Grafton, north of Grand Forks. They had one son, John Paul, a toddler. When their second child, Roberta died at birth, Melvin went with Ken to make the funeral arrangements and select a tombstone for the baby.

"I can still remember how cold it was when I took the snapshot of you and Melvin outside our house," Ken said.

Without an indoor flashbulb, it had been necessary to go outside for the picture. Standing close to Melvin, with her hands clasped together at the waist of her wine colored velvet dress, Eleanor had tried her best to pose gracefully.

"Oh yes, my dress was no match for those North Dakota temperatures," Eleanor laughed, "but I didn't want to cover it with my coat either."

After the meal, Mr. and Mrs. Jorgenson cut their wedding cake together and served each other a frosted piece. Despite the turbulent times in Europe and China, the simple, yet elegant wedding was a festive affair. Everyone seemed to relish the escape from all the doom and gloom of the war. After the Japanese bombed Pearl Harbor on December 7, 1941, America entered the war. Updates from the frontlines were constantly flooding the airwaves of radios and head-lines in the newspapers. More than ever, the fireside chats of President Roosevelt coming over the radio eased the fears of Americans. During World War II, the draft did not affect ordained ministers or young men preparing for the ministry. Consequently, Melvin and many of his friends and family were not called up for the draft. Combined with the boost to the economy from the war, and rains starting again in the Great Plains in 1939, America was finally closing the door to the decade known as the Dust Bowl and the Great Depression.

Chapter Twelve

Jackson

I t was a beautiful spring day with trees yearning to burst from bud to leaf as the bride and groom came to the edge of town in their late 1930s Chevrolet with the spare tire kit on the rear of the car. The Jackson County Courthouse, on 4th Street, dominated their initial view. Built in 1908, it was a large, beautiful stone building, topped with a painted dome adorned with a graceful statue of a lady, similar to the Lady of Liberty or the iconic logo of Columbia Pictures, proudly overlooking the city and its county. By 1940, the Jackson County population grew to 2,840 residents with its southern border touching Iowa. The town of Jackson lay between the Des Moines River to the east, and Clear Lake to the far west, with Ft. Belmont on the south end of town.

"Just so you don't get confused, Main Street is the same as Second Street." Melvin informed Eleanor, "We are only a few blocks away now."

Eleanor watched the signs and windows of the businesses pass by as they headed south on Main Street. Older and newer models of cars and trucks parked at an angle filled either side of the street as pedestrians went about their business. In the heart of the downtown area was the Main Street

Theater with its Art Deco design. The marquee read, "Final Week *Citizen Cane* starring Orson Welles released by RKO pictures." Posters advertising upcoming movies included *Casablanca,* starring Humphrey Bogart and Ingrid Bergman, set in war-torn North Africa.

As the tires of their car rolled onto the dirt driveway on the left side of the building, Melvin was obviously proud to bring his bride home to the Jackson Gospel Tabernacle and the apartment. There wasn't a garage, so he simply parked the car next to the side door that led up a flight of stairs to the second floor. The apartment sat over the front entrance to the church with dark wooden double doors sporting three small rectangle windows marching down and up like musical notes. Over the double doors, cursive writing spelled out "Assemblies of God Tabernacle." The cream stucco building stood on a large city lot surrounded by two-story homes with screened-in porches. Behind the square front of the building rose tall one-story walls with several buttresses curved out from the walls supporting the rounded roof that covered the sanctuary.

"Now you can see how the joke around town started with this being a good building for the 'Holy Rollers'," Melvin laughed. "Well, Mrs. Jorgenson, welcome to our first home!"

He gallantly swung the door open for his bride. Eleanor eagerly climbed the full flight of stairs to investigate the well-built apartment that smelled as new and clean as it looked. As Melvin followed her, he thought of how he had slept in his car, or stayed at people's homes while on the road with Lloyd doing evangelistic meetings. Now all he had to do was walk a few steps from work to home. He was with Eleanor, too. An unstoppable grin spread across his face.

Eleanor stepped across the golden polished wood floors covering the entire apartment except the bathroom. The living room, dining room, and kitchen grouped together to offer a cozy home. Eleanor opened and closed the custom cupboards that someone from the church made, "Oh look, a large slide-out breadboard."

She peered out the two small windows over the sink that sat like two rectangular eyes over the main entrance of the church. The white gas stove and refrigerator weren't overly large, but adequate for their needs, certainly for a turkey at the holidays. No more cooking with coal or cooling with ice as she had in Thunder Hawk. Behind the kitchen was the bathroom with running cold and hot water and an indoor toilet. Still considered a luxury by many, only about half of American homes had indoor plumbing, and less than that with electricity on rural farms. Their bedroom balanced off the other side of the apartment with corner windows and a closet.

"It's beautiful, Melvin!" Eleanor embraced her husband.

"I finally got my lady of the parsonage," he added, making reference to the book Eleanor gave him during their courtship. Their eyes and lips met, enjoying the fulfillment of waiting for this season of their life together.

They began to settle into the typical duties of married life, and overseeing their flock and church property. Melvin didn't have much of a grass yard to cut, but he did put in a garden to tend. Many Americans were encouraged to have Victory Gardens wherever they could find a vacant lot in the city or in their own yards. Eleanor washed their clothes at a church family's house using their ringer washer. Then she hauled the wet clothes home to hang on the clothesline. Melvin didn't think it appropriate to have their laundry strung across the church auditorium, so he picked out a discreet spot in the yard for a collapsible clothesline with a center pole and square spider web design.

In May of that year, *War Ration Book No. 1* was issued by the government. A family of two adults and two children got one hundred and ninety-two points. This allowed them to purchase two pounds of meat a week and other items as long they had the right coupons and cash. Eleanor looked over the red and blue detachable one-inch square coupons. Instead of cash in the offering, some farmers would bring eggs to the church. This enabled Eleanor to bring a couple dozen eggs to the creamery to sell to buy a small Sunday roast for thirty-five cents. At the store, she tore out her coupons for meat and paid the clerk her coins. A month after they got married, selling sugar was banned for a week and then tightly rationed. Some people began buying from the black market telling others that they bought their coffee or gas from "Mr. Black."

One farmer donated corncobs to burn in the furnace located in the church basement, underneath the stairway to their apartment, with a radiating heat pipe climbing up to their living room. As it turned out, the corncobs burned out fast and furiously, so Melvin had to put in the fuel continuously night and day. And the temperature of the heat ran either hot or cold. The worst part though was the unwanted guests that invaded the basement of the church feasting on the cobs like it was a church picnic. Every morning when Melvin shoveled out the ashes into a tin bucket, he would hear the scurries of the mice. After walking to the other side of the basement, he noticed their gnawing marks on the wooden door of the storage room filled with corncobs. Something had to be done and soon! There wasn't room in the budget for spring traps, but he did find some kerosene around the place and set up a line of defense along the doorway pouring a swath of the poison on the cement floor. He went upstairs to report his progress to Eleanor.

"Well, we'll see who wins this battle. In the meantime, I need to look into getting a cord of wood."

Eleanor arranged another air-dried shirt on the ironing board and sprinkled it with water before pressing, "Not to mention planning this Sunday's service. When did you want to go over the music selections? I would like a few days to practice if we pick out hymns I'm not used to playing."

Melvin and Eleanor planned four services held every week. On Sunday there was morning Sunday school followed by a worship service and an evening service. On Wednesday, they held a mid-week service. In preparation, Eleanor and Melvin selected the music together and Melvin worked on his sermon. During the service, Eleanor played the piano to the left of him, while Melvin led the worship. Then Melvin took the offering and presented his sermon, unless there was a visiting preacher in town. The service usually lasted one hour and fifteen minutes. Confidently standing behind the pulpit, Melvin did not feel nervous like his first year at chapel services at North Central. The experiences of going out with Lloyd continued to erase any awkwardness left. Melvin was glad to have the practice runs behind him.

At the end of every service, Eleanor would be at the piano, while Melvin gave an altar call for prayer for those who wanted to get saved, be filled with the Holy Spirit, or other needs of the people.

One time, during a Wednesday night service, mischievous footsteps pounded on the roof. Sometimes young people from town would scale the arched buttresses to gain access to the curved roof intending to aggravate the "Holy Rollers." A deacon went out and chased them off. Although Melvin and Eleanor never saw anyone rolling around in their services, for some reason people started nicknaming Pentecostals "Holy Rollers," and it stuck. Maybe it was because Pentecostals didn't follow the traditional format of liturgical churches. Or perhaps it was because Pentecostals seemed too zealous for people comfortable with a religion they could contain and control.

That summer, Carl Cornelius came to Jackson to visit Melvin and Eleanor. After the warm greeting, Melvin took Carl for the tour of the church and parsonage. Inside the sanctuary, the curved ceiling created a spacious room similar to a bowling alley or a movie theater with nine burnished brown covered opera chairs in each row with no middle aisle. Behind the pulpit was a recessed choir area with a valance of heavy fabric. Two side doors flanked either side of the choir room.

"I'm glad you can stay through Sunday, so you can meet all the children in our Sunday school," Melvin led Carl through the double doors out to the cement walk. "We have a really nice group of young people."

As the two pastors strolled about the church grounds, Melvin said, "Betty Sharp is the oldest student in our class; her father Ray owns the two filling stations I was telling you about.

"Oh yes," Carl nodded his head, "the one you fill in for when he needs to go out of town. That must be hard running a business with gas rationed to three gallons a week."

"Unless you are a trucker or a medical doctor, then it's different," Melvin commented.

"You know, I think I met the Sharp family at your wedding and some other guests from the church here."

"Yes, that's right, we had a pretty good contingent that drove all the way to Minneapolis for the wedding. These people are so supportive Carl, I feel blessed to have them as my first congregation. And we're adding new members to the church every month. There's this one family—Mrs.

Meyers and the children come, but not Mr. Meyers. He only comes on holidays or other rare occasions, but we keep praying for him."

That Sunday, Melvin and Eleanor introduced Carl to the Sunday school class and they went outside for a picture. Twenty-four students from first to twelfth grades, and a few younger, formed three crooked rows with Melvin on the left and Carl on the right. Eleanor looked down the viewfinder trying to get everyone in the picture without cutting someone's head off. Blonde, fair-skinned Betty Sharp stood in the back with Gladys and Adella Buchman and some of the other girls. Click went the camera, "Okay, I think I got it."

From time to time, pastors would stay with the Jorgensons, and assist in preaching. One pastor and his wife from Worthington, Minnesota were visiting for the week. After the Wednesday night service, Eleanor climbed the steps to the apartment to prepare a light snack for their guests. The church could be damp, which attracted spiders. Not little cute ones that artists draw on greeting cards and calendars. They were big, ugly thousand-leg spiders. It seemed to Eleanor as if there were a thousand of the wretched creatures living in her home. Whenever she killed one, another one or two or three took its place.

Just as she was finishing fixing the tray of cheese and crackers, she saw one out of the corner of her eye, "You ugly thing! This is your last day on earth!"

In a flash, Eleanor grabbed the broom and took a swung at the spider like the Yankee Clipper, Joltin' Joe DiMaggio, on a home run. One foot perched on the edge of the steps, she knew she was going to get this one and get it good. Then a slight cry escaped her lips. The broom fell with a slap to the floor. Momentum from her swing launched her down the entire flight of stairs. Head to heel her petite frame hit every step until her head crashed at the bottom.

Through the blood and pain she could hear the pastor's wife from Worthington, "Eleanor! Eleanor, don't stand up. Here. . ." the woman cradled her arms around Eleanor, ". . .just sit here. I'll get Melvin."

Melvin saw the woman's anxious face as she approached him in the church, "Eleanor fell down the steps. We need a doctor. Now." She tried to say it as calm as possible, but the fear in her eyes shook Melvin to the core.

Eleanor lay in her bed with cloth bandages over her head, elbows and knees. Melvin kept trying to tell the doctor what had happened and what the injuries were, but the doctor was hard of hearing. Many doctors had gone off to the war to help the troops so the elderly doctors had done their part by not retiring, and filling in, any way they could.

Finally, the doctor figured everything out and treated her wounds including a cracked head, "You also may have bleeding of the bladder from this type of fall."

The doctor briefly turned toward Melvin, "Keep an eye on things."

Melvin nodded yes, and the doctor continued with Eleanor, "I'll be around tomorrow to check on you Mrs. Jorgenson."

Eleanor closed her eyes and rested while Melvin walked the doctor to his car. Little did she know that one day she would be able to say that Jackson prepared her for some of the creatures she would meet on the mission field in Africa. For now though, she was relieved she didn't have to go to the hospital and that she wasn't expecting. Although, she thought as a whimsical smile worked its way from her heart to her face, it wouldn't be so bad in the future.

That fall Melvin heard about the Bible Quiz contest, "Apparently, the young people are released from school and we can practice with them."

* * * *

Melvin sat at their dining room table sipping his morning coffee. It was Monday, a good day to take his time during breakfast, after the packed schedule they had on Sunday.

Eleanor's curiosity peaked, "How many churches are involved? And how much time do we get to work with the students?"

"All the churches in Jackson County will compete in the contest. I'm not sure on the time frame yet."

"The Lutheran and Catholic churches are so big," pointed out Eleanor, "but the thing of it is, we have some very bright students at our little church."

"We're David going against Goliath," Melvin chuckled with the spark of competition in his eyes.

"Okay then, let's get signed up for the Bible Quiz," Eleanor felt the spark and caught the fire, "This would be something exciting for our young people, and they would learn an awful lot of scripture through the experience."

"We probably will, too," Melvin said in his agreeable tenor voice.

After that, pastor and wife began meeting with several students, including Betty Sharp and Adella Buckman. Week after week, they practiced, drilled, and memorized scripture and Bible trivia. Finally, the day of the contest came and all the students of Jackson County gathered at a large church in a nearby town. The local newspaper had reporters and a photographer ready.

"After all that practice the contest seemed so short," one of the girls said to Eleanor.

All the students and church leaders were dressed in their best clothes that day. Electricity filled the air as students and adults tapped their feet or twiddled their thumbs waiting for the results. Finally, a man walked to the podium in the auditorium, cleared his throat, shuffled some papers, welcomed everyone, thanked everyone, and began to name the third place winner. It wasn't their church. Melvin and Eleanor exchanged glances. Then he announced the second place winner. Nope. Not them either. And then they heard it. Their little church, the Jackson Gospel Tabernacle, won first place! Flash went the camera. The reporter got the scoop, and congratulations were offered from the other churches and students.

On the way home, Melvin and Eleanor couldn't help but sit a little taller and straighter in the front seat of their car. They held hands while humming something or another as they passed by the County Jackson Courthouse with the Lady of Justice standing benevolently on her dome, watching all the festivities.

* * * *

That Thanksgiving, Carl and Ann shared in the turkey dinner Eleanor had prepared in her small, but efficient kitchen. After Melvin said the prayer of blessing and thanksgiving, the potatoes and gravy made their way around the table.

"What a beautiful tablecloth, Eleanor," Ann complimented her friend.

"Thank you, my grandmother crocheted it," Eleanor smoothed out her company-cooking apron tied around her slim waist.

"I hope I don't spill the cranberry sauce on it," teased Carl, "by the way, everything tastes delicious Mrs. Jorgenson." Then he turned to his friend, "You better hang onto her Melvin."

"Oh, I think I will. Nobody's going to get my 'groat' you know," Melvin stated.

Everyone laughed at the table, reminiscing about their romance at North Central and days gone by in Minneapolis. Then talk turned to the war, the new regulations on milk control, War Bonds and the latest headlines about France surrendering Algiers, and Hitler's pompous threats to flatten the American troops in Africa.

"We keep praying for Africa," Melvin paused a moment, "and the rest of the world of course."

"But always Africa," Carl's voice held admiration for Melvin. "Ever since we met during the revival in Crookston I've seen your heart for Africa."

"Well, the Lord placed the call to central Africa in my heart and there's no other place in the world it beats for," admitted Melvin.

A month later, a blanket of snow covered the churchyard and their car while Eleanor thought through her menu. It would just be the two of them together in Jackson for their first Christmas as husband and wife. Eleanor thought she would try to make the Christmas meal like Melvin's mother had over the years. However, while looking over recipes for Swedish Meatballs, she decided she wasn't going to tackle making lutefisk.

On Christmas Eve, Eleanor set the table and put the finishing touches on the meal. The crocheted tablecloth and lit tapered candles were about the only Christmas decorations they had besides the frost on the windows. In the living room, Melvin was tinkering with the furnace pipe that radiated heat from the furnace in the church basement. It was a home-made furnace that someone from the church installed for the apartment. The pipe had a metal plate covering a round opening for a future attachment of a radiating heat stove.

"Eleanor," Melvin called to his wife as he focused on the metal plate on the pipe, "I think there's something wrong with the furnace. Can you come here and hold this plate down for me while I go to the basement?"

Eleanor peered over his shoulder, "What's the matter with it?"

"I don't know, but it seems like it is about to pop off or something. Here, hold the broomstick over it to keep it closed until I get back."

Once downstairs, Melvin knew it was a chimney fire out of control. Slowly he opened the door of the furnace and carefully looked in, which caused a back draft. There was a loud gush of air and then the fire went who-ooh-ooh like the wind twirling up a bass and treble musical scale of notes.

Meanwhile, Eleanor maintained her post at the pipe. She held the broomstick firmly against the round plate. The pressure kept building. She kept pushing until *w-o-o-f*.

Soot spewed out all over the living room and Eleanor. In only seconds, soot-blackened walls encompassed their sur-roundings, coated like the dirt blizzards of the Dust Bowl. The whole room had to be washed and painted! With no heat, they would have to stay with one of the members of the church for several nights until the furnace was back in working order.

Nonetheless, the dinner was ready, so the young couple improvised. They sat on chairs beside the warm gas stove with the oven door open. The large breadboard from the cupboard rested across their laps for a table and they ate their meal. That was Christmas Eve 1942, their first Christmas together.

Chapter Thirteen

Detroit Lakes

66 I wish you were coming instead of going," Mr. Meyers bemoaned the fact that Melvin and Eleanor had accepted the call to pastor a church in Detroit Lakes, two hundred and seventy-seven miles north of Jackson.

Mr. Meyers kept packing the Jorgenson's belongings from their apartment, along with the others that had come to help. Not one to darken the door of a church much, his wife and children had been regular attendees. One time though, on one of his rare appearances, he surprised everyone by walking forward during one of Melvin's regular end of service altar calls. The changes were apparent to everyone and they celebrated with the angels in heaven.

In Jackson, it had been a new work, spiritually speaking, pioneered by visiting evangelists, including Melvin and his brother Lloyd, holding tent meetings. Since then, the fledgling church grew to one hundred people. Just the opposite in Detroit Lakes, it would be an old work where the older people did everything in the church leaving the young people little to do, if anything. The church wasn't in the AG family of churches either, but Melvin hoped to rectify that as soon as they got settled into the parsonage on 504 Front Street on the west side of town. His salary would increase to twenty dollars a week. Again, the AG provided the parsonage, utilities, and maintenance.

Their initial scouting visit revealed a region of Minnesota where lakes, woodland, and prairie merged to create a bounty of wildlife and natural beauty. The city lay on the northern banks of Detroit Lake with the Pelican River to the east. Noble wildlife of eagle, bear, coyote, deer, and badger were plentiful, as well as species of waterfowl, songbirds, raptors, and upland game birds. Duck hunters and those after white-tailed deer flocked to the area every fall.

A man from the church had offered to host Melvin and Eleanor during their initial visit and they gratefully accepted. After driving to Detroit Lakes, the Jorgensons met him at the white church on Rossman Street. It was an average-looking building that currently accommodated one hundred people, mostly from the Broberg and Nelson families. At the next stop, Melvin and Eleanor walked through the small white clapboard two-story parsonage.

From the backseat of their car, their host continued the tour, "Detroit Lakes has everything a person needs. However, if you still can't find what you're looking for, Fargo and Moorhead are only forty miles to the west."

Back in the car they headed for a drive along the three thousand acre lake, "The fishing here is excellent. Throw in a line and soon you'll have a bluegill, black crappie, bass, or even a northern pike."

"Well, I hope the fishing for souls will be as good, too," Melvin chuckled.

The man in his suit, tie, and hat kept driving and talking while Melvin and Eleanor politely asked questions, when they could squeeze them in between their host's running monologue. Then the man began telling about the people of the town, and church, with a bit of gossip thrown in for good measure.

Melvin's frame stiffened, "You know, you don't have to tell me about these people. If I have to know anything about them I can figure that out for myself."

After that, Melvin didn't trust the man.

Later that fall in November 1943, Melvin and Eleanor left Jackson to accept the pastorate at Detroit Lakes. Once acquainted with everyone in the church, they found the young people eager to get involved somehow. Melvin decided to create a special choir and began working with each choir member, and in small groups, teaching them everything he knew from high school choir and North Central's music program. Meanwhile, Eleanor worked on planning activities and outings for them. She broke from tradition and asked the young people to decorate the church for Christmas, including the tree, instead of the adults. The young minister and his wife grew fond of the young people enjoying playing games and going on hayrides with them. One young man, Orvil, fell off the wagon and sustained a few injuries. Back at the church, having hot chocolate and lunch, several of his friends teased, "It would have to be Orvil!"

However, some people were a bit skeptical about all this attention on the young people. They couldn't see the spiritual value of activities and playing board games. During one game night, an elderly lady objected in her sweetest voice possible, drawing out her r's and t's, "Those d-i-r-r-t-t-y games!"

Nonetheless, the fruit of Melvin and Eleanor's labor was blessed as many of the young people began growing spiritually, their souls refreshed by the prayer meetings at church and in the homes. They learned to seek the Lord in earnest, known as pining for the Spirit. One young lady, Dorothy Broberg, kept pining for the Holy Spirit, praising the Lord louder and louder, until she was filled with the Spirit. Then she quieted down, speaking in her newfound heavenly language.

Numbers were added to the church and choir. Melvin took an interest in one young man in the choir, coaching the shy vocalist to become a vibrant soloist. At one point, Melvin decided to have a photographer come to the church and take a picture of the fifty-member choir. Everyone wanted a copy of the photograph framed in cardboard to display at his or her home.

Each week Melvin, went out street-by-street canvassing the town, going to the homes of people to get acquainted with them. The following Sunday, the fruit of Melvin's labor would show up for the service. At one home he noticed an elderly woman had a distinct accent, "Mrs. Olson, where did you come from?"

"I come from Gyland, Norway," she proudly replied.

"My father is from Gyland, Norway. Would you remember John Jorgenson?"

"Yeah sure, I remember little Johnny," her old eyes flickered with joy, "He used to come to my house and jump off the big rock. It was taller than you. The size of a small house. We would take turns over and over, climbing and jumping."

However, not everyone was as happy to meet the new minister in town.

"What are you doing knocking on people's doors, inviting them to your church?"

A nicely dressed lady had confronted Melvin in the middle of the street.

"I'm sorry that you feel offended about it," Melvin offered.

His humble demeanor softened her attitude, but she was still cross about it, "It's just that people are leaving their church—my church—and going to your church."

"Well, maybe we have something to offer them that their church doesn't."

Shortly after moving to Detroit Lakes, word reached Melvin and Eleanor about Mr. Meyers. They sat at their kitchen table at the parsonage, stunned by the news of his sudden death.

"It's sobering to think he helped us pack for coming here only a few months ago," Melvin stated.

"But the thing of it is, God got him ready for a good homecoming and answered our prayers," Eleanor said to her husband and to herself.

"I guess I better get to work on my notes for his funeral," Melvin reflected on the span of one's life and its impact on others. "It was a brief time of serving the Lord. Still, he showed the light of Christ in his changed life, and it will continue to lead the way for his family and others. Yes, that will give his family much peace and comfort in the coming days."

* * * * *

Over the next couple of years, Melvin and Eleanor organized street meetings in order to share the Good News of the Gospel with those who didn't know their Savior. Carl and Ann Cornelius came, as well as many others, to help with the street meetings. A tall silver stand, topped with a rectangular block microphone was set up for a quartet or trio accompanied by a guitarist. Their location in town was perfect, with numerous pedestrians and people passing by until the meetings began growing to the point of interfering with traffic. The city asked them to move, which they respectfully did. Although the crowd dwindled a bit, it still was a good turn out and revival broke out in Detroit Lakes. More numbers were added to the church.

Eleanor's sister, Lois, came to help, living with them for one of her high school years. Of course, sixteen-year old Lois had another motive for moving in with her older sister. Sitting in the front screened porch of the parsonage, Lois peppered Eleanor with question after question, "When are you due? How are you feeling? Are you nervous? How about Melvin?"

"Well, he doesn't have morning sickness," Eleanor teased, "and my due date is in January sometime."

"You'll bring in 1945 with a bang," Lois laughed reaching out to grasp Eleanor's hands, "Oh, Eleanor I'm so happy for you and for Melvin. And I'm almost an aunt."

On January 23, 1945, when Minnesota was frosted over at arctic temperatures with frozen lakes, and cars were reluctant to start in the morning, Richard Wayne Jorgenson struggled to come into the world. Eleanor had been in labor from late Sunday and now it was past noon on Tuesday.

Finally, the doctor decided to take the baby using instruments, "It's a boy Mrs. Jorgenson. Congratulations."

With a slap Richard cried his first song to the world. Eleanor shed tears of joy despite her exhaustion. She cradled him in her arms with the utmost care. "Oh my, his head looks like an egg."

Her heart pained at the site of Richard's elongated skull with raw skin behind his tiny soft ears. Melvin was allowed in for a visit and tears immediately swelled at the sight of Eleanor and Richard together. He tried to say something, and words came out, but they kept getting stuck in the lump in his throat. "Now, we are three."

He bent down to tenderly kiss his wife and get a closer look at his newborn son with the egg head, "Blessed be the name of Lord, and thank you, Lord, for preserving my wife and son."

After two weeks in the hospital, the nurses told Eleanor, "You can leave today Mrs. Jorgenson, but you can't take your baby home until the jaundice is gone."

At the news, Eleanor burst into tears. A bewildered Melvin sat at her bedside feeling useless. Eleanor's mother had come to stay with her and had witnessed everything the past two weeks. Her daughter had fought to give birth and after, got so sick she couldn't nurse the baby. Then Richard would cry so hard he would wear himself out. In sincere interest of Richard's health, the nurses would feed him and he wouldn't feel hungry enough to nurse. Consequently, it altered Eleanor's natural flow of milk, causing her body to quit producing breast milk. Maybe it would be only few days until she could bring him home, but the whole affair was turning into a nightmare as far as she was concerned.

"Come along dear," Hazel Groat comforted her daughter wrapping her arm around her shoulder. "I know it's not easy, but you need to get home to rest so you can come and see Richard tomorrow."

A few days after Richard came home from the hospital, Eleanor's mother left Detroit Lakes. Lois pitched in washing dishes, and ironing clothes. For the next several months, whenever Eleanor drove by the hospital, a shudder erupted from her petite frame. But time passed, and Eleanor found herself enjoying Richard more every day, delighted with each new change in his development. Lois was a comfort to her as well, doting on her nephew after school each day.

Meanwhile, Melvin felt like he had another baby ready to burst on the horizon. The congregation outgrew the small building on Rossman Street, and a building project was under way. At the parsonage one night, he confided all his thoughts to Eleanor.

"The land we bought on the corner of Summit and Front is perfect, but I think I want the front door to be on Summit Avenue. The sound of that address is better than Front Street."

Eleanor agreed, and kept listening to her husband while rocking Richard to sleep. At the kitchen table Lois worked on homework. "And we'll have to get the cross moved too, although it does light up the street for the neighbors at night."

Melvin had always liked the lighted cross that read "Jesus Saves" with the word "Saves" intersecting the vertical spelling of Jesus. "One problem we'll have is finding enough cement. With the war still going on, supplies are hard to get these days."

The war affected everything for daily life in America. With metal and tin used for airplanes, the newly created Jeep vehicle, and millions of cans of Spam shipped overseas, cardboard was one of the few materials in abundance. One enterprising businessman, Clarence Birdseye, had introduced the concept of frozen foods to the public in the 1920's and 30's, but it wasn't until people were forced to go without tin cans that his ideas of frozen vegetables, orange juice, fish, and meats were accepted by stores and the general public.

The Detroit Lakes church had been diligent to intercede for the soldiers, and to send letters. Each month, Melvin would designate a Sunday for people to bring the letters to church. The congregation would pray over the letters and then Melvin would deliver them to the Post Office.

When Melvin went to the hardware store in pursuit of five bags of cement for the building project the store clerk laughed at him.

"You won't find five bags of cement in the whole county!"

Undeterred, Melvin came back home ready to pray and watch the Lord provide. He reminded himself of the time in Jackson when the tire on their car blew out and they only had seven dollars left. It was the exact amount needed to fix the tire. A few days later, a letter came in the mail from a soldier who was part of their Jackson church. Enclosed was seven dollars.

The next Sunday, Melvin enlisted the Detroit Lakes congregation in praying for five bags of cement. Melvin started combing the area. As the weeks passed, he purchased one bag at a time, until he had five bags.

* * * * *

On April 12, 1945, President Roosevelt's fireside chats and confident leadership, since the early days of the Dust Bowl and Depression, ended. America, and the world, grieved the loss of a true leader. The final chapter of the war for America in the Pacific Southwest would conclude with President Truman giving the order to drop the newly developed atomic bomb on Japan. After the decimation of Hiroshima on August 6, and the refusal of the Japanese Army to surrender, an order was given to drop another A-bomb, this time on Nagasaki. Several days later, on August 14, 1945, Americans celebrated V-J Day.

That fall, American G.I.s returned home in droves, shrinking the US Army down to half of its 8.3 million soldiers from the beginning of the year. Woman gave up their wartime jobs, and returned to the home. The economy sparked into prosperity as consumers could finally spend their money on new products they had gone without. Cars, tires, and appliances were snatched up along with new items such as window air conditioners, and five-inch television sets.

Unmindful of the swirling events of history and innovations around him, Richard grew in stature, wisdom, and favor with those around him. His thick, dark hair and curious round eyes melted the hearts of strangers. However, as he learned to walk, and then talk, he did have a tendency to wander a bit. In order to make sure his son knew his address, Melvin continually worked with Richard in repeating 504 Front Street.

"Okay, say it again for Daddy," Melvin coaxed Richard while he sat on the front steps of the parsonage.

Richard stood facing his father, putting his chubby hands together to help himself concentrate. He looked directly at his father and repeated like a parrot; only it came out thickly with the F's sticking in his lips, "I live on F-F-ive-O-h-F-F-our F-F-Front Street."

Eventually Richard lost his accent, but his parents kept repeating the original version for years to come, cherishing those early moments that grow into a warm memory.

In the midst of this, the call of Africa kept sounding. Melvin and Eleanor prayed and discussed their plans. And then they prayed some more. There was a tension of knowing where God had called them, and the work going on in Detroit Lakes. Melvin and Eleanor had explained from the start that they were there until they went to the mission field. The church did not want them to go, but of course, no one would stand in the way. So much had happened. There was the youth choir, the revival, the growth of the church, and a new building to complete. Besides that, deep-rooted relationships between flock and shepherds had cemented loyal friendships that would endure through many years on the mission field.

After Melvin mailed their application to the AG head-quarters in Springfield, Missouri, he walked back to the parsonage for lunch. Richard heard his footsteps and ran into his arms, "Daddy! Daddy!"

Eleanor leaned against the staircase she had scraped and painted when they first moved in five years ago. Richard led his daddy over to the couch where the big stuffed bear sat. It had been ridiculous to buy it, Melvin and Eleanor had to admit, but the way Richard's eyes and mouth had popped when he first saw the stuffed creature in the store had won them over, and the bear was now part of their family.

"I suppose we'll have to bring him to Africa," Melvin shrugged his shoulders. "Well, at least while we itinerate."

Eleanor started thinking about all the planning and packing that lay ahead of them before they would leave America.

Once their application was approved, the AG headquarters would organize an itinerary of churches, primarily in Minnesota and Wisconsin, for the Jorgensons to visit in order to raise funds for their mission work. They would live in their car by day, and stay in homes or churches at night until the benchmark set by headquarters for their monthly budget was met. What Melvin and Eleanor didn't know about the "itinerate phase," as it was called, was that they would be speaking at a different church every night, rarely staying in one place for more than one night.

Chapter Fourteen

Appointment with Destiny

❧

The train stopped at the Burlington Depot in Detroit Lakes and a travel-weary trio stepped off, walking a few city blocks to the two-story white clapboard parsonage, "Here we are at Five-Oh-Four Front Street, Richard." Melvin smiled at his son.

"I want to see bear."

Richard ran through the house to find his friend, while Melvin and Eleanor unpacked, and warmed up their bones with coffee. Their trip to Springfield, Missouri had been exhilarating and nerve wracking. AG Headquarters had asked them to be open to three locations of general missionary service in Africa. The choices were northern and eastern locations including Congo, a Belgium colony. Melvin knew he had been called to central Africa when he was a teenager, but he also had to be flexible. One thing was certain. Wherever they were assigned, their first term would be five years, with no coming back for emergencies or funerals. Their only communication in Africa would be letters.

Eleanor held her coffee cup in her cold hands savoring the steaming aroma, "I can't believe this is really happening,

Melvin. We've both dreamed and prayed about this for so many years!"

Eleanor thought back to Miss Eunice and her stories of children in India.

"And we're going to Congo, now that the board has approved our appointment,"Melvin sighed with relief on his brow until it wrinkled into worry.

"But the thing of it is," Eleanor read his mind, "Now we have to itinerate and raise the funds to go. I wonder how long that will take?"

"Let's do what we always do," Melvin suggested, "Let's lift it up to the Lord and wait on Him for the provision and right timing."

"His guiding hand has brought us this far; I doubt his faithfulness will stop now," Eleanor reflected, as faith stepped in holding up a light for their path.

Richard continued to play with his bear friend and other toys, while his parents prayed about raising funds for the mission field.

By October 1948, Melvin and Eleanor had prepared their flock for their departure. Melvin introduced his brother-in-law and sister, Ken and Julia Olson, to the church and it seemed like the transition would be a smooth one. All their things were packed, stored, or given away. Eleanor and Julia discussed the parsonage and the needs of the church during Ken and Julia's last visit. There was only one thing left to do. Eleanor gathered up four-year-old Richard in her arms and sat on one of the few pieces of furniture in the house.

"Richard, Mommy wants to tell you something."

Richard gazed into his mother's eyes with curiosity.

"Now Richard, we are going to be living in a car and we won't have a home any more. And you have to pick out what toy you want, and it has to be something that can travel in a car that we'll have room for."

"Okay, Mommy."

After the first hundred miles, Eleanor regretted the freedom she had given Richard in choosing the toy himself. Through every country town and populated city, Richard sat in the back seat amongst their belongings with his record player. The red and white plastic toy played Richard's favorite song so often that his parents began to hear it in their sleep, "Here come the firemen to put the fire out. . ."

At every church they visited, the accommodations were as different as the town. They slept in homes, or in church basements where the furnace would wake Melvin with each blast on and off. Then there was the time they slept in the church nursery, and Melvin stretched in the morning, refreshed, "Eleanor, I slept like a baby last night."

Some churches had indoor bathrooms, and some didn't. At one particular church they were instructed to go to an elderly lady's home for the night. The lady lived alone and when they walked up the sidewalk to her front door, she was waiting for her guests with a smile.

"Oh goody, I get a real bed tonight," Richard blurted out before his parents could get acquainted with their hostess.

His parents glanced at the daybed made up in the living room, knowing that the three of them often shared a bed, which made for a torturous night of tossing and turning. A look of embarrassment passed between Melvin and Eleanor concerning Richard's manners, not wanting to put the kind lady on the spot.

She quickly spoke up, "Yes, that bed is just for you."

Melvin and Eleanor breathed a sigh of relief, and thanked their hostess for her considerate accommodations. That night, after they closed the door to their private room, the young couple snuggled for a bit, enjoying the bed that was just for them as well.

If meals were provided, it was usually by the pastor's family on Sunday, after the morning service. Most of the time they ate out, or had a picnic in their car. However, there was one constant thing in their irregular routine, sprinkled in between meeting people and traveling. Prayer was their lifeline and they prayed every day throughout the day about anything and everything. Looking back, they would see the importance of laying the foundation for anything spiritual and physical; seen and unseen battles were won or lost through prayer. There was no substitute.

Their general region assigned to them for raising funds was Minnesota and North Dakota, where they already had contacts, including Sheboygan, Wisconsin. At each church, Melvin and Eleanor set up a display area featuring Congo, their mission focus, and pledge cards to become regular supporters and prayer partners. The pastors were generous in sharing their pulpit, giving the prospective missionary couple the freedom of conducting the entire service. The church would take up an offering for them, and send them off with prayer to their next destination.

Passion and enthusiasm poured out of Melvin and Eleanor as they shared from the pulpit, and with individuals, "Many of you may be wondering if we will be accepting a pastorate on the mission field in Congo. Our intention is to pioneer new works and train the nationals to take over, and have them pastor the people in their own unique cultural ways."

The Jorgensons needed to raise enough funds to meet the benchmark set by AG Headquarters for their budget, before they could go out on the mission field. Over the years, they would come to appreciate the "backbone people" that supported their work in the mission field. The small amounts each month from these people weren't large, but they were faithful, which in the long run, helped more than the one-time larger gifts.

They were visiting a church in Brainerd in northern Minnesota, when Richard set his eyes on the xylophone. The pastor's wife smiled, informing his parents that she was going to sell it. Richard ran his hands over the short and long keys fastened to a richly toned wood, tapping them here and there. Melvin and Eleanor knew Richard loved anything musical. They made an offer and the lady accepted. Once again, generosity moved their hearts instead of their minds. Traveling from town to town, Melvin would lug it out every night and set it up, "It's heavy!"

Richard would stand on the box-like case for the adult-size xylophone so he could play it. Comments were made about the cute boy, and curiosity aroused as to where they stored it.

"It just fits in the floor of the back seat of the car," Melvin explained triumphantly.

Eventually, Richard had to part with his instrument, leaving the xylophone with Lloyd, who was pastoring in Kulm, North Dakota. In its place, he adopted a drum.

* * * * *

Melvin pulled the car close to the high curb along the residence in Lemmon. Hazel came out of the house to greet them. Gray strands threatened to take over her chocolate hair.

"Welcome! There's no wrung chicken, only a plump hen packaged by the butcher, but I did make biscuits and gravy like Great-Grandma Bell used to make at the sod house."

"Grandma Bell?" Richard inquired walking across the yard.

"Yes, Great-Grandma Bell could wring a chicken's neck and have it in the fry pan faster than anyone in the county!" laughed Edward, opening the kitchen door.

His middle-aged eyes wrinkled out to frosted sideburns. Ten years prior, Eleanor's parents moved to Lemmon after her father sold the General Store in Thunder Hawk. Her mother had brought her wringer washer over to put in the basement, so Eleanor intended to make good use of that. Doing laundry while living like gypsies was a challenge. After the last piece of chicken was gone, and biscuit crumbs scattered across plates, coffee and desert was served.

That evening, after Richard had fallen asleep, Eleanor sat at the kitchen table writing letters and thank-you notes. Then she opened the record book, checking over the ledger and making new entries. When they first went out to itinerate they had met with the North Dakota District Council, which gave them an offering of $53.52. The entries continued: gas $4.00 from Lemmon to Regan, Regan Tabernacle gave $27.49, antifreeze for the car $8.67, meals $5.33. They were averaging five to ten dollars a month per church.

Melvin and Eleanor had such a great affection for Detroit Lakes that they would stop in whenever they had the chance. It was wonderful to see familiar faces and hear all that God was doing in their midst. And it was also a chance to rest and catch up on business and personal affairs. Richard's former babysitter, Mrs. Benson, tried her best to make their stay comfortable at her home. A small trade-off she thought, for being able to dote on her Richy. Eleanor was helping Mrs. Benson finish the dishes when Melvin burst in the kitchen door like he was slamming into home base for the winning run.

"Hallelujah! We've reached our benchmark for our budget," Melvin embraced his wife and almost danced a jig.

"Are you sure?" Eleanor asked, "I knew we were getting close."

"I just got word that the churches in Hastings and St. James are each pledging fifteen dollars a month!"

"Hallelujah is right!"

Richard stared in open wonder at his parents, and then joined in with a hallelujah of his own. The trio shared a family laugh and prayed a prayer of thanksgiving together. Melvin walked over to the parsonage to let Ken and Julia know their good news.

That Christmas, as they spent time with both sides of the family, there was a mixture of joy and sorrow. Eleanor, Lorraine, Wayne, and Lois filled the house in Lemmon with their spouses and children. They ate, laughed, and talked about current events. Life in America was good right now. Then the conversation wound itself to Eleanor leaving for Africa.

"What is the mail like there? How do we know where to write you? Are you packing barrels? How much do they allow you to bring? Aren't you going to be in Europe for a year to study French? Why? What about Richard? And what about having more children? I mean, you had such a time of it with Richard. I can't imagine having a baby in Africa."

By now, Eleanor had been asked every question imaginable about being a missionary, so she took it in stride, patiently answering each question.

In Crookston, one last family photo was taken, celebrating John and Anna Jorgenson's 50th wedding anniversary. It was one of those rare occasions that brought the entire family back together, since the Sheboygan days. Melvin stood on the far left in the back row for the picture. Myrtle, Josephine, Clarence, Julia, Lloyd, and Leona filled in the two rows, while his aging parents proudly sat in the middle of their brood.

They took it stoically when they learned about the appointment to Congo, acknowledging the call of God on Melvin's life. Nonetheless, it was hard to watch their boy leave their home on 605 Pleasant Avenue. Who knew what the years would bring?

* * * * *

After 1950 rolled in, Melvin and Eleanor drove their faithful Plymouth, their home for the last fifteen months, back to Detroit Lakes. The peak of excitement after reaching their benchmark fell to a crash when they got the news that Ken, their replacement at Detroit Lakes, was severely ill. The doctors recommended a sabbatical. Their feelings jumbled around with the motion of the car on the road. They felt compassion for Ken and Julia and wanted to help anyway they could. And of course, the people at Detroit Lakes were near and dear to their hearts. Still, the postponing of their departure left them feeling flat lined and drained.

"We'll just have to trust in the Lord, and be willing to accept His guidance."

"Thy kingdom come Lord, Thy will be done."

"We say it. We pray it. But sometimes, honestly, we don't want it."

Back in the two-story white parsonage, Eleanor managed her household like she was still living in the car, only now they had more square feet. Their Spartan lifestyle continued as another page was torn off the calendar, and more prayers were said. Winter passed into spring. Then spring gave way to summer.

On a warm Sunday in the middle of July 1950, Melvin preached his last sermon in America to his flock in Detroit Lakes. Afterward, a final church dinner in the basement, and a herd of well-wishers migrated a few blocks to the train depot. Some walked and some drove, but they all cried. The entire church had come, young and old, and there wasn't a dry handkerchief in the depot. Gayle Lambertson stood along the street and sidewalk to the left of the depot with the others. She was crying her twelve-year-old eyes out along with many of the youth. The Jorgensons were their pastors, too. There were no more formal speeches or prayers. It was a somber moment and audible weeping ebbed and flowed, until the train rolled into town. In a blink of an eye, Melvin, Eleanor, and five-year-old Richard, clutching onto his toy drum, climbed the steps of the train. They turned for one last wave. A few cameras clicked.

Eleanor was dressed beautifully in a fitted green dress, accessorized with a smart-looking hat, and stylish shoes. Melvin stood tall in his suit and tie, his face tender and yet, set like flint toward his goal of reaching African soil. He had always envisioned that they would go out as a young couple in their mid-twenties. Now he was thirty-one. It had been fourteen years since he had graduated from North Central, and longer since he had been a teenager in Crookston, when he had first heard the call of God. Eleanor exchanged glances with her husband. She had been waiting since her childhood for this moment, and now it was here. They turned from the crowd, found their way to their seats, and the train left the depot in Detroit Lakes. Their appointment with destiny had arrived.

Part Two: The Course
1950–1964

Chapter Fifteen

NYC 1950-Brussels

On the train to New York City, Melvin and Eleanor were lost in their thoughts, while Richard dozed with his arms around his drum. The conductor came through collecting tickets and offering newspapers with headlines of President Truman and the conflict in Korea.

"It was a busy time working in Detroit Lakes," Eleanor broke the silence, "an enjoyable time."

"Yes, it was, the Lord accomplished much and we were privileged to be a part of it," Melvin said. "It was harder to leave than I thought it would be."

Thoughts drifted in and out about the ministry in Detroit Lakes. The services, baptisms in the lake, church picnics by the lake, and even a visit from Christian Hild. Then there were visitations in homes and hospitals, and holding services at the TB hospitals, serving communion to the patients.

"I am not going to allow myself to be attached like this again. It bordered on ownership; and Detroit Lakes belongs to the Lord," Melvin reflected, "In the future we need to hold every ministry with an open hand."

Eleanor slipped her hand around his elbow. She leaned into his strong frame and let out a sigh of agreement, "Still having a passion for it, yet knowing it isn't ours to keep."

From Minneapolis they traveled to New York, sleeping on the train at night, in compartment beds. Their plans were to stay several days until leaving on the ship destined for Belgium. Robert McGlasson, known as Brother McGlasson, met them at the New York train station. He had a home set up for the purpose of housing missionaries, coming and going, while also managing the East Office for the Assemblies of God. He assisted missionaries any way he could until their departure, and also when they first arrived back home on furlough. The mission home was in the part of Bronx that wasn't the best part of town.

After organizing all their suitcases and trunks, they decided to go into the city and look around and do some shopping. Navigating around New York was so different than Minneapolis. They needed to find a subway—something they had never used before. Approaching the gate, they encountered a whirly-gig with its three strong prongs hindering their passing. Try as they could, it would not move like the others next to them. Finally, a sarcastic voice called out a suggestion: "You could donate a dime." Melvin dug out a dime and located the slot. The whirly-gig arms rotated and they were on their way to the subway.

After walking up the stairs to street level, the city sites took over. Melvin was noticing all the skyscrapers. Eleanor looked for a café sign where they could eat lunch. The city noises of pedestrians and traffic filled their ears.

"I think that's the Empire State building!" Melvin pointed out. "It sure makes the Foshay Tower look short and stubby."

Richard took it all in stride, enjoying all the excitement and energy New York had to offer. Every department store window featured items stylishly displayed.

Later, back at the mission house, they were introduced to two women about their age who had also booked passage on the Europa to Belgium.

"Hello, I'm Lillian Hogan," she flashed a smile of warm friendship, "So we are soon to be shipmates. I hail from Thunder Bay, Canada, just across the border from Minnesota."

"And I'm Gladys Stock, American, born and bred."

She was shorter than Lillian, and softer spoken. "I'm going to Belgium to work with children. It will be my first time there."

"Our first time too, we're spending a year there to study French in Brussels, the official language of Belgian Congo," Melvin offered.

Lillian spoke next, "It's a lovely language and Congo is a land unto itself. Unfortunately, my linguistic skills are sadly lacking, so I shall be seeing more of you in Brussels as well."

Richard stood alongside his parents, wiggling a loose tooth back and forth. After a few days, he lost his tooth, and

Lillian began calling him "Toothless Tony." They became friends from then on.

On the morning of their departure, Brother McGlasson took them to the harbor and departed with, "Well, now I'll leave you; you're on your own."

They left the harbor and it was quite a feeling, with the final words of Brother McGlasson echoing in their ears. They wouldn't be coming this way again for five years, even if someone in the family died. In their hearts, they said farewell to their friends, family, and the church in Detroit Lakes. The Statue of Liberty glistened in the morning sun as the departing toots of the Europa's horn sounded in the harbor. Slowly, the statue diminished on the horizon, and Melvin and Eleanor said good-by to America.

After looking over their tickets, they managed their way through the throngs of other passengers and descended down to the cheapest rooms on the boat, in sea class. When they opened the door, they discovered they had to go down a ladder to get into their room.

"I can see why they call it sea class. It's under the water line," Melvin observed. "And there's water on the floor!"

Eleanor turned toward Melvin, "What are we going to do?"

After discussing the situation with a steward, they were upgraded to the next level. It was barely enough room for the two bunk beds, but it was clean, dry and had a round porthole.

"Look, I can see the ocean!" Richard exclaimed, "Where am I going to sleep?"

"There's an army cot underneath the bed. We'll set it up for you each night."

"Oh, goody, I get my own bed!"

Melvin and Eleanor laughed, remembering all their nights on the road, sleeping in all kinds of beds while raising funds for Congo. Now they were on their way, and could perhaps relax a bit before arriving in Belgium. They arranged their luggage under the beds and in a few storage lockers. Down the hall were the community bathrooms for the men and women. Richard acquired his sailing legs right away and knew the ship from top to bottom, making friends wherever he went. Melvin relaxed in a deck chair between meals, and kept an eye on Richard. Eleanor was a different story. The motion never stopped. In their small room, the suitcases shifted back and forth, coming out from under the beds. Going up the stairs to the dining rooms and decks for fresh air, she had to hang onto the railings for dear life. Her appetite dwindled as nausea became her constant companion. Lillian Hogan and Gladys Stock assisted Eleanor in any way they could, often watching Richard or sitting with her on the deck, offering soda crackers. In bits and pieces, they learned about each other's lives and what brought them to the mission field. Returning to Congo for her second term, Melvin and Eleanor were especially keen on asking Lillian everything about Congo.

* * * * *

Finally, after two weeks in open seas they were approaching Europe. Eleanor felt revived until she learned about the strike in Antwerp, Belgium forcing a detour to Rotterdam, Holland. Once they arrived in Holland, they had to make their way, with their belongings, to Brussels, Belgium in a taxi. With Lillian Hogan and Gladys Stock and their luggage, it seemed like a logistical challenge, but with the trunks coming later, they were able to manage quite well.

Once in Brussels, the taxi took them to the Ixelles area behind the King's Palace. It was in the heart of Lower Town, the west side of Central Brussels. A large boulevard ran in front of the palace and passed by Park Royal to the north. Between the palace and park was Rue de la Pépinière, the street where their apartment was located, on a busy intersection. It was a large building of several homes converted into apartments. In the neighborhood, the effects of World War II were evident with damaged buildings or bombed-out remains of rubble.

There was a common area when they first walked into the building. The lobby seemed clean and appropriate except for one thing. A portrait hung on the wall of a woman sitting at a table, naked down to her waist. After meeting the landlady, the Jorgenson family realized it was her portrait. She was obviously proud of it as she greeted her new tenants in French and escorted them up a flight of stairs to their apartment. They entered and saw a split set of stairs. Up they went a few steps to see the kitchen, which included a claw foot bathtub. There was a little gas heater on the wall. The landlady demonstrated how to turn the water heater on. Then down a few steps to a combination living and dining room, with one tiny bedroom off to the side.

That night Richard slept on the davenport in living room. It was a cozy room with a little coal stove sitting inside the fireplace. For heat, Melvin purchased a ten-pound sack of coal. After hauling it home, he carried it up the many steps to their apartment. There was no refrigerator so they would need to buy a small one to store milk. With average temperatures of thirty-seven degrees in January and sixty-four degrees in July, it was cold enough to set most other things outside the window on the roof of the next house.

"Just like living in Minneapolis again with the orange crate on the window sill," remarked Melvin, "only this time it's with you, my little Groat!"

Melvin scooped up Eleanor's petite frame and kissed her soundly.

Lillian Hogan lived in the same building. She was company for them and they were company for her. A few blocks away was Park Royal. Once Melvin and Eleanor saw the little pond in the park, they decided to buy Richard a little sailboat. However, shopping for the boat proved no easy task as they walked along streets looking for a store that sold toys. Then they had to figure out the exchange rate for the dollar and Belgian francs. In the stores, people simply went in and asked for what they wanted to purchase and someone behind the counter would go get it.

At one store, Melvin asked in French, "I want butter."

The lady behind the counter corrected with the proper verb for smoothness, "I want some butter."

After that lesson in the store, he remembered the right way to ask for things. For a while, Eleanor would simply point at what she wanted to buy.

Melvin and Eleanor began to learn that Belgians spoke two primary languages, Flemish and French, with a smaller German-speaking district to the west on the border of Germany and Luxembourg. Flemish, a language similar to Dutch, was spoken in the northern half of Belgium, an area known as Flanders. This area included Antwerp, the port where the Europa was denied entry because of the strike. The French-speaking Belgians known as Walloons lived in the southern half of the country, Wallonia, and at times felt more of a connection to France. This tug-of-war between two distinct people-groups of the Flanders and Walloons had been going on since Belgium became an independent nation in 1831. Its capital city, Brussels, was a microcosm of both Flanders and Walloon, with the official commerce and international language of French, which the Flemish did not appreciate. Melvin and Eleanor found it very confusing, reading every town and street sign in Flemish and French. Even the capital was called Brussels by the Flemish, and Bruxelles by the French-speaking Belgians.

On Sunday mornings, they went to a church in a Flemish part of town. It had a double pulpit, one for French and the other for Flemish. The pastors, Mr. and Mrs. Gunter, were from England. However, Mrs. Gunter was originally from Switzerland. Melvin, Eleanor, and Richard sat like stones during the service understanding nothing. They all agreed the music was the most tolerable part of the service. But they were committed to attend church and worship with other believers, even if the bilingual service was twice as long.

During this time, the Jorgensons were supported by the regular giving of individuals and churches that sent funds to the AG headquarters in Springfield, Missouri. Instead of wire transfers, the monthly check was sent to Belgium through the post. Melvin and Eleanor kept in touch with family, friends, churches, and supporters through writing and typing letters.

In August 1950, Eleanor sat down to handwrite a letter to Leroy and Tessie Broberg and their three children, part of the Broberg clan in the Detroit Lakes church.

Greetings and love to you all! Have been thinking and talking about you so much thought I would take time off and write you. Bro. Jorgenson has gone down to the customs office to get our trunk and footlockers. Hope they aren't too hard on us! The import taxes can be high.

My, it's quite a feeling to be in a strange country and hear a foreign language when trying to get around. No one can understand you, and you can't understand anyone. You should see us go shopping for some groceries! I wanted one dozen eggs.

So I pointed to the eggs and put up both hands. Then put up two more fingers. She started to figure it out, and gave me my twelve eggs. Later I found out they sell them in lots of ten. And the eggs were very dirty. They had them in a box with straw. Almost made you feel like you were gathering the eggs yourself. You see, Tessie, you wouldn't have to wash your eggs before taking them to town! The bread here is very heavy and hard and the milk—not worth talking about. Last night before going to bed Bro. Jorgenson said, "Oh, for a good cold glass of co-op milk."

The other night Richy was dreaming and he was saying to your son, "No, Davie, let's not do that, let's go to the barn." The next morning when he woke up he said, "Mommy, I feel sort of lonesome for Davie."

He misses Sunday School. We try to read him Bible stories etc. to make up for it. We may send him to school this fall. They will accept him. It's a private school. Most of the missionaries send their children there—then he will get to be with other children and it won't be so lonesome for him. They teach, of course, in French, but they said in a few weeks he would be talking along with the rest of them.

By the way, you should see them deliver milk here. A cart drawn by a horse comes down the street with a man walking along side of it. In the cart is a large can of milk. If you want some milk you go out with your container and he pours the amount you want and then he goes on to the next house.

How thankful you can be your kiddies have plenty of space to run in. Here there are no front or back yards even. Houses built right against each other. Your front step is the sidewalk. The country of Belgium is densely populated and a very small country. Of course, we miss having a car, especially Bro. Jorgenson.

Richy wants a pair of wooden shoes. He said, "I think I will run in them!"

Greet everyone at the church for us. Write when you can. We miss you a lot!

With our love, Bro. and Sis. Jorgenson & Richy

After folding the letter and sealing the envelope, Eleanor thought about their upcoming social engagement. Through their connections with the Assemblies of God, Melvin and Eleanor met Mr. and Mrs. Scotti, an Italian couple from America, working among the Belgian people with a focus on children's ministry. Once Gladys Stock arrived in Brussels, she began working with Mr. and Mrs. Scotti, and soon became engaged to a Belgian. The young Italian couple had invited the Jorgensons to come to their place in Ans, near Liège, a city one hundred kilometers east of Brussels.

* * * * *

That evening, as they left their apartment, Melvin turned the key in the door and slipped it into his pocket. Down in the lobby, the landlady waved and called out "Au revoir!"

They all responded in the proper reply with their American tongues. The family of three got on the streetcar and went on to the train station. They passed through gates with whirly-gigs and smiled briefly, remembering the last time they had passed through them in New York. They looked for a conductor to help them on the train, but there wasn't one. People streamed in and out of the trains and then whistles blew and the train left. It seemed straightforward to Melvin. He found the train to Ans, Liège. The step to the train was fairly high so he hoisted Richard onto the train and then stepped up himself. Turning to help Eleanor, he reached for her hand.

Just then, the whistle blew and a man with a uniform raised his hand to Eleanor to motion for her to stop. He would not allow her to board the train. Before Eleanor knew it, Richard and Melvin were leaving her.

All time stopped as she watched them float away with Richard's mouth forming the words, "Mommy, Mommy!"

"Now what will I do?" After a moment of collecting herself, Eleanor quietly walked back to the whirly-gig gates.

A man in a uniform asked her in French, "Where's your ticket?"

"I don't have a ticket. My husband has it and the train left before I could board it."

"Where's your ticket?" the man asked again. A man who knew English overheard and helped translate, until finally the uniformed man let her pass through the gates.

Now she had to find the tram to get back to their apartment. She dug in her purse and breathed a sigh of relief as her fingers touched the card. It was a pass that would allow her to travel numerous times. Once she got to the apartment she realized she was in a pickle for sure. Melvin had the key! With little command of the French language, Eleanor tried to explain the situation to the landlady, who opened the door to their apartment. It was then that Eleanor realized Melvin had all the money too.

The landlady knew something was terribly wrong. She knew that three people had recently left and the look of sheer panic on Eleanor's face needed no translation. The landlady said one of the few words she knew in English, "Money?"

Eleanor was ready to burst into tears. She was in a strange country isolated by the language and culture. She had been looking forward to an evening of friendship and speaking English with people.

She nodded to her eccentric landlady, whom she barely knew, "Yes, money."

The landlady smiled kindly and pulled five hundred francs out of her apron pocket and handed it over to Eleanor. Knowing the amount equaled ten American dollars, Eleanor whispered, "Merci, thank you."

Then she ran back to the tram and then to the train station, found the right train and boarded as quickly as possible. She relaxed in her seat by the window, picturing Melvin and Richard waiting for her at the train station one hundred kilometers away.

Only they weren't there. Could they be at Mr. and Mrs. Scotti's house?

Eleanor spotted a man standing nearby with a bicycle. She showed him the address and he said in broken English, "Follow me."

Eleanor followed him like a stray puppy as he led her directly to the house. After ringing the doorbell, she saw anxious faces, including Melvin's, peering at her from a second story window, with coats on ready to head to the train station.

That night the two couples and Richard discussed everything in English over a delicious meal. On the way home Melvin made sure Eleanor had her own train ticket, some money, and helped her on the train, "I guess this will be only the beginning of the Lord watching over us in strange lands."

Eleanor slipped her hand into Melvin's large hand. As time went on, they learned how much the Belgians had suffered through the years of war and religious conflicts, making it hard for people to trust anyone. In light of this,

Melvin and Eleanor's appreciation of what their landlady did for them grew.

* * * * *

As the months passed by, Eleanor was lonelier that year in Belgium than she ever was in her life. No one around her spoke English and she just wanted to pick up the phone and call somebody and speak English! The feeling of isolation was horrible. Whenever she got a letter from home, she eagerly read it and then began to cry. Every letter seemed to exacerbate her situation. Eleanor often cried out to the Lord by her bed at night, "Lord, you've got to help me. I know you placed this call in my heart to be a missionary."

Melvin was making slow but steady progress in learning French five days a week at a government school, augmenting his studies with private lessons. Eleanor took private lessons at home and tried to study around Richard's schedule. After realizing she was lagging behind in her studies, and Richard had no one to play with and the apartment grew smaller with each passing week, Eleanor was ready for Richard to start school in the fall. They enrolled him at School of Mademoiselle's Hamage. Every morning, five days a week, Melvin and Eleanor walked Richard to the tram to meet a teacher and then at the end of the day they would again meet the teacher and Richard at the tram. Richard didn't know a single word of French except for hello and good-by. Every morning, he cried when they left him at the tram.

Then one morning he stopped crying and said hello to his teacher in French. In fact, he picked up the language quickly, getting the verbs right and everything clicked for him. If someone came to the door, Melvin and Eleanor brought Richard with them, because he was the "language master."

Slowly they began making acquaintances through their language studies. Most missionaries in Belgium were passing through to another country after learning French. One couple they enjoyed spending time with were going to Congo through the organization Disciples of Christ. As her social circles grew, Eleanor felt the strain of separation from loved ones lessen. In time, Eleanor's French improved, making it easier to shop and she began understanding conversations around her in the stores and on the streets. Their pastors, the Gunters, had a son close enough to Richard's age to make for enjoyable times together as families. Melvin and Eleanor had wonderful fellowship with them, talking about church life and the spiritual needs of the Belgians. Going from being at the center of the action as active pastors in Detroit Lakes, and then hardly understanding anything or serving in any way at a church had made them feel lost.

* * * * *

About halfway through their year in Belgium, Melvin and Eleanor moved to the east side of Central Brussels known as Upper Town. It was a home with the second floor converted into an apartment, owned by an elderly Jewish couple who fled Yugoslavia during World War II. Monsieur and Madam Savatiavich took an immediate liking to Richard and often invited him downstairs to dine with them.

One time, Richard came back from eating with the Jewish couple and Eleanor asked him, "What did you have for dinner?"

"Well, I had such and such and I drank beer."

Startled Eleanor decided to ask their landlords about a six-year-old drinking beer with them. They smiled warmly explaining that is was table beer, very low in alcohol and very healthy for a person. Over the next several months, Melvin and Eleanor heard the Savatiavich's story of living in Yugoslavia during the war. Before becoming refugees, he was the mayor of their town. They had secretly buried their wealth of jewels and precious things hoping to return one day, but they never did.

The apartment had a much-improved floor plan, with everything on the same floor and an extra room for Richard. The park with the triumphal arch provided a safe area for Richard to play and learn to ride his first bike. Melvin especially enjoyed the view of the park as he sat at his desk to study or type letters. They once again found themselves living close to history, across the street from Parc du Cinquantenaire where the Arch of Triumph stands tall. Many of the trees along the walkways dated back to the time of King Leo II. Built for the Golden Jubilee Celebrations of Independence in 1880, it boasted three arches crowned with a bronze sculpture of a hero raising the national flag while riding a chariot with four horses tethered together to form a quadriga. The ambitious King Leo II had envisioned the arch as the prime entrance to Brussells flanked on both sides with enormous halls. In more recent times, the massive grounds were used to grow vegetables for the people of Brussels during World War II.

* * * * *

On November 4, 1951, Melvin sat down to type up a letter to his family. He placed two pieces of paper between the roller and carriage, rolled the paper to the very top to squeeze in his address. Then the keys began to click and press against the ribbon of ink:

87 Avenue des Nerviens, Bruxelles

Dear Leona, Rowland and Robert,

Greetings in the Name of Jesus! It is just two days now before we are once more on the high seas on our way to the Belgian Congo, so I had better get this letter off to you before then. It is a long time since I have written you, I know, but please forgive as we have been hustling around trying to get ready for the trip. Thanks a lot for all you are doing for us; it helps so much, and we need someone to help us out once in a while. Must get a letter off to Mom and Dad, but I don't where to send it, as they are visiting around. So this is your letter too Mom and Dad. This letter is for Ken, Jul, and family too, and Lloyd, et al.

The pictures in the film I sent are from Norway and parts of Europe. Write me and ask me questions, but you will see where Edvard N. is pointing out where Mom's house stood, and then the beautiful views from this spot over the fjord. Some other views are from Dad's valley.

We leave from Antwerp on the Charlesville, *a Belgian boat, on Tuesday, and arrive on the 21st at Matadi, entrance port. If we get through customs the same day we can take a train the following day to Leopoldville, and leave from there on the 23rd. If we can't get through the same day we will have to wait in Leo. for two weeks to catch the next river boat going to Stanleyville. We are hoping that from there we can go with some of our missionaries who we are hoping will meet us. We haven't heard about that as yet.*

We have just heard that neither our things at New York nor our car has been shipped yet. So now we don't expect to see our car for at least a year, and our luggage we may not see for a year, at least six months to a year. I had advised them as early as last June to send our things and do not know why this has not been done. We learned that one trunk containing Eleanor's sewing machine and my tools is in India. Well, it is not the first setback we have received, and no doubt it will not be the last, so we thank God for what we have and keep on going.

Our address will be: Ndeya, Gombari, Kibali Ituri, Congo Belge, Afrique. And when we get there we are hoping to have a lot of letters from all of you! We won't get any mail now for one whole month! And we won't be able to mail any to you for at least two weeks.

Brother Perkin wrote asking me if I would stay on here, and carry on a work in Belgium. He said they would like to form an advisory board of Europe with a representative from each country, and asked if I would like to consider such a thing. I thought it over and prayed about it, but we thought we should go on to the Congo. Yet there is such a great need here. This Belgian ex-priest we have been working with will be with us this afternoon and will go to a Pentecostal Convention service with us this evening. Last Friday night I got him to speak at another meeting of this convention—about the first time he has spoken since coming out of the Cath. Ch. Is he ever good! Forceful! Full of what he wants to say! He was so happy to speak. After the service, many ministers came up to him and asked him if he would speak at their churches. I hope this helps him to get going!

God bless you all and be with you! Let's pray for one another as we serve and live for Him from day to day. Our next letter will be from the Congo. D.V.

With all our love, Melvin, Eleanor, and Richard Wayne.

Chapter Sixteen

Getting to Congo 1951

❦

Before leaving Belgium for Congo, Melvin and Eleanor put in a call to North Dakota and Minnesota. It was an expensive three minutes for each call, but it would be the last time they heard their parents' voices for five years. Then they escorted Lillian to the airport. For some reason the AG headquarters had routed Lillian on a commercial flight instead of having her travel on the ship.

Loneliness crept into Melvin and Eleanor as they stood there watching her plane take off. It was sad to see their friend depart. They had been through so much together the past year since leaving New York. Still, on the way home, their hearts lifted a bit knowing they would see her again in Congo.

Now it was their turn to leave.

Mr. and Mrs. Scotti drove them to Antwerp where the *Charlesville* was waiting to take them on a two-week voyage to Matadi, a port city on the Congo River. The *Charlesville*, a cargo ship, which accommodated a limited amount of passengers, had recently completed its maiden voyage. Melvin and Eleanor knew from other missionaries that cargo ships gave better service to lower class tickets than regular passenger liners. Once again, Richard got to know all the passengers, this time in fluent French. People assumed he was an adopted Belgian boy of the young American couple.

The *Charlesville* was just getting into the English Channel when a brutal storm whipped up in the Bay of Biscay along France and Spain that lasted for one week until they reached the Canary Islands off Morocco. Eleanor, along with most of the passengers, suffered from seasickness. Melvin tinkered with his new motion camera waiting for calmer seas. One day, his wish came true as the seas became perfectly calm when the Canary Islands came into view.

All the passengers were on deck, taking in the fresh air, watching the islands grow larger with each knot of seawater behind them. Richard rocked on his toes and back on his heels with anticipation of another adventure, "I want to see a monkey!"

"I can't wait to get on solid ground!" Eleanor expressed what so many others on deck thought, "I have hardly been out of bed for a week!"

"After we get back on board, I want to get a bit of this voyage on film to start our documentary of our first four years in Africa. I heard there's going to be a 'Crossing of the Equator Ceremony' in a few days."

It was now 1951. His plan was to visit all the churches he could during their first furlough, which would be in four years, and talk about Congo as the silent film rolled on the projector screen.

The sounds, smells, and sights of the island greeted their Midwestern senses in a tantalizing way. People of various skin colors and attire wound amongst stands of exotic fruit and spices. Clothes, bags, and linens hung from edges of thatched roofs. A beige tablecloth with cutout flowers and leaves caught Eleanor's attention. The island vendor's trained eye knew he had a potential customer.

"Do you like Madam?" he asked in his island accent.

He offered a price and Eleanor declined. The price was exorbitant. Many people in Europe praised the handiwork of the Canary Islands, but it was out of the question. They bartered a bit, something she had never experienced before, but Eleanor left the stand empty-handed.

After making their way back on board the *Charlesville*, Eleanor leaned on the deck rail, taking in one last glimpse of solid ground hoping the calm seas would hold for another week.

"Madam! Lady!"

Someone was trying to get her attention down below on the dock. "Lady, I have your tablecloth."

Eleanor shouted down to the brown skinned man, "I am sorry; it is too much money."

"What will you pay me then?"

Eleanor thought about the twenty-dollar bill her mother sent her in a recent letter.

"All I have is twenty dollars."

"Okay, Lady, that is good."

Eleanor was wondering how to make the transaction when she saw a rope lowered. The man placed the tablecloth in a basket tied to a rope.

"I send you the table cloth and you send me the money, okay Lady?"

Eleanor agreed with a laugh. She kept the tablecloth for special occasions hoping to use it for many years.

* * * * *

A few days later Melvin got his camera ready for the Crossing of the Equator Ceremony. The sun shone through a clear sky, making it perfect for capturing everything on deck as ship and sea merged creating splashes of water nipping at the sides of the hull. As Melvin started filming suddenly someone dressed in a King Neptune costume appeared on deck. The King of the Sea played his part well with spear, crown, and outlandish hair and beard.

"Look, Dad! He's eating raw fish!" Richard exclaimed.

Melvin tried to keep the camera steady as he panned across the expansive deck. Eleanor laughed at the flamboyant display, enjoying the moment with her family. She hoped to have another member along the next time they were on an ocean liner back to the states. Richard was now six years old. Was it the stress of moving to a new culture that prevented her from expecting again, or were there other problems? This thought gnawed at her for a moment and then she let it go with the wind, and turned her focus on Congo and the work that lay ahead. After arriving in Matadi, they would need to ride the train for one day around the rapids to the capital, Leopoldville, and from there get back on the Congo River, taking a riverboat upstream for two weeks to Stanleyville to meet someone from their mission.

After passing the equator, the crew began getting ready for Matadi, while the passengers either organized their belongings or moved restlessly about the dining room and deck areas.

Then, one morning there it lay.

Melvin, Eleanor and Richard gathered with the crowd of passengers on the deck. The sheer size and force of the Congo River took their breath away gushing thousands of metric tons of water from its nine-mile wide mouth to the sea. All seven thousand miles of its tributaries spread out tentacles to form a river basin the size of India. Only the Amazon could rival its power and vastness across central Africa.

Ships came and went going up the river ninety miles to Matadi. The *Charlesville* waited until a smaller vessel approached portside. A river pilot boarded to navigate upstream for its final leg of the journey.

Melvin and Eleanor instinctively moved closer together as their thoughts churned with the steady drone of the ship's engines pushing against the flow of the river. They had looked forward to this moment for a long time. It wasn't about the adventure. For both of them, it was a deep-down satisfaction, a fulfillment.

Melvin softly spoke, "We've finally arrived in Africa. It's the unfolding of a calling."

"God is so good!" Eleanor responded, "I wonder what lies ahead of us."

Everything was overwhelming for her. Still, she didn't feel fearful. She just felt a peaceful confidence that this was God's plan.

Steep hills rose up around them. Later that day, as the ship made a turn in the bend of the deep river, the city of Matadi, clinging to the hillside, came into view. The crew began tying up the thick lines of rope to the dock.

Melvin and Eleanor waited with their handheld luggage to set foot on the soil of Congo. They had waited a long time for this moment and now the waiting was over.

Richard tugged on both his parents' arms, "Look at that rat on the dock! It's the size of a cat!"

Pulled from their thoughts Melvin and Eleanor watched the dark colored creature moving about trunks and boxes, sniffing and snooping.

"Instead of a welcome mat, it's the welcome rat!" Melvin chuckled, "But don't step on it."

They made their way through Matadi to the train station. The heavily populated city looked down on the Congo

River from its southern bank, known as the lower side of the river. A cacophony of mixed languages and smells baked in the African sun along tangled roads of red dirt. Sophisticated European architecture mingled with sheds and dilapidated homes. If Melvin and Eleanor did not get passage on today's train, they would have to wait a week in Matadi. Communicating in French, Melvin got the tickets and found the train that would take them a day's journey inland to Leopoldville. He made sure Eleanor and Richard got on the train first while a man hurried him along in French, "Monsieur, the train is leaving, you must hurry!"

Leopoldville, the capital, was the first navigable port on the river above Livingston Falls, a chain of rapids that dropped nine hundred feet in two hundred and twenty miles. During the time of King Leopold II, before the railroad, Congolese porters were forced to carry goods across a treacherous path that took three weeks of long grueling days, until their bodies dissipated like a morning mist. Once the land was cleared and rocks dynamited, the rails were laid exacting a price of one man's life per rail and tie, until the two hundred and forty-one miles around the thunderous cataracts were completed. Graves of men from China, Africa, the Caribbean, and Europe ran parallel to the tracks.

The open windows in the train helped little with the heat. By the time Melvin, Eleanor, and Richard boarded the riverboat for Stanleyville, their clothes were soaked with perspiration. Once on board they discovered that the riverboat consisted of a paddle wheel with a barge attached to its side, piled high with wood for fuel. Squeezed in with the wood were bales of cotton, and barrels filled with kerosene, gas, and diesel fuel. Every night the boat tied up to a dock on the bank of the river and men went on shore in search of wood, restocking the barge during the night for the next day's journey that would start at four o'clock in the morning.

Traveling up river on the paddlewheel boat, the Jorgensons had more time to observe their new home. It so happened it was rainy season on this section of the river, and its banks were overflowing. Palm trees and huts passed by with every mile. Dugout canoes were parked under thatched roofs with families living in them until the water receded from their homes again. The river kept heading north toward the equator. Once they got to Coquilhatville, the halfway point, they would cross the equator and they would be in dry season until they reached Stanleyville. From there, the river would continue without them turning south below the equator again into rainy season. The great river was always filling with rain somewhere.

At every docking, several passengers would drop coins into the river to watch with amusement as Congolese children dove into the river to fetch their prize. The meals on the riverboat consisted mainly of soup and bread. Eleanor, Melvin, and Richard looked down at their soup in silence. It was stale, but the crew just cooked it anyway, ignoring the little white worms floating on top.

After a few days on the riverboat, Melvin began to feel a tight knot in his stomach. He began making frequent trips down the hall from their tiny cabin to the community bathroom. Fever and nausea took over.

To help Melvin's body core cool down, Eleanor found a pair of scissors to cut the sleeves and collar out of his pajamas. They were crammed into their little room with three cots, making movement in and out of the room difficult. There was no door, just a curtain to pull. Richard informed his parents that people were saying the rats on board were the same size as their "welcome rat" in Matadi.

Melvin would leave his room briefly in his pajamas, making his numerous trips to the communal bathroom, and then collapse back in bed. Eleanor searched for a nurse or doctor on board, to no avail. She went back to their room.

Frustrated and afraid, Eleanor did what she always did, "Dear Lord, am I going to lose my husband before we even get to our first destination? You have got to help me with this situation."

After several days down the river, a doctor came aboard. There were dispensaries along the river and Belgian doctors would visit the dispensaries and then get on a boat to the next dispensary, making their rounds.

When the doctor heard that Mel was sick, he came to check on him, "Yes, you have dysentery, as you suspected. But I have no medicine. You will have to wait until Coquilhatville, a three-day ride. There's a pharmacy there."

Eleanor cringed when she heard that Coquilhatville was three days away. Melvin's fever was so high. His skin was clammy and his eyes were sallow. He was so weak and dizzy he could barely manage to get to the bathroom. How could she find the pharmacy?

Then she remembered the missionaries they had met in Brussels through language school who were part of Disciples of Christ. They had told them they would be in this area. After Eleanor explained the situation to the captain, he sent word ahead, and was able to make contact with the missionaries. Eleanor did all she could with home remedies for three days.

When they arrived at the dock in Coquilhatville, the wife was waiting for Eleanor. After embracing, off they went to get the prescription. Melvin would need a daily injection administered by a nurse. The boat would stop along the river and at each location, a nurse would be found for the daily dose.

To Melvin and Eleanor's surprise, the first nurse was a male African. They greeted each other warmly in French and then the nurse prepared the vial and needle for Melvin's backside. The African had never given a white man a shot before. Common opinion was that whites were a bit on the frail side, especially when sick.

Holding the needle into position he offered, "I'll just go as easy as I can."

Chapter Seventeen

Stanleyville to Ndeya

❧

B y the time they got to Stanleyville, Melvin was on the road to recovery. Joe Nilsen met them at the dock to drive them the remaining five hundred miles through the bush to their mission station located in the Oriental Province.

He greeted them in Bangala, "Sene Mingi, hello Brother and Sister Jorgenson! Welcome to Congo!" He shook their hands warmly. "And this must be Richard."

Richard greeted him in French, "Bonjour Monsieur Nilsen. Comment allez-vous?"

Joe Nilsen had an easy laugh, "Ah, you speak French very well. I see we have a linguist in our midst."

He nodded his head over his shoulder, "The truck is over this way."

He grabbed a few of their bags and they followed their new companion away from the congested river dock to a quieter area near a wide, level, dirt road lined with palm trees and shrubs adorned with scented white flowers.

The three newcomers hardly had time to process the bustling city, named after the controversial explorer Henry Morton Stanley. Rising to fame after finding Dr. Livingston in 1871, Stanley returned to Africa to spend over 999 days tracing the course of the Congo River from east Africa to the mouth of the river on the Atlantic. Catching the keen interest of King Leopold II, the Belgian ruler funded Stanley's further expeditions in order to strengthen his grip on Congo as his own personal country. Although many in the west lauded Stanley's exploits, the Congolese people suffered brutal atrocities and loss of tribal lands because of him.

An African stood watch over the green Dodge truck with the burnt sienna dirt of Congo halfway up the side panels. Round headlights perched over a license plate, with window wipers attached on the top of the windshield. This moment called for a picture! Eleanor searched for the three men in her viewfinder in the camera. Melvin looked happy. He had the soles of his feet on Congo soil and now only needed to get to the first mission station he would call home. Still, he didn't have the relaxed stance or expression of a veteran to Africa like Joe. After the camera clicked, Joe instructed, "Leave your belongings here. It will be safe with Samwelli. We can get something to eat and shop for your provisions."

The back of the truck was packed to the gills with provisions under a framed canvas canopy. Joe met their curious expressions with an answer, "There aren't many stores around the mission stations, only a few Greek merchant stores in Watsa, two hours west of Gombari. Nobody wants to drive five hundred miles just for shopping, so when they all heard I was coming to pick you up, they put in their orders."

Eleanor noticed everything was in case lots, not a can of this or a can of that. She made a mental note of what some of the other missionaries had purchased, and went shopping with a vague idea of what to purchase.

As they wove through the shopping district, new smells assaulted them distinctive to Congo of people, food, vegetation, sewage, and the red earth of Africa. Against a bright sky, the Belgian Congo flag snapped in the wind with a five-pointed golden star centered over azure. Next to it flickered the Belgian flag of three equal bands of black, yellow, and red.

After shopping, everyone piled into the cab in front except Samwelli, who rode in the back, snugly fit between luggage and stockpiles of supplies. Joe turned the key to fire up the Dodge's engine and off they rolled toward the far northeast corner of Congo. At the edge of town, the forest slowly closed in around them. From then on, the vehicle's shock absorbers got a workout until their first destination that evening at the Emanuel Mission Group station. After sharing a meal together, the three newcomers were escorted to a one-room, thatched-roof building. Shutters over the open windows kept insects and other unwanted visitors out. Mosquito netting, hung from an open-beam ceiling, covered the beds.

That night, Eleanor listened to the deep-sleep breathing of Melvin and Richard as she tossed and turned in her bed. All the motion of the riverboat and bouncing in the truck continued. It was pitch dark, and sounds of the night came and went in that darkness. Fear pounded with each beat of her heart. She didn't mind the dark so much; it was what might slink into the room. Eleanor knew she would remember this night forever. Finally, sleep overtook her for a few hours.

* * * * *

After breakfast, they squeezed back into the cab of the truck with Samwelli in the back. Clouds of dust followed them as they curved up and down and around the winding roads toward their first stop of the day at Betongwe. It was one of the four mission stations that comprised the

Assemblies of God organization commonly known by other mission agencies in the area as the Gombari Station. All considered bush stations, Gombari served as the hub for the AG missionaries for a one hundred mile radius. From Betongwe, Gombari was eighty-five miles east. Andudu was roughly in between these two stations forty-five miles southeast of Betongwe. Another forty-five miles to the north of Gombari, lay Ndeya.

On the way to Betongwe, Melvin noticed red spots on his hands and panicked. He kept his thoughts to himself hiding his hands as best he could. Was he going to be sick again, only this time with an esoteric bush disease? They had a short stop at Betongwe, where Joe and his wife, Ebba, were stationed. The Jorgensons met several of the other missionaries and Africans, while Joe had coffee with Ebba. Martha Underwood, who taught school, and Mr. and Mrs. Peck, who did general missionary work, served them filtered water and a light snack of tropical fruit and peanuts.

Gail Winters, a nurse working with lepers at the Andudu station, introduced herself. She had come to Congo from Boise, Idaho, in 1939. She worked with Mrs. Grace Lindholm, a widow with a thirteen-year-old son. After her husband had died in a hunting accident near Ndeya, Grace chose to remain in Congo, having trained as a nurse in the states during one of her furloughs. After returning to Congo, she established a leper colony in Andudu under the supervision of a doctor.

Betongwe was an older, established station featuring redbrick buildings with "soli" grass roofs, and traditional huts that stood in a clearing surrounded by the jungle. Melvin and Eleanor took in the scene of homes, schools, and an orphanage for biracial girls run by Nellie Maloon. Miss Maloon greeted them and introduced the girls, whose fathers were mostly Belgian or other European workers.

"This is Jackie. I've taught her English, and she will be coming to live with you in Ndeya to help you learn Bangala."

Jackie shyly greeted them in English. She was a beautiful young woman in her late teens wearing brightly colored material wrapped around her slight form with a head wrap to match. None of the girls knew their age; only in what season they were born. It could be they were born during the peanut harvest, or maybe the Bakwa rains, when the termites stir and swarm from their mounds. The Belgian government frowned on Congolese learning English, preferring they stick with Bangala. However, a few people did speak French as an international trade language.

From Betongwe, they traveled another seventy kilometers to the Gombari station. This is where their mail from America would arrive. Every station had an African runner that peddled a bike through the bush transporting mail, messages, and goods between the stations. As they approached the station, two hills rose on the distant horizon.

"We're almost to Gombari," Joe said.

A quaint, petite valley lay between the two hills. Graceful palm trees and assorted fruit trees surrounded the church and buildings. Congolese children and adults came from their huts, and the school buildings to greet them. Missionaries stopped their activities as well, to congregate with the others. By now, Eleanor had her hair covered completely with a scarf to fend off the red dust. She had traded in her stylish outfits from Detroit Lakes for sturdy brown shoes and practical dresses for traveling in the bush. Melvin wore the traditional khaki safari pants and shirts with a vest full of pockets. Both Richard and Melvin wore pith safari helmets as well. Once they arrived in Gombari, Melvin felt the urge to scratch the rash-like spots on his hands.

Joe stretched his legs and arms as he conversed in Bangala to the natives, while the other missionaries introduced themselves to Melvin and Eleanor. Lillian Hogan ran over to them hugging Richard first, "Hello, Toothless Tony, only you aren't so toothless anymore!"

"A familiar face in the heart of Africa!" Melvin rejoiced in seeing their friend again.

After shaking a few hands, one of the missionaries said, "I see you've been initiated into the tsi-tsi club."

Embarrassed, Melvin drew his hands behind his back. "Don't worry, they're just fly bites from tiny gnats that live in the palm trees. Everyone gets them when they first arrive. After a while, most of us develop immunity to the pesky creatures. It's best not to scratch if you can help it."

Although relieved by this information, Melvin found himself scratching the bites whenever he let his vigilance slack.

A family with a baby, and a son close to Richard's age strolled over. "Welcome," the six-foot slender man stuck out his hand to Melvin and nodded to Eleanor, "I'm Jay Tucker, and this is my wife Angeline, my son, Johnny, and newly arrived in September, Carol Lynne."

Richard and Johnny discovered they both knew French, and began switching back and forth with English as they sauntered off to other parts of the station. Johnny began tossing in Bangala for Richard to try out, as well.

"So you traveled with Lillian on the boat to Europe?" Angeline asked Melvin and Eleanor. Her posture shifted to one hip as she cradled Carol Lynne. "Before we were married, Jay and I came over with Gail Winters, and the Lindholms. Because of the war in Europe, we all had to bypass Brussels. We came in through Egypt, postponing our French studies until our first furlough. Jay and I spent our first year of marriage at Ndeya. It's a lovely station and I was sorry to leave it."

After Ndeya, the Tuckers had rotated to Betongwe and Andudu, until coming to Gombari the previous year, in 1950, to open a teacher's training station. They were due for another furlough next summer.

"It's good hunting out there," commented Jay. "Legend has it, a missionary liked the hunting so much he thought it would be a good place for a station. I think he and his wife are buried here in Gombari."

"When would that have been?" asked Melvin.

"I would say after the first missionaries arrived sometime in the early 1920s, so maybe Ndeya was established between 1930 and 1935."

Eleanor began asking Angeline about having a baby in Africa, finding out that although there was a government hospital for medical emergencies in Gombari, most of the missionary wives went to Oicha, two hundred and fifty miles southeast to have Dr. Becker deliver the baby.

"Jay had to help Dr. Becker because there are so few nurses to assist."

Eleanor thought of Melvin helping to deliver a baby. Fathers in America were strictly assigned to the waiting room to pace, or read the newspaper, until the doctor came out to declare the gender of the newborn baby.

After a brief time of orientation, the three Jorgensons and Joe Nilsen ate a meal of bush meat and rice before departing for their final destination: Ndeya.

After forty-five miles, the forest jungle had opened up to grasslands. The truck turned one more corner and the bush station came into view. The sun was setting with orange yellow hues fading into fuchsia streaks across the African sky, casting shadows on the surrounding sea of grass, planted palm trees, and red-brick homes with soli grass roofs.

Melvin summed up the past weeks of traveling: "I guess you go to the end of the world—and then head a little bit farther to get here."

A white missionary family and many Congolese were waiting for them. Melvin and Eleanor would spend one month with the Friesen family, and then be on their own while the Friesens left for a one-year furlough.

After greeting the Jorgenson family, John Friesen translated from Bangala to English, "They said, 'we knew you would be here soon. The talking drums told us you were coming.'"

Chapter Eighteen

Ndeya

On Safari

E leanor's hazel eyes fluttered open to morning rays piercing through the white-shuttered windows. The mosquito netting floated above her, attached by a ring to the open soli grass ceiling. From there it cascaded down around the four sides of the bed tucked between the almost comfortable mattress and bed frame.

Something scratched across the redbrick bedroom wall. It stopped, studied her a moment, and went on its business. The green lizard, as long as her hand, startled Eleanor, but at least it wasn't a spider. . .or something worse. Melvin heard her somewhere between sleeping and waking. His sky-blue eyes smiled at her the moment they opened.

His arm reached out for her, "Good morning, Miss Groat."

"Good morning."

She wasn't smiling back, "there's something on the wall."

"Oh, we have a visitor?"

Melvin couldn't help his amusement at her discomfort. Her brunette hair swirled around her wrinkled brow, making her nose lift just a bit above her lips, which he decided needed a kiss.

Eleanor returned the kiss with one eye on the wall. Methodically lifting the netting on each side of the bed, they both checked inside their shoes for other unwanted "visitors" before padding out to the small kitchen. Eleanor caught sight of Richard, still sleeping in the small second bedroom. She made her way over to a covered container of water to wash her face and hands. After running a comb through her hair, she ventured out the front door to find the facilities one needs in the morning. A memory of Thunder Hawk, South Dakota, filled her mind of winters, and dust blowing through the boards of the outhouse strategically placed between the General Store and their home. Eventually they upgraded to indoor plumbing. Still, whenever they had gone to Great Gram Bells sod house for chicken and biscuits, it was back to the biffy where dried cow pies were stacked nearby for the heating stove. Excluding the outhouse, she started craving South Dakota family and food.

Melvin was already talking to John Friesen, so she went to check on Richard again while sending a wave and good morning to John. His reply came back with an offer for coffee and breakfast when she was ready. Eleanor noticed the ground was completely free of any vegetation. No bushes or flowers were set around the house. Instead, a drainage ditch ran around the perimeter of the structure to catch the rain from the roof so it wouldn't flood the house during the rainy season. The bottom edge of the door had been trimmed off, she assumed to keep dry. The grass roof had aged to a weathered brown like the cattails and woods of Detroit Lakes before spring brought new life.

"Hello, Mom!" Richard peered through the mosquito netting with hazel eyes sparkling of adventure. His longer brown hair on top stuck up in all directions. He was sitting crossed legs with a book near his side, "I've been watching a lizard eat all kinds of bugs."

He warmed Eleanor's heart to her core, "We'll let it eat in peace while we go eat our breakfast."

She reminded him to check his shoes as he scampered out of his netted bed while she checked over his change of clothes for anything else that might be clinging to the fabric. That was one of many things they were warned of in their brief orientation in Gombari, concerning health and safety in Congo.

After smoothing his hair as best she could, Eleanor let Richard escape out the door following after him toward the only other house on the property. She was ready for a good cup of strong coffee. To her left there was a church with three open walls, built only four feet high plastered with mud. Tall pillars supported the grass roof. The one full wall ran the width of the preaching area at the front of the church. On her right stood a few other buildings she presumed for school and storage. The rest were bush-type huts and a simple structure of a roof over an outdoor cooking area. The Umma Grasslands surrounded them. It was more of a mixture of savannah and marshlands with a spattering of shrub trees instead of the dense forest surrounding the other mission stations.

Mrs. Friesen greeted Eleanor with a gracious smile, "Good morning! Come in, and have a seat. The kids have eaten, but John and I haven't, so we'll join you."

Gwen, their teenage daughter, was working on clearing off the breakfast dishes, while the other two or three were outside entertaining Richard. Mrs. Freisen called to her kitchen boy in Bangala, to start breakfast.

Eleanor watched the African boy through the glass window begin to work on breakfast, using the outdoor cooking stove on the back porch. Most missionaries had help with daily chores, including washing and hauling water. It provided the locals with an income, and it gave back precious time to the missionary for their work. In fact, it was expected that the white bwana would be generous to the community in this way. Out in the bush, no one stood alone as an independent island of self-reliance. It would have been a cultural blunder to do otherwise.

Mrs. Friesen called in her husband, Melvin, and Richard, whose six-year-old eyes were scanning the trees for monkeys. After exchanging pleasantries, and breakfast finished, the two couples began discussing the next month of transition, while Richard returned to his search outside.

After the Friesens left Ndeya, Melvin and Eleanor would be moving into their house, which was a larger version of the one they were staying in. It had a smooth, clean cement floor with a high ceiling. Unlike the smaller house, it had glass in the windows and a more extensive kitchen area, with a fireplace in the living room that was rarely used. It seemed full of the comforts of home with plenty of furniture. Other missionaries had told Eleanor to bring as little as possible, but now she was regretting that advice as they would hardly have any furniture unless they were able to borrow a few things from the Friesens.

"So, your car will arrive in Kenya?" John asked.

"Yes, at the port of Mombasa," Melvin said. "We also have thirteen fifty-five-gallon barrels coming with our personal effects. We got the barrels from bakeries in Minneapolis. They were used to ship lard in, so we had to hose them down and clean them out, but they were free, and they hold a lot."

"Well, you can use our vehicle for now," John offered. "In fact, we need you to drive us to Stanleyville to catch the riverboat to Leopoldville."

Melvin's orbs widened under his glasses. He thought John was fighting to keep down a grin, maybe reflecting on his early days in Congo.

John quickly added, "We'll have an African come with, in case you have any problems. He'll know the way back."

Then his face went dead sober, "Which reminds me, don't go anywhere without a guide, whether it's for bush ministry, going to a different station, or hunting."

Mrs. Friesen stacked the dishes sliding them to the edge of the table, "We've made arrangements for our houseboys to stay on to help you with any basic living needs on the station. I heard Nellie Maloon is sending over a girl to help you with Bangala, but I'll get you started with basic words for daily life with the boys."

Eleanor let out a nervous laugh, "We just got French down and now we're moving onto Bangala."

Melvin had asked about instruction manuals at Gombari, "Nobody seems to have any language books for it."

"That's because there are none," John said.

Eleanor thought of something, "I noticed the entire grounds are cleared right down to the dirt except for a few trees and gardens."

"It keeps the snakes away," Mrs. Friesen explained. "The nonpoisonous are good for keeping the rodents away, but some are poisonous, especially the mamba. The black mamba can grows to eight feet long, some long as fourteen feet, and is a fast mover. The green mamba is less poisonous. It has some brown to it, but the underbelly and head are green."

Eleanor shifted in her chair and sipped her coffee, while mulling over this bit of information.

John leaned back in his chair and threw one long leg over the ankle of the other, "So what did you bring for guns?"

"We didn't. No one told us to," Melvin's neck and back stiffened. John explained, "out here in the bush, you need guns for protection and food. There's no meat market, save for raising chickens or catching fish. And if you see a mamba hanging from the church ceiling, clear out the people and shoot it on site."

A nervous African face appeared at the door speaking in Bangala, "Bwana, come quickly!"

John rose from his chair and asked a few questions at the door. He spoke over his shoulder to Melvin and Eleanor, "Come along for your first lesson in bush health ministry."

They dutifully followed their mentor. John walked over to one of the buildings Eleanor had spotted that morning. A group of Africans, and the Friesen children and Richard, had gathered on the small porch that held several wooden, backless benches. John greeted the injured man in Bangala and began examining a wounded leg. The gash was from his knee down to his heel. The Congolese man explained what happened through gritted teeth.

"He's been gored by a wild boar. We'll need to wash this leg, apply antiseptic and bandage it. We can get clean water from the house, and the other supplies are inside the dispensary."

John noticed his daughter standing next to him, "Gwen, can you show the Jorgensons what I am looking for? Then ask Mother for warm sudsy water and follow with some water for rinsing."

That afternoon, John asked Melvin and Eleanor to join him for a tour of the station going over everything he could think of for maintenance and ministry.

"You'll find yourself doing the basic ministry work of day school, church services, and bush ministry, along with common medical needs. I'm no doctor, not even close to being a nurse, but out here, you just have to know how to handle injuries and sickness, along with malaria."

Suddenly his eyes caught fire with irritation. "I've told them no alcohol on this mission station, period!"

Melvin and Eleanor swiveled their heads and bodies looking for the evidence of John's provocation, to no avail.

"See that up there in the palm tree?" he pointed to one across the grounds. "Someone has hid a container under some leaves to collect palm juice, and let it ferment in the sun until it turns into palm wine. It's pretty potent and they get drunk on it in a hurry."

He dashed off to get a rifle. After returning he sighted in the container, "I'll fix their wagon."

A shot rang out across the Umma Grasslands and John walked away satisfied. However, later that night, a raucous noise grew. John walked the grounds with Melvin, and found the empty container in the midst of a cluster of drunken men. Their laughter increased when they saw John.

"Bwana, thank you for getting our wine down. It sat in the sun all afternoon getting ready for us."

John set his hands on his sides with a grunt. On the way back to the house, he began to chuckle shaking his head. Sitting around the fireplace, he retold the tale to Eleanor and Lucille, who gave in to the laughter, enjoying the relief it brought.

"All in a day's work for the Lord," John offered, leaning back in his chair and crossing one ankle over the other.

* * * * *

With Christmas inching closer every day, a Christmas Pageant was organized with makeshift costumes. Bedsheets for the angels were gathered, and fabrics were rounded up, or sewn from remnants of this and that, for Mary, Joseph, and the shepherds. Homemade crowns for the three kings were fashioned. The Congolese excelled in acting, and gave their best performance of the birth of Jesus in Bethlehem. African hymns and traditional carols filled the air accompanied by instruments of percussion, and mettle harps made of small wooden boxes. Some of the melodies sung in Bangala were traditional carols. Others were African spirituals with one chorus sung repeatedly until even Melvin, Eleanor, and Richard could join in with the rhythmic swaying bodies, clapping, and raising hands, releasing the joy in their hearts.

The next day, the Jorgensons joined the Friesen family at the larger house for Christmas dinner. When they arrived, Lucille was in her bedroom changing from her work dress into something more appropriate for the occasion. As she sat down at the prepared table of Christmas bounty, someone said, "You've got a spider on your back." "Oh, I forgot to check my dress before I put it on." The cook came running into the room with a stick. Eleanor watched the hairy creature, the size of a saucer, sprouting numerous legs, get gently lifted off the hostess. Then it was deftly whacked into oblivion. As they bowed their heads to give thanks, Eleanor resisted peeking out of one eye in search of the unwanted dinner guest. Of course, during the dinner Eleanor told the story of her encounter with spiders in Jackson, and the fall down the stairs. Melvin followed with their first Christmas, eating dinner on the breadboard in the midst of a soot-filled apartment.

"And now it's our first Christmas together in Africa," Melvin squeezed her hand under the table and nudged his shoe next to her smaller shoe.

* * * * *

The first week in 1952 passed by quietly, with the Friesens making plans to take the Jorgensons out to the bush for a few nights of ministry at Tora, a village north of them by a few hours' drive. John and Lucille packed up the back of their vehicle with cans of gasoline, camping equipment of cots, blankets, mosquito netting, metal eating and cooking utensils, dishes, a one-burner cooker, and a kerosene lantern. Their food supplies included a chicken. Its small beady eyes peered through the open-weaved basket shaped like a chicken. One of the houseboys would be coming. Also included was a first aid kit, along with guns and ammunition.

The two families squeezed in with the houseboy and chicken, and off they rumbled through the tall waving grasslands, over planked bridges and uneven roads barely cut wide enough for one vehicle.

Once they got to Tora, everything was unloaded. Each family would stay in a hut. Then the ministry aspect began of walking around the village, hut to hut, introducing themselves and inviting folks to the evening service. A small band of believers had been slowly growing and plans were underway for a future church building. As Melvin and Eleanor participated in the service that evening under a canopy of stars, they both realized something. Neither one felt strange or out of place. Even with the language barrier, they felt at home somehow, like they were back at Detroit Lakes. Only it seemed deeper spiritually because it was stretching their worldview of the fellowship of believers. In this remote village was amplified the scripture they had read at the end of the New Testament, in the Book of Revelation:

> Lo, a great multitude that no man could number, of all nations, and kindred, and people, and tongues, stood before the throne, and before the Lamb, clothed in white robes with palms in their hands; and cried with a loud voice, saying, Salvation to our God which sitteth upon the throne, and unto the Lamb. (Rev. 7:9-10 KJV)

After returning to Ndeya, John and Lucille went into high gear, packing to leave for Stanleyville. In the midst of this activity, a woman was brought to the mission station on a homemade stretcher of saplings and leaves. Her husband had gotten angry with her, so he threw her into the cooking fire. Melvin and Eleanor winced to see the extensive burns on her legs and arms. While John was cleaning the wounds, the husband walked in from the bush. John looked up and a look crossed his face that resembled a judge in a court of justice.

He stood up to his full height and met the man chest to chest, "Did you do this to your wife?"

The man said that he had to discipline her for not cooking his food right.

"You cannot treat your wife this way. Christian men do not beat their wives, or throw them in a fire when they are unhappy with them. There are other ways to handle these matters in a marriage."

The Congolese man listened, along with all the men gathered at the station. He said he would not do this again when he got angry with his wife.

"Now you must show your words are true by helping your wife."

John showed the man how to apply the ointment on the woman's burnt skin. John later explained to Melvin and Eleanor that this would be humiliating for the man to treat his wife's wounds, but it would teach him, and the rest of the men, to respect their wives.

Finally, the day came for the Friesen family to travel to Stanleyville. After bidding farewell at the riverboat dock, the Jorgensons went into town to shop for themselves, and other missionaries who had passed on their lists. One Congolese guide watched the car, while the other one helped them shop. Traveling the five hundred miles back to Ndeya, Melvin and Eleanor shared their thoughts. The last few months seemed like a year. They had seen and learned so much in such a short time.

Once back at Ndeya, they began moving their belongings over to the larger house. After a few days, they felt settled in, although the furnishings were a bit sparse. A runner had come by bicycle in the late afternoon with their mail. Melvin noticed a copy of the *Saturday Evening Post* was among the assorted letters from North Dakota and Minnesota. After dinner, they read a few letters to Richard, before saying prayers with him, and tucking him into bed under the mosquito netting. At Richard's request, they left a flashlight in bed with him, and a book. Then they carried a lantern and the mail into their own room to escape the hording mosquitoes.

Snuggled into their own bed, they sat closely together under the mosquito netting with one flickering lantern nearby on a stand, creating a shadowed silhouette of their joined bodies against a wall. The African night sounds of the Umma Grasslands drifted in and out of their room. They read every letter twice, repeating some parts aloud to each other. Melvin and Eleanor weren't sure what the future months would bring. But they did know they were content, and the happiest they had ever been in their lives.

Chapter Nineteen

Ndeya, 1952

M elvin unpacked the accordion loaned to him by Lucille Friesen. Hopefully, his own accordion would arrive safely at Mombasa. He inspected everything before slipping his hands under the straps on each side and began pulling and pushing, as air blew through the bellow. The black and white keys on the right came easily to him, but he had to concentrate on the bass, and pre-set chord buttons on the left. As his fingers worked the valves inside, air was released across the corresponding reeds. Music filled the living room with the empty fireplace.

The houseboy stole a glance through the windows, from the cooking stove on the porch. Jackie, one of Miss Maloon's girls sent from Betongwe, smiled and laughed from the kitchen, "Oh, Bwana, that is wonderful! How does the music come out?"

She had moved into the small house. Lillian Hogan and others came and went as well, helping the newcomers to learn all things Congo. Melvin explained to Jackie the workings of an accordion and then he practiced a few hymns for Sunday's service. The heat of the day started making

Melvin's forehead perspire. He swabbed the sweat away with a cloth and moved out to the cooler porch.

Before he started playing again, a voice shouted from an avocado tree nearby, "Ouch! What did you do that for?"

Richard slid down the tree rubbing one hand over his stomach, "Where's Mom?"

"Did Akido bite you again?" Melvin asked from the porch."I've about had it with this biting nonsense. Back at home when a dog becomes a biter, it has to be put down."

Melvin rose from his chair to put the accordion away and retrieve a rifle. Richard ran to his mom to get antiseptic on his stomach and then back to save the monkey's life. Eleanor was working at the school building, organizing the room and preparing lesson plans for the Africans. Then she needed to switch to lessons for homeschooling Richard, who burst into the school like a freight train.

"Hurry, Mommy!" Richard barely held still for his treatment. He dashed back to the tree.

"No, Daddy! Please don't shoot my monkey!" Richard began crying, standing in front of the tree with branches sprawled out perfectly for climbing. "It's not all Akido's fault. I pulled on his red tail. My skin's not even broken really, see?"

Melvin felt his resolve melting. Richard didn't have any friends in the bush, except for his pet monkey. At first, it was a dog, and now this crazy monkey, who would jump on the dog's back and ride it like a horse! It always gave Eleanor the biggest belly laugh.

* * * * *

The next morning after breakfast, out came the quinine pills.

"Do I have to take these pills every day?" Richard complained.

"Yes, just get it over with," his mother advised, and handed him the small white pill, with a sip of juice to help offset the taste.

Richard opened his mouth, swallowed, and squeezed his face and lips like he was eating a lime. There, he had done his duty,"How can something that tastes so bad be so good for you?"

"I don't know exactly how it works, but I do know it's made from the bark of the cinchona trees, which is quite bitter."

"And it's better than getting malaria," Melvin tried to console his son with logic. When that didn't work he offered, "Let's go get some 'soli' for the new roof."

John Friesen had suggested getting the roof done before the rainy season, so Melvin decided it would be his first construction project before attempting a structure using homemade bricks.

Richard's eyes brightened at that and he was out the door, "Bye, Mom."

Eleanor laughed, watching them leave in a work truck, with the open bed filled with Africans. Melvin and Richard could hardly be apart from each other's company.

After father and son had left the station, Jackie came over to help Eleanor work with the houseboys. Besides water collection and purification, there was laundry. Under a simple roof supported with poles, the houseboys boiled water to wash the clothes in a washtub with a washboard. Then a second tub filled for rinsing and hand wringing the clothes. Hung on a clothesline, laundry quickly dried in Congo, unless it was the rainy season.

As the sun increased in its burning power, Eleanor donned her safari pith helmet and headed for a spot in the glaring sun. Before baking bread, the flour was brought out to sit in the sun to kill the bugs and then strained using a woman's nylon stretched over a sieve. Eleanor thought back to the luxury of women's hosiery products during the last World War. Now she was using them for sifting bug larvae out of flour. She certainly wasn't going to wear nylons in this climate.

After the clothes were dry, the irons were heated. As one black iron cooled, the handle would switch to the hot one waiting on the stove. Back and forth it went, until every article of clothing was ironed and folded.

Jackie explained using both English and Bangala words, "The insects fly by your clean laundry and think it is a nice place to leave their eggs. If we do not iron, your britches will itch."

"I can see that 'ants in the pants' is more than a phrase around here," Eleanor dryly observed.

Someone stopped by with fish and eggs to sell. Jackie negotiated, repeating the words for Eleanor. She also showed Eleanor how to place the eggs in the bowl to see which ones were sinkers or floaters.

"Here keep these, they are good."

Eleanor's nose shriveled at the smell of the fish, like Richard had done with his morning quinine pill. Jackie told the seller to bring fresh fish next time.

"Well, I guess it is Spam again for dinner with rice and manioc leaves," Eleanor sighed. She had fried the canned meat last night, so maybe she could bake it whole tonight with mango, papaya, or pineapple, like a ham dinner at home.

Meanwhile, Melvin and Richard drove out several miles through the eight-foot-high elephant grass, interspersed with clusters of trees along the marshes and trickling streams. Birds flew off in all directions with billows of dust in the wake of the truck. After spending all morning cutting and stacking the soli, the Africans climbed on top of the grassy mound, chatting and laughing.

About half way home Melvin hit a bump in the road, "Hmm. . .must have been a tree gone down."

The Congolese began shouting and leaning toward the cab windows, making hand signals. Melvin and Richard looked at each other and shrugged their shoulders. When they arrived back at the station a few of the Congolese looked for Jackie before unloading the grass.

"Bwana, the men want you to know that you rode over a python," Jackie translated.

"Oh, that's why they were yelling so much. I thought it was a tree trunk. I'm glad I didn't stop!"

"No, Bwana, they were not afraid, they wanted to cut up the python to eat the meat."

Melvin took out his small notebook and pencil from his shirt pocket and wrote down python, stop, meat, and food in Bangala. He practiced sounding out the words. Richard ran off to find his mom repeating the words like a parrot.

The next day, a crew of Africans came to refurbish the roof on the main house. Several of the missionaries had explained to Melvin that the Congolese knew what they were doing so the only real aspect to oversee was quality control. Dark-skinned men started tying tufts of the soli together in bunches the size of their arms, with a type of natural string. Then starting from the bottom of the roof, they worked their way up to the top peak using quickly crafted bamboo ladders. A significant overhang was created to prevent rain from eroding the homemade mud bricks. The trick was to make sure the bunches were closely tied together.

As the day wore on, the appropriate spacing was an issue as the men wanted to get home to their villages for the early evening meal. Jackie was at hand to translate and explain the words to Melvin, Eleanor, and Richard.

"Bwana, you know that the word for grass is 'soli' yes?" Her smile illuminated her bright chocolate eyes framed by her colorful head wrap. "Do you see what they are tying it with? That is called 'kamba-na-mi'. . . .'kamba' means string and 'na-mai' means river. It grows in bunches by the stream and it is green when you first pick it and you have to peel off the outer layer and underneath is the part used for cord or string. Kamba na mi can be used thick as a cord for making furniture or walls or animal cages. People in Azande Land use it to make baskets that are beautiful."

While Melvin and Eleanor worked on the Bangala nouns, Richard mentally copied the verbs he heard Jackie using and began working up a sentence.

* * * * *

A few days later, a missionary pulled into the station in a worn-out looking truck, "I thought you might want some fresh bush meat. I heard you have some guns on loan, but not any training on hunting around these parts."

Lionel Fermon tilted his pith helmet to wipe the sweat off his brow under dark hair. "It will only take about ten minutes to walk out to the edge of some of the best hunting lands around."

Melvin decided to change his plans for the day, and take up Lionel Fermon's offer. The Spam, and occasional domestic duck routine was getting old for dinner.

After rounding up some African guides, the two men began trekking north of the station. They came to an elongated marsh and crossed over it. By the time they reached a higher dry spot, Melvin's shoes and socks were drenched.

He paused by a grouping of rocks to sit and peel off his wet socks. Water dripped out of his shoes when he turned them over.

An African guide came over, "Bwana, this is an underground river."

The Africans calloused bare feet were used to the terrain and they didn't bother to warn the white bwana about the water.

"It is safe to cross here, but not over there. Do you see the potopoto?" His brown arm pointed to a mud hole downstream. "Do not ever walk on those."

Melvin could see that no vegetation was growing on it, "It looks so innocent."

"Yes, but if you step on it, you will start sinking in the mud and there is no bottom to it."

Lionel had been talking over the lay of the land with another guide. He walked over to Melvin, twisted off the cap of his canteen, and took a swig of water.

"This whole region is an intertwining of marsh and grasslands with dense woodlands supporting aquatic and dry plants. The galley forests run along the main rivers of the Dungu, Aka and Garamba."

He took another swig of water and wiped off the sweat on his forehead with his shirtsleeve, "This makes for good hunting country with warthog, waterbuck, antelope, hartebeest, all sorts of animals, including the big five: lion, elephant, white rhino, cape buffalo, and hippos. There's even savannah giraffe that you won't find anyplace else in the country, and a host of monkeys, chimps, and baboons."

"Well, I know we have hyena for sure because we can hear them at night."

The Congo sun had baked Melvin's socks a bit, so he laced up his soggy shoes and squished off with the trekking party. A few minutes later, the guides gave the signal to stop. They pointed to a cluster of trees and the group moved through the tall grass.

Lionel whispered to Melvin, "Always stay near a clump of trees if hunting buffalo, it may be your only means of a safe escape. They are smart and can double back swiftly to attack. That's what happened to Grace Lindholm's husband when they lived at Ndeya. The wounded buffalo circled back and his gun jammed."

As it turned out, several warthogs ran out of the bush with their tails straight up in the sky. Melvin took aim and fired his rifle. He missed the target, but Lionel shot one and it dropped to the ground. The African's cheered, and tied it up to haul back to the mission. On the way back, a herd of caramel-coated antelopes with thin, white marble stripes sporting twisted prong antlers grazed in the distance.

"It's the bongo." Lionel said, and then added, "We need to get your gun sighted. I know you've hunted in the States, so something's off."

That night, bush meat sizzled in the fry pan with pangdu, cultivated rice. The Jorgensons sat down with Lionel, and gave thanks for the meal, enjoying every bite. Lionel smiled as Melvin and Eleanor commented on the meat.

"I had no idea warthog could be so tasty."

"Or so tender."

* * * * *

Each day continued in Ndeya, forming a routine. Monday through Friday, Melvin and Eleanor taught adults to read in Bangala, using visual aids and Bible stories, much like a Sunday school lesson. Eleanor also taught basic health care classes for the women on how to care for their babies and children, along with administering government-sponsored quinine pills for prevention of malaria. People came with common cough and cold ailments, burns, and dysentery, but if the need were severe, Melvin would drive them to the government hospital in Gombari.

People also came to the mission station for Bible studies. On one occasion, Melvin read to the Congolese gathered on the cool cement floor, about Jesus healing the lepers. They all knew someone that suffered from this dreaded disease. Leper colonies dotted across the region, with new ones added every year.

On Sundays and other evenings, Melvin conducted services at the open-walled church, with the men sitting together on wooden benches on their side of the church, and the women gathered on their side. They enjoyed the accordion as much as their own African music. After several months of using a translator, Melvin started putting simple phrases together for his sermons. The Congolese told Eleanor, "Bwana's getting it! Bwana's getting it!"

Besides ministry duties at the station, there were evangelistic outreach trips in the bush planned during the two-month break from day school. The next one would be more of a trekking experience, with several missionaries joining them from other stations.

Guides carrying guns for protection led the way. In the middle were the missionaries, followed by several porters toting supplies. Traveling with Melvin, Eleanor, and Richard, were Lillian, Winnie Currie, and Gail Winters. Richard began picking up the missionary children's custom of calling any adult Aunty or Uncle, adding to the close-knit community of the Gombari AG Mission.

Walking through the bush, one was more intimately connected to its every nuance. The sea of vegetation began to show details of various species. Birds with long legs and wide wingspans took to the air, while smaller birds flitted amongst the papyrus reeds, chirping warnings and protest. Talking amongst the missionaries was encouraged, to warn unwanted animals of their presence. Seeing a pool of water in the distance, the guides pointed out hippopotamuses grunting and gurgling while eating. Elephants were making their way to the water hole to drink and cool off. Graceful heads of the savannah giraffes bobbed across the horizon.

After arriving to their destination, Melvin and Eleanor saw that many people had gathered for such a small village.

"How did they all know to come here tonight?" Eleanor asked. "Do they use runners?"

"Look over there," Lillian, instructed, "do you see that wooden thing that looks like a small, child-size, upside-down canoe with the ends notched like an ark or ancient boat? It is the gudugudu, the talking drums of Congo."

Gail added, "They use the gudugudu to send messages about everything. The tribal tongues around here are basically a high/low language; some people call it a singsong language. The drums imitate that. The messages will travel from village to village for miles around."

The chief of the village greeted them in Bangala, rather than using his own tribal dialect. Then he spoke directly to Melvin, "Mbote Bwana, welcome to our village. We are honored to have you as our guest! How was the length of your journey?"

"We crossed three waters," Melvin used the tribal way to express distance instead of miles or kilometers.

"Oh, that's not too bad."

The camping gear was unloaded and the team's cook sought out a "mafika," a cooking shelter. Soon after, a pot perched over a fire simmered with bush meat and vegetables, arousing growling stomachs of the trekkers. Nearby stood a wooden sangu used for pulverizing foods and husking rice.

As the Jorgenson family set up their tent and cots, Eleanor once again regretted not bringing a more generous camping kit to Congo. This wasn't a weekend vacation, it was safari living. Richard could have cared less about all these things as he talked with the children in Bangala, learning some of their tribal words in the process. His language acquisition was uncanny, right down to the accent while Melvin and Eleanor lagged behind as usual.

* * * * *

After returning to Ndeya, it was time to get ready for another three-month school term and go over all the supplies of the infirmary. That night mail and several brown packages sent from Detroit Lakes were dropped off.

"Thank you, Runner. How was your journey?" asked Eleanor.

Somehow, his occupation became his name.

After dinner, they sat around the table to open the packages before the female mosquitoes swarmed in for their evening feed time. The docile male mosquitoes only ate plant nectar. However, the females were feared for their saliva infested with the disease of malaria. Prevention was the best weapon, but eventually all the missionaries succumbed to the flu-like symptoms, spending a week or two in bed.

"Oh, look!"

Eleanor held up two dresses made from lovely print patterns, sent from Mrs. Harry Broberg. There was another one from the women's missionary group, with pajamas and matching slippers for her birthday. Richard opened one package addressed to him from Tessie, Davie's mother. It was schoolbooks, but with reading the same storybooks every day, Richard was delighted and wanted to bring them to bed with his flashlight. And so another day came and went in Ndeya, until it was the end of the dry season.

* * * * *

One morning a man came running into the station out of breath.

"Bwana! A fire is coming!"

Everyone at the Ndeya mission station stopped what they were doing and started a backwash. They needed to burn a four to eight-foot swath around the perimeter of the mission station. Houseboys, school students, and Jackie pitched in with the Jorgenson family side-by-side until they completed their task. Then they all stood within the safety of the ring of burnt grass.

"It reminds me of the prairie fires in South Dakota when I was a girl," Eleanor exclaimed.

Soon the wall of fire came and went like a large rolling wave in the ocean. They later learned that the Africans usually started seasonal fires. These fires assured them new growth, attracting wildlife for the food and sodium created by the burn. The other stations, located in the Ituri rain forest surrounded by the lush foliage of the jamba, were exempt from these cleansing fires as nothing could burn without clearing the land first.

* * * * *

In August, Melvin had the privilege of conducting his first African wedding. He stood in the shade of the porch of their redbrick home with Eleanor and Richard sitting in chairs watching the proceedings. The barefoot groom and bride looked solemn, wearing festive African clothing and headgear. Any combination of this and that was acceptable as long as it was colorful. First, a negotiated bride price between the groom and the bride's father took place.

The groom came forward with a large dishpan, a blanket and three hundred and twenty Belgian Congo francs. "I have already paid one hundred francs, so with the dishpan at eighty francs, and the blankets, one hundred francs that should be enough."

Most brides went for six hundred francs in that area, although an educated girl, who could sew and knit, would be worth more. Biracial girls were usually never considered bride material, and if they did marry, the husband felt it his duty to beat the white out of her to make her black.

Melvin asked the two men representing the bride if they approved of the total sum of money and goods. They gave their reply of satisfaction to Melvin, who then wrote out a note in Bangala confirming the transactions for each party concerned to give to the village chief. The bride remained silent, but she seemed satisfied as well. After pronouncing them man and wife, the newly married couple walked to their hut in the nearby village. The next day, the man came back to the mission station to work.

* * * * *

One thing Eleanor told everyone in the States, before leaving for Africa, was that she was not going to send Richard away to boarding school like so many missionaries did with their children.

So she took along the Calvert Course and set up school for Richard in the mornings, with explicit instructions to the

Africans, "Now when I am in this room in the mornings please don't come, because that is Richard's school time."

People nodded and smiled and everything was fine for a few days. But then someone came around looking for the white lady bwana, "Please come, Madamo, a child got burned badly and the mother is crying for you."

"Tell the mother I am coming." Eleanor organized some papers for Richard to work on, "I'll be back as soon as I can."

She stopped at the dispensary to pick up the necessary supplies, wishing again that she had taken some training for nursing before coming to Africa. After treating the burns on the child's arms and feet, she calmed the mother down and prayed with her, knowing that if the husband got angry enough about the accident he would beat his wife as a punishment. Then Eleanor quickly made her way back to finish schooling Richard before starting lunch. When she entered the room, Richard wasn't there.

She began walking around the station, "Richard, where are you?"

"Over here, Mommy!" a happy voice sounded across the grounds.

Eleanor was not in the mood for hide and seek, "Richard, tell me exactly where you are."

"Up here in the avocado tree!"

She followed the voice to the tree and glanced up to find Richard sitting with Akido. All four eyes looked at her with childlike wonder.

"Oh, brother," she let out a sigh.

If it wasn't one thing, it was another, from interruptions to books being stolen in the mail or lessons arriving late. The thought that Richard needed other children around at his age bothered her as well. Fellow missionaries had told her and Melvin that Rethy Academy was a good, affordable school with terms that ran for three months followed by a one-month vacation.

Later that night she discussed it with Melvin. It was a difficult decision, but they needed to get away for a weekend of rest, so why not stay at one of the guesthouses there and see how it went for all three of them?

They decided to stop at the elephant camp on the Kompandi River near the Andudu mission for a picnic. From there, they continued east past Gombari until their borrowed car broke down. They were stranded for the night, while the African riding with them walked through the forest to get help from Gombari.

"Maybe the Lord is trying to stop us for a reason," Eleanor said clinging to one last effort to avoid leaving her seven-year-old son at boarding school. The next morning, after the repairs were made, they continued their journey.

Rethy Academy was two hundred and fifty miles east of Ndeya over seven thousand feet in the mountains with a view of Lake Albert on a clear day. The aroma of imported eucalyptus trees along the winding drive played among the winds of the cooler climate. Cattle kept in pens were used for milking and food, while the oxen bore burdens of labor, sometimes carting wagons filled with fifty-five-gallon drums of fresh water up the steep road.

"It's really too bad cattle can't survive in the lowlands where we live," Eleanor said, thinking about the fresh milk Richard could drink at Rethy.

Buildings dotted the sloping terrain surrounded by a woodland forest with hardwood trees and pine scented evergreens. Children swarmed around the schoolhouse and dining hall.

"Look! On that hill!" Richard pointed out, "A donkey! I wonder if they ever ride it."

Immediately after leaving the car, Richard gravitated toward the throng of children melting into the group as if he was already a student while Melvin and Eleanor looked for the administration office.

After spending a few days at a quaint guesthouse enjoying the cool evenings, which required a fire in the rock-hewn fireplace, Melvin and Eleanor knew that when they left in the morning Richard would not be coming with them. They both sat in silence staring at the shifting flames and coals of the fire.

When they tried to say goodbye to Richard the next day he hardly looked their way, he was so busy playing with the other children. When they called out to him again he simply waved goodbye. "He's like a thirsty man in the desert," Melvin observed.

On the way back to Ndeya they consoled themselves with how happy Richard seemed when they left. However, within a few days the ache in their hearts for their son became unbearable. A tiny seed of fear began to take root and grow in Eleanor's mind crippling her thoughts and actions. A voice kept repeating. . .*he could be dead and buried and you would never know about it*!

The awful torment continued for a few days until one morning Eleanor went into the privacy of her bedroom and fell to her knees by her bed. In tears, she cried out, "Lord, you have got to help me with this because I can't take it! We came here because you called us here, but I. . .this thing with Richard. . .I just can't take it!"

Then, a peaceful thought came to her, and she knew it was the Lord: *I can take care of him there just as well as I could here. He'll be all right.*

As Eleanor waited on the Lord, kneeling quietly before him, the paralyzing fear left her. She had never experienced that much fear before and it gave her a shudder to think how a fear like that can be like a slab of granite on a person's heart and mind. In the days to come she often cried lonely tears for Richard, but the oppressive fear had lifted and it never returned. Every week they would get a little handwritten note from Richard, and they would send one in return. In another month, he would be coming home for his first one-month break.

Chapter Twenty

Betongwe 1953

❧

After attending "kuvanda," Melvin and Eleanor rumbled back to Ndeya in their newly acquired Carryall station wagon. A mission-minded group based in Minnesota, Speed the Light, supported missionaries by raising funds to purchase vehicles for overseas. The car was shipped to the seaport in Kenya, and the barrels by rail to the border town of Arua, Uganda. Thankfully, Joe Nilsen generously donated his time to help with the task of transporting many of the barrels in the back of his faithful green truck, including drums of gasoline. The much-needed guns had also arrived. Melvin's brother-in-law, Ken Olson, sent a .22 long rifle semi-automatic, and for larger game, a .375. Eleanor's father provided a scope for each gun.

At kuvanda, all the missionaries gathered to vote and decide what station they would live at, and for how long. Ministry focus and furloughs made it necessary to regularly shift missionary duties and rotate to different stations. The Tucker family had left for furlough and the Friesen family was returning to the field, although not to Ndeya. Melvin and Eleanor were assigned to Betongwe, the first AG mission station they stopped at with Joe Nilsen, after arriving in Stanleyville. The Andudu station, forty-five miles to the southeast, would be their closest neighbor.

At first, they didn't know what to think about moving to the older, established mission. Their thoughts drifted along with bumps and dust in the road. It seemed the trick to driving in Congo was to shift from rut to rut while avoiding stones or prickly spikes fallen from a certain type of palm tree that was notorious for flat tires.

"I feel like we are still so new here and now with the move to Betongwe we will be facing new challenges," Eleanor's brow crinkled in doubt, surrounded by her short chestnut hair swirling in the wind passing through open car windows.

"Yes, but it's been a good first year," Melvin reflected. "As a whole, the missionary community works well together. I suppose our bond of camaraderie is forged through survival in the bush. . .and serving a cause greater than ourselves."

"Still, there are bound to be personalities that are harder to get along with just like there are any place else," Eleanor pointed out.

Melvin and Eleanor discussed their concern over rumors that Nellie Meloon could be difficult to work with.

"Well, we are going there, so we'll just have to pray about it and leave it in the Lord's hands," Melvin said dodging another rock in the rutted road.

After the Jorgensons moved into their home in Betongwe, they began to fall in with the ebb and flow of its pulse of life. Congolese woman prepared food under mafikas or gwamos near huts lined up in rows. Short shrubs placed a safe distance away from their homes defined yards swept clean. Nothing grew close to any building, keeping the snakes at bay. Palm trees surrounded the area with banana trees at the edge of the jamba, the jungle forest. Young children played in the open yards, while infants hung in bright cloth nursed or slept close to their mothers Men hunted or worked in the rice and peanut gardens. Older men sat and talked. Their wrinkled, sinewy bodies huddled on the ground together like sticks of wood.

Several African women wove baskets in which to dry rice, or flat trays for sifting. The sh-koom sh-koom sound of the wooden sangu pounded off the outer shell of the dried rice. The flat, woven trays were used for sifting and separating the different parts of the grain. Nothing went to waste. The lighter chaff fell to the ground on a mat leaving the heavier brown rice in the flat, round tray. Chickens lingered hoping for a pecking or two.

Cooking pots on rocks simmered over a fire with manioc root, rice, or bogos (a large cooking banana). A round top of a fifty-five-gallon drum once used for gasoline or kerosene served as the top of a stove. For serving the meal, plates of food were placed on the ground, with little pieces of wood to sit on. When Africans ate, no one had their own plate, but simply dished out of the plates used as a community bowl.

The grounds of the mission station were large enough to accommodate the orphanage for the biracial girls, and a medical dispensary, including leper work. Every redbrick missionary home was a carbon copy. Part of the collection of buildings included the boys and girls' schools for reading and writing in Bangala, and the hub of Betongwe, the church.

Regular safari trips were scheduled to outlying villages for visiting churches and mentoring pastors. Missionaries often worked with native pastors in starting new churches. After a new group of believers formed, they built a small hut-type structure for services. In time, some villages had a church building made from burnt brick.

Without hardware stores in the forest, making bricks for buildings was a part of mission life. From mud to kiln drying by fire, it took about a year to accumulate enough bricks before construction began. Betongwe was next in line for use of the brick machine and Melvin would be a part of that construction team. The simple manual press had two rectangle molds to fill with moist red dirt, after using palm fat as grease. Then a mechanism latched tight to secure the forms while two or three Africans dangled their body weight from the long lever for a few minutes. After the latch was released, two bricks were carefully lifted out to be stacked, ready for the kiln process. When a sufficient pile of bricks was completed, three trenches were dug in the ground and ample firewood gathered for continuously feeding the kiln. Rows of bricks, twenty feet long and six feet high, were neatly stacked and covered with mud. The internal temperature of the kiln had to burn hot enough for three days and three nights to make the bricks hard enough for building walls.

* * * * *

With a mountain of duties to accomplish, it wasn't a convenient time for Melvin to get sick, but in Congo, it was a way of life. It started with a fever. Then his lower back ached. At first he thought it was another bout of malaria, but then he realized as sick as he was, he could still eat something without vomiting. He felt the frequent urge to go to the bathroom, urinating with extreme pain and discomfort. As he lay in bed, Eleanor bent over him with a damp cloth.

Concern clouded her hazel eyes, "Melvin, I really think you should see Grace."

"Okay, let's go," Melvin agreed in a weak voice, "I can't take this anymore." His eyes were red and his skin held a tinge of yellow, "But no Africans."

"But we have to have guides. What if something happens?"

"Eleanor, I just can't have the Africans see me going to the bathroom on the side of the road, with all the blood and everything."

"Well, if that's how you feel about it."

Eleanor left to put a cot in the back of the Carryall.

After arriving in Andudu, Grace informed them, "There is nothing I can do. This is beyond my scope as a nurse. No home remedy will cure this. You need to take him to see Dr. Helen Roseveare at the HAM mission in Ibambi."

Winnie walked over to listen to the conversation.

"How far is it?" Eleanor asked.

"About one hundred miles east of here, a straight shot. Dr. Roseveare is a highly respected physician in this area, who treats tropical diseases."

When Melvin and Eleanor hesitated, Grace firmly insisted, "You need to leave now to make it there before sunset."

"We can take my car," Winnie stated, "I've made the trip many times."

Off they went in Winnie's vehicle, traveling one hundred miles of African terrain. After crossing two rivers via ferries, and Winnie changing a flat tire, they finally reached Ibambi. Once they arrived at HAM—the Heart of African Mission—affiliated with the UK, a nurse took a blood sample.

After a while, the doctor and a few nurses came back with the results. Dr. Roseveare stood with grace and poise despite her humble surroundings. Her family had ties with royalty in England, and whenever she was on furlough, she often found herself on the Queen's list of invites for tea.

A smile played at her lips, "I'm sorry to inform you Mr. Jorgenson that you have leptospirosis, what is known as 'rat fever.'" Her accent made the diagnosis almost charming. "In fact, when we looked at your sample under the microscope, the germs were jumping up and down on the petri dish."

Melvin and Eleanor glanced at each other. Although relieved at finally getting some answers, they weren't scientists and failed to see the humor.

The good doctor continued, "Somehow, you came into contact with rat urine. It could be the rats were running over the canned goods that you store, or your houseboys came into contact with it and didn't wash their hands before cooking. I'll get you started on an antibiotic, a tri-sulfa course, which should clean it up. You'll be feeling much brighter in six weeks."

While recuperating from his illness, Melvin worked on sermons and caught up on letter writing. He scribbled by hand to his parents:

Wondering how you spent the holidays. I was in bed most of the time. I tried to get up Christmas Eve but felt pretty tough. For the first time on this field we had our Christmas evening program on the 27th. I made a lighted star, the Inn door, manger, etc. It turned out fine and everybody liked it. Last Sunday we had over six hundred for service. When we came, it was under two hundred, maybe one hundred and sixty-five, I think. We hope we can hit one thousand sometime during the year.

Melvin thought about how Crookston seemed so far away until he reconnected to his hometown through a letter. News came slowly through the mail, unless they could pick up tidbits from the radios used to communicate amongst the missions. World events such as the Korean conflict ending, and Eisenhower being elected as President, didn't seem to impact them as much out in the bush.

* * * * *

As the weeks unfolded, Melvin and Eleanor found Nellie Meloon to be understanding and kind to them. A veteran to Congo of many years, she took them under her wing, teaching them many things she had learned along the way. Melvin and Eleanor already knew Jackie, so naturally they became acquainted with the other girls, inviting them into their home for meals and game nights. With Richard back at Rethy after Christmas vacation, the girls filled their home with noise and laughter.

One night as they sat around the table Eleanor said, "You all speak English so well. Much better than my Bangala I'm afraid."

Jackie smiled, "Oh, but you are getting it, Madame. Be patient, Sister Jorgenson."

The young woman was interested in nurse's training as was another girl, Josephine. Maria wanted to be a teacher. The girls all had Belgium fathers, men who came to Congo to work on the coffee plantations, and other business or governmental duties. Some of them would take a girl for a temporary wife until returning to Belgium. Marguerite and Clara Barnaby's father was in Belgium, but he seemed to feel more responsible to help his daughters than the other fathers who abandoned them after leaving Congo.

One of the girls said bluntly, "We were never supposed to have been born. We don't fit in with anyone. I don't want to get married and have my husband beat the white out of me like they have done to the other girls."

Melvin spoke up, "Not one of you is an accident. I hope you will see your time here in Betongwe with Sister Meloon as a stepping stone to a better life."

* * * * *

Toward the end of February, Melvin and Eleanor were due for their yearly one-month vacation allowed by the missionary board in Springfield. Rich's term at Rethy wouldn't end for another two months, so they decided to plan their vacation spending the latter part of it at Rethy. In prior visits to Rethy, they met one of Rich's playmates, "Stuffy," who was part of the Stauffacher clan associated with African Inland Mission, or simply AIM. Stuffy's uncle, Raymond and his wife Sarah, were dorm parents at Rethy. Melvin and Eleanor learned that Raymond's mother, Mrs. Stauffacher, ran a guesthouse for missionaries in the foothills of a mountain range hovering on the equator along the border of Congo and Uganda.

After driving to the Ruwenzori Mountain Range, commonly known as the Mountains of the Moon, Melvin and Eleanor got out of the Carryall to a sweeping vista. At four thousand, six hundred feet elevation, the dirt road below them swirled through the forest like a cinnamon hued ribbon. Turning toward a large soli-roofed house they saw a snow-capped mountain peak called Baboon Head looming over the main house and a cluster of guesthouses. Behind the buildings, the Luci-lubi River coursed through a deep ravine with water from the glacier mountain peaks.

As the couple made their way across the bare yard, a stout, sturdy woman with gray hair and hardworking hands came out of the large house to greet them. At the last minute, Rich's dog, Tags, was brought along to surprise Rich when they saw him at Rethy. Now the Rhodesian Ridgeback was running circles around the car and barking with relief from escaping the Carryall.

Grandma Stauffacher, as everyone called her, laughed at the dog's antics and welcomed her guests. After settling into their own little cottage, Melvin and Eleanor walked to the large house for the evening meal.

The next day Melvin and Eleanor strolled along a path to the Luci-lubi River until it led to waterfalls with caves overhead. They crossed a natural bridge of rocks enjoying the freshness of the falls. Eleanor wore a full pink skirt popular for the 1950s, with a pink, fitted shirt trimmed out with a white pointed collar. Her saddle shoes completed the outfit she was looking forward to wearing on vacation. Most of her clothing usually consisted of the practical kind. Melvin slipped his arm around her petite waist as they reached the river.

"Here, I'll hoist you up on this log for a picture with the river behind you."

Their eyes met and then their lips. For a moment, they felt like they were back in a park near North Central Bible Institute in Minneapolis.

When they got back to their cottage, they spent the rest of the afternoon sleeping or reading, enjoying the cooler climate. During the evening meal, they swapped stories with other guests and their hosts while the houseboys came and went with dishes and filtered water taken from the Luci-lubi River. Melvin and Eleanor listened as Grandma Stauffacher told her story. She, and her late husband, had come to Congo in the early 1930s with their children, spending two years trekking inland from the East Coast.

After several days of pure relaxation, it was time to leave the Mountains of the Moon. On the way back to Congo, Eleanor felt a knot in her stomach.

Soon she was running a fever, "Melvin, I need to get out of the car."

"Are you going to throw up?"

"It's more than that, I'm afraid."

They decided to stop at Oicha, where Dr. Carl Becker operated the largest leprosarium in the world with over two thousand lepers. Eleanor got treated with the necessary medicine to kill the parasite and rested. She also decided to switch from quinine to aralen for malaria.

"The other missionaries said they like it better," she told Melvin later that night as she rested in bed at Oicha. "Maybe it will help with the ringing in my ears."

Eleanor closed her tired eyes. The new information concerned her, but at the moment she was slipping into a cozy sleep after all the stress of the day. It was the worst case of "trots" in her life—up to this point anyway. Later they found out the houseboys didn't run the water through the filtration system properly after boiling it for twenty minutes, and Grandma Stauffacher fell victim to amoebic dysentery as well.

* * * * *

When Melvin and Eleanor returned from visiting Rich at Rethy, the loneliness of an empty house greeted them. Of all the adjustments and sacrifices they made as missionaries, nothing compared to the pain of separation from their son for three months at time. To make matters worse, the upcoming kuvanda for the local pastors they were hosting fell over Rich's next school break in April.

Knowing that missionaries from other stations would be guests in their home Melvin glanced at the ceiling thinking about repairing it before kuvanda. Instead of an open ceiling like their home in Ndeya, most of the homes in Betongwe had panga ceilings. It was a light-colored wood harvested from deep within the forest that was light and porous like bamboo. Once the rows of round panga sticks were in place, a layer of mud was applied on top of that, and then banana leaves, followed by another layer of mud. Panga ceilings created insulation from the heat, but eventually succumbed to termites. The rustling of insects in the ceiling grew with every week. Whenever Melvin clapped his hands loudly, the ceiling grew quiet for a few moments.

Deciding to replace the panga ceiling with plaster, Melvin set to work on removing the ceiling while Eleanor was teaching at the day school, and attending to medical needs. Piece by piece, he worked around the edges until *wham*, the whole ceiling fell. All the school kids came running out of their classrooms to investigate. Melvin laughed at their curiosity, while the teachers coaxed their students back to their studies. Once the opened ceiling was repaired to Melvin's satisfaction, he moved onto the next task.

Right before kuvanda, in the midst of all the details of hosting the conference, Melvin made plans to go hunting. As the host station, they needed to provide the fresh meat for cooking meals for three days.

He left toward evening, taking some of the Africans along as guides and drove to a site where he could sleep in the car overnight, knowing early dawn was the best time of day to hunt. Hopefully, he could get it back to the mission station in time for the conference.

The next morning Melvin woke up to find all the trees were down around the car. As he got out of the Carryall to survey the debris and damage, the guides who slept in the safety of nearby trees scurried over to him, "Bwana, a herd of elephants came through in the night. The elephants could have turned the car over!"

Melvin blew out a whistle of relief. He had slept through the night not hearing the elephants plundering past. "Lucky I didn't have a clump of bananas placed under the car like I do sometimes; otherwise they *would* have turned the car over to get them."

* * * * *

Working on a letter, Melvin was happy to report to the folks in America starting out with his usual salutation:

Dear Ones at Home,

Kuvanda is over—and all the rush connected with it for those who are on the host station. There were meetings morning and evening and business meetings with natives in the afternoon. Different native teachers were shifted around. We got two more this year and they were put in two new places. The teacher's salaries were raised from eighty francs to ninety francs a month. That's $1.80 now and the native church itself pays them. Services were held all day Sunday with the baptismal service and communion in the morning. There were twenty-six baptized from Betongwe, more than from any other station by far. Bro. and Sis. Nilsen were able to come in spite of her broken leg. She ate in our house and not with all the others in the schoolhouse. They stayed here, too.

Also, during the business meetings for the missionaries at the end of kuvanda they elected the new field superintendent as Bro. Griffin is leaving on furlough soon. I was chosen as field sec-treasurer, but not because I wanted to be. It is really a lot of work. The treasurer takes care of all the finances on the field. Maybe I can get out of it when Winnie Curry gets back. . .Martha Underwood who has it now and the girl's school is leaving in two weeks. Then Miss Meloon is leaving in about five weeks, which will leave us on the station alone until Winnie gets here. I'll have to take Miss Meloon's place supervising and teaching in the boy's school. We'll have our hands full—and our pockets, too. It looks like El will be teaching school all the time now as there will be no one else to take the girls' school.

That's too bad as there is so much other work to do in the spiritual work; women's work, Sunday School, etc. Now these will suffer because we can't do everything. But I AM starting a young people's Christ Ambassadors group out here. The first on the field. I think this is so important I am going to neglect some other work to do it and get it started.

God bless you all and be with you as you live for him. Pray for us during these busy times.

With our love to you all, Melvin, Eleanor, & R. W.

Chapter Twenty-One

Betongwe 1954

A s Melvin and Eleanor got acquainted with the local pastors and natives they often got invited to weddings and funerals. If the family was Christian, they could be asked to officiate. At one outdoor Christian wedding, Eleanor played an old pump field organ, wearing a hat with a wide floppy brim while the solemn bride and groom walked as slowly as possible toward Melvin. Bought at an Army Surplus store by a missionary, the portable instrument folded down for an easy transport to almost anywhere.

While weddings were a quiet affair, where the bride must keep her composure at all times, a funeral was a stentorian affair. Grief was expressed through wailing and crying, even rolling in the dirt. Deemed as proper to show sympathy this way, the more important the person was, the louder and longer the wailing and crying. The burial took place right away, but the wailing went on for days, depending on the person's rank in the community. People painted themselves white and wailed through the night, beating the toms and jumping as high as they could.

At one Christian funeral Melvin and Eleanor attended, the deceased woman's body lay on banana leaves while people waved palm fronds over her body to keep the insects away until everyone was gathered under the gwamu. Then the body was covered with a cloth, lowered into a grave and placed on a shelf carved out of one side so the dirt wouldn't fall directly on it. The Christians sang songs and read scripture. After closing in prayer, the service was over and everyone went home. There were tears and sadness, but also joy that their loved one was safe in the arms of Jesus until they were reunited in eternity.

With recent events on his mind, Melvin squeezed in time to compose a letter and sent it with their runner forty kilometers to Mungbere to make the long journey to America, to be passed around to families, friends, and churches.

Dear Ones at Home,

While the radio is on and we are listening to some English, I will try to type off a few lines to you. It is now nine o'clock, and it has been a busy day. Sorry that we didn't get to write a letter home last week. But the Griffins surprised us last Friday with a request to go with them to Paulis to help them and Miss Meloon. They can't speak French, so we had to go along to help make arrangements for their plane tickets through the bank and have them sent to Nairobi, Kenya. I also had to get francs for the field fund, and change a lot of little change into larger money for the Betongwe church. They had a little locker full of coins and it was so heavy that two men found it hard to carry. It amounts to about $250.00, which is a good sum for a native church. And it is growing.

A baby, seven-months old (or eight) died on the mission during the night. I was over to the hut twice, and El was too. In fact, during the night she got out of bed without my knowing it (easy thing to do) and was over there with a girl for about two hours. She got to sleep at four. The baby had pneumonia. They buried it at noon, just off the mission grounds. She had the baby out in the rain when it had a cold. The father was a Christian and the mother was not. They were both very much afraid because someone has to bear the blame for the death and both were afraid he or she was the one. The relatives beat up whomever they think is guilty. He was really scared, and had a right to be—it's the women that beat him up! Scores of them. I let them stay on the mission for protection. She threw herself on the ground and wailed and hollered in their fashion until our Christian women stopped her. While she was doing this she was looking around to see what the effect of it was on the rest of us. They both feared that if they didn't show enough grief they would be beaten. Thank the Lord for enlightenment back home. The native preacher gave a good message.

Rich wrote two nice letters and says the term is going by very fast. We bought twelve rabbits; ten young ones and two females. . .that's the only hitch until we get a male. Also, we got Griffin's nice white kitten. So, we still have our pets—mostly for Rich's sake. I have about 12,000 bricks hit now, and when I get about 20,000 hit I will burn them. But before I do that I have to repair the roof on the kiln as a wind blew it over. Then I want to build a chicken coop—three sections, with one section for R's pets. I have to keep hitting more brick, too, for the other necessary buildings to be done. I am trying to get all the gardens clean, too, and am cleaning the coffee gardens too. This is a real farm!

Across the room, Eleanor wrote a letter to her sister-in-law, Leona, including life in Congo with the houseboys.

I really cleaned house today—my houseboy wasn't too happy as I guess he thought I worked him too hard. They're most happy when they aren't working. How I wish we didn't have to have them. They all but wear me out. I think Mel wrote home about our cook. He had stolen three blankets (for the bush) and some canned goods—then when we found him out, he ran away. So now I'm training another one. He says he understands things I tell him and then I find he hasn't understood or as he says "I forgot."

* * * * *

After the summer months, Melvin and Eleanor started some activities to promote Sunday school. They began by organizing the teachers and having weekly meetings with them. Then working with other missionaries, they started translating the quarterly materials sent from Springfield into Bangala for the teachers to use, including rolled-up wall charts, and flannel graphs. Once they established these practices at the Betongwe station, they implemented the same program with the pastors in the bush.

Stepping out into new methods, they held a Rally Day in Sunday school called "Mikolo Mokuru," kicking it off with a parade through the Betongwe mission station and into town, which consisted of ten native mud stores and a dispensary. Participants marched along singing while holding Belgian and Congo flags and a poster written in Bangala. Once they reached the town, an outdoor service was held inviting people to come to Mikolo Mokuru.

In the evening services, Melvin began showing movies taken from film sent to the States to be developed and shipped back. Shouting and laughter broke out as people recognized themselves and their surroundings, and shock as they witnessed life in America. Even Belgian officials would attend these film nights packed out with five hundred

Congolese. One missionary was able to secure a film on the life of Christ that could be narrated in any language. Watching the intense interest of the nationals made Melvin want to find more materials on film.

On October 17, 1953, Melvin finished typing another letter to home with one final paragraph:

The parade worked out so well we are planning on having another one. I wish I had some banners in Bangala wording. Also, a couple of trumpets. The things we lack out here are the same as at home in many places—teachers, materials, sufficient room. We have classes on porches, and crowd together any place we can find. But praise the Lord for a people that want to get together to hear the Word of God. But there are many here, too, who are indifferent, uninterested, and hostile. Surprising how much the same it is here as at home. So much the same and yet different.

* * * * *

Right before Christmas Melvin drilled holes in a bamboo pole at an angle. Then he organized the branches from the fir trees they had cut when they picked up Richard at Rethy. He smiled at the thought of the branches piled high on top of the Carryall. After making a stand and inserting the branches Melvin stood back to survey his work.

"It's hideous!" Melvin laughed, "but it's a Christmas tree, nonetheless."

"It just needs some decorations from the barrels!" Eleanor beamed. "And the smell of pine is heaven to my nose."

Richard watched from the couch with Koko sitting mildly on his arm chirping, "Pretty bird, Koko, pretty bird."

The African Grey parrot with clipped wings showed up one morning in a small, woven chicken basket outside his bedroom door. Brought by a fellow missionary to Betongwe, it came from a pygmy tribe in the Oicha area. Koko sat most of the day on an outside perch off the front porch. Mimicking all kinds of sounds, the parrot quickly learned to make the sound of a traffic cop whistle. One day, Melvin noticed all the workers on the construction site and gardens went home early. The next day, he found out they heard the whistle blow, which signified the end of the workday—but it was really Koko. After that, the workers would come to the house to check if Melvin or the parrot sounded the whistle.

* * * * *

Christmas came and went, and Richard was back at Rethy for another term, sending his weekly notes to his parents. He always put up a brave front when leaving the station or writing letters, but inside he was torn up about the separation. After Melvin read his son's note for the second time through, he walked out of the house in Betongwe into what felt like a kitchen oven.

"The hot, dry season is living up to its name!" he exclaimed to himself.

When they had first come to Congo they wondered why the other missionaries complained about the heat so much, especially during the dry season. Although they knew it was hot, they didn't feel it that much. But every year the heat worked a little more into their bodies, getting their attention. Walking across the yard to put in a cement floor in Winnie Currie's storehouse made Melvin feel like he was being cooked for dinner.

Meanwhile, Eleanor went to check on a woman who recently had a baby. Another woman was helping the laboring mother at the time of delivery, and panicked when the baby seemed stuck in the birth canal. The woman reached in and pulled the baby out, injuring the mother. Eleanor applied medicine to the torn area and prayed with the new mother. Returning home, she felt the heat smoldering through her body. The upcoming trip to Rethy could not come sooner. Everyone said this was the hottest dry season in thirty years. She made a mental list of what to pack—Tags and Koko for Richard—but not the monkey, cat, or rabbits. They were also going to bring the croquet set they bought from the Nilsens. And they had something to tell Richard that couldn't be sent in a letter to him.

* * * * *

On February 23, 1954, another letter-writing session for the whole family was underway at Rethy.

Richard wrote in large, grade school cursive to Grandma and Grandpa:

How are you? My dog ate our rabbits. He jumped in the pen and ate them. We were sad. Daddy gave him a spanking. We are hoping to get more. We have a croquet set. The boys like to play it. Yesterday we watched a pig get killed. It was fun. Love, Richard Wayne J. oxoxoxox

Melvin typed on stationary with the new letterhead he created for their AG Gombari Mission. In the left-hand corner there was a logo of a national preacher inside of the continent of Africa, caring a sack of seeds, with the sun on the horizon behind him. Below that, a side bar listing all the stations and their initiatives. At the bottom read a verse from Romans: 10: 14-15 (KJV). "How shall they believe in of whom they have not heard? And how shall they hear without a preacher? And how shall they preach, except they be sent?"

After Melvin finished typing his letter, Eleanor wrote a brief paragraph on the back, hardly able to contain her joy.

Hi—have only a few minutes before Mel must go with the mail. Had intended to write you a long newsy letter in detail but will have to wait. Anyway—get ready for some news! The baby we have been waiting for is on her (?) way—I'm in my fourth month, which means baby will arrive in Aug. Went to see the Dr. here. He said everything is all right & he doesn't see why things shouldn't go along o.k. Haven't been feeling too well, but better since being here. Dr. said I needed a good rest & gave me pills to make me sleep. So I was sleeping morning, afternoon & night. The heat has been so terrific down our way. Martha will be here in May to take over the girls work. We're so excited about it all! Haven't told Richy yet—he won't come down to earth for a while I'm sure. Must close, more later—oh yes—could you send me a crochet hook No. 3 in your next letter? I borrowed one as I'm crocheting a sweater. Thanks—Love—El.

After Melvin and Eleanor told Richard about becoming a big brother, the entire Rethy school and mission station were talking about the baby. Everyone knew he had been talking and praying about a baby for over a year. At first, he told his parents he was praying for a sister, but after quite a few months passed, he told Eleanor he didn't care what kind of baby it was and that he would take anything, as long as it was a baby.

As much as Eleanor enjoyed the cooler mountain climate of Rethy, she felt fatigued and had a growing pain in her side. After the Dr. discovered that her white blood count kept climbing to a dangerous level, he wouldn't hold off operating anymore. Thinking it could be her appendix the doctor made another discovery during surgery. An ovary had twisted, as the uterus was being pulled up because of the baby. It was twice its size with a cyst on it. Instead of removing the ovary, the doctor drained it and put the ovary back in its correct position. Toward the end of the surgery, Eleanor began to feel the doctor stitching her up. The spinal tap was wearing off because she vomited right after it was administered, thus delaying the procedure. The doctor was so concerned about the stitches holding with her pregnancy that he kept on stitching and stitching. Finally, the surgery was over and the doctor and nurse went out to tell Melvin the good news.

"Your wife and baby are doing fine. In fact, we could see that the baby is about the size of a papaya, a cantaloupe."

Later that night Melvin prayed while sitting beside the fireplace in his guest cottage, "Lord, I don't understand why you would let Eleanor go through an operation right now, but I thank you that this happened where there was a doctor."

* * * * *

At the end of March, Eleanor felt ready to travel to Betongwe. They took their time over the uneven roads stopping over night at many places. When they arrived in Betongwe, a revival at the nearby Heart of African Mission, was in full swing. Before they had left for Rethy, there had been some stirrings of revival at the HAM station, with visits of the Holy Spirit bringing repentance and gifts of the spirit, including healing and praying in tongues. Some of the missionaries at Rethy, which was part of the African Inland Mission, favored the revival. However, others were not open to Pentecostal traditions. Meanwhile, at the last kuvanda for the AG group, a missionary pastor in a leadership position had openly confessed sins. Melvin and Eleanor hoped this confession would open the door for revival in the future.

Although HAM was previously not Pentecostal, the revival had taken hold and they began sending out speakers to any mission station that wanted a touch of the Spirit. After Melvin and Eleanor attended several of the meetings, they put in a request to have people come to Betongwe to encourage and strengthen the national pastors and Christians.

Three evangelists were sent over from HAM, and the revival meetings at Betongwe grew in size with each passing night. African men came dressed in suit coats sent in barrels from the west, coordinated with red hats and African style men's pants. The women sat on their side of the church with head wraps and babies in slings of cloth. No one sat in reverent silence, but chatted and waited until the music started, while a dog wandered inside searching for a possible morsel. When the music started, bodies were in motion and singing filled the air. At times, they would compose their own songs. Someone would belt out a line and everyone else would repeat it many times until a new line came along. Then dancing and jumping would break out with even the white missionaries dancing.

One woman, part of the HAM contingent, exclaimed one night in her English accent, "I've never danced so much in my life!"

Meanwhile, Melvin captured the meetings on film, wishing he had the capability of recording sound. He thought for sure the Congolese had springs in their calves!

One night, in the middle of a revival service, Africans were hopping on the chairs and flying out the open windows. When the rest of the congregation saw that a snake had fallen down from the grass roof, the people dissipated like a mist in the wind. Melvin went for a gun and came back to the church looking for the poisonous mamba. It took a bit of coaxing to get people to come back inside the church, but they did, and the meeting continued with preaching, singing, dancing, and jumping.

More than enthusiasm and exciting meetings, the fire of revival spread to village churches in the bush, transforming lives as the message went forth of salvation, a spirit-filled-life, Biblical healing, and the Second Coming of Jesus Christ for his bride. Although many missionaries came to Congo not believing in actual manifestations of demons, or that witchcraft was anything more than a superstitious practice, they soon changed their minds. Confrontation with the powers of darkness increased their desire for earnest prayer and guidance from the Holy Spirit. Pages in the New Testament previously skimmed over, thinking those days were of a special dispensation, were carefully read and gleaned for insight in dealing with situations, including witch doctors.

At one village, the Sunday school had grown to eighty-five people. A witch doctor who gave his life to Christ two weeks prior was greatly feared in his village because he had a piece of wood the size of a large hand that he called his drum. If he wanted someone dead he would do his incantations with chicken blood, tap the piece five times, and then say the person's name that he wanted dead, and that would be it. Sometimes a person in the village might pay the witch doctor to get rid of somebody.

During the revival, a large fire burned in the center of the village. The witch doctor brought all of his relics to burn, including a basket of spiritual medicines. A thick pillar of black smoke rose from the crackling fire as Christians circled the fire, singing songs with their new brother in Christ.

His face radiated peace, "I'm free! Jesus has made me a new person!"

* * * * *

In the midst of all this, preparations were made for the Jorgenson baby. During the vacation break for the boys and girls school, Melvin began putting up much needed shelving in their house and making furniture. Some of the wood came from the forest and some came from shipping crates. First, he made a vanity for their bedroom, a chest of drawers for Richard and then something for the baby. What it would be he wasn't quite sure yet. They were able to get a crib from Friesens, so he took that apart and refurbished it. Eleanor ordered baby clothes, diapers, and bottles, and sent requests to Leona and other relatives for baby food. It was a challenge getting ready for a baby on the mission field, but they were all excited and Richard didn't want to leave for another trimester at Rethy. He helped Melvin with everything and watched for notices of packages for the baby waiting at Mungbere.

"What if the baby comes while I'm at school?" he complained.

"We want you there too, Richy; Oicha isn't that far really. We can radio Rethy and someone can bring you down to the station," his parents promised.

Richard didn't seem convinced, so he started asking the Lord to help him be there for the baby's birth.

* * * * *

It was the first week in August when Melvin and Eleanor began the two hundred and fifty mile journey east to Oicha. Melvin drove with extra care, while Eleanor tried to find a way to sit comfortably.

"This baby is a regular jumping jack!"

About halfway there a tree blocked the road.

"A storm must have knocked it down." Melvin said.

A few Africans came over with machetes, "Bwana, we will cut the tree so you can pass through."

Melvin offered his thanks and waited for an hour.

"This is too big of a job; we'll have to turn back and stay at the Mennonite Mission we just passed."

The next morning they headed out again and found the tree cut through. They continued onto Oicha and were shown to a one-room guesthouse made of red brick and an aluminum roof with a cement floor extending out to the sitting porch.

Melvin and Eleanor ate their meals at Dr. Becker's house and waited for the baby to come. Richard finished his term at Rethy and a family dropped him off at Oicha, and then the family of three waited.

Two weeks later, after dinner at Dr. Becker's house, Eleanor knew it was time. She waited in the guesthouse until the late hours of the night. After Eleanor eased into the stretcher, Melvin and an African nurse carried her up a hill to the hospital. The sound of a generator hummed behind the hospital, which provided the power for lights and equipment in the delivery room. Unlike Eleanor's previous surgery on her ovary, Melvin stayed in the room to assist the doctor. As her labor increased, the contractions grew closer until she began to feel the urge to push the baby down the birth canal.

Suddenly the room went dark and the night was silent except for the voice of Dr. Becker, "You'll have to hold it while I work on the generator."

Melvin stood next to Eleanor in the room illuminated by lamps. His nervousness was obvious, while Eleanor panted, trying to hold back a baby that was coming with the force of the Congo River churning toward the ocean. Minutes ticked by as if hours until the generator sprang to life and lights flickered on in the room. Smelling of fuel and grease Dr. Becker scrubbed, gloved, and donned a fresh white surgery coat, "Okay, Mrs. Jorgenson, push."

* * * * *

Dear Ones, Oicha   August 24, 1954   Congo Belge, Africa

Aldene Anne was born on Sunday morning, August 22, 1954 at five o'clock. (Eleanor had been having "false" pains for two days, since Friday. El says they were anything but false; guess they were the real thing but didn't do anything for her.) Then Sunday morning at two she woke me up and told me to go get the nurse. As I had called her before, I got around to it this time at four o'clock. She called the doctor right away and after examining her said, "Get the stretcher". The doctor had arrived at 4:15 and the baby was born at five o'clock. We were both so happy about that, and thank the Lord for it all. Guess we had those who were praying for us back home. (We couldn't help but remember the time when Richard came and what a time that was.) I was with El all the time, and I wouldn't have missed it for the entire world. I heard her first cries as she took in the first breaths of life, and watched as they washed her and put drops in her eyes, and wrapped her in blankets. She was cute even when she was hanging upside down in the doctor's hands! El had some ether.

We were back at the house where we stay by 5:30, and I wanted to get Rich right away, who was sleeping in the doctor's house for that one night. But the nurse wouldn't let me. But at six I saw him opening the doctor's front door and stealing out, so I secretly waved to him to come on and hurry over. He sat all morning long by the baby just looking at her. He is a big help too in taking care of her. The first night she slept well but last night she cried most of the night.

Now as to whom she looks like—we really don't know yet. As soon as we make up our minds about that we'll let you know. She weighed two kilos 920 grams, about six and a half pounds; her length is nineteen and a half inches; her cheeks are so fat, and she has a double chin; black hair, and eyebrows and lashes. Hair not as long as Rich's was. Her head, shape of it, was absolutely normal.

I suppose we'll be here about eight days more; we arrived on the tenth. Rich is now anxious to get home and says he doesn't want to go to Rethy anymore and leave the baby. Don't blame him! God bless you all and thanks for praying for us during this time. God is good!

With our love to all of you, Melvin, Eleanor, Richard, and Aldene Anne

* * * * *

On the way back to Betongwe the family of four stayed overnight in a "gite," French for resting house. Similar to a mud house with mud floors with an unlocked door firmly latched shut to keep out animals, it was an unfurnished house put up for Belgian officials if they were traveling in the territory. The gite was also available to anyone if a government official did not occupy it.

Melvin and Richard set up sleeping cots, bedding and cooking utensils.

"Can I light the Primus?" Richard asked.

After a nod from his parents, he pumped the primer and lit a match to the single kerosene burner.

As dinner simmered, and then a bottle prepared, Richard kept an eye on his baby sister, "I'm nine and Aldene is zero."

"Yes, that's right," Melvin said, "I will always be able to remember your age because I can just flip the numbers around from '45 to '54."

Eleanor smiled watching Richard dote on his little sister. Her heart was full of gratitude to the Lord for the blessing of another child and seeing her through the pregnancy.

Chapter Twenty-Two

First Furlough 1955–1956

A fter Richard left for the fall term at Rethy, Eleanor soon found herself going about her daily life in Betongwe. She felt much stronger after having Aldene than she had with Richard's birth. Making her rounds to nearby villages, Eleanor took her daughter with her, or left her sleeping on the front porch in a buggy under netting with Melvin. Samwelli, another houseboy that Eleanor trained to do daily household chores, couldn't get enough of the baby. He often babysat Aldene when Eleanor was off teaching classes or other duties. Unlike the other boys who stole things or got drunk when Melvin and Eleanor left the station, Samwelli was a dependable young man.

That November, rain pounded down outside their house in Betongwe while the wind howled across the mission station. Aldene smiled and cooed during her bath until Eleanor took her out of the water. A protest of crying filled the air as Eleanor wrapped her daughter in a towel, "There, there, Miss Aldene Anne, it's okay."

Finally, the cries subsided and Eleanor began slipping clothes over tiny arms and legs. The rash from using regular detergent on her baby clothes was almost gone thanks to

Angeline Tucker giving them a bar of Ivory Soap. Eleanor quickly sent a request to Leona to order a case of Ivory shipped to Mungbere, along with cod liver oil and briefs for Melvin.

"Wait until you slip a quinine pill in her mouth," Melvin said, looking out the window.

The rain came down in torrents making it impossible to see anything. He glanced at a calendar on the wall. Three more weeks and Richard would come home for Christmas vacation. Eleanor was already planning special meals and treats for their boy. Both Melvin and Eleanor thought the addition of another family member would help to fill that aching void when their son left for school, but somehow it seemed worse. Eleanor began pushing the bitter pill into Aldene's mouth. Her tiny body arched while her angry face pinched her eyes tight. Then she bucked and twisted.

Melvin braced himself for the onslaught, "It's the wind up, the pitch, and the swing!"

On cue, Aldene announced her feelings about the quinine pills to the world in record decibels.

Eventually, the rain subsided enough for Melvin to see across the mission station. Debris lay everywhere. He sucked in his breath in shock, "Eleanor, our church is gone!"

He grabbed his pith helmet and ran out the front door.

The entire roof was gone. Brick walls lay crumbled on the ground. Benches were broken from the supporting beams and bricks were falling on them. Melvin knew how much time and labor it took to build a structure like this in Africa. His heart sank to the bottom of his feet.

"Lord, you brought me here and you're working mightily. . .but this I don't understand. I need your strength to stand against discouragement. I know the devil works to steal, kill, and destroy, but you have come to bring life, abundant life that is more than bricks and mortar."

That Sunday, outdoor services were held under the bright sun. Melvin stood before the people sitting on repaired benches or the ground.

"By the grace of God, we are moving forward and trusting Him that all things work together for good. This year's Christmas program will be held on the Sunday after Christmas with the children's nativity play in the morning and the young people's choir in the evening. In the meantime, I need help in building a temporary shelter, something like a large gwamo, until the church can be rebuilt."

After the service, Sara Anabote came up to Melvin and Eleanor, "Blessings Brother and Sister Jorgenson!"

Her smile spread across her radiant face, "Do not be discouraged. It is only a building. We, the people of God are the true building of living stones. What seems like bad, God will use for good."

Her heart of faith encouraged Melvin and Eleanor. If anyone knew about sacrifice for God's kingdom, it was Sara Anabote. As a young girl, she was sold to the Paramount Chief of the Mabudu tribe. Every village had a chief, but the Paramount Chief was chief of the entire region and because of his status, acquired many wives. Sara was one of over three hundred wives still living in her own village, until she became one of his favorite wives and moved into his household.

However, there was so much jealousy with the wives that their constant fighting and bickering drove the chief to send them to a local Protestant mission station. He heard that the Christians taught people to be respectful and kind to each other.

After a time, his favorite wives came back and he was satisfied with the changes in his household until he told Sara to cook a batch of beer. She refused his request, stating that it was his idea to send her to the mission and that she decided to follow Jesus Christ. This meant she would serve him by cooking his food, working in his gardens, carrying water and wood, but she would not make him beer.

No one ever dared refuse the chief above all chiefs, and certainly not one of his wives! For a punishment, he made her a slave, doing long hours of menial labor, and refused to give her more children, a woman's honor and legacy in the community. She was allowed to keep her one baby daughter, but she was not allowed his intimate company.

As the years went by, Sara's respectful attitude and ardent faith won him over, and the Paramount Chief allowed her to return to her family village. From there Sara moved to Betongwe to help with God's work supervising the girl's school, teaching and training young women.

Now her legacy was the hundreds of Congo daughters mentored by their spiritual mother, Sara Anabote.

* * * * *

On Christmas Eve, sixteen people gathered around the Jorgenson table by creatively borrowing tables from the school and other homes. Melvin had met Richard in Watsa and picked up the Friesen family along the way. When Aldene first saw Richard, she laughed for the first time and Richard's hazel eyes swelled with tears. Also seated at the table were Winnie and her missionary friend, five of the orphanage girls, and Edith McClennan.

Edith was a nurse from England. She held quite a few credentials as a midwife and surgical nurse. The young woman in her late twenties listened attentively to the conversation surrounding the bush trip Lillian and Martha took to Azande Land.

"They'll be up there three weeks to help pioneer a new work close to the town of Biodi."

"What kind of work?" Edith asked.

This was her first term, and she was approaching her first furlough, as were the Jorgensons.

"Well, mostly evangelism, but there are so many lepers in the area," Melvin replied. "Grace has talked about the need to start a leprosarium up there."

Edith's eyes sparked with interest and then clouded over with other thoughts. The conversation switched to other subjects, dishes were cleared, and dessert was served

* * * * *

Christmas day came and went quietly, with the Friesen family as guests in their home for a few days. Together the two families shared a duck dinner with all the trimmings. Watching the children enjoying their new gifts lightened hearts that were saddened by separation from loved ones.

"Look what I got from Auntie Lillian, it's for my monkeys!" Richard held up two small outfits that looked like doll clothes.

In on the secret, Eleanor divulged some information, "She sewed them herself! I don't know how she got the measurements though."

He promptly went outside to look for Akido and Bootsey.

"I better get the camera ready for a photo shoot," laughed Melvin.

Later, the primates sat passively in the wire basket of Richard's bicycle posing for the picture with red vests and hats sporting green zigzagging trim. Richard straddled the bike holding the handlebars. He wore a blue and white wide striped shirt, blue shorts, and his pith helmet.

* * * * *

The following Sunday, both Christmas programs went off without a hitch and attendance at Sunday school soared over eight hundred. Melvin preached the message, wearing his new pants he got in the mail. Lately, he had resorted to wearing khaki shorts because his pants had thinned down to bare threads. He thought back to the dress code at North Central. He would have been written up for sure, wearing shorts behind the pulpit!

The annual missionary kuvanda came with business meetings at the end. Furlough schedules were ironed out and Melvin happily resigned as field secretary-treasurer. Missionary kids played in the yard or hung around the porch of the Jorgenson home. Richard and Gwen were playing a board game of *Sorry*. Aldene slept in her buggy on the porch while Edith rocked in a chair enjoying the thought that she wasn't included in the business meetings.

"What are you going to do with your monkeys when you leave?" Edith asked Richard.

"I don't know. But I'll be back soon. Mommy and Daddy said furlough is only for one year."

Edith stopped the rocking chair declaring, "I'm not coming back until I bring me a man!"

Richard and Gwen gazed at Aunt Edith. She set her jaw firm with determination and kept rocking, the chair creaking in rhythm. The two missionary kids shrugged their shoulders and continued their game.

Suddenly, Congolese men and women content in the slow pace of daily life sprang into action as if called into battle. Some grabbed sticks to burn for torches. Others snatched baskets. Everyone was yelling, "BAKWA!"

"All right! Yippee!" yelled the missionary kids ready for some excitement. They followed the Congolese in Pied Piper fashion to the termite mounds.

Once a year, the bakwa rains came to break up the dry season. These rains softened the hard termite mounds arousing the insects to swarm by the thousands to start new colonies. Hence, the annual harvesting of termites was known as "bakwa."

The Africans started a fire nearby the large red mounds of dirt, which were taller than Richard, while others feverishly dug holes for their baskets. As the insects erupted into air, flaming torches waving over the mound singed the wings, and termites dropped into baskets.

The dead insects were stored in large baskets hung under the roof of the gwamo to use for roasting, cooking, or just for snacking. Once the starchy root of manioc was prepared into creamy fufu, the women would stir in the roasted termites. Then they would roll up the mixture into a leaf, tie it with a string and steam it in a boiling pot of water. They also fried the termites in palm oil and then mixed them with peanut butter freshly ground between two stones. The gorging lasted up to three days until the Africans lay on the ground immobilized. It was the African Caviar, rich in protein, and free for the taking.

Richard watched termites sizzling in palm fat until they were crispy. Hot off the pan, they were eagerly devoured, as brown and white hands reached out begging for a sample.

"It tastes like bacon!" said Richard, crunching on a few.

* * * * *

Once kuvanda was over, preparations for furlough were in full swing. The tension of getting permission to leave, and the funds to purchase tickets, all coordinated by long-distance correspondence, was finally over. Before leaving Africa, Melvin checked on as many of the village pastors as possible. There was one pastor, Tandarua, who was blind and a leper. A boy would lead him around with a stick from village to village while Tandarua held onto the other end of the stick. His wife was sick with dropsy, but he still wanted to serve the Lord and tell people about Jesus and salvation in his name.

Arriving at the village Melvin greeted the pastor and they sat under a mafika visiting.

"Bwana, would you go with me to a village to share the gospel? It is only an hour's walk."

Melvin agreed and they left for the village. On the way, Melvin noticed the sky darkening and the wind picking up. Tropical storms blew in without much warning and now they were caught in one. Searching for shelter, Melvin saw a small structure held by poles and a grass roof.

"Come with me Tandarua, this way. I see a gwamo."

The wind had come in with such force that they clung to the poles while the rain pelted their faces. The blind pastor with leprosy lifted an arm toward the sky and prayed a Bangala prayer to stop the storm, "Atikisi mbula oyo."

Melvin watched in awe as the rain stopped and the wind settled down.

* * * * *

A few months later Melvin, Eleanor, Richard, and Aldene, along with Koko the gray African parrot, boarded the vintage DC-3 plane operated by Sobelair. Departing from Irumu the pilot followed the Nile River north to Khartoum, Sudan. By the time they checked into their hotel their bodies had wilted. At one in the morning, it was over one hundred degrees. Protesting the heat, Aldene stood in her crib bawling. The next night they spent in Cairo, after following the Nile for a second day, and then flew west over the Mediterranean Sea to Naples.

On the fourth day, they landed in Brussels. Memories flooded their minds and hearts as they spoke French. There were so many white people, so many cars, and streets with pavement, and no scorching heat. They tried to visit with friends between business errands, before leaving on a ship to New York City. The boat ride across the Atlantic gave them the first chance to catch their breath from the whirlwind preparations and travels of the last month.

* * * * *

Arriving in America, Melvin and Eleanor stood together on the deck of the ship with ten-year-old Richard, straining to see the Statue of Liberty, while ten-month-old Aldene bounced in Eleanor's arms. She was living up to Eleanor's predictions that she was going to be a regular jumping jack.

"Well, the Lord has brought us through five years and here we are again," Melvin said, slipping an one arm around Eleanor, and the other reaching for one of Aldene's waving arms.

"Yes, the Lord has brought us through a lot," reflected Eleanor, with a grateful heart.

After checking into the missionary guesthouse, they went to an American café with another missionary family in transit. While Melvin and Eleanor were chatting with the couple at one booth, Richard sat with their son in the next booth. A waitress brought a tall dessert made of three round balls all different colors with something red on the top.

"I think I ordered this," Richard said, "it looks like the picture."

"It's an ice cream sundae," the boy sitting with him offered. "Don't they have those in Africa?"

The next day they went to a zoo. Richard could identify so many animals that he knew from Africa, but he felt sad for them. They didn't seem the same in a small cage.

"How about if we get a hamburger?" Melvin suggested.

As they stood in line at the food stand, Richard wondered what that smooth black thing was on the counter. He set his hand on it and started yelling, "Owe! It burned me!"

The man at the food stand handed Melvin some ice and a wet rag. "Can't you see it's a hot plate?"

Melvin explained as he comforted his son, "He hasn't lived in America for five years."

It wouldn't be Richard's last adjustment. After moving into their rental house in Minneapolis, Richard's parrot flew to a yard across the street. Cars honked and brakes screeched as he ran after his bird. Melvin and Eleanor worked with their son, "Every road is dangerous, always look both ways. It's not like living on a mission station."

Well-meaning relatives hugged the breath out of him, declaring the standard, "My, how much you've grown. Just like a cornstalk."

Before they went to Crookston and Lemmon, Melvin and Eleanor had tried to remind him of people's names and where they fit in the family. However, Richard was used to his aunts and uncles in Congo, he just couldn't remember his relatives enough to feel comfortable with the onslaught of names and faces.

In Crookston, Melvin and his family stood on the porch of the white house on 605 Pleasant Avenue. His mother and father were saying the long Minnesota good-by with promises to come visit them in Minneapolis at their rental house. After five years, Melvin could see the changes in his aging parents, but they both seemed in good health and he was thankful for that.

After Aldene's first birthday, Richard started school and things seemed better. He was happy to come home every day to his family instead of the boarding school routine. On weekends, they began to travel to churches to report on their work in Africa and raise funds for their next five-year term. Melvin set up the portable white screen and projector and narrated the silent films he had spliced together. Many churches had a room designated for mission supplies, overseen by the women's group. The women would get together to sew, knit, and pray for the missionaries. Eleanor was free to "shop" for home items and clothing. She browsed past shelves of homemade quilts and child-sized dresses and pants. There was even a section of bandages made from old sheets. Knowing more of what she truly needed in Africa, Eleanor made sure to bring plenty of bandages for the lepers. Not only did she want to bring clothing for the Africans, she needed to plan for her growing children as well. How many sizes would she need for Richard and Aldene for five years? And how many pairs of shoes?

A woman from the church in Detroit Lakes had a farm that offered to cut corn and can it at a nearby cannery to pack in shipping barrels. Another woman, Mrs. Patterson, had a large bakery and knew how to package things for restaurants and nursing homes. She canned cereals, cake mixes and other boxed items that wouldn't last long in Africa with the heat, humidity and bugs.

Melvin worked with the Speed the Light group again in securing another vehicle. The faithful Carryall from last term had fought a good fight and succumbed to the roads of Africa. Their next vehicle would be a 1956 red and white Ford station wagon.

Over the course of the year, barrels of clothing, home goods, medical supplies and canned food slowly filled their rented house. Now all they had left to do was finalize their travel plans, update passports, and get medical checkups.

* * * * *

"I'm sorry but your blood test showed some kind of infection," the doctor in Minneapolis seemed concerned, "I can't give you clearance to travel."

"It's probably filaria," unfazed, Melvin shrugged his shoulders, "it's from a red fly bite. The next thing you know, there's a worm traveling through your body. If your arm or leg swells up a bit, you know where it is that day. We all get it out on the field. It's not contagious."

The doctor's curiosity was peaked, "How do you treat it?"

"Sometimes you can get some kind of concoction the medical doctors in Africa create, or you wait until it crosses your eye and take it out with tweezers," Melvin replied.

"I see," the doctor said. "Well, in that case, if I can verify that what I am seeing is filaria, I will give you clearance for Africa."

Melvin smiled in agreement.

Chapter Twenty-Three

Andudu 1957-1959

❧

On January 23, 1957 Richard celebrated his twelfth birthday in Stanleyville at a swimming pool, until a tropical storm ended his short swim. The Jorgenson family of four made it back to Congo in record time, flying from Minneapolis to New York on a Northwest Airlines Boeing Stratocruiser, and then crossing the Atlantic onboard American Holland Lines to Belgium. From Brussels, they flew eleven hours on a DC6 directly to Stanleyville, bypassing the paddleboat ride upstream from Leopoldville.

During Melvin and Eleanor's short time in Stanleyville, they observed the mistreatment of the Congolese by some of the white Europeans. Navigating through the crowds, Belgians rudely broke through a crowd of Congolese, kicking shins and yelling at them to get out of their way with cruel remarks of "sale macaque"—filthy monkey. The attitude of many Belgians was that the Congolese had recently come down from the trees and were not as developed as whites.

In light of recent racial tensions in America, the Jorgensons were acutely aware of the segregation of restaurants and public places in Stanleyville. While on their furlough, Rosa Parks made national news when she was arrested December

5, 1955, after she refused to give up her bus seat to a white man in Montgomery, Alabama. This sparked a sixteen-month bus boycott in Montgomery by the black population. One of the organizers of this boycott, Rev. Martin Luther King, Jr. urged all blacks to follow the path of nonviolence after his home was firebombed on January 30, 1956. President Eisenhower found himself in the middle of desegregation of buses and schools, and voting rights for blacks in America.

* * * * *

After a three-day stay in Stanleyville, Melvin, Eleanor, Richard, and two-year-old Aldene boarded a DC3 flying northeast to Paulis. After the three-hour flight they hitched a one hundred-kilometer ride southeast with the Friesen family to Andudu. Their new home for the next five years lay in the heart of the Ituri Rain forest. Leaving Paulis, the vehicle passed small villages of tribal populations of the pygmy Aka and Mangbetu in the northeastern region of the forest with the Sua toward the west near Betongwe. In the north and east lived the nomadic pygmy Efe and Lese groups who were more Sudanic-influenced speakers, mixing in Swahili. The Mbuti and Mamvu lived near Andudu with the Bila, toward the southeast of the rain forest. The Boko was a tribe of the Bomokandi River near Andudu.

There were also Bantu-speaking farmers who traded their crops of peanuts, rice, manioc, and other produce with the pygmy tribes. The Mamvus and Mangbetus no longer practiced cannibalism. However, there were rumors from time to time of a select few natives secretly making *dawa*, a medicine made from humans.

Interspersed among these tribal lands were the Belgian and Greek coffee plantation owners and the mission stations of the numerous Protestant and Catholic organizations.

Named after the Ituri River, the Ituri Rain Forest is the only place in the world where the okapi lives. Under a canopy of mixed foliage, with a crown height of thirty to forty feet dwells this shy, elusive animal that is part of the giraffe family. The okapi has a robust body with long legs and a shorter neck than a giraffe. Their dear-like ears alert them of their predator, the leopard. An okapi humorously mimics a child dressing in seemingly uncoordinated colors and patterns. Zebra-striped front and hind legs contrast with a solid body of dark caramel red reaching up its neck between its ears down to a black nose separating a white face. The okapi have skin that repels the heavy rainfall and moisture of the forest, and the males have ossicones, short skin covered horns. A cud-chewer, with a stomach of four chambers, its long flexible tongue easily strips the leaves off many plant species poisonous to humans. Not a small animal, at five to eight feet long and over five to six feet tall at the shoulder, an adult can weigh over seven hundred pounds.

The mission station lay four kilometers north of the Nepoko River and the town of Andudu. An elephant camp on the river drew visitors for picnics and watching the elephants lumber into the tea-colored river to spray water through their agile trunks. Not far from the station, a pond formed by a brook attracted hippos.

A spur of the Cape-to-Cairo highway ran by Andudu. The Cape-to-Cairo was never completed, but the spur provided a nice flat road, creating the west border of the station. Two main redbrick houses sat close to the spur. A small plot of coffee trees grew between them, with the Griffin house to the south, and the house to the north for the Jorgensons.

The Griffin family didn't always live in that house, but that's what everybody called it because Herbert Griffin had moved the mission station to its present spot after living on a lower elevation near a river. Plagued by insect and mosquito infestation, Herbert decided to scout for a better place to live and work. The new location sat up high on a plateau, offering a stunning view of the rolling hills and distant mountains of the densely forested jungle. North of Jorgenson's home ran the road from the spur to the Bible School, leper village and hospital, and also a dispensary. In the southeast corner of the station stood a garage, storage and lumber sheds. Directly behind the Griffin house, stood the nurses' house. In the center of the station was an open park-like area within steps of the Jorgenson home and the church.

People carried water from the cement-lined square water hole at the northwest corner of the station along a dense jungle-walking path filled with butterflies. The path hugged a stream until turning uphill to the road and station dotted with papaya and other fruit trees.

Their vehicle, covered with red dust, pulled into the roundabout near the sheds with a honk of hello from its horn.

"Mbote Bwana! Mbote Madamo!" people huddled around the newcomers.

"Mbote mingi, serna mingi!" Melvin replied.

"Oh, you speak the older way of saying hello," one African replied to Melvin.

The language of Bangala was a simple form of Lingala and was slowly being replaced by Lingala. Other dialects were spoken by each tribe in the rain forest, but most knew enough of Lingala to communicate with people outside their village.

"I guess I will have to adjust to Lingala," Melvin said.

A tall, strongly-built Congolese strode forth and offered the African handshake to Melvin and nodded his head toward Eleanor, "Mbote Bwana, Mbote Madamo, I am Bomo."

His smile and countenance were friendly and held something attractive to those who recognized an honest, faithful friend when they saw one.

"I have cooked for many missionaries and now I will cook for you."

Richard walked right up to Bomo and looked up into his brown eyes, "Mbote Bomo, I'm Richard."

"Yes, I know you are Richard," and in that moment Bomo became a cook and a mentor.

Grace Lindholm came over to greet the Jorgensons. She oversaw the medical needs of over three hundred lepers in Andudu and was helping to pioneer leper work in Biodi.

"Welcome back!" she embraced Eleanor. "Oh, look at Aldene, she's walking. . .no running!"

Grace laughed at Aldene's pent-up energy after riding in the vehicle all day, "Hello, Miss Aldene, I'm Aunty Grace."

Aldene turned for a moment to cast a glance at Grace and then ran to chase after Richard, who was following Bomo over to their house.

The next morning, Bomo walked to the station. He stepped onto the back porch of the Jorgenson home that faced the road coming to the station. He placed his cooking apron over his head, tied the laces in the back, and set to work loading the cooking stove with wood. The mauve-colored apron patterned with small blue flowers and green trim contrasted sharply with his formidable stature, yet somehow in Congo, it went unnoticed. After the fire settled into a bank of coals, Bomo's strong hands worked to cut nut berries from a large bunch harvested from a palm tree.

Richard came around the corner, "Mbote Bomo, are you making mamba and chicken tonight?"

"Yes, Richard," Bomo smiled. "Do you like mamba sauce?"

"Who doesn't?"

Unlike coconut-bearing trees, palm oil trees bear compact heads with one to three thousand fruitlets in each bunch. Each fruitlet is a hard kernel enclosed in a shell surrounded by a fleshy mesocarp. After felling the tree, the fruit head is separated and thoroughly boiled. Then the cooked berries are pounded with a big round stick inside an earthen jar until the skin separates from the nut. Only the skins are kept to wring out every drop possible of palm butter. Then a second process of cooking begins and the fat rises to the top, becoming a healthy palm oil.

Inside the house, Melvin and Eleanor sipped on coffee brewed over the single Primus burner.

A voice called from the middle bedroom.

"Mommy! Daddy!"

Trapped under mosquito netting tucked under her mattress, Aldene wanted freedom.

Eleanor padded into Aldene's room that also had a side door to the master bedroom, which wasn't much larger than the two single bedrooms. It seemed such a luxury to Eleanor that each child could have his or her own bedroom. Before she reached Aldene, something scurried across the cement floor.

"Oh, you nasty thing!"

Eleanor grabbed a flyswatter and went after the spider the size of a fifty-cent piece. She slammed down the swatter, killing the intruder. Eleanor's smug satisfaction turned to horror as babies ran off the dead spider's back. Eleanor raised her weapon for attack—*swat-swat-swat!* Aldene watched through her netting. There were many types of insects in

Congo ranging from nonpoisonous to deadly, so Aldene and Richard were never allowed to go barefoot except for bathing and sleeping. Every pair of shoes needed to be inspected before slipping them on. Sometimes during the night, Aldene would awake needing to use the indoor pot in her bedroom. By the time Eleanor slipped from her mosquito-netted bed, grabbed the flashlight, checked her slippers for critters, and passed through the side door to Aldene's room, it was too late. The bed was wet and needed to be changed.

After breakfast that morning, Melvin and Eleanor discussed arrangements for getting Richard to Rethy, and the upcoming kuvanda the end of January. Then Eleanor worked on unpacking and talking over household duties with Bomo and the houseboys. She set out bread pans and granulated yeast. To her surprise and delight, Bomo was an excellent baker, making their future look promising for meals.

A few weeks later, Eleanor started the dreaded task of packing Richard's suitcase for Rethy. Tears welled up in her eyes as she looked around his room, digging through newly arrived containers. Lost in her thoughts, she didn't notice Richard standing in the doorway.

"It's okay, Mom," Richard consoled his mother, "I'm the one who has to go."

He left to search out his bike and Akido. Of all his pets from Betongwe, the monkey was the only one left, for now. Tags had died from tick fever and Koko stayed in America with Grandma Groat. Richard was grateful a missionary adopted Akido in his absence. However, he quickly found a replacement for Koko. Roostie, a Rhode Island Red rooster, was three times the size of the small bantam-like chickens found in Congo. The rooster had his own special cage, but spent some of his time riding in the basket of Richard's bike. From time to time, Roostie would go missing and Richard would find him in a local village. Years later, it was said the chickens in the Andudu area were noted for their unusually larger size.

Meanwhile, Melvin began making plans for the coming year of ministry, and improvements to the station. Looking over the grounds, he spotted a nice clearing, perfect for a garden away from shrubs and trees. Knowing the Africans made their rows five or six inches high to protect the seeds from torrential rains, he followed suit and set to work on several eght by ten foot plots. He knew what American vegetables would work best in the African red soil and dropped to his knees sowing the seed. Fleeting memories of sugar-beet fields and Crookston came and went. Later, dripping with sweat, he stood with satisfaction rubbing the dirt from his hands while looking over his new garden.

A few months later, the garden looked the same as the day Melvin had planted it. Frustrated and bewildered, he mentioned it to a few of the Africans that lived on the station.

"We knew you weren't going to have anything there," they promptly replied.

"Why not?"

"Well, because the dirt you gathered together was from old houses."

When their huts became worn out, they would simply tear them down and build a new one out of fresh organic supplies from the earth and forest. The old, useless dirt was spread out in the open areas of the mission.

"I didn't know that; why didn't you tell me?"

"You didn't ask us."

The months passed quickly as Melvin and Eleanor worked on the Andudu station with outreaches to the bush. Eleanor taught school in the afternoons, helped in the dispensary giving out anti malaria medication, and visited women in the surrounding villages.

In addition to church services, Melvin became director of the Bible School, teaching and planning courses. Students of all ages came from the other mission stations to live and study. Masiokpo, the son of a village chief, came to the station when he was a young man to join the Bible School. Eventually he became a teacher and Melvin enjoyed working with him. When his father died, the people of the village came to Andudu and forced him to go back to his village to take his father's place. Another man, Komobondri, met Melvin in his village in the jamba. After thinking and praying about which village pastor would be best suited to be trained as a teacher for the Bible School, Melvin asked Komobondri if he would be willing to come to Andudu. In time, the village pastors in the area asked Komobondri to be their leader.

* * * * *

One morning, as the sun peeked its first rays over Andudu, Melvin and Eleanor began the day with their usual routine of prayer and reading scripture. As the day unfolded, a short man clothed with natural forest coverings walked into the station. Standing less than five feet, almost eye level with Eleanor, and about the same weight, he smiled and said hello. Eleanor smiled back and asked him to wait while she got her husband. By the time Melvin got to the school building, a group of pygmies had gathered. Melvin greeted them and invited them to school and services at the church.

For several weeks, the pygmies went to school, attended meetings and welcomed the rice and peanuts offered them. Then one day they packed up and left just as quickly as they had come.

Eleanor was disappointed, "Why did they leave? Here I thought things were going so well."

Bomo explained, "They are hungry for the bush, the forest. It is how they live, going from one place to another trading bush meat and honey with the villages, then back to the forest to live for a while."

"It seems so disruptive to live like that. Don't they want to better themselves with an education?"

"When they stay close to villages too long, they pick up sickness and disease easier. They are also very educated in the ways of the forest knowing many uses for the plants. That is why they can poison the tips of their hunting arrows without killing themselves. They know which poison to use that will be temporary or deadly."

* * * * *

Besides his teaching and administrative duties for the Bible School, Melvin was also in charge of construction projects. Although the school building needed improvements, the housing for the students was sorely lacking. Melvin plotted land next to the Bible School along the incoming road for eight dormitory houses. He decided his choice of material for building the houses would be cement blocks, rather than bricks that needed to be fired. After stating the needs of the students through letters, a generous donation came from someone at their former Detroit Lakes church for cement.

Normally the ratio for mixing cement could be one to three or one to four. However, cement was a scarce commodity that took an enormous amount of effort to haul to Andudu. At first, they mixed the cement one to six. When the supply started dwindling they ratio became one to ten with a prayer. The houses went up, the soli roofs installed and the students moved in.

Inside the Bible School Melvin painted black paint over a cement wall for a blackboard. Gleaning mahogany from Herbert Griffin's lumber shed, he made the first desk. Then he trained the nationals to make the rest of the desks.

At the graduation service, people came out of the bush, walking with chairs or tying them to bicycles. Men sporting reed hats made from kumb-na-mai accented with parrot feathers wore bark cloth and American-type t-shirts. Women wore traditional sarongs, a dhoti, and head wraps. The students wore cast-off suit jackets and shirts from missionary barrels and men's ties sent from Melvin's brother, Lloyd.

* * * * *

Life for missionary kids in Congo had its ups and downs, and Richard and Aldene had their own unique growing pains, mixed with memories to treasure. At Rethy, one of Richard's teachers threatened to tie his left arm behind his back, insisting he learn to write with his right hand. However, Richard enjoyed his piano teacher much more, who managed to bring her harp to Africa. He even got to ride the donkey he saw on his first day at the school. But he did manage to get room-grounded for raiding the pantry one night with Andy Englebrecht. They had just lit a one-burner Primus to make hard-boiled eggs when they were discovered. At least he didn't have to endure the dreaded spanking machine like another student, Johnny Tucker, did for knocking a bees nest down with rocks. The thing suddenly dropped in the schoolyard creating chaos as swarming bees stung any target possible. Soon after, a chain of older students waited for

Tucker to crawl between their legs, ready to pound and swat with hands.

Melvin and Eleanor never knew what Richard would bring home from Rethy. One time it was a Golden Crested Crane, another time it was a pair of common hawks raised from chicks. When he brought them home, Aldene was entranced by the way they sat on Richard's arms.

"I want King and Queeney to sit on my arm too!"

Richard gently shifted the birds to his sister's arm. Melvin walked by and stopped in his tracks, "I don't know about this hawk business, Aldene. Those hawks are still immature and their sharp beaks might be attracted to your eyes."

Later that night, during dinner on the front porch overlooking the coffee trees and rolling hills of thick jungle, Richard told the story of his classmate from Rethy, "Stuffy climbed a tree and asked God to help him to fly! He said, 'I believe, I believe.' Then he jumped from the tree and broke his arm!"

After the meal was finished, the family of four sat a few minutes to watch the parrots fly and the monkeys play in the trees. Cicadas buzzed all around them. Aldene tapped the table loudly with a spoon. The monkeys stopped their play.

"Look, I can still see the monkey's tail!"

Aldene giggled, her eyes radiating under her shortly cropped bangs. Melvin joined in with a chuckle, "Yes, it thinks it's pretty clever hiding from us."

Growing up on the mission station Aldene's friends were her dolls, her pets, and workers on the station. However, her best friend was Butch, a doll with a hard rubber head and a cloth body. Butch went everywhere with Aldene. In the morning, she would set him on the potty. Then she would take him out to the cooking porch to read books to Bomo. Sitting on a short stool, Aldene "translated" her storybooks into Bangala. She didn't know how to read, but her preschool mind rapidly memorized every book she owned, as her parents read to her each night before bed.

Bomo's white smile laughed and his eyes danced, "Read me another story Aldene!"

Another friend of hers was Grace Lindholm. After falling off her bike one time, she ran to find the nurse, "Aunty Grace, my blood is bleeding!"

In fact, Grace felt such affection for Aldene that one time when Aldene came down with a severe case of malaria Grace hesitated to administer the injection. She knew it could be dangerous for a young child. Finally, Grace confided to Eleanor, "I just can't do it. I'll have to ask Toma."

The African nurse slowly administered the cure and Aldene recovered. Soon she was back to her jumping-jack speed coming into the house in time to run into a hot cookie sheet Eleanor was pulling out of the tiny kerosene oven. It hit right between her red shorts and white polka-dot shirt.

Another time Aldene ran across the station after Eleanor who was checking on the health of a nearby village woman. Aldene felt a bug slip into her right ear. Her yelling brought out Melvin from the Bible School, Toma from the leper hospital, and Eleanor from her visit.

"It's buzzing in my ear! Stop the buzzing!"

"Stand still Aldene, I don't want to injure your eardrum," Toma instructed as he carefully prodded with a tweezers. When that didn't work, they tried oil.

Melvin thought a moment, "What attracts bugs?"

He went to fetch a flashlight. Holding it up to Aldene's ear, the bug crawled down the ear canal and out. Toma grabbed it with the tweezers.

"Give me that bug!" Aldene took it to the nearest cement floor and stepped on it as hard as she could, "Take that you nasty thing!"

* * * * *

The adult day school finished another three-month term, and Melvin and Eleanor got a request from a Christian in an outlying village to come for an evangelistic outreach. A man had heard the Gospel of following Jesus, and he wanted someone to come and have meetings in his village. They would have just enough time to fit in the trip before Richard returned from Rethy. Melvin and Eleanor packed up the car with army cots, bedding, water to drink, and a bit of food knowing that they would also eat some African food.

With a couple of guides along, they rode in the car with Aldene in the back seat, until reaching an impassable river. Leaving the car, the three of them got into a dugout canoe and a guide paddled them to the other side. The guides made more than one trip with the canoe filled with supplies. Then they started going through the forest walking along a footpath.

Just as they were arriving to the village, Eleanor noticed an odd sensation, "Melvin, I must have touched something poisonous."

Melvin looked at his wife in shock. Her hands were swollen, her feet were swollen, and her face was swollen!

"Eleanor, I think we better turn around and head back home."

Eleanor shook her head, "No, I don't think so. I think the devil is just trying to keep us from being here."

Someone showed them to a hut. On the ground there was a layer of freshly packed mud to make it clean. Melvin and Eleanor knew the kind village people thought they were doing them a favor, but it felt damp and musty. They set up the three cots on the mud floor getting things ready to spend the next few nights in the bush village.

The next morning Melvin went with the Christian man to the peanut and rice gardens to share the message of faith in Jesus. Wanting his wife to rest, Melvin decided to bring Aldene along.

After Melvin and Aldene left, Eleanor noticed the man's wife was under a mafika cooking. She could at least keep the woman company, so Eleanor hobbled out to the mafika and sat down for a visit. It wasn't long before a lady came down the walking path wailing from the deepest part of her soul. In her arms, she carried a little, lifeless child. As Eleanor watched the distraught woman, the Spirit of the Lord said to her: (a strong thought came to her that she recognized as the Spirit of the Lord saying to her), *I want to manifest myself here today.*

The woman dropped to her knees. Rocking back and forth, with tears streaming down her face she blurted out that she had gone out to cut firewood for the evening meal and set her two-year-old child down.

"And I told my baby, 'Now you stay here and I'm going to go cut the tree.'"

But as she began cutting the tree, the child got up and toddled over just as the tree fell crushing the child. Eleanor now knew why she was in this village. "Please, come closer and sit with us."

The Christian man's wife sent word to her husband and Melvin. Then she gathered banana leaves and placed them on the ground for the mother to lay her child on under the roof of the mafika. Eleanor comforted the mother and began telling her about Jesus and that he could heal her little girl if they prayed together.

Melvin, Aldene, and the Christian man came down the footpath from the peanut and rice gardens. Their faces froze when they saw the little, lifeless form on the banana leaves on the ground. The child's father came from behind them and started beating the mother. Aldene's eyes widened at the display of violence.

Melvin spoke up, "No. Stop that! As Christians, we don't do things like that."

The husband quieted down and Eleanor told the group what the Lord had said to her, "We need to pray and wait on the Lord. I believe he wants to heal this little girl."

Then the small group gathered together, calling on the name of Jesus and praying. They continued to sit for several hours quietly looking to the Lord. Eleanor knew what God's Holy Spirit had said to her. Aldene took in everything, listening to her parents pray.

And then, the little girl stirred. She opened her eyes, sat up and said, "I'm hungry."

The relieved parents gave her a banana, and watched in awe as their daughter munched down the banana.

In the meantime, the message had gone out to all the villages around using the gudugudu that this little girl had been killed. People began coming, wailing, and doing all the things the way Africans do when there is a death. But when they got there, they saw that the little girl was all right. The news spread out all over the villages. That night, the little mud church that the Christian man had built, overflowed with people inside and out, and those people heard the Gospel.

The next day Melvin went back again to the gardens, and was asked to come to a hut where a lady was dying. There were no windows and it was so dark Melvin couldn't really see her, but he talked with her and prayed with her and led her to faith in Jesus as her Lord and Savior.

After three days, it was time to pack up and go home. While Eleanor was folding bed sheets and blankets, she glanced at her feet. She looked over her hands and felt her face. The swelling was gone!

Before returning to Andudu, Melvin heard the news that the lady he prayed with in the dark hut had died, "Someday in heaven I will see the lady I led to the Lord, but never saw."

A few days later, the father of the healed child came to the door of the Jorgenson home with a chicken in a basket. He had walked to the mission station spending one night in the forest."This is for you Madamo."

Touched by his gratitude, Eleanor went to the barrel filled with children's clothes to find something to send back with him. Then she thanked him again for the chicken, reminding him that the power of Jesus healed his daughter.

"Yes, Madamo, Jesus healed my little girl and I thank Him every day. But today I want to thank you for bringing Jesus to us."

Chapter Twenty-Four

Independence 1960

❦

"The tires are worn out on the bicycle you gave us." The African man explained further, "it needs new tires."

Melvin made another mental note of the cultural ways of the Congolese. The expectations of the national were that if Melvin supplied a bike he should also supply tires. As the provider of the gift, it was also his responsibility to take care of the gift.

"I see. Well, then I will check in the shed for some new tires."

As Melvin finished his conversation in Bangala, a vehicle rolled into the Andudu mission station.

A young couple with an infant emerged from the vehicle. Melvin waved and strolled over to greet them, "Mbote, Edith and Philip, I see you've brought the newest member of the Gombari mission community. Congratulations!"

Edith proudly held their first child, Philip John. She had left Congo with the declaration that she was coming back with a man, and she did.

Philip Cochrane, quite a few years younger, married Edith and her call to medical missions. His heart of kindness matched Edith's, making them an attractive couple in looks and character. They were traveling through on their way home to the Biodi mission, where Grace Lindholm was overseeing the leper work until their return.

Eleanor came out of the house with Aldene behind her, "Oh, let's see the baby."

Aldene peered at Philip John, "He's so little."

"I hope we're not a bother," Edith said handing her one-month-old son over to Eleanor.

"Not at all, Edith. I'm so glad you can stay the night. Richard is still at Rethy, so don't worry about crowding us out. Come on in for some iced tea. Our newly-acquired *old* kerosene refrigerator provides a bit of luxury in the bush."

The women and Aldene headed for the house, while Melvin and Philip went to the shed looking for bicycle tires.

Later that night, gathered at the dinner table illumined by candles, the two couples talked about raising children on the mission field and the challenges of mission work. The chrome and Formica-topped table typical of the 1950s with red-padded chrome chairs had been easy to disassemble and ship oversees. The couch was a different story.

"Melvin built the frame out of mahogany wood from the forest and I ordered cushion covers thinking I could stuff them with cotton from your area around Biodi," Eleanor explained with a laugh, "Well, the problem is I couldn't get all the seeds out, so when you sit on the davenport it pricks you!"

Aldene played in the adjoining living room, entertaining Philip John lying in a travel cot by showing him her dolls, "And this is Butch. He is bigger than you."

"It's been quite a first year for me," admitted Philip. "It's one thing to hear about leprosy and another thing to see it firsthand. Calling the lepers every day for their medication, I was overcome by the white scaly scabs and their stumps of what once were feet or hands covered with rags."

"Yes, I know. It's a sight and odor that can make a person sick to their stomach," Melvin agreed.

"It's such a ravenous disease," Philip said, "but then, I began to get to know them by name, and hear their stories. And God gave me grace to look past their deformed faces and begin to love them."

"Did you know that one of our houseboys gave to the work in Biodi?" Eleanor said as she stacked empty dinner plates into a pile. Then she leaned back in her chair, her hazel eyes lit with the memory, "It was during one of the kuvandas in Andudu when we lived in Betongwe. We were praying about having a mission amongst the northern Azande people. So, we took an offering. People were giving a chicken, or eggs, or maybe produce like pineapples—and here comes our houseboy, Setephano Pengberie, with a kerosene lantern that he saved up for months to buy. He set it down at the altar and then left the church for a few minutes. When he returned he said, 'I forgot the matches.'"

Eleanor's eyes brimmed with tears. "I'll never forget the devotion of that young man for his own people in Azande Land."

One morning while Melvin and Eleanor were eating their breakfast, a Bible student came to the door."Bwana, teacher," his concerned face peered through the screen, "one of the lady students expecting a baby is dying. She has been in labor three days."

Melvin and Eleanor immediately left their breakfast table.

Eleanor instructed her daughter, "Aldene, stay by Bomo until I come back. Don't run after me."

"Okay, Mommy. Butch and I can read books to him."

"I'll get the car ready to take her to the government hospital in Watsa," Melvin said.

Eleanor headed out the door following the student to a hut nearby the mission station.

As Eleanor walked into the hut, her eyes adjusted to the dimness. She recognized the still form lying on a bamboo bed covered with banana leaves. Ruth and her husband had come to Andudu from Azande Land. They were a taller people than the bush peoples of the Ituri Rain Forest. Blood trickled out of her mouth and her eyes were set. A distinct voice said to Eleanor's mind, *there's no use in praying. . .it's too late.*

Pushing the thought aside, Eleanor started to pray. Shortly after her arrival, an African pastor working with the Bible School came into the hut. Pastor Simona Karada paused, as if startled for a moment, before joining Eleanor in prayer. Then Pastor Karada and Melvin carried Ruth to the car on a stretcher. After gently placing her onto the bed made up in the vehicle, her husband climbed into the car. It was a one hundred kilometer drive to the gold-mine city of Watsa that would take at least four hours.

Melvin slid into the driver's seat. Before he shut the car door, Eleanor leaned her face in close to Melvin. "We'll be praying," she brushed his face with a kiss.

As the Ford station wagon left in a cloud of dust, Eleanor, Pastor Karada, and the Bible students went to the church to pray. All studies and duties in the Andudu station were suspended. From morning through afternoon, they all stayed in the church praying, no one left, and everyone had an urgency to pray for the couple from Azande Land. It was like a burden sitting on their hearts and minds that they couldn't stop. All they could do was pray. And they stayed in the church praying until four o'clock in the afternoon. Then it seemed like the burden of prayer lifted like a cloud floating away in the breeze. No one said a word. They all just got up and walked to their homes.

About eleven o'clock that night, the sounds of a car engine could be heard in the distance. Soon, headlights came down the spur of the Cape-to-Cairo and turned into the mission station. All the students were coming from every direction to hear the news. Eleanor held her breath waiting for Melvin to get out of the car.

His tired eyes held hope mixed with pain, "At four o'clock in the afternoon the doctor came and told me that Ruth would live. They removed the baby surgically. The child had been dead for three days."

Later, Eleanor found out that when the African pastor first walked into the hut he had heard the same words as Eleanor, *there's no use in praying. . .it's too late.*

"But God heard our prayers!" she exclaimed to Pastor Karada. "Isn't it something how the Holy Spirit works and ministers? It wasn't until four o'clock that all of us felt the burden of prayer lifted and it was four o'clock in the afternoon when the doctor came in and told Melvin that she would live!"

* * * *

That year, Richard learned to hunt starting with the .22 rifle. Melvin taught him everything he knew about gun safety, and hunting in Africa. Away from everyone at the mission station, Melvin showed Richard how to site a gun using a tin can nailed to a tree.

"Oh, I almost forgot to tell you, always drop off something for the local chief on your way home."

A smile played at his lips, "When I first started hunting I got into a little bit of trouble because no one told me I had to ask the local chief for permission to hunt in his area."

Richard took note. He only needed to ask the village chief once for permission to hunt on his land. After that, it was a simple matter of dropping off the best cuts from the animal—the head or the organs. In the days that followed, if Melvin wasn't available for hunting, Richard went looking for Bomo. Shedding his apron, Bomo went from bread maker to safari guide.

Meanwhile, Aldene kept Eleanor on her toes. It seemed if there wasn't anything going on for Aldene, there soon was. One time she got into the malaria pills and had to have her stomach pumped by a doctor who happened to be passing through Andudu. After placing Aldene on his lap, the bald-headed doctor with round glasses inserted a tube down her throat. Blah! Stomach fluids splattered into a bowl. There was only one pill counted.

"I told you so!" Aldene pouted.

Then there was catching her and an African boy killing a snake in the yard with a stick, not to mention the time Aldene's cat nipped at Eleanor's leg while she was giving Aldene a spanking for sassing. Aldene thanked her furry friend later for coming to her rescue.

But nothing compared to the horrible day when Butch's head fell off. Her screams filled the mission station, "Mommy! Mommy! Butch is dead!"

Eleanor rocked her daughter on her lap, "I am so sorry, Aldene. It must be the tropical weather; it rots out everything."

That year for Aldene's birthday, a huge green crate arrived with a swing set inside. Melvin made a playhouse out of the shipping crate. It had a child-sized door and window. Everyone was happy about it except the Africans.

"Bwana, you must get rid of Aldene's little house. The snakes like it."

* * * * *

That fall, Jay and Angeline Tucker and their three children came back from their furlough in America and moved into the Griffin house.

"We're not totally sure what our next five years will look like. There's something about a work in a city that pulls at our hearts," Jay told Melvin, while the generator-powered saw buzzed through another board of mahogany.

Most of the wood in Griffin's lumber shed came from the forest. After felling the trees, the men cut the timber into boards to store in the shed until it dried enough for woodworking. Melvin's latest project was a hutch for the dining-living room.

"Well, Jay, I know we've always been focused on being a bush-station ministry, but the cities have great needs for the Gospel too."

"We just want to make sure it's a pioneer work, not duplicating what someone else is doing, or infringing on another organization's territory."

Across the mission station, at the swing set near her house, Aldene was sizing up the Tucker's youngest son, Crickey. "So how long are you staying?"

Aldene was always asking the same question of anyone her age who stepped onto the station, calculating the days she would have a playmate.

"I leave for Rethy when school starts," he pumped his seven-year-old legs, swinging higher and higher.

"Isn't your real name Melvin?" Aldene interrogated.

"Yep."

"My dad's name is Melvin." Her eyebrows pinched together under her short-cropped bangs. "How come they call you Crickey?"

"'Cuz when I was first born my dad thought I looked like a skinny cricket." He kept swinging.

A woman's voice called from the door of a burnt-brick house, "J-o-h-n-y!"

Richard and Johny strolled out of the Jorgenson's house. They were both teenagers, coming of age.

"Let me know about hunting tomorrow," Richard was saying.

"Okay," Johny said, "Come on Crickey. It's best not to keep Mom waiting for dinner."

* * * * *

In the spring of 1960, Melvin and Eleanor went into Paulis to do a little shopping. Aldene packed a few dolls and books for the trip. Pastor Karada Simona, who taught at the Bible School, rode in the back seat of the Ford station wagon with Aldene. Along the way they stopped in at Betongwe for a visit with Winnie Currie and Lillian Hogan who offered to take Aldene, after she dropped a couple of not-so-subtle hints.

Then Melvin slid behind the steering wheel of the car with a smile. When the new red and white Ford first arrived in Congo, it created quite a stir.

One missionary, while looking it over commented, "It's a mite fancy for Africa. You're going to have trouble hitting the high places on the roads. That car rides too low."

Melvin was careful to not let that happen to his chosen vehicle. But one day, *bump,* and the bottom of the Ford needed to get fixed. Melvin promptly brought his lovely car to Watsa to have it repaired. However, he decided to keep this bit of information from a certain missionary.

After arriving in Paulis, Melvin navigated the car through the streets of the city looking for Jay and Angeline's house. Compared to the bush stations, Paulis seemed electrified with activity. Besides the airport, it boasted a train depot, several hotels, government offices, a hospital and even a club and swimming pool. The Tuckers moved to Paulis in February after meeting Mr. and Mrs. Colin Buckley, who worked with the Heart of Africa Mission. The Buckleys had assured the Tuckers there was plenty of room for another Protestant society in the up and coming city.

Driving past the ballpark, Melvin spotted the Belgian rental house located in the European sector. They only planned to stay a couple of nights, leaving in time for Sunday service in Andudu. However, torrential rains blew in Saturday morning, turning the roads into thick mud.

"We'll never make it through to Andudu."

Melvin conceded to the change in their schedule, to the delight of Jay and Angeline who were holding their first service of the new church plant in Paulis. On Sunday morning, the sun shone bright and hot as the Ford followed Tucker's Opel into the African sector. The church was temporarily meeting in a front yard under a palm tree. The owner of the yard, Bodaka and his wife, Mombi, had lived in Betongwe until moving to Paulis. When Mombi first saw the Tuckers at the Buckley's church, she cried with joy knowing the Lord had answered her prayers for a church closer to her home. Even though Bodaka was no longer an active Christian, he quickly agreed to host the new church and to deposit the weekly offerings.

Angeline asked Melvin to play her accordion. Soon strains of hymns filled the open air as men, women, and children sat on benches and stools under the shade of a large palm tree. Then Jay Tucker turned to Pastor Simona Karada and asked him to lead the rest of the service. It was a divine appointment for the pastor and flock to meet each other.

In May 1960, Pastor Simona was released from his duties in Andudu to become the national pastor of the new church in Paulis. Shortly after, several Bible students moved from Andudu to assist him in the new work.

* * * * *

The next month, on June 30, 1960, independence came to Congo.

A century before, when Leopold was crowned the king of Belgium in 1865, the hunt for a colony began. A shrewd man with a small-country complex, he lusted for more land, resources and power. War was not an option. However, Africa had possibilities.

In 1884, the chiefs in Congo began to sign their lands away and Henry Morton Stanley sailed to Europe with a sheaf of papers giving Leo claim to his slice of Africa. Under the guise of good will and philanthropy, Leo tightened the noose around its inhabitants. After America recognized Congo as a colony, other European countries followed suit. In 1885, Congo, neither a place he had never seen nor a soil he never set foot on, became Leo's personal country and pawn for twenty-three years.

After rumors about the atrocities of the brutal mistreatment of the Congolese in order to profit from the countries resources of ivory and rubber proved true, a public outcry forced Leo into a public relations corner— not to mention the pressure of his accruing debts. He bequeathed his African country to the Belgian people in 1908 for a tidy sum. For the next fifty years, Congo waited for independence until the rumblings of freedom took hold of men's hearts.

In January 1960, two political prisoners, Patrice Lumumba and Joseph Kasavubu, would rise to political prominence as they joined 200 Congolese attending negotiation talks with Belgian officials in Brussels. While in Brussels, Lumumba and Kasavubu worked for the same thing: Independence.

An overly-hasty decolonization plan led to elections in May. After Lumumba won, becoming the first Prime Minister of Congo, he asked his opponent Kasavubu to serve as President to help form the new government.

An official ceremony was scheduled for the transition of power to be held in Leopoldville the end of June. Belgian King Baudouin spoke, followed by President Kasavubu who gave a positive speech, ignoring the Belgian's patronizing remarks paying homage to King Leopold II. However, when Prime Minister Lumumba spoke, he snubbed Baudouin with searing remarks of the unjust oppression of the Congolese by the whites through the years. Anyone listening to the speech knew the underlying message. It was time for the whites to get out.

* * * * *

Most people in the Oriental Province, the territory in the northeast corner of Congo, were still wondering what independence was all about when a Belgian official knocked on Melvin and Eleanor's front door. Home on another one-month break from Rethy, Richard listened as Melvin spoke to the official.

Speaking in French the man ordered, "You must leave immediately and go to Paulis."

When Melvin inquired about the order, the government official explained, "The soldiers at Watsa have mutinied. It is not safe for Europeans, especially women."

Although the abrupt announcement stunned Melvin for a moment, he soon felt the need to protect his family. Without bothering to contact Jay Tucker via the HAM radio, he made plans to drive to Paulis. In a matter of minutes, the Jorgenson family packed up, leaving their house just as if leaving for a walk across the mission station. Two biracial girls working with them at Andudu squeezed into the station wagon with Aldene and Richard.

Before Melvin and Eleanor left, an African came up to them, "Bwana, when is this Independence going to be over?"

* * * * *

That night, when the station wagon arrived in Paulis, the city seemed calm. Not having any other place to stay, they were at the mercy of the Tucker family to accommodate them. To Melvin and Eleanor's surprise, Lillian and Winnie were already there, and Grace Lindholm came later, making fourteen people squeezed into the rental house. Everything was happening so fast no one was quite sure what to do about the situation.

In the morning, Jay found out that evacuation planes from other countries were coming into the city every couple of hours. Running lights were set up for evening flights. Belgian officials and coffee plantation owners were sending their wives and children out of the country.

The new flag of Congo gently waved as cars and people rushed past the ballpark to either fly out or buy provisions from the Greek storeowners before driving out to a safe border. The only difference in the new flag was the addition of six gold stars along the pole representing the six territories, including the Oriental Province. The blue background and solid gold star remained.

Back at the Tucker house, all the adults were discussing the situation. It seemed the anti-white feelings were mostly toward Europeans and not white missionaries. Jay and Angeline described the peaceful ceremony on Independence Day in the ballpark as the Belgian colony flag went down and the new Congo flag was raised. However, the official ceremony in Leopoldville had created ripples of unrest. Four days after the ceremony, the black military mutinied against the remaining white officers and chaos ensued in Leopoldville, Stanleyville, and the most southern diamond-mine city of Elisabethville.

Reports were coming in of riots and violence toward Europeans. Men were shot, women raped, and houses looted. Catholics priests and nuns were not exempt; nor were the educated Congolese, who were viewed as white sympathizers.

Missionaries and Belgians continued to pour into Paulis creating tension. Nerves were strained deciding whether to ride out the storm or escape it. The Congolese in Paulis were friendly and supportive, but reports of violence kept coming and evacuation planes kept landing and taking off.

After Melvin and Jay spoke with an American Air Force captain, they learned he would be back at the end of the week on Saturday. They would need to decide by then if they wanted their families to be on the plane bound for Uganda, an English colony.

As the week wore on, pressure kept building in the city as fearful Europeans continued to flood the streets and cram into hotels. For the sake of the children, it seemed better to get them to a quieter place than the swirling chaos of Paulis.

The decision was made to send the women and children to Uganda. Melvin and Jay would stay back and send word when Paulis had settled down again.

That Saturday morning, Melvin and Eleanor waited at the Paulis airport with Richard and Aldene. Jay and Angeline, and their children, were there along with Lillian and the orphanage girls. A small clump of suitcases and belongings waited to be carried on board.

The plane arrived. It was time for Eleanor to say good-bye to her husband, "Oh, I hate to have you stay."

Melvin slipped his arm around the small of her back looking into those hazel eyes that still had the key to his heart, "Would it help if we drove out and met you and the children in Uganda?"

Jay and Angeline stood nearby having a similar conversation. At that point, only women and children were allowed to evacuate by plane.

Eleanor heard the rain spatter on the old DC3 US airplane as she adjusted her seat belt. It was a cargo plane with bench seats attached to the sides of the plane, instead of the cramped rows of a commercial flight. At the thought of separation from Melvin, panic swept over her body, churning in the pit of her stomach. As the plane rolled to the runway, she wondered if she would ever see her husband again.

After arriving in Kampala, the capitol of Uganda situated on Lake Victoria, there were people waiting to assist the refugees fleeing Congo. An English couple, working in Uganda for business reasons, greeted Eleanor, Richard, and Aldene and took them to their home twenty minutes away in Kampala, on the north shore of Lake Victoria. Eleanor should have slept soundly that night, but all she could think of was Melvin. Prayer was her only option at that point. And it was a good one. Pouring out every fiber of confusion, fear, and uncertainty of the future that wove angst inside of her, she cast her burdens before the Lord. And she knew that he heard her cries.

A few days passed and word came to Eleanor that Melvin and Jay managed to drive out, with Winnie following them in her car. The reunited family stayed one night at the English couple's home and went to a Canadian Pentecostal Assembly mission station near Kisumu, Kenya for several weeks. It seemed as if they were living in a bizarre dream. No one had anticipated anarchy to roll across the country like a grassland fire. When things seemed to calm down, they drove into Congo. Hopefully, they could return to their normal routine of life.

* * * * *

After getting back to Andudu, fifteen-year-old Richard had a decision to make. Sitting on the front porch overlooking the coffee trees and rolling hills, Melvin and Eleanor discussed the options with their son. Aldene moved from the table to the edge of the porch watching for monkey tails in the trees Cicadas chirped their constant buzzing like an electric current in the background.

"It's up to you, Richard, you're old enough to make up your own mind."

"Well, with Rethy still closed, that leaves either Rift Valley Academy outside of Nairobi, or living with Uncle Lloyd in North Dakota."

Richard's dark eyebrows burrowed in thought. He ran a hand through his thick brown hair cropped short around the ears and nape. Then he shrugged his shoulders.

"I guess I'll go to the States. You'll be coming on furlough in a year anyway, no sense starting at Rift Valley for that short of a time."

* * * * *

At the airport in Uganda Eleanor tried to be brave for Richard. She looked him over, trying to memorize everything about him. He stood almost as tall as Melvin. His build was filling out with firm muscle tone. When they first came to Congo, he was a little boy riding his bicycle with his pet monkeys. Soon he would be driving cars. Richard didn't seem fazed by it all. In fact, his confidence told Eleanor he would make it, but her heart was still breaking. She avoided glancing at Melvin's eyes to keep the dam of tears from bursting until her son left.

"It's going to be okay, Mom," Richard embraced his mother, "It will go by quickly, you'll see."

Then he hugged Aldene giving his sister last minute instructions about certain pets he was bequeathing to her.

"You came here a boy—and now you're leaving a young man," Melvin choked down the lump in his throat, verbalizing Eleanor's thoughts.

Eleanor cried most of the way back to Andudu. To make matters worse, once they got back into Congo, they suddenly realized they were cut off from the rest of the world. All forms of communication crumbled. It was as if a "bamboo curtain" had fallen overnight! They couldn't get word to Richard, and he couldn't get word to them.

Chapter Twenty-Five

Second Furlough 1961-1962

M elvin checked the wires on the HAM radio and the battery.

"Hello, this is Melvin Jorgenson at Andudu," he said into the radio receiver.

Someone's voice crackled back, "This is Jay, come in, Melvin, over."

Melvin asked how things were in Paulis.

"Things are tense, but seem under control." Jay replied, "Rethy is making plans to reopen for students. What about Andudu?"

"We are all fine here," Melvin answered back, "But we're more cautious, even locking our doors at night. We still haven't heard from Richard and we can't get word to him."

Eleanor and Aldene listened from the breakfast table as Melvin finished, "Okay, over and out."

Then he said over his shoulder, "I'm going to contact the Friesens."

They had returned to Gombari, but Edith and Philip Cochrane left on furlough, while Grace Lindholm decided to continue her nursing career in Queens, New York. Since then, the Andudu station just didn't seem the same without her.

After the evacuation out of Paulis, everyone in the Oriental Province was on their own. There would be no more warnings from Belgian officials. Instead, missionaries and organizations kept in touch through the HAM radio. Mail wasn't coming in or going out. Radio broadcasts on the larger radio were tuned in for updates concerning the political tensions in Congo and the upcoming presidential election in America. In November, voters would decide between Republican nominee Richard Nixon and Democratic nominee John F. Kennedy.

* * * * *

Eleanor checked her watch; it was 9' o'clock in the morning, "Come on Aldene, we've got to go to school."

Mother and daughter walked over to the Griffin's house. Now that it was empty, it became a convenient place to have school away from distractions. The sounds of an airplane came over forested hills before it swooped over the mission station so close that Eleanor could make out the writing on the Soviet aircraft. Surveillance planes were a common occurrence these days. Prime Minister Lumumba's courting of communistic allies did not sit well with Americans in the midst of the Cold War.

Inside the Griffin house, Eleanor pulled out the Calvert Course lesson plans for the morning. Aldene worked on her lessons while occasionally sneaking a look out the window. Women were cooking under mafikas, while children were playing in the yard with metal bike rims propelled by sticks. Aldene was just getting the technique down herself.

A few hours later Eleanor announced, "Time for lunch, Aldene."

Aldene skipped back to the house, "Mbote, Bomo!"

"Mbote, Aldene," the cook smiled from his post on the back porch tending the stove and dinner, "How was school?"

"It's over," Aldene's tennis shoes bounded for the door, her ponytail bouncing with every step.

After lunch the battle began, "Why do I have to take a nap?"

"Aldene, we've been over this before. I don't want you to get run down, it makes you more susceptible to malaria and other things. You can either get some rest now or go to bed at six o'clock."

Aldene reluctantly went to her room to serve her sentence of solitude and boredom. After several minutes she heard her mother creak open the door. Playing possum, Aldene fought the desire to peek through the cracks of her eyelids and gave her best impression of sleeping.

After Aldene finished her "nap," she stopped by the Bible School on her bicycle. Melvin looked up from correcting papers and waved at her. Then she went on her way, riding around the station. Eleanor was at the dispensary checking over supplies when Aldene rode past going around the turn about a few times. She knew her parents were worried about Richard, but she was so used to having him gone at Rethy, she felt like he was there instead of living in America. With little to do at the station, she decided to ride down to the waterhole. She wasn't exactly supposed to go there without anyone, but one of her favorite things to do was cross the stream, balancing on wet rocks, pretending she was one of the butterflies dancing over her head. Content in her imaginary world, she rode back to the house to tell her dolls about her latest adventure.

That night after dinner, a Congolese came to the door asking for Eleanor.

"Yes, of course," Eleanor stepped out onto the back porch, "just a minute. I'll be right back."

When she came back into the house Eleanor informed her daughter, "Aldene, I have a job for you."

"What is it?"

"I need you to hold the flashlight for me while I dig out chiggers."

Chiggers, also called jiggers, would burrow themselves into the African's feet. Trying to remove the tiny flea-like insects caused the fleas to burrowed themselves in deeper. If a female laid eggs, then there was a cluster sack under the skin. Sometimes Africans would come and stand on the back porch made of cement, it was considerably cooler, and all of a sudden, the tiny chiggers would scatter out of their feet.

Aldene held the flashlight while Eleanor dabbed a little kerosene on the man's swollen foot to suffocate the chiggers. Then she struck a match and held it under a sewing needle. After the needle was sterilized, Eleanor started carefully probing for a sack of eggs. If she broke the sack, the chiggers would start digging in to get away. The trick was to poke holes around the cluster and then remove it.

"I am sorry, but this is going to hurt," Eleanor said in Bangala.

"It's okay, Madamo," the grateful Congolese said gripping the bench he was sitting on.

*　*　*　*　*

In early October, Melvin awoke one night from a dream. The mosquito netting floated over him as he tossed and turned.

"What's wrong?" Eleanor could wake at the drop of a dime on the floor.

"I think something has happened to my mother."

"Why?"

"I don't know if it was a dream, or what it was, but her face appeared in front of me."

"What else did you see?"

"That was it, but it was so strong, it woke me up."

Eleanor reached for her husband, "Maybe it was the malaria pills. Sometimes I get weird dreams from the medication."

* * * * *

A few months later Eleanor looked through the barrel marked "Christmas" in the back storage room of their house, and took out a few decorations. She didn't feel like celebrating Christmas, but for Aldene's sake she decided she'd better do something. As Christmas approached and no word came from Richard, Melvin and Eleanor were beside themselves with worry. They knew Richard had traveled more than most boys his age in America, but to not know for sure that he had made it to North Dakota was unbearable.

Meanwhile, the political landscape of Congo kept shifting. Neither Prime Minister Lumumba nor President Kasavubu were prepared for the eruptions of violence that followed Independence Day, including the diamond-rich southern province of Katanga declaring succession. After a plea for help, the United Nations (UN) sent in troops to help stabilize the Congolese military forces as Belgium began withdrawing its troops. Feeling snubbed by the United States, Lumumba also turned to the Soviets for help. By September, Lumumba and Kasavubu faced off again, attempting to remove each other from the newly formed government. Kasavubu backed

Joseph Desire Mobutu, after Mobutu led the charge to crush the rebellion in Katanga.

Previously serving in the Belgian-controlled Force Publique, Mobutu was never able to break through the white barrier to becoming an officer. However, after independence, he swiftly became the officer who had the most controlling power over the renamed Armee Nationale Congolaise or ANC. Although the Congolese legislature remained loyal to Lumumba, the UN stood with Kasavubu as he called for the arrest of Lumumba. The ANC forces began splintering into factions of government soldiers and rebel soldiers. No one knew who was actually in charge, or which side to be on, including the soldiers. The fast track to decolonization became a house of cards.

* * * * *

In the midst of uncertain times, Melvin kept himself occupied working on lesson plans, Sunday sermons and visiting local village pastors. He also labored on improvements on their house, checking over the plumbing for the indoor bathroom and reworking the cistern for the mission station. One day he realized all the activity he could find in a day couldn't keep at bay his concerns of Richard and the tensions in Congo. Despondent in heart, Melvin stole away to a secluded place in the jamba.

Alone in the trees of the forest he looked up to the sliver of blue sky peering through the thick canopy of foliage, "Lord you placed me here, and you gave me a definite call to be a missionary to Congo, and now this has come upon me and I'm asking you to take care of it for me."

In the middle of January, political tensions reached a boiling point again. Melvin spent a lot of his time listening to the larger radio and HAM radio for updates. One night after Aldene was in bed, word started coming in from the European and American consuls, strongly advising evacuation from the Oriental Province. The next morning a radio broadcast came from Rethy, stating that it may be closing due to the request their organization received that all Protestant missionaries evacuate immediately. Eleanor started packing items in suitcases and barrels while Melvin frantically worked on materials for the Bible School. Africans around Andudu complained there was too much fighting and they didn't know what it was all about.

After contacting the other mission stations via HAM radio, Melvin and Eleanor told Aldene they would be leaving first thing in the morning. "Where are we going?"

"To Uganda."

That night Melvin and Eleanor fervently prayed together for guidance and protection. The Tuckers and other parents were driving to Rethy to collect their children and leave the country together in a caravan.

Just as the first rays of dawn streamed over the Ituri Rain forest, Melvin, Eleanor, and Aldene left Andudu for the border towns of Aru, Congo and Arua, Uganda. No one else drove with them. A fairly simple drive in the past became bogged down with checkpoints in every town along the way. Soldiers questioned where they were going and why. A few looked through the trunk of the car asking questions about the suitcases.

At one barricade they got through by giving out Gospel literature, tracts, and booklets printed in the African tongue. Even during this time of trouble, a portion of scripture would often turn the thoughts of a soldier from his evil intent. At the next barricade, a soldier was reluctant to let them through, but finally gave his permission. Then on further thought, he requested a gift in money. As Melvin took the forty cents from his pocket, he kept the conversation going by asking the soldier what he was going to do with the money.

"I'm going to buy some beer and have a good time," the soldier replied.

Melvin hesitated for moment and then told the soldier, "I'm sorry, but I cannot give you money for that purpose."

Then Melvin slowly backed up to the car. He got into the car. The barrier had already been removed. No command was given to halt as Melvin started the car and started to drive down the road. In the rearview mirror, he could see the soldier standing in the dusty road gazing after them.

Finally, in the late afternoon they reached Aru. At the border, there were two gates, one to enter Congo and one to exit. Melvin found a place to park the red and white Ford and went into the customs office, leaving Eleanor and Aldene in the car.

While Eleanor waited, she felt a tension creep into her. Everything around her was different from the previous times of crossing the border. Something was wrong. People were screaming. Yelling, drunken soldiers waved guns taunting travelers. Eleanor flinched as a white woman was dragged to a hut. . .rumors of white women being raped by Congolese soldiers had been confirmed by valid reports of eyewitnesses.

A soldier strode over to Eleanor, "Get out of the car and come with me!"

"No," replied Eleanor firmly, "I can't leave my daughter."

Another soldier, taller with a robust build, came over and said, "No, she doesn't have to get out of the car, leave her alone."

The other soldier reluctantly backed away. Eleanor softly thanked the Lord while glancing at Aldene in the back seat.

"Get out of the car and come with me!" He nodded toward the hut the soldiers were using to defile any women they chose to drag in there.

Eleanor froze at the soldier's abrupt return to her car window. He leaned down toward her face. His breath stunk and his body odor hung in the air.

Once again, the larger soldier came over and said, "I told you she doesn't have to get out of the car. Now leave her alone!"

As soon as Melvin got back to the car the larger soldier opened the gate for people coming into Congo, "Just go out this gate, quickly, now."

Melvin drove several miles into "no man's land" situated between the two countries and stopped the car. He now knew more of the details of why the soldier had sent them through the wrong gate. The family of three got out of the car and thanked the Lord for their deliverance. Once they passed through customs in Arua, Uganda, Eleanor reached for her husband. She held his strong hand and calmed herself for Aldene's sake.

"You know, Melvin, that one large soldier didn't seem to fit in with the other soldiers," she said, reflecting on the unusual size of the soldier compared to the other soldiers from the areas that were much smaller in stature.

"Do you suppose he was an angel?"

"Either way, I thank God he was there for our protection and safe crossing into Uganda."

* * * * *

They stayed in Arua one night at a guesthouse for missionaries and then left the next day for Entebbe on January 23, 1961. Once in Uganda, they found out the reason for

the unrest and increased violence. On the run from his enemies, Lumumba had been captured, and later assassinated in
Elisabethville.

When they arrived in Entebbe, they went straight to
the tower at the airport to place a call to Bismarck, North
Dakota. After the operator made the connection, they could
hear the phone ring. Not wanting to miss a thing, Aldene
stood as close to her parents as possible.

"Hello?"

"Hello, Richard, it's Mom and Dad." Melvin choked out
the words, the best he could.

"Mom? Dad? I can't believe it's really you! Are you okay?"

"Yes, we are fine, but we had to evacuate again to Uganda,"
Melvin said, then he held the phone out so could Aldene
could join in as the three of them said, "Happy sixteenth
birthday!"

"Thank you, now it is a happy birthday," Richard said.
"You called just at the right time. Uncle Lloyd and I were
just stepping out the door for Grandma Munyon's funeral
in Lemmon."

Eleanor felt a mixture of emotions digesting all the
information and the relief at hearing her son's voice. They
also learned that Melvin's mother passed away on October
1, 1960. After placing the phone call, Melvin, Eleanor and
Aldene stayed at a missionary guest resthome in Nairobi,
Kenya. Eleanor continued homeschooling Aldene while
Melvin wrote letters and monitored the situation in Congo.
After two months passed of waiting in limbo, Melvin and
Eleanor made plans to leave on furlough. From Nairobi,
they flew directly to London and took the ocean liner Queen
Mary to New York City.

* * * * *

Waiting to greet them in New York City was Eleanor's mother. Hazel Groat wrapped her arms around the three travelers, "Thank the Lord you are all safe!"

The aging woman sparkled with joy, "Everyone in Virginia is anxious to see you, including your father, but I just couldn't wait!"

It amazed Eleanor how comforting it was to see her mother. For a moment, she felt like a girl again in Thunder Hawk, South Dakota, instead of a forty-two year old woman with a family of her own.

Once they found their luggage, Melvin picked up the 1960 Nash metallic-brown four-door sedan he had ordered. They drove south to Washington D.C., and then to Alexandria, Virginia, across the Potomac River to stay with Eleanor's sister, Lois, and her husband, Alan Durick. After a joyful reunion and a memorable visit to Mount Vernon, it was time to be reunited with Richard. Aldene rode in the backseat between her Grandma and Grandpa Groat, listening to all their stories and telling some of her own stories about Africa. Melvin thoroughly enjoyed driving on the smooth black-tarred roads that were organized and maintained. He couldn't believe the distance they could cover in one day!

Before arriving in Minneapolis, they stopped at a fruit stand and at Melvin's request, bought a watermelon to have with their picnic lunch. Away from hectic metropolises, they could enjoy the peaceful spring air with the hope of tree blossoms, tulips and daffodils bursting from their winter rest. Finally, Melvin couldn't resist the green grass any longer and took off his socks and shoes.

Eating a wedge of watermelon he walked over the tender soft grass and spit black seeds as far as could, "I feel like we are on another planet!"

"Where are all the animals?" Aldene wondered.

"Instead of crossing the road here and there, they are on farms in pens and pastures," Eleanor explained while her parents packed up the picnic supplies.

* * * * *

Meanwhile, on Easter vacation from school, Richard left Bismarck on a Greyhound bus bound for Minneapolis. When he first got back to the States, Richard had started ninth grade in Kulm, North Dakota. Although he often thought about his parents, the adjustment to American culture and everyday life blocked out his gnawing feeling of worry, and the loneliness of separation. For one thing, he didn't even know how to dress properly to fend off the harsh northern winters! After getting his ears severely frostbit, Uncle Lloyd and the other relatives patiently worked with him, helping him out as if he were an immigrant. Just because Richard could speak the language, it didn't mean he knew how to live in America. It was also his first Christmas without his parents. His only link to Congo was his pet parrot, Koko, who lived with Grandma Groat. After Christmas, he was uprooted and started a new school in Bismarck. At first, his Uncle Lloyd didn't have a house, so Richard lived with the Samuelson family for a while, and then, Oscar Reid and family.

* * * **

When the bus rolled into the station, his parents and Aldene were waiting for him, and he was not ashamed of his tears. After embracing everyone, he took a small velvet pouch out of his pants pocket, "It's a little early, but here, Happy Mother's Day."

"Why—thank you, Richard," Eleanor ran her fingers over the little heart pin with stones on it that read *Mother*. "It's beautiful; it will always remind me of this day."

Later that week, the reunited family of four were visiting Eleanor's sister, Lorraine, and her husband, John Dunser, at their recently purchased lakefront home in Mound, Minnesota.

"Have you found a place to live yet?" Lorraine asked as the afternoon sun drifted into their living room with furniture arranged around a brick fireplace.

"Well, we're looking for a place to live," Eleanor said, "but our budget doesn't fit in with what we've found to rent."

"The rent has gone through the roof in the last five years," Melvin joked.

John threw in a suggestion, "Why don't you buy a place?"

"Well, we hadn't thought about that because we didn't have any money," Melvin said.

"Yes, I'm afraid Melvin's right," Eleanor echoed her husband, "we don't have any money. We don't have anything."

"Well, let me look into it and see what I can find," offered John.

After Easter, John lined up a couple of properties in Minneapolis for them to consider. One was a three-bedroom rambler on the corner of 106th and Russell Avenue South in Bloomington. The current owner had an assumable GI loan at a four and a half percent interest rate. The asking price was $16,000, with $1,600 for a down payment. Melvin and Eleanor knew they didn't have the money, but they also knew they could pray about it and see what the Lord would provide for a place to live. Then they left for the Assemblies of God Bible Camp in North Dakota with Aldene and her homeschool books. There was a prayer room in the main lodge and they prayed about the house and their finances.

Then they went to the AG camp on Lake Geneva in Alexandria, Minnesota.

One day at the Lake Geneva camp, they came out of the prayer room and standing there waiting for them was Eva Larson.

"Hello, Eva," Melvin and Eleanor said together.

Eva had been the Sunday School Superintendent when they were in Detroit Lakes. Now she was a teacher at the AG Bible College in Springfield, Missouri.

Eva came right to the point, "God's been speaking to me and told me that you have a need."

"Well, we do, but it's a big need," Melvin said.

"I know it's big. What do you need?"

Melvin and Eleanor explained to Eva about the house in Bloomington and the amount of the down payment.

"I'll loan you the sixteen hundred. And you can pay it back as you can."

* * * * *

That summer Melvin, Eleanor, Richard, and Aldene lived together in their own house on Russell Avenue South. It was a typical-looking rambler like the other houses on the block with a sidewalk out front. White shutters accented the blue shake siding under a black-shingled roof. They had running water, electricity, and no mosquito nets over their beds. There was even a small yard with green grass for Melvin and Richard to take turns mowing.

On August 22, 1961, Aldene turned seven and Eleanor enrolled her in second grade at the local public school. A few days after school started, Aldene walked by herself to the bus stop and came home by herself. It was the first time her mother wasn't her teacher. Her playmates on the playground were all white and nobody spoke Bangala. The girls were afraid of bugs and snakes, but they did play with dolls.

And Grandpa and Grandma Groat moved to Minneapolis making visits with them convenient.

One day when she got home from school "someone" was sitting on the couch of the living room. Melvin and Eleanor exchanged smiles as Aldene walked over to the couch.

"We took him to the doll hospital," explained Eleanor, "and they made Butch a new body."

"He looks smaller," Aldene cautiously inspected the best friend she ever had in Congo.

"Well, Aldene," her father suggested, "I think it's because you're bigger now."

* * * * *

During their furlough, Melvin and Eleanor traveled to many churches, showing movies and telling people about the work of the Gospel in Congo. A church nearby, in Shakopee, bought them an electric washer. All they needed was a small generator and then no more washing clothes on a scrub board trying to rinse the soap out by hand! One church west of Jackson, in Worthington, had adopted Richard as their missionary child for years, even through high school, praying for him and sending gifts to Congo.

At the Summit Assembly in St. Paul, a woman married to a chiropractor came up to Eleanor, who greeted her: "Oh, Mrs. Satterberg, how nice to see you again!"

Eleanor thanked the kind woman who served tirelessly with the women's mission auxiliary, as so many women did in the churches they visited.

"Well, you are most welcome, Mrs. Jorgenson," Mrs. Satterberg politely spoke, "I just have to tell you that one night this winter, in the middle of the night, the Lord woke me up with such a burden to pray for you."

"Oh, really? When was that?"

"It was the middle of January this year," she replied.

They discussed the time and even the day of the week. Instantly, the day at the border crossing flashed into Eleanor's mind, "Thank you for obeying the Lord and praying for me; I was in a very dangerous situation and the Lord delivered me from the hands of my enemies."

* * * * *

The months passed as the Jorgenson family lived in their miracle house for their one year on furlough, and then it was time to go back to Congo. Their funds were raised for the next five years, and people were interested in renting their house. The turbulence following Congo's independence seemed stabilized and many missionaries from the AG Gombari station group were in Congo or heading back.

However, there was one caveat for Melvin and Eleanor.

* * * * *

They sat on their bed in their home discussing the situation," I don't know what we should do," Eleanor confided in her husband, "Richard only has one year left of high school and then he could be off to college."

"Well, the mission board only allows so many months for furlough," Melvin said, "Maybe we should stay home and take the consequences."

Richard knocked on their door. After stepping into the doorway he confessed, "I'm sorry, but I overheard the last part of your discussion."

He stood as tall as Melvin now, drove a car, and had the whisper of a mustache that he faithfully shaved. Richard crossed his arms and leaned against the doorframe, "I don't want you to stay home because of me. I can do my last year of high school via correspondence through the University of Minnesota and go back with you."

Chapter Twenty-Six

Letters from 1963

❧

Dear Grandma and Grandpa, etc.   *Sept, 16*
Hotel Metropole, Bruxelles

*I guess it's about time I sit down and write you a letter! I
can see my first line is already slanting. I find it impossible to
keep my lines straight.*

*We had a most enjoyable trip to Europe. When we left
Mpls. we were served dinner. Our stewardess wasn't very pretty,
but the food was good. They had no more than collected our
plates then we started to descend. Our flying time to N.Y. was
2 1/2 hours.*

*Auntie Grace met us in N.Y. (Mrs. Grace Lindholm, her
husband you remember was killed by a buffalo). We were taken
by car to the Pan Am terminal. We had supper there; it was
good. I had lobster. We had a good visit with Mrs. Lindholm.
Her son, Steve is in India now. (U.S.A.F.)*

*Our plane was a 1/2 hour late in getting started because of
provisioning of the air craft. (really they were working on no.
3 engine.) We left N.Y. at 9:30 PM. They served us supper
at about ten o'clock. We had stuffed chicken, it was really
good. There were only about twenty people in the plane so the*

stewardess (we had two, but one was <u>so</u> cute you couldn't believe it!) took the armrest out of the center two seats and it made into a very nice bed. We all had our own beds. We landed in Ireland at about eight o'clock their time. Coming into Ireland was really beautiful. I took some pictures from the airplane, I hope they turn out.

We landed in Belgium at ten o'clock. The crew was very nice and made you feel very welcome, of course they're paid for it. Flying time from N.Y. was about 6:15 min. We flew on the Jet Clipper Caroline.

We stayed at the Metropole hotel the first night. Aldene and I had a very nice room with a balcony. You could look right out into a narrow street and watch all the people. They walk right in the street, it's fun to watch the cars try and get through.

Mom, Dad, and Aldene are staying at a home now. They pay by the week for their room and meals. I'm staying at the Gunter's. Bennie, their son, is twenty and is studying piano at the college. He's a terrific player, really good. He has his own grand piano in his room. It's out of tune though.

Well, I think I must close, it's getting late. I already miss the lot of you. Lord bless you (I'm having a ball by the way).

Love, Richard W. Jorgenson

Dear Ones at home,   *Sept 17, 1963*   *Brussels, Belgium*

We have been here a week today. It has gone by quickly as there have been so many things to do and take care of. We have had beautiful weather for which we are thankful, as Belgium can be cold because it is so damp. Just hope the weather stays this way.

Our visas were applied for today. We are hoping Mel gets in on being a teacher in the Bible School for teachers do not have to pay for their visas. Otherwise, we must pay thirty-three dollars for each visa! Americans have to pay more. Also, we are going to have to wait for our car. It so happens that the '63's are all sold out and they are waiting for the '64's to come out. Mel has made a number of calls to Paris and is awaiting a call from them tomorrow concerning the car. It may be that we will have to wait until Oct. 15 for the car. We surely hope not. But there is nothing more we can do.

Melvin, Aldene, and I are staying in an old folks home. Mr. Gunter got us the place here. We have a room and eat our meals here. The meals are excellent. The lady who cooks has won blue ribbons in France for her cooking. We do not eat with the old folks, but with the Spinsters in their dining room. We are happy for this place as the hotels are so very expensive. This place is very reasonable, $5.60 a day for the three of us (room and board). Richard is staying with the Gunters. Their son, Bennie, Richard used to play with him when we were here before. Richard is working on his French. He is getting to hear plenty of it. Bennie is studying music at the university and practices three hours a day in the mornings on a grand piano in his room. Richard practices on a piano downstairs.

Mel has spoken twice since being here. When things get settled here with our visa, car, etc. we want to go over to Holland for a couple of days. Where we are staying they speak only

French, so we speak only French when we are here. Aldene is beginning to say some words. There is a twelve-year-old girl at the Gunter's she enjoys playing with. They seem to manage to understand each other somehow.

I keep thinking of all those things I left piled in your living room. I hope Lorraine had time to help you get them packed and mailed off. I wonder if you could possibly send Aldene's writing paper right away to Congo. It is the one with the two lines. I can't get the paper here—I thought I could. Send it to Paulis, B.P. 99, Province de l'Uele, Republic of Congo, Africa. That is Lillian's address and she will be sure to get it should it happen to get there before us, which I doubt, but anyway we will be sure of getting it.

We did not leave you money for sending the packages. If you have not yet cashed the check we left with you, Mother, write it out so it will take care of the packages and I still owe Dad $5.00, so add that on too. Just be sure you let us know the amount so we can keep our books straight.

Richard is wondering if you have gotten any more calls about the bird, Kukulu. He said he started you a letter, but doubt he got it finished. Mel has also been wondering about the car. Do hope it can be sold for a halfway decent price. We must take the money from the car and apply on the loan we made for our house. Have you met our renters yet?

Must get to bed. Mel has to leave here at eight o'clock for the Gunter's as he is expecting a call from Paris around 9:30. He had given them the Gunter's number before and didn't want to confuse them by giving them another number. It takes about 45 minutes to get there, as he must take a tram and then a bus. He also has to be at the Congo Protestante Council at 10:30. I will stay here and have school with Aldene in the morning. It is quiet here. Will be writing again soon. Am beginning to look for a letter from home!

Bye for now and God bless you each one. Much love to you all,

> *Eleanor, Melvin, Richard & Aldene*

Mr. and Mrs. E.J.Groat Minneapolis, MN U.S.A.

Dear Dad,   *Sept. 24, 1963*   *Brussels, Belgium*

I wonder if you could do me another favor. I left our prayer folders (the ones with our picture on it and a song on the inside) in the garage. They are in a small cardboard box. Could you send them to Leona and Rowland in Fergus Falls for me? I will be happy if you can do this for me.

Everything has gone along very well for us here; everything, that is, except the car. We received a booking on a boat from Trieste, Italy for the 22nd of October. The agent says we are very lucky to get a place at this time of the year (all traffic is going south) on a boat at such short notice. We also got our visa—the same day we applied for it; something unheard of.

But we have had some difficulty getting a car without paying the government tax. But we have finally arranged for it and will pick up the STL car (Speed the Light) in Paris on the 5th of October. We had to take a 404 French Peugeot Familial instead of a regular station wagon as none else were available. The Familial has the three seats in it seating 7/8 people. It is a luxury car with very nice soft seats; better than we had intended. I am having some extras put on it, including an extra wheel and tire, and extra set of shock absorbers, luggage rack, etc. I will also have a trailer hitch put on.

God bless you all. Wish we could see you. Love,

Melvin, Eleanor, Richard, Aldene Anne.

Dear Ones at home,   *Oct. 8, 1963*   *Brussels, Belgium*

It is 3:15 and I just came upstairs from the dining room. I sat and talked for two hours with the two Spinsters here. They speak only French so I have been getting a good work out. Mel left at 8:30 this am to take the car to the garage and hasn't come back yet. His dinner is being kept warm on the stove. He just called and said he may soon be coming. What a time in a foreign country to get things done. One place tells you one thing and another place another. Let's see where shall I start?

We left for Paris on Friday. On Sat. am we went for the car. It was all ready except for some papers, so it was almost noon before we left there. The traffic in Paris is something to see and never to be forgotten! There is no rhyme or reason to anything. Cars come at you from all directions. It's more or less a game of dodging I think. Sat. afternoon we took the children to the Eifel Tower. Rich and Aldene went clear to the top. They really enjoyed it. One gets a beautiful view of the city and the Seine River.

Today Mel took the car to the garage here to have a trailer hitch put on. He is taking care of some papers that he must have for the car. They told us in Paris we did not need these papers. Here—where we got our boat bookings they told us we must have papers—signed by two people here in Belgium that own their homes—that the car is ours, and we must have this to get the car on the boat! Mel has secured one man and now must find another. Besides that, he must go to the Congo Embassy to get a permit it to take it into Congo! You chase from here to there. Then the offices have different hours. We had planned to go to Holland today—everything is so much cheaper there to buy, but we may still be kept here tomorrow by the looks of things.

Rich is anxious to get to a warmer climate, but that won't be until Italy. It is cold and damp here. How I wish I would have brought my red car coat. I had planned to all of the time and then changed my mind the last minute. Oh, I haven't suffered. I have been living in my beige knit dress. It is warm. That under my raincoat isn't bad. Now we have the car so we won't be standing, waiting for street cars. Rich called this afternoon and said he was going to a museum of music. They show the original music of Bach etc. He has so enjoyed the different museums. Aldene has been out this afternoon with one of the old ladies picking up walnuts from the ground. She brought up a big sack full to the room. We have a little heater in the room and she puts the nuts on the heater so they will dry out. I have school with her every morning.

Have been washing out clothes everyday so they won't pile up. Then, too, it is hard to get them dried as it seems to rain every day. The ones I put out today pretty well dried, as there was a wind.

Europe has changed since we lived here in 1950-51, as far as living costs are concerned. Everything is so high. Paris is terrible. On Sunday, I bought some bread, cheese, ham and some pastry cakes and we had our lunch in the car. We will be doing that all along the way as we cannot afford to eat out three meals a day. I think I will buy a little one burner stove so I can heat water for coffee or tea. Then we plan to buy a couple of sleeping bags, so Mel and Rich can sleep in the car. It would be more pleasant traveling if one could afford to stay in hotels and eat out along the way.

Eleanor, Melvin, Richard, and Aldene

Dear Grandpa and Grandma,   Nov. 3, 1963
                  Lloyd Triestino Europa Ship

Well, I guess it really is time I make myself write a letter. It's easier to send a card, but I think a letter is nicer, especially when I haven't written for such a long time.

We have had the most exciting trip. Mother hasn't been seasick at all. The girls wear the most daring bikinis! Some of them really cute. The ships activities are very well planned. The temp. is 87 and humidity 78% which makes it quite uncomfortable. We have been following the coastline now for two days. It's all sand.

On the 31st we had to stop over at Aden (City in Yemen). It's a free port, so things are really quite cheap. You can figure on just about 1/2 the price. The trouble is you have to barter for everything. You never give what they ask for. We bought a very nice shortwave radio. Dad was really happy too, he got a telephoto lens for his 35mm camera for only $11! In the states it's about $250 I think.

I suppose Mother wrote to you about me taking a trip to Cairo! I really enjoyed myself. Our guide could speak 7 languages. We left the ship at 6 a.m. and drove by bus from Port Said to Cairo while our ship continued down the Suez Canal at 4 knots per hour. The people in the country are really poor. At Cairo we visited their museum of old arts. It was really interesting. I saw a mummy that still had fleshy look to the skin. Also, a mummy coffin made of pure gold. We also visited the Alabaster Mosque. It's breathtaking. If you can, picture a building made of pure alabaster. Also visited the pyramids, rode a camel to get there. They also took us to the famous Cairo perfume makers. They sell pure liquid from flowers, no alcohol or oils are added. I got some for Mom, it's really quite expensive, but you can't get it any place else. I got her Adder *of Roses & Scent of the Desert. It's composed of 14 different flowers. I also got a footstool, pure gazelle leather. It's all white, really nice. I paid $5 for it! I've run out of space and also we're being called for dinner. So good bye for now.*

Lord bless you and keep you, Rich

Dear Mother and Dad,   Nov. 14, 1963   Kampala, Uganda

We are now in Kampala. Arrived here yesterday late afternoon. We stayed longer in Kisumu waiting for your letter and got it yesterday a.m. We read it in the car as we were driving. I was so happy to get it.

Just now, I am sitting in a bank writing this. It is pouring rain. Our car is in the garage and will be until four o'clock this afternoon. Some default from the factory with the oil pan. Glad we caught it before getting into Congo. I have spent the whole morning in a wholesale house. Bought up groceries in case lots and will have it sent to Arua, Uganda to an AIM mission station. Mel will have to make a trip to pick it up.

Nov. 15th—Didn't get this finished yesterday—such a busy day and was so tired last night. Now we are on our way out of Kampala and I suddenly remembered I hadn't finished and mailed your letter. Am writing as we're driving along so hope you can read it.

Had forgotten to get stuff to fumigate our house. A native has been staying in it to keep away thieves. We are going to the border a different way as the customs man is very mean where we had planned to go in. We plan to stay overnight tonight at Rethy. We hear roads in Congo are quite bad. So don't know what kind of time we'll make going to Andudu. We'll stay a day or two at Andudu and then go into Paulis. Will write you from there and let you know how we find things.

Oh yes, we have an addition to the family. Got a dog in Nairobi. It's a pup, six weeks old. The father is Great Dane—a huge dog and the mother is Doberman Pincher. The kids are hoping he will be as big as his father. The owners of the pups gave the cutest one to Aldene.

So sorry you are not well—but since you both have to watch your diets and now that you are alone—you can just plan meals that will suit you—don't keep other things in the house that will tempt you. Do take care of yourselves now.

Much love to you both, Eleanor, Mel, Rich & Aldene

Dear Grandpa & Grandma, Nov 1963 Congo

I hope this reaches you before too long! We are now in Paulis. Had a most wonderful trip all the way. The roads are really quite bad, we average about twenty to thirty MPH most of the time. We are staying in the Tucker's house. Mom says that Angeline left her house intact so it can be used. It is a huge house. Four bedrooms. Typical Belgian style. I found my piano in pretty good shape. It got scratched up a bit. I think it's from the Tucker kids' feet.

When we arrived in Mombasa we stayed overnight at a beach hotel, really nice. Aldene and I had a nice long swim in the Indian Ocean. It was really warm. We spent 2 days in Nairobi and also stopped in at Rift V.alley Academy; saw a lot of old friends. We then went to Kisumu, left for Kampala and spent one whole day shopping for food supplies. We can't get very much in Congo. Only a few canned goods sometimes. We also stayed over the weekend at Rethy. It took two days to go from Rethy to Andudu. It made me sick to see our beautiful station. It was mostly all grown into weeds. I guess it can be fixed. I am having a time getting some parrots. I guess there can't be much of a market for them now because there are so few white people.

We were all sick when we heard of Pres. Kennedy's death. I was driving from Tucker's house, and turned the radio on, and just happened to turn to Voice of America. When I reached Aunt Lillian's and Gail's I knocked on the door and told them he was shot, but not dead yet. They rushed to the radio and left me outside. Really a tragic thing and shameful! We took black cloth and made bows and I got some pictures out of magazines and made a display in the window of the bookstore. Even the Africans are grieving. All stores here are closed until Tues. morning. If you could, could you please send me those three LP records. Gram, kiss Kukulu for me if you dare to. Hope you are both feeling well, think of you so much.

God bless you, Love Rich

Dear Dad and Mother,   *Dec. 18, 1963*   *Andudu, Congo*

It is hard to imagine that it is almost Christmas time. In some ways, it is just as easy not to think about it. Anyway, I wonder what you all will be doing. I don't suppose Lois and Alan will make it to Mpls. this year.

We got back to Andudu last Friday night. Couldn't do much on Sat. as there was no one around to help us. We started in on the house Monday. I have never seen so much filth in all my life—including the dead cockroaches and rats. The rats really had themselves a time in my kitchen cupboard. I had several bottles of Germ-trol left over and I've made good use of one bottle. We now have the three bedrooms painted and scrubbed, windows washed etc. also the hallway and kitchen. Some of the barrels we packed in such a hurry we didn't write everything down—now to find things is quite something. For instance the casters and clamps for the bedsteads! I didn't want to start unpacking barrels until the house was clean but I did some today—hunting for the bed clamps—but didn't find

317

them. I'm so glad we hung the mattresses up in the attic. We kept the original cartons and paper. They really kept nice and clean. Only thing we found was silver fish on one of the box springs. We haven't opened our wool rug yet but I'm keeping my fingers crossed.

One thing we found out today is that our deep freeze is ruined. I think the rats chewed on it underneath somehow and let the fluid out—anyway the bottom of the freezer has several holes eaten through. One quite large one. It made us all just sick as were so planning on the freezer. Meat is so very difficult to get. Rich, Phil Cochrane, and Mel were planning a hunting trip and we thought we could fill the freezer! That freezer was such a big help to us last term. Then to top it off a piece from our fridge. is missing. There are two others fridges on the station, but we can't get either one of them to work. I had bought some lovely bacon in Kampala and it has all spoiled. Bacon is unheard of here. I also bought up quite a bit of butter. So far the butter hasn't spoiled.

I washed clothes yesterday with the washing machine and it still works ok. Mel spent a day working on the motor—getting it cleaned up etc. It started right off. We have lights tonight for the first time here in the house. Quite a change from kerosene lamps.

The boy who cleaned the house for me last term came to see us and said he would help us all get settled. He would like to work for us again, He has been cleaning dresser drawers, washing windows, etc. for me. Then the two men who are teaching in the Bible School have been painting. I told them I wanted to have it all done before Christmas and they are pitching right in. They are so happy to have us here as they were afraid we would go to Paulis.

The Cochranes and the girls (Lillian and Gail) are coming the 24th. Then a Dr. and his family are coming to stay overnight the 26th, so we will have two full houses. I asked Mario if he would bring me a turkey and some vegetables this week. He said he was not going past Andudu, but would leave them off at Paulis with the girls. I only hope he doesn't forget—which he often does. Haven't heard anything about our freight yet. Wish it were here as there are a lot of things in the food barrel that I would like to have. We could make use of some clothes too! We are still waiting and hoping for our packages. Guess I told you we got some of our books.

The guns are all ok and the scope on the big gun is as good as ever. Mel got his permits when in Paulis—so he can hunt now. Richard has gotten excited because the Africans come saying the elephants are eating up their gardens—and want someone to shoot them—but there won't be any elephant hunting around here!

Did I tell you we located our trunk that we had sent home? It is in Mungbere in the warehouse there. Mel will have to go as soon as he can get it. It's the one that had my sewing machine in it. Wonder what state will find the thing in.

Mel wanted me to tell you that we sent rolls of film from Kisumu to you. Maybe you have them by now. They must be developed and Mel will see to it that you get paid for it. There is no place here to get it developed. All of our projectors are at your place, so you will be able to see them.

Have been trying to get some of the forest cut away. This has always been such a pretty station, but it's going to take a lot of work to get it looking decent again. It isn't easy to get workers either. Not many people are anxious for work around here.

Didn't hear from you this week, but I imagine you sent it to Paulis. The girls will bring it when they come. I am hoping this letter goes out tomorrow. It is supposed to. We haven't gotten into the full swing of things yet.

319

We do hope you are both well and that you will have a happy Christmas. Our thoughts will be with you and I know your thoughts will be with us. We miss you so very much. At times, it doesn't seem possible that we can be so far away. Our prayer is that the Lord will watch over us while we are absent one from the other.

Much love to you both, Eleanor, Mel, Rich & Aldene

Chapter Twenty-Seven

Before the Storm

❦

Eleanor sat at the kitchen table writing another weekly letter to her parents, while Rich listened to the Broadway production of West Side Story on the radio in his room. Aldene's giggles came through her bedroom door. Charleston, the Great Dane-Doberman mix they acquired in Uganda, lay outside her door whining for attention. A missionary had given Aldene a kitten for Christmas and the fluffy white ball was the new star of the family.

"I hope nothing has happened to my records," Richard said loud enough for Eleanor to hear.

Relaxing on his bed Richard crossed his ankles and folded his hands under his head after spending the day working on algebra and French.

She turned toward his bedroom, "I heard the postman thought we were still in Paulis, so he sent our mail there from Mungbere. The girls will keep a look out for your package. I wish we would hear about our barrels. The only one of us with enough clothes is Aldene, not to mention the groceries we packed. I was lucky to get eggs and get some baking done today."

Eleanor turned back to her letter telling her folks about spending New Year's Day with Philip and Edith Cochrane in Biodi. The family of five was stopping for the night on their way to Rethy for a month's rest. Edith seemed so worn out lately with three live-wires, "real clippers" Eleanor wrote. Sadly, their youngest, Andrew succumbed to cerebral malaria before his first birthday and they buried his little body in the red earth of Congo. At Andrew's birth, Edith had taken the doctor's advice to be sterilized because of her health. And yet, against all odds, after the medical procedure, she was expecting a child that spring.

"Do you think you could ask Gram and Gramps to tape a few shows for me?" Richard interrupted his mother's thoughts, "Even if their recorder is different, I think Dad's new tape player he picked up in Germany has enough tracks to adapt."

"Which shows were you thinking?"

"The Judy Garland Show, Bell Telephone Hour, and Andy Williams."

Meanwhile, over at the Bible School, Melvin sorted through papers in preparation for the new term starting in two weeks. As director of the school, he was hoping to translate a third-year curriculum into Bangala in-between bush ministry and construction projects.

After finishing in the Bible School, he walked across the road, coming into the mission station to the side of their house to check on the cistern. The round cistern collected rainwater from the corrugated metal roof or "linzanza." He had cemented the walls and floor and then sealed the inside with paint. A 55-gallon drum barrel sat over the cistern, filled with different size rocks to strain the water covered by a screen to keep off leaves. A pipe ran into the house for the indoor bathtub, sink, and toilet. There was also a septic system, and a drainage pipe that ran from the inside toilet to the outhouse, which had a pipe running into the jamba. Although Melvin was quite satisfied with his handiwork, he hoped to install a filter in the kitchen to run water directly through, instead of first boiling the water and then slowly drip filtering.

Bomo spotted him from his post at the stove on the back porch wearing his mauve print apron, "Mobote, Bwana, did it pass inspection?"

"Mbote, yes, Bomo, I just hope it holds up for another five years."

Melvin went inside to greet his family. Eleanor looked up from her letter, "I'm almost done here and dinner is almost ready."

"Don't forget to ask about the hair color, Mom," Richard suggested from his room. "You're looking a little gray around the edges."

"Oh, dear me, Richard! Well, if we could get the barrels I would have some."

Melvin bent over to kiss his bride, "Well, Miss Groat, you look fine to me."

Eleanor smiled back at him, almost married for twenty-two years and he still made her feel like she did when they met at North Central Bible Institute. Eleanor returned to her task, requesting Loving Care, warm brown, sent via airmail. Then she folded the lightweight sky blue paper in half, and then in half again with the address to her folks on the front and their address on the back of the air letter.

* * * * *

Before Melvin and Eleanor arrived in Congo for their third term, they both wondered about the political climate.

A missionary couple leaving Congo to go on furlough told them that things were calm and back to normal. But it was not back to normal. When they first arrived, it was an eerie feeling as they saw the contrast before independence had come. Roads previously kept up by the Belgians were in disarray. Mail was erratic, with more items stolen from packages. Only basic staples could be found in Paulis and other cities that were once bountiful with choices.

They also saw more soldiers. Some were government soldiers loyal to President Mobutu, others were rebel soldiers, and some switched back and forth, depending on the situation. The troubled area of Stanleyville was some distance from Andudu. Of course, that did not mean much as things could move fast as they witnessed when they evacuated the second time. So far, as long as they stayed on the mission there were no incidents, but they had to get out sometimes for necessities, and in the normal course of their work.

During their first term, there was not much discussion about politics. The Belgians were in control, gaining riches for the products they produced from elephant ivory, rubber vines, and the gold and diamond mines. Most missionaries tried to be neutral. Still, there were times of internal conflicts and struggles of one's place in Congo as non-Belgian whites. Some whites came to serve and love the Congolese people, while other whites came solely for profit. Most missionaries felt that the Belgians did not treat the Congolese with respect. But again, would a Congolese President be even harder on them? Only time would tell if the new government or the people of Congo would realize the potential of Congo.

One thing was sure though, Congo was different, it had changed and would never be the same again.

* * * * *

"Here we are sitting on the front porch again looking over the Ituri Rain Forest." Melvin sipped on his after dinner coffee, "Sometimes when we eat out here it seems like we never left for furlough."

Aldene watched for monkey tails hanging from trees, while Richard listened to his folks chat.

"The house has been a job to clean up these past couple of months." Eleanor sighed, "But it's coming along and as soon as the barrels arrive I'll finally feel settled in."

"The coffee trees still need to be cleaned out," Melvin noted looking over the hector of trees infiltrated with random trees and shrubs, "it's too bad the community didn't see the possibility of cash crops to support the church and school."

"Well, our ways are not always their ways." Eleanor stated and then asked her son, "How did your studies go today Richard?"

"About the same, algebra is slow but steady and the French is okay, but I think some tutoring with Monsieur Toulon would help."

"And after your lessons you and their son can go hunting," Melvin suggested the obvious.

"Sure, why not?" laughed Richard. "He's homeschooled so there's not much else for him to do and not many kids around his age. Besides, I can continue French while hunting!"

Melvin and Eleanor agreed with laughter that it was a worthy cause to befriend the young man. Four years younger than Richard, Mark, was an only child of Belgian coffee plantation owners of 1600 acres just a few miles down the road. A late-in-life baby, his mother, Madame Toulon was well into her forties when he was born.

"Monsieur Martian is more than happy to let us come and hunt baboons on his property as well." Richard said and then he added, "Too bad Frenchy isn't around anymore otherwise it would have been fun to study with him."

"Who's Frenchy?" Aldene asked, suddenly interested in the conversation.

"Gerald Collet, I met him at Rethy when I was about eight. He was one of the few Belgians at school. He lived in Watsa," Richard explained, "His father works in the gold mine there. Now he's studying in Brussels."

"You know, I should go visit Madam Toulon sometime to get some tutoring on my flowers," Eleanor said as she crossed her legs and sipped her coffee. "She does such a great job with her flowers."

After dinner, Richard went to his room to study and Aldene walked around the station rounding up her dogs and cats, including her newest addition Fi-Fi. The fawn-colored petite dog was mostly Pekingese breed. Every evening it was Aldene's job to get the pets ready to bring them inside for the night so the wild animals wouldn't kill them. First, she had to search through all their fur for ticks. She started with the cats pinching her fingers together like a pair of tweezers to disconnect the blood-sucking insect from its host. Some were so bloated they were the size of blueberries with tiny legs sticking straight out from their bodies like needles on a pincushion. Aldene strategically sat close enough to the hot cooking stove so she could deftly toss the ticks to their impending doom. *Pish-iff-Splat!* The top of the stove sizzled. Search, pick another *tick, toss. Pish-iff-Splat.* A smile formed on her nine-year-old face. Mischief twinkled in her eyes as she thought of Bomo scolding her in the morning.

"Aldene!" he would say in a stern voice while scraping off the burnt remains of the ticks, "Quit putting the ticks on the stove! Open the burner door and throw them right in the fire."

And she would diminutively stand before his towering presence with her short-cropped bangs and bobbing pony-tail, dressed in a white and red polka dot shirt and red shorts, "But then I can't watch them pop!"

Inside the house, Richard heard scratching at his bed-room window. "Bwana, a baboon is in the peanut garden!"

Richard looked up from his desk to find two locals peering through the mesh screen, "Okay, I'll grab my .22 and be right out!"

Peanuts were one of the primary food crops in the area, supplemented with fruit of nabogos, a cooking banana, and roots of manioc. The peanut gardens were cleared out of the jamba through a slash-and- burn method. First, they would fell the trees and let the plot rest through a dry season. Then any wood wanted for cooking was collected, before setting a fire to everything including the tree stumps. Later, the cooled ash was worked into the ground and peanuts planted around the charred stumps. After the crop matured, the nuts, a large, classic size similar to Virginia peanuts, were pulled from the ground. Many babies were saved by peanut milk. If a mother died when the baby was born or it couldn't be nourished, they would give the infant peanut milk. After boiling the raw peanuts, the water would be used to feed the baby.

* * * * *

In April, Phillip and Edith stopped by Andudu on their way to Oicha. Knowing how worn out Edith was with her latest pregnancy, Melvin and Eleanor had agreed to care for two of their children. Aldene strolled out of her house, across the cement porch, and over to Cochrane's aging VW Kombi van as children, parents, and luggage trickled out.

"Who's staying and who's going?" she asked looking over the situation.

"Phillip John, and Elizabeth will be staying with us, and David will go on to Oicha," Eleanor replied then turned her attention to Edith, "Welcome dear, do come in and let's get your feet up."

Melvin was greeting Phillip when Aldene asked her standard question, "Well, how long are you staying?"

Advanced in communication for his age, five-year-old Phillip John responded, "After Mommy delivers the baby at Oicha, Liz and I are to be picked up on their way back to our station."

He was trying his best to be brave in light of separation anxiety from his mother.

"Okay," said Aldene and they ran to her swing set.

David trailed his older brother while the youngest, three-year-old Liz, decided to follow her parents into the house.

The next morning Phillip and Edith left and the Jorgenson household livened up considerably for the next several weeks. For one thing, the rainy season was in full swing bringing on colds and bouts of malaria. Eleanor nursed her larger brood through illness including digging out a pocket of jiggers from one of Richard's toes. Their broken transmitter finally repaired by an AIM's missionary, now needed to be returned through a creative shipping route of being passed like a racing baton from city to city via traveling missionary or native. Then the big radio went out. Thankfully, the one they gave away to a houseboy before their last furlough was kindly lent back to them.

Besides all his duties in Andudu, Melvin made monthly trips to Paulis, straightening out bookkeeping, working on the broken-down printing presses, and coordinating permits and plans for the construction of the new church.

One night before drifting off to sleep in his bed in Andudu, he murmured to Eleanor, "I'll be glad when the Tuckers return from furlough in July. In the bush, we just ask the Paramount Chief for permission, he picks out the land for us, and then we clear and build. In Paulis, it's back to red tape and the run around like in America."

He rolled on his side to face his wife, "The highlight though, is that Pastor Simona and I found a set of plans in the builder's catalog that can be converted to African building needs."

"How many can it seat?" Eleanor leaned on her elbow toward her husband.

The mosquito netting swayed over them. "It seats one thousand and can be built in stages," he answered, then chortled, "The name of the design is called 'The Conqueror,' which seems appropriate for the situation!" Then he kissed her soundly.

The next day Eleanor spent most of her day going through the long-awaited barrels. They had finally come at the end of March, only to sit in Mungbere until the proper paper work was found. Then they learned the paperwork had to be redone.

"It's rather unhandy being in the middle of nowhere!" exclaimed Eleanor while she stacked items in piles.

Liz followed her like a shadow and helped Eleanor carry clothes to the table for sorting.

"Thank you dear, you're such a good helper," Eleanor smiled at her little companion. She laughed to herself, thinking about how cranky Aldene had been lately about not having things. All her shoes were too small except one pair of sandals that would allow her toes to hang out a bit. And the rest of her dolls, toys, and future presents for birthdays and Christmas were in the barrels.

Last term, whenever Aldene needed something she would tell Eleanor, "Well, just go to the barrel and get it!"

"Oh look, the blender, now I can make peanut butter." Eleanor felt like she just won a shopping spree at a store, "And the vacuum sweeper!"

Several of the fifty-five gallon barrels were filled with donated clothes for the children, Bible School students and their household workers. Eleanor had also made sure she brought something for each one of Bomo's five children.

The weeks passed and word got out about the clothing. One day, two little children from the area stood on the cement porch calling for the Madamo.

"Mbote mingi," Eleanor called to them as she opened the back door of the house.

"What can I do for you?"

"Lamba" they said, which in Bangala means clothing.

They each had a chicken under one arm for trading."Of course, just wait here and I'll be right back."

Eleanor found a beautiful dress for the girl and a matching set of pants and shirt for the boy. She gladly took the two chickens knowing that to refuse would be insulting to the parents.

"Aldene," she called for her daughter, "we have two more chickens."

Aldene's latest endeavor was watching over the hens and their chicks. Often Liz would tag along, making the scene heartwarming and comical as hens and chicks clustered around Aldene for safety, and scattered in fear from Liz.

Both Melvin and Eleanor thought the Cochrane children were wonderful and enjoyed them immensely. However, Phillip John was quite mischievous at times. One morning, Melvin was on the back porch giving the workers instructions for the day concerning chopping wood, carrying water, and working in the gardens. Phillip John stood near the African workers, none of whom wore shoes. While Melvin was talking to the men, he noticed Phillip John nonchalantly lean toward a worker and step on his toes. Annoyed, the man moved away a bit. Amused Phillip John found another set of toes to step on.

Inside the house in the kitchen, Eleanor turned when the door creaked open to see Phillip John going to his designated bedroom during his stay. A few minutes later, Melvin came in, walked to the same bedroom, and closed the door.

Inside the room Melvin sat on the bed next to Phillip John to talk about his behavior, "Jesus wants us to treat people with respect and kindness and I think we should pray about this."

Melvin didn't know why, but for some reason he said, "Phillip John, why don't you pray."

Kneeling down by the bed the young boy folded his hands and closed his eyes as tight as he could. Then he said in a deep, slow voice, "Dear God, you know how people are."

Melvin tried his best to keep a straight face until the boy got out of earshot and left the house. Alone in the kitchen with Eleanor he repeated the story mimicking Phillip John's prayer: "He sounded just like a minister in a cathedral."

* * * * *

At the beginning of May, the VW Kombi pulled into Andudu."Mommy! Daddy!"

Phillip John and Liz ran into the arms of their parents and then hugged their brother, David. After peeking at her newest sibling, Liz squealed with delight, "I have a baby sister!"

That night after dinner, Aldene sat on the couch in the living room cradling the newborn in her arms. She had thoroughly enjoyed having the extra company the past month and had informed Eleanor that plenty of families had oodles of kids and they should too.

"Ruth is a fitting name for such a beautiful baby," Eleanor commented. Thinking of the medical procedure Edith had undergone to prevent any further pregnancies, she stated, "One can only wonder what plans God has for a child brought into this world under such unusual circumstances."

* * * * *

As June approached, Madame Toulon paid Eleanor a visit. As they walked toward the house for a cup of coffee, Madame Toulon commented in French on the vibrant hibiscus plant, "Oh, look at those bright pink flowers, they are almost the size of a dinner plate!"

A patch of poinsettias that favored the side of their house caught her attention as well. Walking onto the front porch Eleanor said, "The rainy season has really brought out the color hasn't it."

Once inside, Eleanor pointed out the two bronze planters sitting on two little tables placed on either side of the archway of the dining-living room. Dark green leaves with red centers mounded gracefully over the edges of the containers, "I just planted those caladiums this spring."

After finishing her cup of coffee Madame Toulon drew something wrapped in fabric out of her large purse, "Madame Jorgenson, I would like to give you this in appreciation for your son's kindness to Mark."

"Why, thank you, Madame Toulon," Eleanor stammered, "I don't know what to say."

"You don't need to say anything; your actions as a family speak for themselves!"

The middle-aged Belgian woman's eyes brimmed with tears as Eleanor held the handcrafted porcelain Belgian vase slowly turning it to admire the exquisite colorful patterns.

A few weeks later, the Jorgenson family returned to Andudu on Saturday evening from a two-night stay in Paulis. As the car turned into the station a houseboy ran up to the car before Melvin parked the Peugeot.

"Bwana" he spit the words out breathlessly, "thieves came to the mission!"

"What happened?"

"After you left, I noticed some things were missing. At the same time, the woodcutter boy saw things in the road and told Bomo. We started looking in the forest, searching for the thieves. We didn't find them, but we found a sack full of your things, and a car battery next to it."

He finished his story with, "We locked everything in the house."

Melvin and Eleanor thanked their loyal worker and headed for the house, followed by Richard and Aldene. In the kitchen sat the large gunnysack and the battery.

Shock and relief filled their hearts as they sorted through stolen household items, a bicycle inner tube, and blankets.

When Melvin got to the car tools, he couldn't believe his eyes, "They must have taken these right out of the car the night before we left! What if we would have had car problems? Not to mention there's no place to buy these items."

"Look, they even took the dog's hair brush!" exclaimed Aldene.

The next morning several of the local Christians came over to talk to Melvin to talk about the incident.

"We are so sorry this happened to you."

The other suggested, "Bwana, maybe you should get a night watchman."

Melvin listened while rubbing his back with his hands. He wasn't sure what injured his back this time. The pain still bothered him but at least he was able to walk. At the last kuvanda in May, he spent most of the week in Betongwe in bed. After finishing his conversation with the men, he turned his thoughts to the Bible School. One of the teachers, Masiokpo, was still living in student housing. With his wife and four children, it made for cramped quarters. It was also a matter of honor and respect due a capable teacher. The project was moving slowly acquiring seven thousand bricks from Mungbere to add to the eight thousand stockpiled.

Then there was the tin roofing and cement from Paulis, and many trips of harvesting sand from the nearby Nepoko River. When Melvin first dreamed of being a missionary, he never envisioned spending so much time on building projects and the necessities of daily life. Although he was more than happy to see that Masiokpo and his family had a decent place to live, it just seemed that in this country a person got everything the hard way in more ways than one.

* * * * *

On the last day of June, the fourth year of independence came and went quietly. Lillian and Gail had decided to spend the national holiday in Andudu in case any tension developed into serious trouble. The girls ate one last breakfast at the Jorgenson family table before their departure to Paulis. Aldene cleared her dishes off the table and scampered outside to check on her hen and chicks.

Richard excused himself as well, "If I'm ever going to have a chance at learning to fly I need to get this higher algebra course finished."

As Richard left for his bedroom, Melvin confessed with a laugh, "It's been quite stimulating for my brain as well. Sometimes I'm not sure who is assisting whom on the lesson."

"How is Aldene feeling about going to Rethy this fall?" one of the girls asked.

"She seems okay about it and Phillip John is going too, so it will be a new experience for both of them." Eleanor replied and then her eyes clouded over. "Honestly, I think it will be harder on us."

Melvin nodded and sighed, "It always is."

"Well, thank you for hosting us these past several days."

Gail leaned back in her chair hoping the change of subject would help shift Melvin and Eleanor's thoughts to something else, "Paulis does have the conveniences of the city, but it's so relaxing here in the bush."

"We have to be on our guard more in the city than before," Lillian set down her coffee cup, "With the Friesens relocating to Tanganyika it's just the two of us until the Tuckers get back the beginning of August."

Other families had moved or left for furlough diminishing the personnel of the AG Gombari Mission group.

"One wonders what the future holds for Congo. Sometimes it doesn't look too bright in the natural, with our earthly perspective."

Melvin shrugged his shoulders while crossing his arms, "We hear about Uncle Sam sending one hundred birds to Stanleyville, and other countries supplying the airplane fuel. Meanwhile, the communists keep their foot in the door as well."

There was a pause in the conversation around the table as personal thoughts reflected on the current situation.

"Seems like it has been a constant struggle since coming back," Eleanor said flatly.

"The old devil is doing his best to keep us down, but we know there is victory in the Lord." Melvin stated, his blue eyes flashing in confidence.

"Yes," Eleanor agreed leaning toward the table, "It makes us realize, so much more, our utter dependence upon the Lord. It is only *He* who can give us the grace, courage and strength to remain faithful and true."

Aldene bounded into the house with the back door swinging behind her, "The pinching ants got into Richard's pigeons!"

Richard came out of his room and went outside to inspect the damage, followed by his parents and the girls.

"They got the babies," he observed opening the cages. All that was left were the skeletons picked clean. Also called driver ants they crawled together in a horde eating everything in their path or pinching with stinging pain driving the larger victims in search of a river for relief. After cleaning out the bones, Richard tried to coax the adult pigeons back in their cages, but they just fluttered their wings and cooed in fear.

∗ ∗ ∗ ∗ ∗

On July 16, 1964 Eleanor wrote another weekly letter to her parents.

We know you are concerned about us but so far things have been quiet around here. We have been concerned ourselves at times. Things never have been too quiet in Stanleyville. However, I think things are settled down now. One wonders with the new government just how things will be. In some ways, we feel encouraged and in other ways, we wonder about some things. Things have been awful in the Katanga Province on the borders of Rhodesia and Tanganyika. I think the Kivu Province, directly south of us, is quiet again now. Seems there are always flare-ups. This old world is in quite a mess, good thing we know how to pray.

We had a very nice time at Biodi. We went on Wednesday. Richard and Phil went hunting on Thursday. The services started on Friday. Some of the national pastors spoke and did very well. Melvin spoke on Sunday and had a wonderful service. The Spirit of the Lord was really present. Twelve came forward for salvation. The service lasted until about six o'clock in the evening. It was wonderful to see these people as they wept before the Lord. Some of the others got a refilling of the Spirit. In the evening service, they had a testimony service and it was a real thrill as we heard the different testimonies. We wish for more services like that. Another thing that was a real thrill was to see the pastors at Biodi and how they were growing in the things of the Lord—and to see how they conducted the services—with the anointing of the Holy Spirit upon them. All of the teachers but two had been in the Bangala Bible School under Melvin's teaching. I know Melvin felt encouraged. The Lord knows we need to be encouraged these days!

Chapter Twenty-Eight

August 23, 1964

❧

With just enough clothes packed for a few days, the Jorgenson family drove to Paulis. Once there, they opened up Tucker's rental house and unloaded their few pieces of luggage. Discovering there were no bed linens, Eleanor sent Richard to Lillian and Gail's apartment over the print shop across town. As Richard navigated through the roundabout with the white Peugeot, he turned out to the right and parked near the cement steps leading to the girls' apartment. Suddenly he found himself surrounded by four policemen.

"What are you doing out past curfew?" one of them asked.

"I didn't know there was a curfew. We just arrived today and my mother sent me here to get some bed sheets for the house we're staying in."

"Get in the car with us!" another one said.

Richard looked at the four men and their car. One of them had a machine gun slung over his shoulder. He didn't trust them. There was no telling where they would take him or the Peugeot, "No, I will not get in the car."

They stepped closer to Richard. All he could think of was grabbing the wrought iron railing connected to the steps.

His dad's previous warning to not get in a car with anyone echoed in his mind, "No, I'm not going in the car."

Then the leader ordered the other three to pull Richard off the railing. As six arms engaged in a tug of war, the railing lost, and came off the cement steps!

"Come with us!" the one leader commanded.

They tried to shove Richard into their car, but he kept his back ramrod straight and they couldn't shove him into the back seat of the car.

Tired of the struggle the officer barked, "Fine, then you can walk!"

Richard began the two-kilometer walk to the city jail flanked by two officers and one leading the way. The fourth man lowered his machine gun at Richard's back occasionally poking his captive's back.

Waiting at Tucker's rental house for the bed sheets, Eleanor happen to glance out the window, "There's Richard! With a gun at his back!"

At the jail, Richard was locked in one of the better cells, where he waited for his father. A few minutes later, Melvin came and discussed the situation with the police and they released Richard.

* * * * *

After that first night of excitement, things calmed down and Melvin helped Lillian and Gail at the print shop and bookstore, while Eleanor worked on getting the house ready for the Tucker family's arrival. Richard kept working on his studies and Aldene finished third grade in preparation for starting Rethy. A knock on the front door revealed someone selling a baby monkey for one dollar, and Richard and Aldene quickly put together some change before Eleanor realized what was happening!

Things were peaceful in Paulis and everyone went about their business until the first week of August when reports came in that Stanleyville was attacked and taken by the rebel soldiers. The military conflict was some distance away, but everyone understood its significance with Stanleyville being the capital of the former Oriental Province. After Lumumba's death, Mobutu created nineteen provinces to replace the original six. He also replaced the 1960 Independence Congo flag of one large solid yellow star over a blue field and six smaller yellow stars along the pole. The new flag had a diagonal red stripe across the solid star on a blue field. The red stripe represented the martyrs' blood spilled for independence and the large star for unity.

On August 8, 1964, as merchants and plantation owners were either leaving or sending wives and children back to Europe, the Tucker family arrived on a plane from Leopoldville that came specifically to evacuate people from northeast Congo. Melvin and Eleanor were at the airport to greet them along with Pastor Simona Karada, Sara Anabote, Lillian and others. Gail was sick in bed with malaria. The next morning, Sunday services were held in the French chapel behind the bookstore and then at the Congolese church.

Melvin and Eleanor made plans to leave on Monday, August 10. However, in the morning, fighting broke out when a group of young people affiliated with the opposing party to Mobutu tore down the red-striped Congo flag in front of the government building and replaced it with the former six-star flag in honor of Lumumba. Riots followed with windows broken and people fleeing the streets until the police could contain the disturbance. One police officer waving a gun commandeered the Volkswagen shared by

Lillian and Gail. Fortunately, Jay Tucker was able to get it back for them. Roadblocks were set up and government soldiers called in from Gombari and Watsa. The entire city of Paulis was in lock down. The Jorgenson family was essentially under house arrest until further notice.

Walking downtown for an errand that day, Melvin had witnessed the attempt to change the flags. As he discreetly made his way back to the Tucker's house he saw the blood from numerous people killed, running down a hill, mixing in with the red soil of Congo. Some estimated the dead to be from fifty to eighty. That evening after the children were in bed Melvin and Eleanor prayed and sought the Lord for wisdom and direction.

Before falling asleep Eleanor softly said, "I'm going to try to get one more letter to my folks. Maybe I can send it with someone going to Kampala like the last one. We need to let people know what is going on." Then she added, "We need prayer."

The next day Eleanor wrote, *"This is a letter that is a bit difficult to write."* Then she proceeded to recount the events since coming to Paulis. She wrote of continuously sudsing the few clothes they had brought with them never thinking they would have been stuck in Paulis so long. And then she continued with:

We understand the road to Andudu has roadblocks and we don't want to take chances. We are praying the Lord will lead and guide us in His will. When I pray I feel peace in my heart. There are planes coming in to evacuate people. We can't know just what we will do. We are thinking some of going to Biodi for a time as it is quiet there and the men found out the road is open and no trouble. Anyway, we don't like to think of flying out, and leaving the Cochrane's behind with four babies. We feel confident that the Lord will lead and guide us. He has never failed us. Please try not to worry—but we do covet your prayers.

Eleanor thought of the torn land of Congo hoping the future would bring healing. Then she finished her letter.

Would you please call the Lindquists and also Bro. Rohde at the Dist. office telling them about conditions here and asking their prayers. Tell them we asked you to do this. Will write again soon. Our love to you all, Melvin, Eleanor, Richard & Aldene

* * * * *

On Saturday, August 15, it was about five o'clock in the morning when Melvin, knowing Eleanor was awake, said, "I feel that we should leave and go back to our mission station."

"Well, I feel the same way."

Quietly, they got up and told Jay and Angeline that they were going to leave for Andudu. They sat in the kitchen discussing the situation and their options.

"Oh, don't leave, because if anything happens we have the airport here," Angeline said.

Melvin responded, "Well, the airport is the first thing they'll take."

After the conversation ended, Melvin drove to the government-soldier camp to see if the roads were open from there to Andudu.

"They are open," one commander said, "but there was fighting the night before. One of the soldiers barely escaped the rebels and he is injured. You may leave if you take him to the hospital in Gombari."

When Eleanor saw Melvin drive into the yard with a soldier in the Peugeot, a shiver ran through her body. Her last experience with soldiers sitting in the back seat with loaded guns hoping Melvin would not hit a wrong bump on the road was unpleasant to say the least.

After finishing packing their few belongings in the trunk of the car, Melvin and Eleanor, along with Richard and Aldene, bid farewell to Jay and Angeline standing in the yard of their rental house.

"Please consider going to Biodi for a while," Melvin suggested. "The last time the rebels came there, the locals ambushed them giving them a sound beating and they never returned."

"We'll think about it," Jay managed a smile, "In the meantime, we can stay in contact through the transmitters."

* * * * *

They had only been out of Paulis a few miles when they spotted a truck on the road, full of government army soldiers fleeing from the rebels. The soldiers in the back of the truck yelled, "Stop! Halt!"

The injured soldier instructed, "Don't stop! Go down around them and keep going or they will take your car and you'll be left in the jamba."

Meanwhile, the soldier driving the truck stuck his head out the window to get a better look. Melvin steered off the road to pass the truck while the soldiers kept yelling to stop. Richard and Aldene's eyes widened, but they never said a word. Eleanor thanked the Lord for this provision and kept praying.

* * * * *

At Andudu a crowd of African faces with white smiles surrounded the Jorgenson family as they opened the doors of the white dusty Peugeot to get out.

"Bwana, Madamo, we were so worried!"

"The Lord delivered us!" Melvin exclaimed and he briefly retold the events of the last three weeks.

That week seemed the happiest of their present term in Congo as they planted vegetables, made necessary repairs around the station and continued work on the home for Masiokpo and his family. At night, the generator hummed for a couple of hours providing light in their house and energy to run the blender for making peanut butter.

And then, calmness shifted into a brewing storm. One night, footsteps crunched on the gravel outside their bedroom windows. In the morning, Melvin, Eleanor and Richard walked around the house. "Look!" Richard pointed out, "Footprints from soldiers' boots right outside my window."

Were the government soldiers there to protect them or escaping from the rebels?

After that, there were signs of the advance units making preparations for the coming of the main band of communist rebels. Many soldiers of nearby Gombari deserted while others sought to join up with the rebel forces. Cars were commandeered and all who wanted to gain favor with the coming horde had to put flowers and palm branches on their homes and gates, and if traveling, on their bicycle and person. Fear and apprehension filled the hearts of the Greek and Belgian plantation owners and the tribal peoples. All knew that the coming of rebels was evident and most of the people were ready to capitulate without a struggle.

Every day, usually after the AIM broadcast ended at 1:30 pm, Melvin contacted Jay in Paulis and Phil in Biodi through the radio transmitter. Both men reported that things in their area were relatively peaceful. However, in Paulis there continued to be checkpoints at every roundabout and roadblocks at the edge of town. One afternoon, Aldene felt tension in the air as she stood watching her dad contact Jay.

"Are you able to leave?"

Jay's voice crackled through the speaker, "Negative. Negative, not now. Negative."

Almost ten years old, Aldene noticed the uneasiness of her parents and Rich after getting the message on the HAM radio from Jay Tucker that they weren't able to leave. But she kept her thoughts to herself.

The next day Melvin contacted Phil in Biodi, "I can't make contact with Tucker, can you?"

"No." responded Phil, "I think his transmitter was starting to fail. But he knows we have tentative plans to meet here if things become critical."

* * * * *

On Friday, a message from the British Embassy asking all Brits to evacuate came via the AIM broadcast. As a precaution, Melvin had mapped out from their house a steep footpath that went down through the coffee trees to the road if they needed to avoid any soldiers. That night, the family of four ate dinner on the veranda near those trees. They all thought how beautiful the view was from a house that sat on top of a hill enchanted by the treetops of the rain forest on the rolling hills like a majestic carpet.

* * * * *

The next day, on Saturday Aug 22, 1964, a message from the American Embassy was relayed through the AIM broadcast, asking all Americans to leave.

"Well that's it," Melvin turned toward his family, "we're leaving tomorrow morning."

Amidst the preparations to leave, they tried to celebrate Aldene's tenth birthday the best they could, playing their first and only game of badminton in Congo. Then for lunch, Eleanor cooked a duck dinner for a birthday meal. Aldene looked at the last, scrawniest duck they had left on the station served on a platter. Poor little thing, she thought to herself, it died in vain. After dinner, her parents and brother sang "Happy Birthday" and she blew out an assortment of ten previously used candles. That afternoon Eleanor made peanut butter in the blender for sandwiches and sliced homemade bread. Most of their clothes were packed. She walked through every room of the house looking everything over deciding what to take and what to leave. The dining-living room looked so nice to her that day with the drum chandelier floating over the table covered in a tablecloth that matched the fabric of the curtains. Against the one wall sat the handcrafted mahogany china hutch Melvin had made for her. On the wall over the sofa were large pictures of Richard and Aldene brought from America. Other pictures of extended family dotted the room. For a moment, Eleanor forgot all the ants, spiders, snakes, and rats that constantly tried to invade her home. Although it was a hard life in Africa, it was a good life and she hated to leave again.

Outside near the lumber shed, Melvin and Richard debated what to do with their guns.

"I don't think we should get rid of the rifles completely, "Melvin said, "all the Africans know white Bwanas have them for hunting and protection."

"Right," Richard agreed, "and I've done plenty of hunting monkeys and baboons for the local Africans for food. So they will probably tell the soldiers there are guns here."

"My main concern is that the soldiers will take it out on the people around the mission station if they can't find the guns. However, I don't want them used to kill people either."

"So let's get rid of the ammunition and a few of the working mechanisms." Richard suggested.

"Yes, I think that is best," Melvin nodded.

"Then store the guns where we normally put them."

"Sounds good. If they are still there when we come back we can bring new bolts."

Richard took the bullets and working mechanism out of the rifles and threw them down the outhouse toilet. Then he put the guns where they were normally stored. Meanwhile, Melvin checked on the jerry cans for fuel. It was a necessity in the bush to routinely haul gasoline to the mission stations by drum barrels from the larger cities. He hoped and prayed he had enough for the journey.

That night they ate a meal with the African Christians, who warned them to leave early while it was still dark. One of the Bible School teachers advised, "Bwana, you need to get past the railroad terminal of Mungbere just at dawn before people are stirring. That will be the safest."

Another teacher spoke up, "We will be praying for you until the burden is lifted! Go in God's protection and peace!"

Tears were shed and farewells exchanged. No one knew how long it would be until they saw each other again.

* * * * *

On Sunday August 23, 1964, at four o'clock in the morning Aldene felt her mother touching her arm, "Aldene, wake up. It's time to go."

Aldene padded to the bathroom and slowly got dressed. Then the four of them left as if they were going out for the day.

Leaving the mission station in the Peugeot, Aldene felt an odd sensation of leaving the home that she knew best. Silently she said good-bye to her little world of dolls and pets and everything familiar. She hugged her fawn-colored, black-nosed Pekinese sitting on her lap. At the last minute, Fi-Fi got to come, but Richard's dog, Charlton, didn't like uniformed men, so he was left behind. Her father warned her that if Fi-Fi started barking, the soldiers would likely shoot her dog, but she kept begging and won her dad over. Sitting in the back seat next to Aldene, Richard stared straight ahead. He glanced out his window as they passed the Toulon's coffee plantation wondering when they would evacuate.

From Andudu they turned west to Mungbere and then north through Rungu and Dingba. On their way to Biodi, they saw car tracks coming from the area of Paulis. Melvin and Eleanor were hopeful that perhaps the Tucker family got out after all and they would meet them at Phil and Edith Cochrane's house.

Arriving in Biodi, the Jorgensons realized the car tracks in the road they had seen were not from the Tuckers, but from the rebels. The town was infested with them. After lunch that day, several African Christians rode their bicycles to the mission station, dropped the bikes in the dirt, and ran to the front door, "You don't know what our eyes have seen today!"

"Don't leave tomorrow it's not safe!" said another man. Then they told about all the killings of the government workers and other people that they had seen.

Feeling trapped at the mission station in Biodi, they all had the same question: How are we going to get out?

Through prayer and fasting they would seek the Lord for guidance.

On Monday morning, Melvin and Eleanor went to their bedroom to pray and Edith Cochrane went to her bedroom to pray. Phil went outside to talk with a government soldier who stopped by looking for gasoline. When they started to pray, Eleanor felt the powers of spiritual darkness. It was hard to break through the suffocating oppression, but finally she said to Melvin, "I feel that God wants to speak to us through his word."

Someone had sent them a record from the Klout Indian Family and together husband and wife sang one of their songs, "Sheep, O Sheep, do you know my voice? Yes, dear Lord, I know your voice. I know your voice by the reading of the word."

And just as they finished singing Edith knocked at the door. She had her Bible open in her hands, "I've come to share with you the word the Lord has just given me from Psalm 41, verses 1 and 2."

Melvin and Eleanor stood at the door of their room as Edith read the verses: "Blessed is he that considereth the poor: the Lord will deliver him in time of trouble. The Lord will preserve him, and keep him alive; and he shall be blessed upon the earth: and thou wilt not deliver him unto the will of his enemies."

Later that day, Melvin felt impressed to read Acts 27:22 in his Bible, "And now I exhort you to be of good cheer:

for there shall be no loss of any man's life among you, save the ship."

He reflected on the account of Paul's' journey to Rome on a ship caught in a violent storm on the Mediterranean Sea. This chapter in Acts included the Lord's promise to Paul that although the ship would be lost, all passengers would survive.

As their parents prayed and discussed what they should do and their concerns of the situation, Aldene ran outside with Phillip John and David to play on the termite mounds. The three of them climbed up the towering red hills and then slid down soiling their clothes with the red dirt of Congo.

A decision was made to leave the next day for East Africa. They would depend on the word the Lord had given to them to keep them safe. During the night, Eleanor couldn't sleep and went out to the living room to pray. And in the middle of the darkest part of the night a thought came to her that she recognized as the voice of her Lord and Shepherd. *Take as little as possible and I'll see you through.*

In the morning, she told Melvin what the Lord had told her and he went to the car and started sorting through everything and repacking. Richard was helping him when Melvin saw the leopard skins under some blankets.

"Are you sure we need to bring these?"

"Of all my collection of skins I chose only these two," Richard's eyes met his father's eyes. "They are worth a lot of money."

Melvin thought back to Richard leaving Charleston at Andudu and left them in the station wagon. Now they were down to three small overnight bags, peanut butter sandwiches, drinking water, gasoline, travel documents and their Bibles.

On Tuesday, August 25, after praying with the African Christians and listening to the 9:00 a.m. broadcast, the two vehicles pulled out of the Biodi Mission Station. The newer, solid white Peugeot dusted in red dirt led the way, followed by the older tan Volkswagen Kombi bus. They would head twenty miles north to Dungu. From there they would travel east to Aba on the border of Sudan and then turn south following the less-traveled road along the Congo border until reaching Aru, and crossing into Uganda to wait out the storm.

Chapter Twenty-Nine

Dungu

❧

That morning they heard word that one of the many dismantled bridges was repaired. This left one option for choosing a route to Aba. They made it down the road not very far, when three government soldiers stopped them, "Are you running away?"

Melvin replied, "We are going to Dungu."

"They don't have much stuff back here for running away," one soldier reported.

"Don't be running away and leave us," one soldier said with a mock smile and let them go on their way.

In his side mirror, Melvin watched the officers wave the Cochrane's van on and they continued on their way. He knew the main problem confronting them was getting through occupied Dungu, planning on arriving there just before noon to stop to get permission from the new authorities to proceed.

As the two vehicles drove into the town they found thousands of people gathered to witness executions that had just taken place. But a side road was clear. Placing their trust in the Lord, they discarded their original plan of stopping and continued through town. Usually there were dogs, goats, and whatever meandering on the roads, but that day there wasn't anything.

It was then that they saw a line of rebel soldiers standing alongside the road. The soldiers turned their attention from the violence to watch the vehicles drive past. But they did nothing. It was as if they were frozen, glazed-eyed statutes, looking—yet not seeing. Standing there with their guns of various sorts, as well as more primitive weapons of spears, bows, and long machete knives, they didn't move a muscle.

The rebel soldiers were easily recognized by their dress. Government soldiers deserting to the rebels stripped down to the waist. They wore an assortment of chosen embellishment of palm leaves tied to their bodies, lion skins on their wrists, or fur caps. Many of them marked their bodies with colors or whitewash. All rebels saluted by putting their hand to their waist instead of their forehead while sounding their battle cry—the word for lion: "Simba!"

The Simba, as they called themselves, were often drunk or drugged out on hemp. They feared no one, thinking they were protected from bullets that would melt like the rain if fired against them. The Simba would not shake hands or touch anyone. When giving them something, the item must be placed on the ground or somewhere else, and then they would pick it up.

As Melvin drove past the sixty soldiers, he fought the urge to press the accelerator pedal down harder while going at a snail's pace to cause no angst on their part. Richard watched from the back seat of Peugeot 404. Despite the Bible on his mom's lap, open to Psalm 41, and knowing his parents had listened to God's whispered voice for many years, he still felt that at any minute they were going to get ambushed and that would be it.

Eleanor looked over her shoulder to her daughter, "Aldene, close your eyes and put your face in your hands until we get out of Dungu."

At first, Aldene obeyed her mom's admonition to not look and bent over her quiet dog laying on her lap, but soon her head worked its way up a bit and she spilt her fingers open enough to peer out her car window. On the other side of the line of soldiers, there were black men lined up on a hill. She wondered if they were going to be shot or hanged. Tortured screams filled the air. Men's throats were slit and hands sliced off with machetes and women dragged into huts, violated by the Simbas.

Quietly Eleanor sang songs and hymns of praise in between praying the words of Psalm 41:1 and 2, "Blessed is he that considereth the poor: the Lord will deliver him in time of trouble. The Lord will preserve him, and keep him alive; and he shall be blessed upon the earth: and thou wilt not deliver him unto the will of his enemies."

Finally, after what seemed like an eternity, they were out of Dungu and they continued to worship the Lord and to pray his word as they turned east toward Faradje and then Aba.

After an hour of winding roads, they encountered a ten-ton truck of rebel soldiers parked in the middle of the road. The sixty soldiers quickly surrounded both vehicles. An officer who rode in a white Volkswagen got out to interrogate them. He asked Melvin in French if he had a "Laissez-Passer." The possible options of what this band of Simbas could do to them passed through Melvin's mind. *Would they beat us? Take our cars? Take us as hostages or kill some or all of us?* Any of these alternatives was entirely possible and had been experienced by others. Melvin knew they had no guns or other weapons upon which to rely, but he also knew they had the sure Word of God and the promises He had given to them before beginning this journey.

When the leader heard they had no traveling permit he said, "All right, we will be your traveling paper. No one will hurt you as long as you are with us. We will take you through. We are the Liberators!"

That was another popular phrase of the rebel soldiers, wanting to be known as the liberators of their people. To the despair of the Jorgensons and Cochranes, four so-called Liberators joined them. One of the soldiers got inside the back of the Peugeot station wagon and one climbed on top holding onto the luggage rack. The soldiers riding on top of the station wagon and the Kombi began yelling along with the soldiers in the truck, "Mai, mai, mai, mai—Simba, Simba!"

Thinking Melvin and Phillip were not driving fast enough they changed their chant to, "Noki noki na libosu!"

Melvin didn't dare drive any faster. If any soldier fell off the car or van and was hurt, they would be responsible and face terrible consequences.

The Jorgensons and Cochranes followed the white Volkswagen and truck into a village. The Simbas dispersed out into the village, killing people and looting. Aldene's young eyes saw a rebel soldier grab a teenage girl by her arm and drag her toward a hut. The terrified girl clung onto the wood post of the hut. The soldier kept pulling her inside. Despite her shrieking and thrashing, no one came to her rescue. Gradually the soldier got his victim loose and pushed her into the hut. Cries of protest died down to silence. Aldene sat in the back seat of the car waiting for the girl to come out, but only the soldier came out of the hut.

When the rebels were satisfied with their work in that village, they went to another and more violence ensued. Screaming and hollering mingled with the sounds of gunfire.

This continued until they stopped at a village and ordered Melvin and Phil to turn their vehicles around and park in such a way that they were prevented from a hasty escape if the opportunity were to present itself. For added measure, a machine gun on a tri-pod blocked their way. Then the soldiers ordered the families out of their vehicles and made them sit on logs in the shade. Phillip John, David, and Liz huddled close to their parents. Edith soothed her children and the baby in her arms as best she could. Not far from them sat Melvin, Eleanor, Richard and Aldene.

Apparently, a government official ran into the woods to hide at the last village. This outraged the band of Liberators and they were determined to not let any officials slip through their lines.

One Simba sauntered over to the two families and boasted with a sneer, "We're going to get them and we're going to bring them back here and slit their throats right in front of your eyes."

To illustrate this they forced a local man to lie on the ground. His fear-filled eyes glanced up at his captor then closed as a machete swung viciously through the air and struck the ground inches from his head.

"Only next time," the soldier's eyes flashed with murder, "I will not miss!" He let out a hideous laugh, "We made the Catholic priests and nuns watch an execution. They covered their eyes and turned their faces!"

A cluster of soldiers nearby joined in the joke enjoying the disgusted looks on the faces of the white missionaries.

That was the only time Richard said anything, "This, I can't take."

"Please, think of the children," Melvin implored, "You don't want these children to see something like that do you?"

Suddenly two crazy-eyed officers waved guns at Phillip, "We need you to drive us to get those officials before they get away!"

Phillip hesitated and tried to reason with them to no avail.

Edith stood by the side of the road with her four children watching her husband leave with a group of rebels. Eleanor went over to her side and put her arm around her friend. She began to pray, "Lord we don't understand this, but please keep Phil safe."

As time slowly passed, rebel soldiers stopped by to report their exploits. One soldier brashly stretched out his arm for them to see the watches all up and down his arm, "These are the watches of the people I killed today."

Finally, a leading soldier said, "We need to get to Watsa. Send someone in the car to get the men back here."

The Jorgensons and Edith and her children squeezed into the station wagon with a few soldiers and headed back five kilometers to the village where Phillip was detained. Huts were burning to the ground. When Edith saw her husband, she cried with relief. The officials were still missing, but their car was found hidden in the jamba. It seemed a real prize to the soldiers and in their exuberance, they began to forget about the need for the Peugeot and Kombi.

"Let's go! We need to get to Watsa!" a soldier yelled. Throughout the day tidbits of information gathered from the rebels talking was that their plans were to kill all the Belgians, Greeks and Americans they could find in Watsa.

At one point, a commanding soldier had asked Melvin where he was from.

"We are from Minnesota," Melvin wisely and truthfully answered. None of the soldiers knew where Minnesota was and the answer seemed to satisfy them.

It was getting late in the day and the shadows were growing longer. By now they had been traveling as hostages for over five hours and were only a short distance from the junction of Faradje and the road south to Watsa, where the truck of rebels were headed. If they stayed with the rebels, they would potentially be in the middle of a massacre. Something had to change.

Right before the Peugeot got to the village, Phillip had narrowly prevented a local man from being executed by a people's court set up by the rebels asking the people if the man was good or bad. Of course, everyone out of fear said bad. Phillip boldly asked if he might talk to the man about God before he died and it changed the tone of situation.

It was then that Edith asked her husband who was in charge. He pointed to the Volkswagen. Edith walked over to the car with four-month-old Ruth. The baby was restless and fussed in her mother's arms. Edith spoke to the commanding officer in French. After thanking him for their "protection," she told him that the milk she had packed for the day had spoiled in the heat and she needed to get to Aba to get something for the baby to eat. As Edith asked for a traveling permit, Melvin and Philip joined her.

Through the course of the conversation, they learned that this rebel leader had been schooled at a Catholic mission. Melvin talked with the commander on a positive note of benefiting from the education at the Catholic mission while Ruth, hungry for milk, kept fussing. The commander looked at the baby for a long time. Then he ordered his assistant to get a paper and pen.

After scribbling, using the hood of the Volkswagen for a desk, he gave Phillip and Melvin the Laissez-Passer, "Keep this. If you run into any other soldiers show them this pass to leave. They will know that I am highest commander of this region and will let you pass."

Ten miles later, the Jorgensons and Cochranes passed the turn off to Watsa and continued east to Aba.

Chapter Thirty

Aba and Aru

A fter their release from the Simba rebels, the Jorgenson and Cochrane families continued through Faradje toward Aba. Window washers swung back and forth to clear the rain pouring down around them. It was the perfect amount of precipitation, enough to clear the streets of people, but not torrential to the point of preventing their passage to Aba.

Eleanor asked Richard to dig out the peanut butter sandwiches. They hadn't eaten much all day, and hadn't felt like it either. Normally everyone savored the flavor of homemade peanut butter between slices of bread made from scratch, but now it seemed dry as the Congo dust sticking in mouths lacking saliva. Although they all were thankful and overwhelmed with gratitude for God's deliverance from the will of their enemies, their minds and bodies were drained. The rain provided a cocoon of tranquility until they reached Aba.

The light of their headlights pierced the darkness as they made their way to the AIM mission station just outside the town of Aba. After ascending the rugged hill to the station, they turned the engines off on their vehicles. Getting out of the car, Melvin noticed a blow out on one of the tires that would need to be replaced with the spare.

An elderly white woman and a few Africans came out to greet the weary travelers.

"Oh my word," Mrs. Kleinschmidt hurried over to the bedraggled group, "it's the Jorgensons and Cochranes! Please come inside."

Then she turned to the people from the station clustered at her side, "Let's get a meal ready for these tired travelers."

Later, sitting around the widow's generous table the adults recounted the past several weeks and their harrowing events of yesterday spent as hostages of the Liberators. They all knew each other quite well from Doctor Kleinschmidt's routine visits to the leper colonies while helping Grace and Edith to pioneer the hospital in Biodi. The good doctor had died that spring and was sorely missed by all who knew him.

After the refreshing meal, they made their way to red brick homes recently vacated by the resident missionaries leaving for safety across the border to Sudan. Melvin and Eleanor adjusted the mosquito netting over their bone-tired bodies and drifted off to a restless sleep holding hands. A last whisper of thanksgiving to their Banner of Protection, their Father God, escaped their lips.

In the morning, they begged Mrs. Kleinschmidt to leave with them, but she refused, "I feel perfectly safe here alone. In fact, several rebel soldiers stopped by before you arrived and were quite nice to me."

The Africans at the mission urged them to walk and go across the border into Sudan, offering to guide them through the bush. Although it was tempting to skip the customs office at Aru, it was a long journey for small children. There was also the concern for the Tuckers and other missionaries coming after them. If the authorities found out they had left illegally, the other missionaries would surely face the ramifications.

During the next one hundred miles south, the winding, bumpy road hugged the Congo border. The journey was relatively peaceful with only one bridge washed out from the rampaging river swelled to the edges of the high banks from rain. The bridge before them looked like an old man's smile with missing teeth. Nevertheless, there were still enough wood planks left to assemble a path across half the bridge's frame. After placing wood planks over the remaining beams, each vehicle crawled to the other side and they continued to Aru on the border of Uganda stopping once for Philip to change a tire on the older Kombi van.

On August 26, before the sun had reached its highest point in the sky, they arrived in Aru to find the city still in control of the government. Coming from behind the lines of the rebels, then through lines of the rebels, and now ahead of the rebels—they wanted to keep it that way. Their first stop was the mission station at the edge of town. A missionary and his wife were still there, but they had their papers and permits for leaving that afternoon. After a meal, the entire group went to the customs office. Before crossing the border, the missionary put in a good word with the custom officials on behalf of the Jorgensons and Cochranes.

Eleanor sat in the Peugeot 404 watching the long white pole lift to allow the missionary and his wife to leave. Hopefully, before too long it would be lifting for them! Her Bible was open to Psalm 41 on her lap. Richard and Aldene sat placidly in the back seat. Aldene clung to Fi-Fi, who had kept quiet through the entire ordeal of yesterday. Melvin sat behind the car wheel waiting for the customs officer to come out for him after he was finished with the Belgian mine workers from Watsa. Their wives became agitated when government soldiers began going through all the items in their vehicles taking whatever interested them. Tension grew when their husbands stormed out of the customs office muttering there was more than one way to cross the border. They climbed into their vehicles and roared off toward the main part of town.

Finally, Melvin and Philip were told to come into the office.

It was then Eleanor noticed people cleaning up the simple monument in honor of Lumumba and placing palm branches and flowers around it. Others were painting the nearby trees white. Then two bold rebel soldiers appeared and lowered the red striped Congo flag replacing it with the original six-star independence flag.

Time dragged on and Melvin and Philip were still in the office. Dusk was approaching. Eleanor knew the Africans never worked this late. Something was wrong.

A truckload of government soldiers rumbled into the customs area and began combing the grounds. One soldier sauntered over to Eleanor's side of the car, "So, you have made it this far have you? I thought you said you were going to Aba to see the doctor. Or was it to take the children to school?"

She recognized him from the threesome that had questioned them right after they had left Biodi.

Then he demanded, "Give me the keys to your car!"

Eleanor had a set of keys, but she answered evenly, "My husband is in the office."

He left and went into the office to find Melvin. When Melvin came out of the office followed by the government soldier, Eleanor's heart sank. The look on her husband's face told her they were about to lose the Peugeot.

Eleanor opened her car door and marched right up to the soldier. She rose to her full five- feet-two-inches while pointing a finger at his chest, "This is God's car!" she declared in Lingala mixed with Bangala, her hazel eyes flaming with righteous indignation, "He gave it to us to use for his work. And if you don't take care of this car God will punish you!"

Then she abruptly turned from the astonished soldier and attended to her daughter. Aldene had distanced herself from the car. Tears streamed down her face. She was almost squeezing the breath out of Fi-Fi. Then the dam burst and she cried her ten-year-old heart out. Her last haven of refuge was gone. Eleanor tried to console her in vain.

Melvin and Richard unloaded what few things they had under the watchful eyes of soldiers looking for anything that would suit their fancy. When Richard uncovered the leopard skins Melvin lowered his voice, "No. Leave them in the car. We don't want anything so symbolic to stir up emotions."

Then Melvin explained to the soldier how to shift the transmission from park to reverse, neutral and drive. He also explained how the steering wheel would lock up as theft prevention if they didn't start the car properly.

Melvin walked toward his wife and sobbing daughter, "They have our passports. We will have to come back tomorrow. We've lost the ship, but not our lives."

Numbly, the Jorgensons walked over to the older Kombi van with their three small overnight bags and climbed into the vehicle. Then the group of ten made their way back to the mission station for the night.

That night they were the only white people at the mission. After scrounging through several of the houses, Eleanor and Edith put together a meal and got the children ready for bed. An African midwife on the mission had given them bread and fresh milk. Melvin and Phillip spoke with the local African Christians about a last resort plan to trek through the bush to Uganda if things deteriorated again at the customs office.

Then they finished the night with prayer, thanking God for His guiding hand, looking to Him for provision for tomorrow.

* * * * *

Down to one vehicle, on the morning of August 27, 1964, the two families arrived at the customs office before eight o'clock. Melvin and Phillip stood around in the office, wondering where their passports were stored. All the workers in the office were busy working on nothing. Scared out of their wits, they were anticipating the main forces of the rebels to show up at any minute.

Meanwhile, in the van Eleanor and Edith prayed with their Bibles open to Psalm 41 with the border in sight. The two men were still waiting when at 10:30 the head customs official asked Melvin, "How long do you expect to be in East Africa?"

Melvin decided it was finally time to pull out the traveling paper given to him by the high ranking rebel soldier, "I have this Laissez-Passer allowing us to travel unhindered, written and signed by a commanding officer."

Just as the custom officers eyes began to scan the permit to pass, Edith burst into the office with Ruth in her arms. The baby fussed and wriggled with agitation in her mother's arms. Edith addressed the official in French, "Why are you keeping us here like we are criminals? What wrong have we done to you?"

All eyes in the office locked in on Edith as she continued, "Have not I as a missionary nurse cared for your children and delivered your Congolese sisters at their time of childbirth? Have not these men taught you the way of life eternal through Jesus Christ? One of my babies has already died and is buried in this soil, your land. Must this baby die too?"

As if to punctuate her mother's plea to leave Ruth writhed, screamed as only babies can, and projected the entire contents of her stomach over herself, her mother and the floor of the office.

Edith broke down into tears, "Oh my baby, my poor little baby!"

The officer's mouth dropped open. He sucked in a breath and threw up his hands, "You may all leave. Go!"

He reached for the passports in the drawer of his desk and stamped them as fast as possible, "Madamo, please sit down, do not cry, you and your baby are leaving."

Eleanor had watched Edith deftly pick up Ruth from her sleeping cot inside the van and march into the customs office. A few minutes later, the tenacious missionary nurse was marching out of the office toward the van followed by her husband and Melvin.

They were leaving!

A few soldiers, not in a hurry, meandered through their frugal belongings taking a few things including the one last stuffed animal belonging to the Cochrane children.

And then, with the engine of the Kombi humming, the white pole lifted ever so gently to the sky.

Phillip simply pressed down the accelerator and the two missionary families passed over the border of Congo. Behind them, the pole lowered silently blocking the exit again. Yet, to Melvin and Eleanor it seemed almost a thunderous crash of steel.

When—if ever—would they return to their beloved Congo and its people?

For the next five miles, they were laughing, crying, praying, and shouting praises to God. After reaching the border town of Arua, Uganda, and passing through the entrance gate, the ten refugees slipped out of the van and onto their knees.

Now it was time to formally thank Him and mark this day for the rest of their lives, as the day they were delivered from the will of their enemies!

* * * * *

In Minnesota, Eleanor's mother, Hazel Groat, opened the Western Union Telegram addressed to 10821 Thomas Avenue South, Minneapolis, with shaking fingers. She had not heard from her daughter since Eleanor wrote from Paulis. The top line of the telegram was dated: Aug 27 64

"Edward," she said to her husband who walked over to her to peer at the small yellow piece of paper, "our prayers are answered!"

She handed the telegram to him and sat down melting into the living room chair with tears streaming down her joyful face.

Eleanor's father read the four words of the message in a hushed voice:

ARRIVED SAFE UGANDA JORGENSONS

A week later, an air letter arrived in Bismarck, North Dakota addressed to Rev. Lloyd Jorgenson and Mr. John Jorgenson. After unfolding the two thin pieces of light blue paper, Melvin's brother Lloyd read the letter to his father. They both sat at the kitchen table, with cups of coffee waiting to be sipped.

"It's dated August 28, 1964 from Arua, Uganda," Lloyd looked at his father, "it's confusing how they have the town of Aru in Congo and Arua over the border."

"Yes, but what does the letter say?"

"Dear Ones at home," Lloyd began to read the letter typed by Eleanor on behalf of the family.

We trust that by now you have our cable and know that we are safe in Uganda. There is so much to say I hardly know where to start, but before I say anything I want to first of all give praise and thanks to our wonderful Lord who so miraculously delivered us and brought us to safety.

Then Lloyd read about their time in Paulis and returning to Andudu, only to leave the mission station a week later to meet up with the Cochrane family in Biodi. His breath caught as he read the ordeal in Dungu and the five hours that followed of being hostages of the "Liberators" while they clung to the scripture in Psalm 41. After reading another page recounting their two days at the border, losing the new Speed the Light car and God using the Cochrane baby to soften the custom officer's heart, the letter ended with:

We covet your prayers for this time that the Lord will lead and guide us. It was hard to leave our Christians. They cried like their hearts would break.

I am sure the Lord had a purpose in bringing us back these few months—we pray that we have been able to encourage the church— we feel we have. Anyway, we did what we felt the Lord would have us do. In it all we have been drawn closer to the Lord and have seen the mighty hand of the Lord working miracles in our behalf. For the children it has not been easy but they too have seen the power of our God and have realized His word is truth and the power of His word. Our hearts are filled with praise and worship to Him who has delivered us from the hand of the enemy. During this time, we have thought of what the Lord showed Melvin in a vision at the time he called him to Congo. He saw men trying to take his life, but the Lord would not permit them to touch him. We wondered at that when we first came to Congo as the people always seemed to be so friendly and happy to have us. This has meant much to us this past week and we have thanked the Lord for revealing this to Melvin.

God bless you all and do remember us in prayer. We have felt that many have been praying with us.

Our love to you all. Mel & El, Rich, Aldene
Write Nyang'ori Pentecostal Mission, Kisumu, Kenya

Part Three:
The Completion
1964–1999

Chapter Thirty-One

The Decision

✦

When the barrier was finally lifted, everyone in the Kombi van waved good-bye to the gate official. And then, the Jorgenson and Cochrane families crossed into no man's land, a five-mile swath of red dirt, brush, and a cement bridge. Melvin, Eleanor, Richard, and Aldene sat as in a dream as the vehicle bumped along the seventeen miles to the British AIM station, not fully realizing that after a month of uncertainty and suspense they were out of it all.

The refugees were kindly greeted by the mission station community and shown to their accommodations. They had little to unpack. Warnings on the radio instructed people to try not to bring out musical instruments, recorders, typewriters, cameras and anything else of value. However, Melvin did manage to get his 35mm camera out, but other than a few days of changes of clothes, that was it.

Later that night, after a warm meal, the Jorgenson and Cochrane families slept soundly, awakening to peace and safety. During breakfast, a nurse at the station recounted, "We heard you were kept at the border and had lost one of your cars, so we all gathered together for a time of prayer."

"Thank you! We count ourselves blessed and happy that we are not on the other side of the palm tree curtain, as they call it." Melvin exclaimed with relief beaming from his face, "We would still be there if it were not for the direct promises of God to us. We would never have dared attempt the uncertain journey without them."

Then he added, "But mingled with our joy we think with sadness of heart of many friends still there. We must continue to uphold them in prayer before the throne of God."

Many around the table murmured their agreement. Phil and Edith were as anxious as Melvin and Eleanor to learn of news about Lillian, Gail, and the Tuckers, along with many plantation owners and Congolese friends.

"Rest up and feel free to stay as long as you need to get your bearings," a doctor in the group said, "I am sure you have many decisions to make."

"Thank you, it will be nice to catch our breath and figure out what to do next." Eleanor held her coffee cup in both hands close to her last clean blouse, "We do know we will head to the mission in Kisumu for the time being, it's a good central location between Kampala and Nairobi."

"The higher elevation and beautiful scenery of Lake Victoria will be a healing balm for you all right now," the nurse said.

Another missionary woman offered, "You know, I am leaving for furlough and need to leave my car in Nairobi for when I return. It's available if you want to use it until I get back."

"Are you sure?" Melvin inquired and then stated, "It would be a great blessing as we have to take care of so many business matters right now—after we figure out a plan, that is."

Later that day, reports came in from natives clandestinely crossing the border on foot trails known only to them. "Bwana, you were the last ones to leave Congo by that road. After that, the rebels came and they closed the border. They were so mad at the customs man for letting you go that they cut out his tongue."

Melvin and Eleanor flinched at the news. Richard strode over to hear the report, while Aldene played with the Cochrane children.

"The rebels could be cruel couldn't they?" Melvin spoke softly thinking over the many acts of brutality he witnessed since the riots in Paulis.

"Yes," Eleanor sadly agreed, "humans are most cruel at times."

As the conversation ended, a doctor approached the group, "Did you mention that the car you lost was a Peugeot 404?"

"Yes, why?" Melvin's interest perched his eyebrows above the rims of his glasses.

"Well four men, government soldiers, have just come to the station looking for medical help after wrapping a car they took around a tree," the doctor continued, "I think the description matches your car. One of them sustained multiple fractures and the rest are severely bruised."

Melvin replied in a matter of fact tone, "They did not heed my wife's warning. They took God's car, did not care for it nor brought it back as they had promised."

Rich was intently listening, "I heard Aunt Edith give the soldier the same admonition as Mom did, so he had a double warning."

"We treated them," the doctor said, "but we can't have military personal stay here at the mission so they are going to the government hospital."

* * * * *

The next day after Aldene tearfully said good-bye to Fi-Fi, she walked to the car and climbed into the back seat of the weatherworn yet dependable vehicle. The British nurse who adopted the tawny little black-nosed Pekinese promised to let Aldene know how she was doing.

"Good-bye my pupper-dog, I'll miss you!"

Aldene waved one last time to her faithful travel companion as they pulled out of the station. Richard reached out his hand to give her a brotherly pat of assurance that it was for the better. Even so, he didn't like leaving all his pets either. He didn't blame his sister for crying buckets.

The Kombi van and Jorgenson's borrowed vehicle headed 776 km southeast to Kisumu, a port on the northeastern corner of Lake Victoria. The eleven-hour journey would take them two days. However, on the way they could pass the night at a mission station in Kampala near the northwest shores of the lake before crossing the border into Kenya.

As they traveled the last few miles to the Assemblies of God mission in Kisumu, the lake came into view against the lush background of the foothills of an extensive mountain range running north, known as the Rift Valley. To the southeast, the mountains led to the notable Mt. Kilimanjaro in Tanzania. Once again, the displaced travelers felt welcomed as they settled into their temporary home. The question was—would it be a month? Or would they linger for several months waiting for guidance and direction from the Lord, and the mission board in Springfield.

A few days later, a letter arrived from Poppy Agnew, a missionary located at Mvara Mission, Arua, Uganda dated September 2, 1964. Melvin read it to Eleanor as they sat in the kitchen of their guesthouse.

This is just a short letter to tell you about the news, which Margaret's boy, Yosam, brought us yesterday evening, the evening of the day you left Arua.

Yesterday, Yosam came back for evening duty all excited at the Congo news from his village near the Border. The "Liberators," or "Rebels," as he calls them, have destroyed Aru, broken the fine cement bridge out of the town on this side, killed not a few, and chopped off hands. The mutilated swam the river and ran the seventeen miles to Arua hospital for treatment. An Alur Evangelist, who traveled by bus from Goli via the Border road yesterday to Arua, said that the Congo people, many, all the way down, were standing shirtless on the hills shouting to Uganda for help and food. The Evangelist said the Goli mission station was besieged with refugees. I, with you, thank God again, that you got out in time. With greetings to you all. May your journey have been safe to Kisumu. Yours, Sincerely (signed) Poppy.

Melvin folded the letter and slipped it back into the envelope. He placed his glasses on the table in order to dab the tears at the corners of his eyes. After taking a moment to collect his thoughts he sighed, "I wonder if things will ever settle down there." And then he added, "Maybe we aren't going back there. Maybe we have answered the call and the completion will be somewhere else?"

Eleanor reached across the table for her husband's hand, "Remember the first year we spent in Brussels studying French?" She studied her husband's face. "Remember the great need we saw there and how we prayed for the Lord to send missionaries there?"

"Yes, I do. There has always been something tugging at my heart about Brussels and Europe."

"Well, there's the connection to Congo being a colony."

"And if things calm down in a few years we could always come back," Melvin offered, "I know many missionaries are finding work in Tanzania or South Africa, but I just don't feel a freedom to go there. Do you?"

"No, I can't say that I do."

* * * * *

Over the course of the next week, Melvin and Eleanor prayed together and with Phil and Edith for their friends left behind the palm curtain and the future of Congo. After much discussion it seemed best to enroll Aldene and Philip John at a school two hours northeast in Eldoret. Situated high in the Rift Valley Mountains, the boarding school was working with other missionary families fleeing from Congo, in addition to teachers from Rethy. After David made a plea to attend as well, he was added to the mix, making it a trio heading off to school. Perhaps, their parents reasoned, with other children around and studies to focus on, school would help take the terrible incidents they had witnessed off their young minds.

At first, Aldene looked at it as a coming-of-age moment when she was finally old enough like Rich, to attend boarding school. There was a dorm room full of girls her age that would play late at night using their flashlights to make silhouettes of their dolls on the walls. A posted lookout alerted them to the footsteps of the dorm mother coming. All flashlights and dolls were hastily tucked under covers and sleeping faces pasted on every girl until the door closed and the footsteps faded down the hall. Then out came the dolls and flashlights.

The grounds of the school consisted of two story dormitories, classrooms, a dining hall and other buildings for offices and maintenance. In the center of it all was a swimming pool. Not allowed to swim in Congo, Aldene made up for lost time, wearing a blue wool suit her mother bought her that itched her to pieces, but she was determined to keep swimming and put up with any soreness from the wet, rubbing fibers.

Each week, the students wrote a letter to their parents telling them of tidbits of school. Aldene wrote to her parents about playing the part of a queen in a play. She bit on the end of her pencil, thinking of what to write next. She didn't want to worry them or have the school read her true thoughts. Every week was getting harder to be there. At night, she woke up wet in her bed from nightmares. A man with a machete swinging over a young woman's head flashed in her mind before the woman was pulled in to a hut never to be seen again. In the morning, the dorm mother would scold her about a girl her age wetting the bed. After a few times of that Aldene figured out where the linens were stored and started changing her bed sheets at night. Everyday her emotions ran a constant rollercoaster of highs and lows.

The only one who understood her was Philip John, but sometimes he got irritated with her for smothering him, "Stop taking care of me, you are not my mother!"

"Well, I am three years older than you!" returned Aldene. She didn't care if he got angry, at least she could think about him instead of herself.

* * * * *

Meanwhile, Melvin and Eleanor decided to take a trip to Arusha just across the border of Tanzania to see AG missionaries, Norm and Norma Correll, and the work they were doing there. Thinking of all the hunting possibilities in the foothills of Mt. Kilimanjaro, Rich heartily agreed to the trip.

The mission station in Arusha was similar to Andudu with a church and Bible School. Walking around the grounds, Melvin and Eleanor felt at home and knew they could easily slip into the routine of managing the station while the Corrells and their two children left for their upcoming furlough. A cooler climate with the convenience of the bustling city nearby, nestled between coffee plantations, made for a desirable location. Added to that was a view of Mt. Kili on a clear day. Still, they would have to learn Swahili to be effective.

John and Lucille Friesen, who were working in another location in Tanzania, came to comfort their friends and see if they would be willing to join them at their mission station. Melvin and Eleanor appreciated the chance to talk about the evacuation and discuss their future with their former coworkers from their early days in Ndeya. They knew from experience that they could work effectively with John and Lucille, yet something kept pulling their minds toward Belgium.

Once again, Melvin and Eleanor found themselves deciding between Africa and Europe. The Cochranes were heading back to England at the end of November for a time to reconnect with Edith's family and raise funds by speaking at churches. After that, Phil and Edith would wait on word from the AG headquarters in Springfield as to their next move. The possibility of being adopted by churches in northeastern states could lead to another term in Congo if things ever calmed down there.

* * * * *

It was during this time that Melvin came back from doing business in Nairobi with some disturbing news to tell Eleanor and Richard.

"I saw Mr. Martin," Melvin began telling the story of the local coffee plantation owner not far from the Andudu mission where Richard used to hunt baboons and monkeys, if he wasn't hunting with Mark on the Toulon's property. "The rebel soldiers came through the area three hours after we left our mission station. It's a good thing Mr. Martin had sent his wife and children ahead of him to Belgium, because they took about twelve people hostages and tied them up, including the Toulons. Then they drove to the Nepoko River and started tossing people into the crocodile-infested river. Mr. Martin managed to keep his arms taut and in position so that after he hit the water he was able to free himself. Hiding under a bridge downstream a bit, he saw Madame Toulon float by, and grabbed her by the nape of her hair. They hid under the bridge until the next morning and floated downstream to an island. After a couple of days they were rescued by UN soldiers."

"And Monsieur Toulon. . .and the boy, Mark?" Eleanor's hazel eyes darkened with trepidation.

"They both drowned. I guess Madame Toulon told Mark to take three deep breaths of water and it would be all over quickly."

Eleanor's breath caught, "Oh, that's so sad!"

Melvin continued, "Mr. Martin also told me that he heard that the rebels had gone through our house in Andudu and taken Richard's picture off the wall to identify him. People told the rebels about Rich hunting around the area. When they found the guns useless they were furious."

Everyone sat in stunned silence their hearts torn with the horrific news about Monsieur Toulon, Mark and the loss of the other people. Only Mr. Martin and Madame Toulon had survived.

"And here we were one step ahead of the rebels pursuing us." Eleanor shuddered before turning her thoughts toward Madame Toulon, "We need to lift up that poor woman to the Lord. What a thing to live through! To wake up every morning and wonder why?"

"Those are questions we will never have the answers for," Melvin softly remarked.

"Not in this world anyway," offered Richard soberly.

* * * * *

One night, while staying in Arusha with the Correll family, Eleanor couldn't sleep. She hadn't been that restless since the last week of their evacuation. She slipped out of bed not wanting to disturb her slumbering husband, and quietly padded out to a chair in the living room of the Correll's home. It seemed they had finally turned the corner in transferring their missionary appointment from Congo to Belgium. After discussing their options and praying, they both agreed the Lord was guiding them to Brussels. The only problem was—they didn't have any money. Their account was in the red! After writing to Springfield to ask permission to come home to itinerate for a little bit to raise some funds, the board responded, "No, your term is not up yet."

Eleanor thought about feeling sorry for herself, it was a situation beyond their control. How were they supposed to get an apartment and set up housekeeping? She didn't even have a winter coat and they would be arriving in Brussels in November! Then she did what came natural, "Lord, how can we go there? We have no money. We have nothing."

And then a thought came to her and she knew it was the Lord's voice, her Good Shepherd's voice: *Haven't I always supplied your needs?*

Chapter Thirty-Two

Thanksgiving 1964

❧

A week before Thanksgiving, Eleanor stepped off the plane, wearing a borrowed coat of Norma Correll's to fend off the cold, dank November weather of Brussels. Unconsciously, she pulled the black coat with a fur collar closed without touching the buttons. Eleanor glanced down at her worn white practical shoes for life in Congo. They were the only pair she owned. Knowing her shoe size, five-and-a-half extra narrow, would be hard to find even if they did have the money didn't help her anxiety of moving to a different climate and culture. A lot had changed since 1950 when they spent their first year as missionaries learning French in Brussels. It was one thing to pass through the country filled with beautiful cathedrals, museums and rich history—and another to make it home.

The Sundells, a missionary couple working in Brussels, greeted them and walked with them to catch a taxi. There were not any large pieces of luggage to carry, just three, small tattered suitcases and the clothes on their backs. But they had their lives, and each other, and Eleanor was grateful. A spark of hope fluttered in her heart.

Before their arrival, Mary Greenaway had gone to the Embassy and gotten them a family visa. To Mary's relief, government officials were sympathetic with people coming out of Congo and visas were quickly obtained. Her husband, Charles, was the field representative for Assemblies of God Europe, traveling extensively while living in Brussels with his family. The Greenaways had been missionaries in West Africa before transferring to Europe. Melvin had briefly met Charles during their time in Brussels while securing the Peugeot 404 in 1963. Now a year later, Melvin was back in Brussels, minus the car.

Charles welcomed each of the Jorgensons, including Aldene, with a hearty handshake and booming voice. A northerner, he was just the opposite of his wife Mary, the petite Southern belle of his life. While she preferred to have her hair done at a salon followed by a manicure, and dressed with attention to detail, looking poised in every situation, Charles was earthy and combed his hair only when necessary. Their personalities were night and day and yet they shared their love for each other and their work in a captivating way. They had two children, a daughter, Sandra, who was in the states in college and a son, Phil, who was close to Aldene's age.

The Greenaways had a rented office space on the ground level next to the entryway of their apartment building. Mary led them into the office, her Southern belle voice ringing out sweetly, "It isn't much, but we set up beds for ya'll. There's no kitchen, but our apartment is just up the stairs or elevator on the second floor and you are welcome to take your meals with us."

Across the street from the Greenaways was another large apartment building under construction with large rectangle apartments on three floors. Eleanor smiled with a tongue-in-cheek laugh, "I used to say when we were here traveling through, 'I sure would hate to live in one of those!' Now I'll be searching for one to rent!"

Soon after their arrival, Melvin was invited to speak at a service men's retreat in Germany. Melvin accepted and traveled there, with his family to the Bible School at Erzhausen, near Darmstadt. They arrived in time for the evening meal with other European missionaries enjoying the time of fellowship that followed dinner.

The next day on Thanksgiving, morning and evening services were scheduled. That afternoon, Melvin chatted with the military men, asking where they were from and what their duties were. A few men came over and introduced themselves.

"Someone told us you used to live in Congo, is that right?"

"Why, yes," Melvin said, "We evacuated out of northeast Congo into Uganda the last part of August. Then we spent several months in East Africa until we flew to Brussels last week."

Just before the evening service began, the news came over the armed forces radio out of Frankfurt that Jay Tucker had been taken as a hostage and held captive at the Catholic mission in Paulis, along with forty other men in confinement. On November 24th, the day before one hundred Belgian paratroopers landed in Paulis, Mr. Tucker was brutally beaten to death. His body was thrown into a crocodile-infested river along with many other victims.

Melvin sat in his chair stunned until someone came up to him, "Brother Jorgenson, we need to get you near the podium, it's your turn to speak."

Melvin slowly made his way to the platform. It seemed like everything around him was moving in slow motion and he was in a time-warp tunnel. Jay Tucker's face flashed in his mind and the first time they met in Gombari, when his daughter, Carol, was a baby. Melvin heard his introduction. With his notes in his hands he walked to the podium, greeted the crowd of four hundred service men and their wives looking to him for a word from the Lord. Somehow, he started talking and the Lord met him in that moment and he preached from his notes and from his heart. Afterward, four men came forward to pray for salvation. One young man leaving for Minneapolis the next day asked for the address of the Lindquists and Eleanor's parents, "I taped the service and I think the Lindquists and your parents would enjoy hearing it."

Afterward, when Melvin gathered with his family they had a time of grieving and praying for Angeline and the children, Johnny, Carol, and Crickey. The next day, on the journey back to Brussels, they talked about all their memories of each person in the family and the legacy Jay Tucker left of a dedicated missionary and devoted husband and father.

* * * * *

As soon as the Jorgensons got back to their temporary home in the Greenaway's rented office, they learned of a plane coming in from Congo with evacuees that night. Melvin and Eleanor made plans to be at the airport in the morning.

That morning, when people started coming off the plane Melvin and Eleanor thought it was a sight they would never forget. Some wounded, they all looked haggard and worn. Most of them just had Congo things on, men wearing dirty short pants, women in summer dresses, many carrying their pith sun helmets. The Red Cross met them with coats for them to put on. One young boy, about twelve, had his face covered in bandages and an arm in a sling. His mother's face, laced with cuts, was sad and drawn from fatigue and terror.

Women in the waiting crowd stopped each woman coming through the line asking if they knew their loved one. Some heard news, good or bad, while others heard nothing. Melvin and Eleanor asked various people if they had come from Paulis. In addition to white people being killed, estimated reports at the time were that about four thousand Congolese had been killed in and about Paulis.

One tired-looking man nodded his head, "Yes, I was in confinement with Jay and heard him beaten to death. Mrs. Tucker and the children are in Leopoldville on their way to America."

"What about two single ladies, Lillian Hogan and Gail Winters?" Melvin asked, with Eleanor clutching his arm.

"I'm not sure if they went to Leopoldville, but I heard they were safe."

Melvin learned another man had also been with Jay at the time of his death and approached him, but the man refused to talk. In a daze, the man shuffled over to a friend of his trying to get the man's attention. A few minutes later the friend made a point to tell Melvin, "I'm sorry he could not help you. It took him awhile to recognize me and we have been friends for a long time. Maybe someone else will be able to help you with your questions."

Throughout the day, Melvin and Eleanor made many trips back and forth to the airport, waiting for every plane that was coming in from Congo. The next day they went back to the airport, and Richard went with them, while Aldene stayed with the Greenaway family.

After one plane arrived, Richard ran breathlessly up to his parents, "I spotted the Davis family and another missionary lady from Paulis. They went with the Red Cross people!"

After the government officials working with the Red Cross learned the Jorgensons were missionaries from Congo, they helped them to locate the Heart of African Mission people in transit on their way to England.

Meeting at a facility for housing incoming refugees, they were all shocked and happy to see each other. Through the HAM missionaries, the Jorgensons found answers to their many questions. Just the night before, the Davis family had been with Angeline and the children, and Lillian and Gail.

On November 24th, Jay was killed during the night at about eleven o'clock, the usual hour for the killings. His body was repeatedly struck with a stick and his face slashed across with a broken glass bottle. Jay had been in prison three weeks and beaten every day. Angeline was able to call the Catholic sister to ask about Jay and that evening the sister told her the dreaded news, "He is in heaven."

The rebel soldier in charge ordered one of the Africans to come with a truck to take the bodies away. There was no grave dug for the dead. The soldier in charge told the driver to take them out about seventy kilometers from Paulis and throw them into the Bomokandi River. Reluctantly, the African did what he was told to do. It so happened that he was a Christian and when he got to the river and saw Jay's body, he went to pieces in agony. Throwing the bodies into the crocodile-infested river, the Christian slipped Jay's wedding ring off, later secretly giving it to Angeline.

After Lillian and Gail learned of Jay's death, and the deaths of many other men at the Catholic mission, the girls were allowed to stay with Angeline and the children until they were airlifted out of Paulis.

Prior to Jay's death, the girls had their own brush with violence.

In August, Lillian and Gail's apartment over the print shop and bookstore were riddled with bullets. The next day rebel soldiers demanded they leave. Walking down the stairs the girls were hammered with the butts of the rifles and taken to jail for questioning where they were accused of hiding those of the opposing political party.

Boldly, Sara Anabote saved the girls from being killed. All the people there knew her and said she was a good woman of God and that she could witness for the two girls. The rebels told her, "If you are a preacher then let us hear you preach."

Under the anointing of the Holy Spirit, Sara Anabote preached to them and when she finished, they let the girls go. After Lillian and Gail were miraculously released, they were driven back to their apartment in their commandeered car where a soldier actually helped nail boards over the broken glass on their entry door.

Chapter Thirty-Three

Stepping-Stones

Returning to their office apartment from running errands, Melvin stated while closing the door, "These have been terrible days."

He removed his cloth scoff-cap and smoothed his slightly thinning hair back into place, "Yet, how gracious the Lord has been to us."

"Yes, we have been virtually living out of suitcases since July, and they weren't large ones either!" Eleanor slipped off her borrowed black coat and hung it on a coat stand, "Yet, we will have a happier Christmas than others we can think of won't we?"

Then Eleanor impulsively stepped toward her husband slipping her arms around his waist. Sinking her chin into his chest while looking up into his face, she gave him the look that begged for a kiss. Melvin promptly delivered enjoying the moment of closeness.

Sitting at the office desk used for a kitchen table at times, Aldene let out a groan, feeling embarrassed and delighted at the same time about her parents' display of affection for each other. Richard laughed at his sister and went to flop on the borrowed cot he slept on at night.

"Well, that's what married people ought to do, Aldene," Melvin crooned and then he started a chorus in his tenor voice, "I will sing of the mercies of the Lord forever."

* * * * *

After reading the letter, Richard handed it to his parents. For the time being their mail was sent to the office apartment they lived in on 57, Avenue du Derby Bte 13, B - 1050 Brussels, Belgium. Reading over the typed-up letter with the University of Minnesota letterhead, Eleanor let out a gasp, "What? They didn't get enough of your assignments so you can't graduate?"

"I just hope I can finish before I leave for college. In fact, I hope North Central will let me register for fall classes."

It was a blow to Richard to find out his lessons didn't get through to the UofM, but it didn't completely shock him.

"Looks like it's back to the books for both of us then," Melvin sighed.

"All they left out was Merry Christmas," Richard noted sarcastically, "Oh well, I guess I will be twice as good at all my subjects."

Ten-year-old Aldene threw in her two cents, "Our whole family will be in school, me at the International School, Daddy and Mom at the Bible School in Andrimont, and you at Avenue du Derby in our new apartment."

"Technically our apartment address will be Avenue d'Italie," Richard teased his sister.

In the past few weeks since arriving in Brussels, the questions of what and how were answered for the Jorgenson family. What had seemed muddy and unclear became a path of stepping-stones to forming a new life after Congo.

Melvin was approached by a missionary about a position at the Assemblies of God Bible Institute in Andrimont, a country village ninety minutes east of Brussels near the German border. Started in 1959, missionary Victor Greisen had arranged for the purchase of a chateau majestically situated on sixteen acres of woodlands and Ecole Biblique Emmanuel began classes. Melvin's duties would be much the same as they were in Africa, only now in French and English. Instead of huts built of natural materials, or buildings made from burnt kiln-brick, his working environment was an ornate, old-world chateau filled with exquisite woodcarvings in the stair railings and former bar of the men's smoking room. Eleanor would help teach as needed, in between her duties of setting up a household and getting Aldene registered for school.

On January 1, 1965, the Jorgensons were handed the keys to their second-floor apartment across the street from their current living quarters. The newly built, modern-style building resembled a cement grid of rectangles filled with windows. It had a concierge office on the ground floor with a spacious entryway that included stairs and an elevator. The apartment took up the width of the building with windows running the entire length of both outside walls. The top half of the tall windows were clear and the bottom half frosted for privacy. To the left of the entryway was a door to a bathroom and to the right, a closet door. Past this was a small kitchen with a cement-walled balcony overlooking Greenaway's office on Avenue du Derby and a set of tram tracks. Facing the same street were the two bedrooms with a small bathroom at the end of the hallway. The hallway split the floor plan in half with a generous line of built-in cupboards and closets for storage. The other half of the apartment facing Avenue d'Italie consisted of a small sitting room immediately to the right of the entryway with a balcony. Beyond the sitting room was a spacious combination dining and living room, which faced an eastern exposure of sun, unless it was another day of rain. With half the month normally receiving some kind of precipitation, cloudy days were a common occurrence for the oceanic climate of Brussels, with Fahrenheit temperatures falling in a range of thirty-three to forty-two degrees in January and sixty to seventy degrees in the summer.

After setting up cots in the master bedroom, and bunk beds for Richard and Aldene's shared room, all borrowed from the Bible School in Andrimont, they were done moving in. Walking around the empty apartment, Melvin and Eleanor envisioned what it would look like when they had furniture and put up a wall in the living room for Richard's room. Maybe they would get a TV for the sitting room, something they went without in Congo. There was nothing to cook with in the kitchen, and only a towel for each person to bathe. Yet hope stirred in their hearts.

Soon after they had returned from the conference for the military service men and their wives in Darmstadt, Germany, Melvin received a phone call from a service man saying several soldiers had gotten some things together and were going to drive to Brussels with it. And they did!

Melvin and Eleanor could not believe their eyes when the car pulled up with a washer and dryer tied to the top of it. Like a trail of ants, pots and pans, bedding sheets and Army blankets were carried into their empty apartment.

"Usually customs will give a person a little bit of a bad time when you take anything from one country to another," one of the service men said, "But we explained who these things were going to and that you had just come out of Congo with nothing and they said go through. No more questions asked!"

As the weeks went by Eleanor sought out furniture from auctions, flea markets and cast-offs from people moving. Some of the items needed to be refinished, while others were of excellent condition. The auctions were in French with people raising their hand for the price of furniture and trays of items. Eleanor looked over trays of dishes and eating utensils, not knowing what some of the things were, but she had to buy the whole tray. One bargain she found was two chairs with cane seats for five dollars each. Later she found out that, as antiques, in America their value would be over five hundred dollars each!

One of their first major acquisitions was a sturdy, heavy wooden dining room set with eight chairs, a buffet-style hutch, and a wine cupboard all for six hundred American dollars. When they finished eating dinner, they simply turned the chairs around for the living room furniture. Visiting friends from Holland were surprised that they had so little furniture in their house, but as the weeks and months passed by, the Jorgensons slowly gathered what they needed and eventually the apartment became a home.

Eleanor contacted a plumber to hook up the washer in the only full bath off the entryway. She would have to carry the wet laundry into the kitchen to use the dryer, but these were the only two spots available for the machines.

When the plumber came he shook his head with disbelief at Eleanor's request, "How can you do this?" he continued in French, "How can you live without a bidet?"

"Well, it's the only place I have extra plumbing. I can't afford to send my laundry out like most people do living in this neighborhood."

She didn't bother to add that most people also sent out for their food as well, or ate out, reflected in the design of the tiny kitchen. Eleanor had little counter space and one small sink, making cooking meals for her family and frequent guests no small challenge.

$$* * * * *$$

At night, Aldene would lay in her bed watching the lights from the tram on Avenue du Derby go by her bedroom window distorted by the windows. The combination of the rumbling rhythmic sound of the tram and pulsing subdued lights was a comforting thing to Aldene in a strange world that was now her home.

Deciding the Belgian school would have been too much of an adjustment for Aldene with all her studies in French, her parents chose the international school where the classes were in English with a French language class included. It was difficult for Aldene to have such a change from Africa, and yet at the same time, it was fun to be with other kids that were used to traveling and living abroad. Miss Morison was a nice teacher and the class size was only fifteen students including Donna Sundell, one of the other few missionary kids attending the school. The other classmates were a collection of American, English, French, and Italian whose parents held prestigious positions of business or government, such as ambassadors. The main school building, previously a home, was a large, white chateau with stately pillars, wood floors, and high ceilings. Nearby there was an addition to the property of a newer building for fourth and fifth grades.

One night, while Aldene watched the tram lights through the frosted windows Richard leaned over his top bunk to avoid vomiting in his bed. *Splat,* the contents of his stomach hit the floor."Y-e-w-e-w!" Aldene drew her hand to her nose.

Then the top bunk creaked and swayed as her brother leapt to the floor with a thud, bypassing the top bunk's ladder.

Next she heard retching sounds coming from the bathroom at the end of the hallway.

"Mom! Richard's sick," she yelled from her bed, afraid to travel over the floor to deliver the message in person.

The next morning the neighbor man whose apartment was below them knocked on the door complaining of the racket over his mother-in-law's bedroom, "She is recovering from a heart attack!"

Speaking in French to the Belgian, Eleanor apologized, "I am sorry Monsieur, we have recently returned from Congo and my son has a relapse of malaria. He jumped from the top bunk bed to get to the bathroom."

The man's stern face softened at the news, "Oh, I see, Madame. Well, I understand completely and I am so sorry for your son, and for your leaving Congo. Terrible things have happened there."

* * * * *

A week later, Richard announced one morning after breakfast, "I'm meeting Frenchy at his place to chum around a bit for the afternoon."

After getting over his disappointment at having to redo his senior year of high school, Richard decided to make the best of it and started searching for friends he knew from Congo. Gerald Collet was one of the few Belgians who had attended Rethy Academy. His father worked at the gold mine in Watsa, and during the massacres, was killed in the mine. When Richard arrived at the apartment, Frenchy was already outside on the sidewalk waiting for him, despite the cold weather.

"Bon jour," Richard greeted his friend who was a few years older, "Where do you want to go?"

"Bon jour," Frenchy smiled then added, "You won't believe who's inside in there visiting with my mother."

"Who?"

"Madame Toulon."

"Really?"

"Somehow they got in touch," Frenchy explained, "we didn't see the Toulon's too often, but you know how Belgians stuck together in Congo, especially after Independence."

Then Frenchy offered, "I can let Madame Toulon know you are here. I'll be right back."

After a few minutes the young man returned, his face clouded over with darkness, "I told her you were here and she just froze and shook her head no. It must be too much of a reminder of happier days with Mark and you hunting together."

Later, after Frenchy returned home, he asked his mother if she would help set up an appointment for Madame Toulon and Richard to meet at a café or somewhere. The arrangements were made for a future day and Richard and Frenchy waited for Madame Toulon, but she didn't come and Richard never made an attempt to see her again.

* * * * *

From the sidewalk along the street, the Jorgenson family of four walked down a long hallway independent of anything else, and then came to a small courtyard that led to a house, and then to the church. Located near the south train station, Gare du Midi, the AG church was fifteen to twenty minutes from their apartment.

The auditorium of Rue Joseph Claes could hold fifty or sixty people, but usually only about half that attended Sunday morning services. According to city code, there was another door of escape from the auditorium that opened to an enclosed garden with no exit save back into the same door, yet it seemed to satisfy safety requirements. In the front of the auditorium was a pulpit for preaching in French. Swedish missionaries had been there for a year or two and then Pastor Maurice Knops and his wife, came to take over the fledgling church. They were an older couple, with grown children. Before the service started, a girl about Aldene's age took a seat at the upright piano to the left of the double pulpit. When it was time for the first hymn, she played the melody line with one finger. Melvin and Eleanor glanced at each other and began singing.

After the service, Melvin offered his services of playing the piano and in the following weeks, the Jorgenson family became an integral part of the French-speaking church and dear friends of the Knops.

* * * * *

From taking meals with the Greenaway family, Aldene and Phil became friends as their two families shared life and work together. They soon discovered two of their favorite activities were making fudge, and playing outside after the occasional snowfall. The tram tracks between their apartment building lent itself to an experiment of rolling a gigantic snowball onto the tram tracks and hiding behind one of the cement pillars of the apartment. Soon the ding-ding-ding of the tram mingled with giggles of the conspirators while watching the conductor exit the halted tram to roll the white ball off the tracks.

Then they would head over to Aldene's apartment, "Mom, we're going to make fudge," she announced, starting to pull out the ingredients and a pan for cooling the fudge.

"Okay, Aldene, just make sure you clean up the mess when you're finished," Eleanor instructed from the dining room table.

Working on another letter to her parents, she overheard Aldene and Phil's conversation. After a while, the two friends got into an argument. It was like a regular routine for them, as sure as the setting sun and rising dawn.

"I want to lick the pan," Phil stated.

"No, you can lick the spoon," Aldene countered. "You always get the pan."

"Take the spoon or nothing."

"That's it, I'm leaving!"

"See ya," Aldene said with little concern in her voice knowing she would enjoy licking the spoon and the pan.

After a few hours there was a knock on the apartment door, "I came back to get some fudge."

"Sorry, there have been kids here and it's all gone."

Working on the evening meal in the kitchen, Eleanor suppressed a burst of laughter choosing to let the two friends fight their own battles.

Aldene's other friend in the Greenaway family was Uncle Charles. She enjoyed exchanging jokes with him and laughed at his mutterings whenever he got mad about something. Then Aunt Mary would spout in her soft delicate southern voice, "Oh, Charles!" and Aldene and Richard would hold their sides from laughing so hard. Melvin joined in the laughter except for the time Aldene burst into a board meeting of all the mission representatives of Europe at the office on Avenue du Derby.

"Uncle Charles, I got a joke for you," beamed Aldene from head to toe.

"Well, let's hear it!" Uncle Charles waited expectantly while the rest of the men blankly stared at Aldene with polite smiles. Melvin looked up from his notes to listen as well.

"Why don't elephants smoke?" she piped out the question.

"I don't know. Why?"

"'Cuz, they can't get their butts in the ashtray!"

Uncle Charles roared with laughter slapping his knee and pounding the table with his other hand. Melvin absently adjusted his tie and avoided eye contact with the other European committee members.

* * * * *

That first winter in Brussels, the Jorgensons added another member to their family. Still missing their pets left in Congo, Richard and Aldene found a brown envelope and wrote the words "Pet Fund" on the front of it.

"You can get a dog if you get a small one. It will be easier to keep in an apartment and you won't have to leave it behind when we go on furlough," Eleanor said, confidently laying down the rules of pet ownership.

"We agree," brother and sister replied, and Melvin witnessed.

When Christmas came, the two siblings put any money they got in the Pet Fund envelope. Then Richard turned nineteen in January and he donated his birthday money to the fund. One day, Aldene received a thoughtful card with a five-dollar bill in it from a woman in America.

After the growing stack of bills in the brown envelope seemed adequate for their goal, they headed down the city sidewalk toward the south train station past food stands of hot, crisp Belgian waffles and restaurants serving mussels and fries, called "moules and frites." Finding the pet store,

they walked in to find a charcoal puppy with tiny, black-jel-
lybean eyes staring up at them. It was love at first sight, and
total commitment after learning the breed.

"It's a miniature poodle," assured the storeowner.

"How much is it?" asked Richard in French.

After hearing the price he used his bargaining skills from
Africa a bit, "We only have fifty American dollars and we
would still need to purchase a collar and food."

When they returned home with Gigi, Eleanor didn't
know what to think, "Is she okay? She looks like the runt of
the litter. I didn't know you were going to get a dog today. I
thought you were going to shop around for a while."

The siblings fortified their defense.

"She's the one."

"She just kind of chose us I guess."

At first Gigi wouldn't eat her food and she became so
weak she couldn't stand on her four short legs. However,
after getting dewormed Gigi made up for lost time and rav-
enously ate her food, gaining weight and growing in inches.

After a few months went by Eleanor complained, "If that
dog grows anymore I won't have her. This is an apartment,
not a mission station!"

But that was just talking into the wind, as Aldene would
say to her brother. They knew Mom was strict on certain
matters, but they also knew she felt bad about all the pets left
behind in Congo. Once Gigi reached her full, standard-poodle
height, her head could easily reach the kitchen counter. Now
that Richard had his own room, the dog's ebony, curly-haired
body filled one of Aldene's new set of twin beds. In fact,
over time it became Gigi's personal bed.

Chapter Thirty-Four

Brussels 1965-1966

❧

Early in the morning, while it was still dark, Melvin drove their red 1965 Mercedes diesel to Ecole Biblique Emmanuel twenty minutes southeast of Liege in the German-speaking part of eastern Belgium. The 180D four-door sedan with no power steering made Eleanor's arms ache after driving it, but other than that Melvin thought it a fine means of transportation for meandering 125 km of cobblestone roads through towns dotted with village homes, castles, churches, and old Belgian estates until he reached Andrimont.

A narrow drive lined with trees led up a hill to the chateau converted into the Bible Institute. The brick and stone two-story building sat on a wooded lot. Beyond that was a pasture, and horse stables with a hayloft used during the horse and carriage days. A cobblestone courtyard and outdoor pool completed the charming scene.

Inside the chateau, hand-carved wood adorned the windows, and doors in between the wood floors and wood beamed ceilings. Figures and faces of women served elegantly for the balusters under the banister as staff and students passed up and down wooden steps to the second level. A prince with thoughtful eyes, and a queen holding a delicate rose stood majestically over the former men's smoking bar. The details of their faces and their clothes were so intricate it seemed as if they could tell stories of the past patrons.

That summer, after classes ended at Ecole Biblique Emmanuel, several tents were erected on the grounds of the Bible Institute in Andrimont for Bible youth-camp meetings. Eddie and Ruth Washington, working in Germany with the service men, were the main speakers for the services held in the largest tent. Off to the side, a smaller tent was used for times of prayer. Happy to be done with fourth grade, Aldene wandered in and out of the chateau and over to the horse stables in between the tent meetings.

After one particular service ended, everyone walked over to the prayer tent, including Aldene. People began waiting on the Lord in prayer. Some were praying for specific needs, or speaking words of worship, while others were interceding in tongues, a spiritual prayer language given by the Holy Spirit. Suddenly Aldene's eyes flew open. Someone was distinctly praying in Bangala! She turned her head in the direction of a young Belgian man that she recognized as someone from their French-speaking church in Brussels. Not wanting to interrupt his intercession of prayer she ran to find her parents, "Mom, Daddy, hurry! Someone is praying in Bangala!"

She dragged her parents from their duties toward the prayer tent. After the young man finished praying Aldene approached him, "Do you know Bangala?"

"No, what's Banga. . .what did you say?"

"Bangala, it's a language spoken in Congo and you speak it perfectly."

"I was praying in tongues," the college age man explained, "I don't know what I was even praying, but I know it was a burden of some kind until it lifted."

"Well, I know what you were praying."

Aldene then translated, "You were praying for the Christians in the uprising and to keep angels around the Christians for protection."

* * * * *

After the summer camp at Andrimont was over, Melvin and Eleanor said good-bye to their son at the airport in Brussels.

"You're always having to make adjustments," Eleanor's eye's filled with concern while her voice cracked with worry.

"It's okay, Mom," Richard shrugged, "I'll be at North Central four years, so that's pretty long at one place, and I can keep an eye on Gram and Gramps Groat for you."

"Well, we will see you when we come on our furlough," Melvin left out the part about it being in three years until 1968. He could feel his heart breaking again, but on the outside he tried to be brave, "Although you are probably going to find you've experienced more of life than most of your fellow students, it's still your time to walk the bridge to becoming an adult."

Richard gave a crooked smile and nodded. Then he hugged his little sister and strode toward the gate for his flight to America with his carry on thrown over his shoulder. His senior year of high school was finally over and now he would be a freshman at college. He turned for one last wave and then left.

* * * * *

That fall the one-year anniversary of their final evacuation and departure from Africa came, leaving Melvin and Eleanor reflective. Relaxing in their now furnished living room they each sipped a cup of after-dinner coffee enjoying an evening at home, while Aldene worked on her studies for fifth grade.

"It's been such a drastic change being back in Brussels."

Melvin sat in one of the matching upholstered chairs facing the couch. "There's no comparison between working in Congo and Belgium."

"It was far easier working in Congo than here in Belgium as far as our work goes spiritually," Eleanor said as she set her cup and saucer down on the side table between the two chairs.

"Well, we knew we were supposed to be there. Having the call to Africa and the Lord kept us steady."

"Yes," Eleanor agreed, "but the thing of it is, the Congolese were appreciative and they had a need, where the people in Belgium—they don't have that type of need really."

"Don't I know," chuckled Melvin, "When I tried to serve communion during hospital visits people panicked, thinking I was serving them their last rites, so I had to quit doing that."

Eleanor sighed, "It just seems so hard to plow the field here. There is so much spiritual darkness, much worse than Congo."

"Well, they have their religion and they think that's all they need."

Melvin offered his thoughts, "They don't read their Bibles leaving the job of spiritual matters in the hands of their priest or minister. They don't know about the fellowship of Christ and the abundant life that only He can bring."

Eleanor's hazel eyes held her husband's blue eyes, "I really thought we would have made more inroads with the French-speaking people, but there is so much resistance."

"It's going to take a lot of time and prayer to win their trust. They have been through so much with the wars that you can't blame them for being afraid of new-comers telling them how to find a deeper faith in God."

"We just have to keep our eyes open to what the Lord has for us," Eleanor said, and then added, "You know one thing that really surprised me was the number of Americans working in Brussels."

Later that night, Aldene woke up from another nightmare. This time the man with the machete was standing at the border crossing, waiting for her. She reached for Gigi sleeping on the floor by her bed. Aldene's hand stroked the poodle's soft curly fur. A flickering of tram lights through the windows and the rhythmic rumble of the track lulled her back to sleep. She awoke in the morning to face another day of cold, dreary weather with a sea of white faces concerned with the tasks to conquer for the day. She missed the leisure of relationships, the good cooking of Bomo, and the relaxed pace of life on the mission station.

* * * * *

It was during this time, as 1965 drew to an end, that Eleanor met a woman while attending a service at the American Protestant Church in Brussels.

"Are you American?"

"Yes, I am," Eleanor smiled at the woman.

"Oh, and do you live here?"

"Yes, I do, at the intersection of Avenue du Derby and d'Italie," Eleanor replied, and then asked, "How about you?"

"I live two or three blocks from you on Avenue Franklin Roosevelt," she replied, "My husband works for the Federal Aviation Aeronautics for all of Europe." Then she offered, "I'm going your way, could I give you a lift home?"

On the way to the car the woman introduced herself, "My name is Bess Malloy, but please, just call me Bess."
"Eleanor Jorgenson. It's nice to meet you Bess."

Once in the car Bess found out Eleanor and Melvin were missionaries with the Assemblies of God. "Well, praise the Lord!" her face lit up like a Christmas tree, "I'm a spirit-filled Methodist."

Soon after her encounter with Bess, Eleanor received a phone call at their apartment."Hello, I am with the American Protestant Church here in Brussels," a woman's voice came over the phone line that Eleanor did not recognize. "The Women's Guild was wondering if you would consider teaching their Bible Study this winter."

"It depends," Eleanor hesitated, "what are they wanting to study?"

"Well, we thought we would like to study the Book of Acts."

"Well, if I teach it," Eleanor stated with conviction, "I will teach it like I believe it."

"We wouldn't expect you to teach any other way," replied the voice on the phone.

* * * * *

On December 13, 1965, Melvin sat down to type a letter to his son:

Dear Rich,
Greetings in the Name of Jesus.

We got your note this evening, with the form for traveling. Thanks a lot for even just a note, as we know then that all is well. Do it when you don't have time for anything more. I know how busy you can get and occupied with things in school and dorm life. I will send the form in right away.

Mommy hasn't been feeling very well again for several days. We went to the Doctor and she has to take blood tests and other things as well as x-rays. All of this slows us up and we are not able to do what we want. And this is the Christmas season when we want to do special things. We haven't got around to getting what you wanted us to get as gifts, the crystal, so we will have to send something airmail to get there in time. To make it light we will send some lace instead. Will that be O.K.? We will get the crystal too, and send after Christmas so you will have it there when you want it.

We don't know yet what is wrong with Mother, but these tests ought to help us find out. But pray with us that everything will go along alright, and that she will regain her strength again quickly.

I went down to the Arcade at Louise with Aldene after school today to get her some ski pants. She needs them for gym class. And to think that we unknowingly walked in Au Jardin just when this one item was on sale, so got them for $6.00. She has let us know all of the things she wants for Christmas, and if we get all of them we will end up in the poor house.

When I take the mail out in the evenings (it is nearly 10:00 p.m.), I take Gigi out with me for the walk. She knows now just where I walk as I take her the same way each time so she will learn. But she is still afraid and is always glad when I turn around and head toward home.

If you do go to D.C. I hope that you won't be neglecting any of your studies or piano by doing so. Let us know definitely if you go and we can send you $25.00 for spending money. I wish it could be more but we must look forward to your coming school bills. Why don't you arrange for either the school, or you yourself—no, ask the school to send it to us—an itemized list *of what we owe and have paid. Oh, I guess I will write directly to the school. I like to know what is being paid out and for what.*

I am going downtown tomorrow and do some of my own shopping. I am not going to leave it any longer. Already it is getting late. Aldene has made a calendar and put it behind her bedroom door. It shows the number of days left until Christmas. She says there are eleven days left, so I had better get going.

God bless you good and keep you. Make this Christmas season a good one! Greet Claude for us!

Love to you, Mother, Daddy and Aldene

* * * * *

As the months passed, Melvin integrated his duties at the school with the French-speaking church and working with the small missionary community of the Assemblies of God. He also began to realize the need for more study materials in French, for not only the Bible School, but also the churches. While the school had a curriculum to follow, the churches had no Christian literature besides the Bible for growth and development. After much prayer and thought, Melvin embarked on his first translation project, *Knowing the Doctrines of the Bible*, by Myer Pearlman. Jacques Knops, Pastor Knops' son, helped design the cover of the book. Other people began translating other works such as, *The Daily Manna from Heaven*, a booklet, into French. After meeting Bob Hawkins, a former missionary to Beirut, Melvin and Eleanor soon found themselves in the Christian literature distribution business. Bob's focus of work became a publishing house based in Florida serving missionaries who needed a source for ordering reprints of translated materials. Soon a large amount of space at the office on Avenue du Derby was dedicated to this new ministry of literature distribution.

"Do you think you could blend a dove to symbolize the Holy Spirit with a book inside a circle?" Sitting at the conference desk at the office on Avenue du Derby Melvin spoke with Jacques.

As the book and literature ministry grew, Melvin incorporated a brand called VIDA . . .signifie la vie, meaning life. . .significant life; for light in the heart and to fortify the spirit.

"Somehow I want it to convey the idea of books of inspiration and encouragement," Melvin added.

Jacques began to doodle with his pencil on his sketchpad, "How about the bind of a book dipping down to the left and looking like the nose of the bird and the wings flaring up to the right looking like two fluttering book pages?"

A few weeks later Melvin slipped the VIDA letterhead with its round logo into his typewriter at his office. He smiled with satisfaction at the contrasting navy blue on the top half and black on the bottom with the white dove-like book splitting the image diagonally.

In order to reach out to a secular market, Melvin began renting space at the annual book fair in Brussels. People came from all over Europe to stroll through the large maze of tables advertising books and literature of all types of genre.

Chapter Thirty-Five

Berlin, London, and the Women's Guild

❧

E leanor heard the phone ringing in their apartment. When she picked up the receiver, an anxious female voice relayed the news, "Mary Greenaway has been in a car accident."

Melvin's secretary at the office on Avenue du Derby, Virginia Sasscer, was driving the car when a tire hit a patch of wet autumn leaves on the street. It was a chronic problem in Brussels every fall, with the mixture of constant drizzle and trees shedding their leaves. The car skidded into a lawn area and hit a tree. Riding in the passenger seat, Mary flew out of the car. The hospital staff was shocked to find tread marks from the tire across her chest. Sustaining only minor injuries, Virginia felt terrible about the accident and no words could console her.

Mary survived, and Charles was on the first flight he could find across the Atlantic. While working at his new post in Springfield, Mary had remained in Brussels to wrap things up concerning their move. Charles was told she could not travel and would require several months of bed rest.

With no place to live and needing regular care, Mary moved in with the Jorgenson family and everyone settled into a new routine. Aldene slept on the couch in the living room. Phil slept in the TV room. Mary slept in a hospital bed in Aldene's room and a bed was set up for Charles at the office.

One night after Mary retired for the evening, Charles sat around the apartment, tossing a caramel on the floor for Gigi. He roared with laughter while the poor dog tried valiantly to work the caramel off her teeth with her paws. Yet, the next night it was the same thing. When he began unwrapping a caramel the black poodle's ears perked up. Instantly, she was in front of him wiggling and wagging, ready for the treat. With most of his duties passed onto others, and wanting to be near his Southern belle, Charles would remark how Gigi kept him from going crazy.

Aldene laughed from her spot at the table where she was working on her homework. She traded daily jokes with Uncle Charles, and liked to listen to his stories. She also admired his devotion to Aunt Mary remembering what he had told her father one time, "I know people think Mary is prissy, but that's just the way I like her!"

As Thanksgiving approached, Eleanor decided to buy a new electric stove to replace the old gas stove. Then she purchased ingredients for a traditional turkey dinner with all the fixings and even pumpkin pie. She turned on the new stove waiting for it to heat up to the proper temperature. After sliding the stuffed bird in the cooking pan into the oven, Eleanor left to work in the office confidently looking forward to the roasted turkey.

Home from school, Aldene and Phil were in the living room with Charles when a loud bang went off in the kitchen.

"Let me see what it is," Uncle Charles said protectively as he went to inspect the situation.

No sooner had he walked into the kitchen when Aldene and Phil heard a stentorian, "OH HORSE-MANURE! There goes our turkey dinner!"

Alarmed by the noise, Mary came out of her bedroom slowly making her way to the kitchen. Aldene heard Aunt Mary declare in her southern drawl, "Yes, Charles, HORSE-MANURE! There goes our turkey dinner!"

Walking into the kitchen, Aldene did not know whether to bust a gut or be in shock over the mess from the exploded stove. Glass from the oven door and the stuffed turkey was everywhere, but all she could think of was prim and proper Aunt Mary's echoing of Uncle Charles horse manure!

That night six people gave thanks and ate their meal of canned beans and wieners cooked in an electric skillet while discussing the different kinds of electric voltage around the world.

"I specifically asked if the voltage was high enough for our apartment and they assured me it was," lamented Eleanor.

"We seem to have a way with holidays and explosions," Melvin reminded her of their sooty first Christmas dinner together as husband and wife in Jackson. The story was told and after Charles stopped laughing, he reached for a caramel.

* * * * *

The following year on March 18, 1967, Melvin and Eleanor celebrated their twenty-fifth wedding anniversary at their apartment in Brussels with a few friends and Aldene. The couple posed for a picture standing behind the dining room table covered with a cream tablecloth and laden with food, special-occasion plates, and coffee cups. Brightly displayed on one end of the table sat a silver service for coffee, sugar, and milk resting on an ornate silver tray. The office in Springfield had sent them a check of appreciation for caring for Mary during her recovery and Melvin and Eleanor found the formal service set during one of their trips to West Germany. On the top white cake between two burning tapered candles stood a decorative number twenty-five in the middle of a circle of lace. Just before the camera bulb flashed, Melvin slipped his right arm across Eleanor's petite back to the shoulder of her white, short-sleeved belted dress. Tilting her head slightly to the side, Eleanor's left arm found the back of her husband's dark suit. Her softly curled brunette hair framed her hazel eyes and radiant smile. Melvin mirrored her expression with silver-blue eyes behind combination glasses, a thick plastic brow line frame connected to a lower round metal chassis. His slightly thinning hair above his forehead took nothing away from his handsome features.

* * * * *

Later that spring, Melvin and Eleanor took a family vacation to Spain to let their bones soak up the sun and listen to the waves of the ocean. After traveling through most of France, Melvin started looking for a place to sleep in the car overnight so they could save money for the hotel room near the beach.

"This looks good," he pulled off the side of the road into a little clearing, "I think I'll check to see if I can pull the car off the road just a few more feet."

Leaving the car running with the lights on, he ventured a few steps past the front of the car and disappeared.

"Where's Daddy?"

"I don't know Aldene," Eleanor gasped. "One minute he was there and one minute he was gone!"

Suddenly a form appeared as if rising out of the ground. Melvin opened the car door, "Eleanor, I need a towel."

"What happened?"

"I fell in the creek in front of our car!"

* * * * *

One memorable destination for the traveling trio of Melvin, Eleanor, and Aldene, was Berlin. After passing through the last of many checkpoints going through East Germany, the red Mercedes passed into the west side of Berlin. Melvin began looking at the handwritten directions the German couple sent him with the invitation to come speak at the week of meetings. The Jorgensons were familiar with West Germany, traveling to Frankfurt and Darmstadt to work with the service men, but traveling through East Germany with the multiple checkpoints was daunting. Although the countryside was beautiful, signs of weariness and neglect showed on the buildings and people. The lack of trust in the eyes of East Germans was unmistakable.

Melvin turned the car onto the next street on the list of directions, "It's interesting that communist-controlled East Germany is called the German Democratic Republic when there's nothing democratic about their government."

"How did East Germany end up with Berlin split into a free side and a communist side?" Aldene asked from the back seat.

"After World War II," Melvin began explaining, "Germany was divided into four zones occupied by the Americans, British, French and Russians, or Soviets as they call themselves. They did the same thing to the then capital, Berlin, with Stalin agreeing to allow access to the city. Over time, the four governments couldn't agree on much, especially America and Russia and political divisions morphed into physical barriers. Berlin is a city version of this political division tucked inside the northeast corner of East Germany."

"When did they put up the wall?" Aldene was full of questions.

"About five years ago," continued Melvin, "the wall separating the city in two sections west and east, went up after what they call a 'brain drain' of people leaving East Germany by either flying out of the free side of Berlin or obtaining the documents to travel to other countries and never returning. The Soviets tightened their controls even more in East Germany, East Berlin and other countries of the Eastern Bloc, creating what Winston Churchill called the Iron Curtain."

Melvin smiled at his daughter, "There ends the traveling history lesson for the day."

"Just think, kids in America read about the Iron Curtain while you see it first hand," Eleanor commented.

"Yes, it's kind of like going on field trips," Aldene mused.

Despite feeling like an only child at times, the travel in Europe fascinated her and she could never get enough of it. One of her favorite ways to travel was riding the train through Gotthard Pass on their way to Locarno for the annual meeting of the European representatives of AG missionaries. They would drive until they reached the other side of Zurich, the German-speaking part of Switzerland. Then cars would drive onto an open flatbed car of the train designed for securing personal vehicles. For almost two hours, Aldene and her parents rode through several tunnels carved out of the mountains, one of them eleven miles long, before reaching the other side of the pass in the Italian-speaking section of Switzerland. Then her dad simply released the emergency parking brake and rolled off the ramp to finish the final hour of their drive by road.

"I think this is the house," Melvin said pulling into the parking area off the street. A middle-aged German couple came out of the small two-story house surrounded by flower and vegetable gardens. The rotund husband of average height wore a navy blue suit and tie. His wife wore a dress protected by a cooking apron. Her black shoes matched her dark coal hair combed back into a tight chignon bun with not a stray hair out of place.

"Guten Tag!" they greeted as they came toward the car.

"Good Day! Guten Tag!" returned Melvin and Eleanor, while Aldene emerged from the car. Delighted to have a young person in their home again, the older couple ushered Aldene into their humble kitchen and offered her a cookie from one of the three ceramic jars that reminded Aldene of the three bears from the story of Goldilocks.

"Bitte, please," the German woman encouraged Aldene to reach into the jar after lifting the bear's head to reveal freshly baked sugar cookies.

"Danke," Aldene politely took a cookie and sat in a chair at the small kitchen table to nibble her treat.

Later that night, after a dinner of wurst sausages, sauerkraut, homemade bread, and applesauce the two couples sat into the night talking about the meetings and the culture of the church in Germany.

"Sister Jorgenson, I like the way you style your hair," the straightforward woman spoke her mind on the subject, "the first woman who cuts her hair in Berlin, I'm the second."

"So you are reluctant to cut your hair then?" Eleanor inquired.

"Well, it is considered a sin for a woman to cut her hair short," she pressed her hands on her apron smoothing it out on her lap.

The hand-carved wooden cuckoo clock chimed and Aldene watched the little door open above the face of the clock. She giggled as the little bird popped out briefly and then the door closed again until the next hour.

Then Aldene thought of something, "Women in Congo have short hair, the Pygmies don't have long hair either."

The two couples broke out into laughter.

"Out of the mouth of babes comes wisdom," Melvin said.

"The thing of it is, "Eleanor began, "every culture has its dos and don'ts. In Brussels, women are expected to wear a headscarf in church. I usually keep one in my purse for such occasions. Well, one time I was asked to play the organ at a church Melvin was speaking at and," a laugh bubbled out from her as she tried to continue while the German couple waited expectantly.

"Oh, I know what you're going to say, "Melvin suppressed a laugh also.

"I didn't have a scarf in my purse and the minister told Melvin, 'You've got to tell your wife she needs a headscarf on.' I told Melvin I didn't have one, so I just slipped off my matching jacket to my skirt and slipped it over my head! So there I am sitting at the organ with a jacket over my head, but it was covered."

The room burst with laughter until Eleanor could finish, "Finally, a lady came up to me and said, 'Here, please borrow my extra scarf.' And then, I played the organ for the service. After that, I bought myself a blue hat with a tiny brim and just wore that."

"All the things we put our emphasis on," commented their German host, "instead of the great grace of God who, by the sacrifice of Jesus, tore the wall of separation down so we could have forgiveness of sins and fellowship with Him."

"Yes, sometimes we let the rules of religion get in the way of the true path of holiness of loving God and others," agreed Melvin. "Having right attitudes, words and actions should be our aim."

That week, between the regular meetings, the Jorgensons and a group of Christians met with the Burgermeister at the local town hall to pray for that city district and for Berlin. Using a translator, Melvin spoke to the young people, inviting them to the tent meetings, "We will have a brass band, a Swedish girls' choir, and words of inspiration."

Before leaving for Brussels, the Jorgensons went into East Berlin. Not allowed to take their personal car, they boarded a bus for a tour of the communist-controlled city. At the only entrance for foreigners, known as Checkpoint Charlie, Aldene read the large, black-and-white sign written in three languages to her parents, "You are leaving the American Sector."

Silence filled the bus as the vehicle passed through the dead zone of empty space, hidden land mines, and rolled barbed wire. Soldiers with guns and dogs patrolled the area known as no man's land. Soon they saw the Brandenburg Gate topped with the Goddess of Victory and the four horses of her chariot, built during the 1700s for traffic to pass through the wall to the palace. The once-celebrated gate was sealed off, adding to the oppressive state of East Berlin. The dismal streets were lined with bombed-out buildings and rubble from World War II. A once-beautiful city echoing grand Prussian heritage lay in ruins in contrast to West Berlin, which had been quickly revived through the Marshal Plan. It was as if Berlin had experienced a stroke, and its right side was paralyzed.

At the end of their three-week stay, the Jorgensons bid farewell to their hosts and retraced their route through East Germany to the border of West Germany. Before leaving the Iron Curtain into the free area, they had one last checkpoint.

"Pull your car over there for inspection and then get out," the soldier instructed.

Aldene watched as a team of soldiers looked through the inside of the entire car and removed their belongings from the trunk. After inspecting the luggage the soldiers removed the back seat.

"What are they doing all this for?" Aldene asked her parents. "We don't have anything illegal do we?"

"They are looking for people trying to leave the country by lying under the back seat," Eleanor explained, "Watch how they even take the spare tire out. People will curl up tight like a ball to fit in that small space."

Before putting the car seat back in place, the team ran mirrors under the body of the car, looking for people secretly riding on the frame. Aldene watched with interest noting several soldiers walking the perimeter of the checkpoint with dogs. She didn't feel any of the fear she had in Congo when they last escaped, still it was an odd sensation to think of the people desperate to escape communism.

* * * * *

After returning to Brussels, Melvin typed up a report and made an audio tape entitled, "ISLAND CITY" TENT CAMPAIGN, to be sent to the AG staff of *Mission News* and supporting churches.

Brother Jorgenson reports that he left Berlin, Germany, refreshed and blessed after participating in a three-week, citywide tent campaign. He says that the tent was filled almost every night and that there were many, many testimonies of blessings received from the meeting.

Among those saved was a teenager who, while wandering down the street after having been thrown out of a beatnik dance hall, was handed an invitation to the services. A middleaged man, who wandered drunk into the tent, also gave his heart to the Lord.

One woman, unable to raise her arms because of arthritis, testified to being healed immediately and raised her arms high in the air. A man who intended to be operated on the following day for serious ear trouble was saved. Two nights later he was back in the service, to report that the operation had not been necessary—he had been healed the night he was saved!

Street meetings were held in the most important parts of the city. A thirty-five-piece brass band and a fifteen-voice girls chorus from Sweden helped in many services.

Another sidelight of the meetings was a half-hour service before Berlin's Mayor Albertz on the city hall steps. After the band played, Brother Jorgenson spoke of the international aspect of the Assemblies of God.

Berlin is known as an island city because of the walls and fences that close it in. But even as on Melita [Malta] and Patmos, God worked in wondrous ways to the salvation of souls and the strengthening of His church.

* * * * *

Heading in the other direction for another summer camp Melvin, Eleanor, and Aldene crossed the English Channel on the ferry with their car to England. Melvin navigated to the missionary hostel, finding that driving on the left side of road with their car's steering wheel on the wrong side of the car was quite a trick. After settling into their room, Melvin dug out his speaker's notes to review the messages he had prepared as one of the camp speakers.

One of the highlights in the midst of the camp was reconnecting with the Cochrane family who were making plans to return to Congo.

"What a surprise!" Eleanor exclaimed, "We didn't know you would be here!"

After many warm embraces, and a tear or two of joy at the remembrance of their escape from Congo, Phil said, "It's too bad Richard isn't here, it would have been so good to see him as well. Unfortunately, we didn't have a chance to see him with all of our travels in the States to raise funds."

"Yes, he would have liked to see you all," agreed Melvin.

Eleanor asked her dear friend, "What did you think of America?"

"I found myself a bit dizzy in that big country of yours," Edith exclaimed.

Their children Philip John, David, Elizabeth, and little Ruth surrounded Aldene, who enjoyed seeing Ruth toddling about the grounds of the summer camp.

"The children look so good," Eleanor beamed seeing them again. She always had a soft spot for them even if they were "real clippers." Naturally, talk turned to the Congo and any updates they had heard.

"Do you remember the sisters, Margaret and Clara?" Eleanor asked, "They were brought out by missionaries and their Belgian father took them in until he could bring out their Congolese mother for them to live with."

Eleanor smiled with delight, "They've even come over to our apartment and cooked Congolese food for us."

Then she continued in a serious tone, "In March when they came over, they said Betongwe and Andudu were still in rebel hands and that the chief and sub-chief in Betongwe were killed. They were the ones Richard had his picture taken with. Margaret also said the National Army is giving the Belgians and Americans a hard time."

"We haven't gotten much word from anybody in Andudu," Melvin said, "Maybe they are still hiding out in the forest."

"So you are sure about going back to Congo?" Eleanor searched her friend's face for answers not found in spoken words.

"Yes, we know people wonder what in the world we are thinking bringing our children back in there again, but we truly feel the Lord's guidance in returning next year," Edith replied.

"We've prayed about going back after our next furlough," Melvin interjected, "but so far the Lord has said 'I have need of you here.' But maybe after Aldene graduates from high school we will return."

"Yes, maybe someday you will return to Congo," Phil answered.

A time of rest and touring in England following the week of tent meetings was cut short for Eleanor when word reached her that her mother had suffered a stroke and wasn't doing well. Someone was gracious enough to loan Eleanor the amount needed for a plane ticket and she departed from London to Minneapolis. After two weeks of caring for her mother, Eleanor returned to Brussels. Although Eleanor's mother would recover, her frail state was constantly in Eleanor's thoughts as she resumed her life in Brussels. First though, was getting Aldene ready for another year at ISB, International School of Brussels.

Meanwhile, Melvin began working with the staff at the Bible School in Andrimont, and welcoming incoming students. He also picked up another duty of welcoming new missionaries to Europe, sometimes making trips to Holland or other places to greet them at the airport and get them acquainted with their new surroundings. When Melvin relocated to Brussels after leaving Africa, there were only twelve AG missionaries in all of free Europe, but as the need became more apparent, a slow but steady growth of missionary interest brought more appointments to Europe. With Charles Greenaway's transition to a new position at AG headquarters in Springfield, the baton would be passing on to Melvin as director of the Bible School in Andrimont, with increased duties over Europe.

Melvin also continued regular trips to West Germany to speak at chapels for the servicemen. Often times, groups of military personal and their wives met at AG fellowship groups throughout Germany such as Stuttgart, Wurzburg, & Nuremberg. And on American Holidays they would gather at Erzhausen Bible School as one big fellowship meeting, having dinner afterward. During one such meeting, Melvin heard a voice calling him. He turned at the top of the steps to the lower level.

Down at the bottom, an attractive young woman with dark brunette hair waved at him, a smile of surprise crossing her face, "Brother Jorgenson! It's me, Gayle Lambertson from Detroit Lakes!"

Melvin retraced his steps down to meet her, "Why, Gayle, I recognize the voice, but you are a grown woman now."

"Well, now I am Mrs. Detert. I haven't seen you since I cried my eyes out at the train station when you and Sister Jorgenson left for the mission field."

"Oh, my, that's," Melvin calculated since 1950, "about nineteen years. What a wonder to meet you here in Germany."

"My husband, Ken, is on a three-year tour. We so enjoy what Dick Fulmer is doing here for the fellowship groups, and Eddie and Ruth Washington are at every meeting in Erzhausen."

"Yes, we have the Washingtons come to summer camps in Brussels."

"Is Sister Jorgenson with you?"

"Yes, let's go find her, if you can spare the time."

"Oh, I can," Gayle smiled, "But let me find my husband first!"

* * * * *

Meanwhile, in the midst of spiritual camps and delightful reunions, there were frustrations. As for Eleanor, to her disappointment, there was continued resistance to women's Bible studies or any type of women's ministry in the French-speaking church. However, the Women's Guild of the American Protestant Church, or APC, was a different story. That past winter when Eleanor taught on the Book of Acts, she witnessed something she knew was the working of God's power in the lives of the women, as they read and studied God's word together. Most of the women traveled in the affluent circles of diplomats, or government officials with a direct line to the White House, or VP's of car manufacturers. Some of the women came willingly, some hesitant at the invitation of others, and some didn't know why they were there. But as each week passed these wives of elite businessmen and ambassadors of English-speaking countries experienced the life of the Spirit in Christ Jesus.

They all had the creature comforts of life at their fingertips, and yet there was something missing in their lives. Now these women had found an abundant life of living waters that quenched that deep longing in their souls nothing else could touch. Many surrendered their lives to Jesus Christ as their Lord and Savior. Through the Book of Acts, Eleanor let the Word of God speak for itself concerning the infilling of the Holy Spirit in a believer. Curious as what this second experience after being born-again was all about, the women asked Eleanor questions to satisfy their spiritual hunger. Eleanor answered their questions directing them to the examples in the Book of Acts, beginning with the final words of Jesus instructing his disciples to wait in Jerusalem until they were empowered by the promised gift of baptism with the Holy Spirit.

The choir director at the Methodist church in Brussels told her pastor, "I gave my life to Jesus and got filled with Holy Spirit at the Women's Guild, where Mrs. Jorgenson is teaching on the Book of Acts!"

"Good, I hope some more of you ladies get as happy as you," her pastor replied. He wondered what the choir director was talking about, but it seemed like a positive experience so he thought he better encourage her.

It was also during this time that one morning at eight o'clock, the doorbell rang at the apartment door, "Could I please talk you about something?" the woman asked Eleanor. She was married to the pastor of the Methodist church.

"Why of course," Eleanor ushered the woman into their living room.

"I am really stirred up about what you said the other week about saved through grace rather than through good works," the pastor's wife began, "I asked my husband about it and he said, 'Oh, I can't help you. Go see Mel Jorgenson.' So, here I am looking for answers."

In addition to the Women's Guild, Eleanor's new friend Bess, asked her to consider teaching a study in her home on Avenue Franklin Roosevelt.

"I'll invite some of the women I've met through our social circles and the women from my husband's office," then she laughed, "they don't dare refuse me."

After the first study at her large, beautifully decorated apartment, Bess confided to Eleanor, "My husband told me, 'Bess, would you leave those women alone.' But I am trusting in the Lord that he will come around. In fact, I have an idea about the next time I host another VIP party of inviting you and your husband."

Another woman in the group at Bess Malloy's apartment, an artist, would get angry in the middle of the Bible study and leave. However, the next week she would be there again, well dressed in her two-piece suit with fashionably styled mid-length brunette hair.

This happened several times until one day Eleanor got a phone call from her, "Can you come over to my place?"

After Eleanor arrived the woman shrugged her shoulders, "I'm not sure if I am ready to see you or not, but come in anyway."

Eleanor silently asked the Lord for help and then buckled in for the ride. The woman led Eleanor over to the buffet. Then she pulled out a painting from behind it, of a beautiful woman in the nude, "You see this? This is the gal that my husband is stepping out with. Don't you think it's big of me to paint a picture of her?"

Eleanor decided her best strategy was to just listen.

"I do everything I know how to do to be a good Christian. I pray every day to God. I give fashion shows for the church and other things."

"Isn't there something missing?" Eleanor asked, then she continued, "We need to pray to God, but we need to pray to Him through His son, Jesus. Asking Jesus to forgive you of your sins and calling upon *His* name is the only path to salvation and eternal life. That feeling of being poked around inside is the work of the Holy Spirit drawing you to God. Is today the day you are ready to accept Jesus as your Lord and Savior and follow Him the rest of your life?"

"Why hasn't anybody told me that before?" she asked. Then she declared, "Well, I know what you are going to say next. You're going to say we need to pray."

And they did.

The two women knelt down on the floor near the davenport and when the woman started to pray Eleanor knew she would never forget her words, "Dear God, I come to You for the first time in my life in the name of Your son, Jesus."

Shortly after that, the woman's husband was transferred back to the States, and she called on the phone, "Eleanor, can I come over for prayer before we leave?"

At the apartment, a small group of ladies gathered around their sister in Christ and prayed for her husband and their move to America. The finely dressed woman began weeping to the point that Eleanor needed to get her a box of tissues to clean up her face.

After they finished praying, she threw her arms around Eleanor, "And to think I didn't used to like you!"

Another woman in the group offered, "Well, now that you've really found the Lord, some people might not like you either."

Later, Eleanor learned that after moving to the East Coast the woman's husband was invited to a Full Gospel Businessmen's meeting and gave his life to the Lord and their marriage was restored.

Chapter Thirty-Six

David Wilkerson

ॐ

On November 28, 1967, Eleanor typed a letter on their electric typewriter to send to Minneapolis.

Dear Richard,

While I am over at the office and waiting for Daddy to help me with some things, I will start a letter to you. As the mornings and evenings go by and not a word from you—I can't tell you the disappointment. I know you are busy, but it seems to me you could at least find a few minutes to write at least a note now and then. We haven't heard from anyone for weeks now. When we hear from Mother that always helps although it certainly isn't the same as a direct word from you. Guess I shouldn't start my letter by scolding you, but I'm about in that mood.

It is a rainy, dreary day. Not really too cold. I am so thankful for a nice warm apartment. So many places I have been in lately are cold. Perhaps Daddy told you that Andrimont has been sold. We still have another year before having to be out. Really not that long.

We thought of you on Thanksgiving Day and wondered where you were. I thought of calling you but didn't. Maybe *we can talk to you at Christmas time. We just don't know what to get for you this Christmas. Is there anything you would like especially? Don't know what to send the folks. Thought it would be nice to send them something together since we did not send them anything for their Golden Wedding Anniversary. We must take some time and go shopping. I did do some shopping at the Crystal factory when we were at Berchtesgaden. It is sometimes hard to make the money stretch. We got Aldene a crystal punch bowl. She has wanted one for a long time and has been saving her money for one—however, in the meantime she uses it for something else. Last week she bought ice skates. Grandpa Jorgenson had sent her $10.00 and she had some birthday money so she used that for her skates. Aldene went shopping on Friday as she had vacation from school. She got Gigi a new collar and leash for under the tree. She made a big deal out of it with Gigi when she got home and told her she couldn't see in the package. Gigi got all excited.*

Daddy is to leave for Warsaw, Poland, next week. That is if his visa comes through. I don't know why it wouldn't. I wish I could go with him. I think he is looking forward to going. It should be an interesting trip.

Suppose you will be working through the holiday season. Will you be able to put in some extra hours? Would be nice if you could earn a little extra for yourself.

Meant to mention if you are wondering about something for Aldene she really needs a white, dressy sweater. Also she could use a band for her watch. She has a leather one on it now. Just to give you an idea.

Daddy is ready to go and I see it is 1:15 already. Do write. With our love and prayers, Mother, Daddy and Aldene

Before folding the paper in thirds for inserting into the envelope, Eleanor turned the paper sideways and wrote with a pen in the left margin:

Richard - Do not spend a lot on me & Daddy for Christmas. There's no use making it difficult for yourself when we know you can't afford it. A nice long letter or a tape would be a big gift for us!

It was a few weeks later, on December 11, that Eleanor received a letter from her mother and set to typing reply.

Dearest Mother,

Your most <u>welcome letter</u> came just this morning. I have read it over twice. It is hard to keep from crying. It has been so long since we have heard from Richard. There have been times that I could hardly stand it and wanted to go to the phone and call. Melvin has been equally disturbed. No, we did not know that Richard had moved. Why he has been so neglectful in writing I do not know. We know he is busy with school, working, and flying lessons, and that he does not have much free time, but it can't be he is so busy he hasn't a moment to write. What did you mean that he is in no school activities this year. Isn't he even in the men's chorus? He was so much taken up with it last year. Will write him today and hope to get an answer. Will send the letter to the school.

Ever since Richard left us last summer both Mel and I have been so heavy. I do hope everything is all right. As far as the boys he is staying with, I guess they are nice boys. I only know Dave Nelson. He has always seemed to be a good kid as far as I know. We have always been so grateful that Richard has never caused us undo concern. He has always been so thoughtful and we have appreciated it so much. I suppose it is handier for him to be nearer the school—although I liked it when he was staying with you.

Melvin left for Warsaw, Poland on Saturday. The plane was late leaving here. It was supposed to leave at 1:40 and it didn't leave until six o'clock. I didn't wait with him as I was supposed to meet a Belgian lady at three downtown. I hated to have him get into Warsaw at night. He had a forty min layover in East Berlin. He can't call home as he is behind the curtain. He was to be at the dedication of a new church in Warsaw yesterday. He wasn't feeling too well when he left. He recently had the stomach flu, which has been going around. I hope he is OK and has a warm place to be in. Don't know how it is there. Will be happy when he gets back home. He was excited about going and looking forward to the experience. Of course, he always hates to leave home. I'm glad he is that way.

We have been having meetings at the Hilton Hotel and last night was our last service there. We are now looking for a permanent meeting place. There are so many complications. However, we must find something soon, as the school out at Andrimont has been sold. There are so many responsibilities here and problems. We are looking to the Lord to help us with them all. They are too big for us.

No, we did not know Lorraine had been to D.C. I never hear from either Lorraine or Lois. Wonder if Lois will soon be moving to her new home. I would almost think a part-time job as stenographer would be easier than getting out and selling, maybe not. Would be so nice to hear from her.

I don't think Melvin was really serious when he mentioned going home for Christmas. It was just wishful thinking. He has so wanted to be with Richard. I don't know if we will go home in June or July. Depends on things here. School isn't out until the middle of June. I don't know what we will do with our apartment—and our things. Will take care of that when we get to it I guess.

Will try to get your package for Christmas mailed off today. Hope you like it. It isn't exactly what I wanted but, what I wanted I couldn't get. It will be for both of you together.

Melvin wants a bathrobe, but the ones I like are so expensive. Will have to do some more looking. Aldene has a long list taped on her door with her name signed to it! A watchband isn't on the list. By the way her band is gold. She wants a bag for her skates. She just got new skates with her birthday money. She also wants a five-year diary with a key!

I must tell Lorraine if she sees any sale on shoes in my size. I have gone through the walking shoes I got while home. These streets are death on shoes. I like Aldene's so much—wouldn't mind some like hers. Or on that order. I know after the new year, Oricks usually has a sale on shoes.

Must get a letter off to Richard. I am trying to get out Christmas cards as well. But I wanted to write you first of all, Mother, I appreciate your letters so much. We want to talk to Rich at Christmas time. I suppose he will be at your place.

God bless you and keep you. I am so glad that you are feeling as well as you are, Mother. Surely, the Lord has been good and we do thank Him for His goodness.

Love and Prayers

Eleanor signed her name after pulling the letter out of the electric typewriter. Then she began on a letter to Richard.

* * * * *

To Eleanor's delight, she soon received a letter in the mail from Congo. Walking over to one of the upholstered chairs in the living room Eleanor sat down to read over the form letter from Lillian and Gail. It was the girl's second Christmas back in Paulis "following a whole year of blessings from the Father's hand."

Perusing over the news brought a flood of memories to Eleanor. How she ached to see everyone again.

Our reception last Christmas revealed the joy our very presence brought to all. The glow of that welcome lingers still. We have never felt so wanted in all our lives! We spent four months going from mission to mission in evangelistic trips and short-course Bible classes for two weeks in each area. What joy to minister!

A few paragraphs down, Eleanor read about donations coming in for peanuts, and rice for seed, as well as twenty bicycles for pastors "to speed the light." Now they would be able to "wheel" rather than walk to the many villages with the Good News. Wiping a tear from one eye, Eleanor continued to read.

A week ago we took our superintendent and two other pastors to a village about fifty miles from here on the way to Biodi. The young village chief had replaced his father, who was killed along with many of the tribes elders, has been asking for a pastor for a long time. Toma Ngbetima has been chosen by the Betongwe Church to go there. They had several services in the few days they were there and eighteen accepted the Lord as Savior. So they already have a good start for a Church.

Did you know we are in "Real Estate"? The "Gold and Diamond" kind for the kingdom of Heaven. Our Bible School opened September 20th. Twenty-five adults and nineteen children ,and "no room at the inn." We are purchasing lots adjoining the church property where housing will be provided.

The second page ended with the Cochrane's hunting for a house again in Paulis and upcoming birthdays for Gail and Elizabeth Cochrane and the new "luxury" store that just opened featuring high-price items like cereal, candy bars, cheese and sausage, etc.

Eleanor heard Aldene come into the apartment, "Mom, why are you crying?"

Aldene walked over to the chair Eleanor was sitting in, "What's wrong?"

"We got a letter from the girls today." Eleanor wiped her tears away. "It's just so good to hear from them and see what the Lord is doing there."

"Do you want to go back?"

"Sometimes, but I know the Lord has something for us here."

"You mean with the ladies Bible studies and the Bible School?"

"Yes, but the thing of it is, there's something about the French-speaking Belgians that keeps pulling at Daddy's heart and mine."

Eleanor reached for her daughter's arm, "While we pray and look to the Lord to provide for when the time is right, you, my dear, will be going to high school here when we return from furlough. So, no worries about moving."

At first when Aldene came to Brussels, she never thought she would call the city home. There were too many changes from life in the bush in Andudu. Different noises, smells, and food, assaulted her senses. The pace of life and so many white faces compared to black African faces made her feel like she was on another planet! But then, each passing day turned into a month, and then a year. A tiny seed sprouted and the first hair like strands of roots bravely emerged into this new soil called Brussels. Roots growing and anchored by familiarity with people and places, and tender memories to recall made this place home for Aldene. And now, she was looking forward to coming back and she hadn't even left for furlough yet!

* * * * *

It was during this time, that a book caught the attention of Melvin called *The Cross and the Switchblade*. Co-authored by Rev. David Wilkerson, and John and Elizabeth Sherill, the authors spent three years writing about Brother Wilkerson's riveting story of working with street gangs in New York City. After its release in 1963, *The Cross and the Switchblade*, swept across America like a prairie fire. In addition to this, Wilkerson founded the first Teen Challenge center in Brooklyn, New York in 1958 to provide a long-term treatment program for drug and alcohol addiction based on the principles of faith in Jesus Christ and the Bible. In 1967, Wilkerson began Youth Crusades with a focus on what he referred to as "goodniks," good kids bored with the good life tempted by the false glamour of drugs, drinking, and the sexual revolution of the 1960's.

After Melvin translated *The Cross and the Switchblade* into French, the office on Avenue du Derby became a hub of distribution for the book. The message crossed all denominational lines with Protestants and Catholics clamoring for a copy, with many of the books sent to France.

On March 6, 1968, Eleanor wrote to Richard about the book: *Must go over and fix lunch for Daddy. Have 10,000 more Cross and Switchblade books coming off the press—so now it means work to get them wrapped and mailed off.*

She also wrote in the same letter: *Have a prayer meeting with the ladies this afternoon. One of the ladies says the Lord has told her that she needs to have more power in her life. These ladies are really so different to work with. They come from all denominations.*

Although the spiritual ground had been hard plowing, the Lord was organizing a mighty work of the Holy Spirit intertwining separate pieces of the ministry in Belgium. Eventually, Brother Wilkerson and his team came to Europe for Youth Crusades including Brussels. Melvin and Eleanor rented a hall, called Salle Regina, for a youth meeting. It was old and musty, but it was in a good location in the heart of Brussels, close to the trams and train station.

Collaborating with as many groups as possible, Melvin invited the Methodist minister from the American Protestant Church to encourage the youth at his church to attend the meeting.

David Wilkerson gave a powerful message and asked those youth who wanted to make Jesus Christ the "Boss" of their life to come to the front to pray. As the young people went forward for prayer after the service, Melvin went to the back of the hall where the parents were gathered. Some of the parents were mildly concerned while others were plainly upset.

"Oh, they don't need that, poor so and so."

"Just to think those children, those little innocent children went down there."

Later, when Melvin told Wilkerson what the parents were saying the preaching evangelist replied, "Well, if they had heard what some of those young people said to me they wouldn't think they were so innocent."

The Methodist pastor invited David Wilkerson to his home for dinner. While eating the meal the pastor admitted, "If someone came up to me and asked me how to find the Lord I wouldn't know what to tell them."

Recognizing the divine appointment Brother Dave explained to the Methodist pastor how to find the Lord, and the pastor did!

In the midst of this, a man – who audited the bookkeeping for the book distribution so that the proper taxes were paid to the Belgian government – began telling Eleanor about his terminally ill wife, "The doctor told me she has cancer, but I can't bring myself to tell her even though she is a nurse."

"I see," Eleanor sensed she was to do more than lend a sympathetic ear, "Would it be alright if I go visit her?"

"Please do, Madame Jorgenson."

After several visits, the woman confessed to Eleanor, "You know I've always had it so good I never felt I ever needed God. I remember the prayer you said and I pray it every night."

Chapter Thirty-Seven

Furlough 1968-1969

O n March 9, 1968, Eleanor started another letter to her parents thanking them for the birthday card, the blouse and especially the letter. How she craved news from home! Making phone calls was so expensive; they just couldn't squeeze it into their budget.

Haven't heard from Richard for a while so it was nice to hear about him and what he has been doing in part. So nice of you to let him have his dinner party there. I have never been able to do things like that for him. Maybe next winter I will have a chance. That is something I have missed. Guess Aldene is making up for it—seems she always has something going on. Always some girls around. Today she went down town with a girlfriend. They did some shopping and had lunch downtown. She seems to think Saturday is her day off. The sun is shining today. I hope it stays that way.

Thursday I went down to the school with Melvin. We left around seven a.m. The ground was covered with snow—and the roads were a bit slippery. I very seldom get to go out to the school as Mel always leaves around six a.m. but this week it was later as there was another teacher from France there this week. He comes every so often. Too bad the school is so far out. It is a very nice building and we wish it were closer to Brussels.

Tonight we plan on going out to a home for a hymn sing. They will all be Americans. She said she was expecting around twenty. They are Baptists. Said she got lonesome for some good singing once in a while. It is interesting as there will be people from many different churches there. There doesn't seem to be that difference over here—which is good. Tomorrow night we go to another American home to show a Cathedral Film on the Life of Christ. Tomorrow afternoon a couple from Germany will be coming in for a few days. He is a Sgt. in the Air Force. A very nice couple. Two ladies from Holland are spending the weekend at Virginia's. They will be coming over for coffee tomorrow afternoon. So we never look for something to do.

Yesterday we cleaned the living room. I washed the curtains and did a bit of changing around. Claudia washed the wood-work and windows. So that is done. Only thing, the windows do not stay clean here very long with wind and rain.

After closing the letter Eleanor thought about how much had happened since she first met Bess Malloy. Not only did Bess continue to host Bible studies in her home for women she also invited Melvin and Eleanor to the VIP parties.

"Just mingle with people," Bess would say with an adventurous smile.

When people asked what company they worked for, the Jorgenson's would tell them what they were in Brussels for and their experience coming out of Congo. Keenly aware of the unrest following independence, the guests listened intently. Eventually, this led to Melvin working with the men and showing a Biblical film series to mixed groups.

When Aldene would come home from school, she never knew whom she would find at her house. Some of the women came for prayer for children addicted to drugs, or husbands that traveled a lot and were not faithful to their wives. Recognizing the significance of God working through Eleanor, one artistic woman, Dottie, whose husband worked for a petroleum company, painted the classic picture of praying hands as a gift for Eleanor.

* * * * *

As the time drew near for furlough, Melvin arranged to temporarily move the Bible School during his absence to Rue Joseph Claes. At the suggestion of Charles Greenaway, it seemed best to start fresh at a new location convenient to transportation in Brussels. Meanwhile, the decision was made to keep their apartment and try finding someone to stay there for at least part of the time they were gone. Now, what to be done about Gigi.

"Aldene we have no money in the budget to ship that dog to America." Eleanor informed her daughter, "I told you and Richard to buy a small dog so we wouldn't have this problem."

"What if we breed her and she has pups?" Aldene laid out her strategy to save Gigi, "We can sell the pups and she will earn her own way."

* * * * *

In July, Eleanor typed a short letter to her son:

Dear Richard,

Just a quick note before Virginia leaves for the post office. We have been so busy and have had so many irons in the fire we hardly know which way to turn. We have been working on MISSION NEWS and hope to get that out in the mail tomorrow. Besides trying to type stencils, entertaining, keeping appointments etc. I haven't had much free time! I wrote you that I couldn't leave Daddy the 15th. Now I'm almost wondering how I can leave next week the 25th. Anyway, I have made reservations for the 25th. Will spend the weekend with the Duricks and come to Mpls the Monday after. I think the plane gets in at 6:45. Will check for sure and let you know. It will be nice for Aldene to see the Duricks and see D.C. a bit as well.

I really hate having to leave Daddy. It really takes away the joy and excitement of going home. By that, I know you know what I mean. Poor Daddy is counting the days now. He keeps talking about the freezer full of TV dinners! I tell him he will be so busy he won't miss us! Greenaway comes the first to the fifth of Aug. Youth camps start, although I guess he doesn't plan to be there too much of the time. Zimmerman comes in Sept. and he is to take him around a bit I guess.

We received your letter last Saturday. Were we ever glad to hear from you! Daddy was pleased that you are taking night school and will have that over. When that is finished it shouldn't take too much longer!

Here is Daddy with the page he had done on offset. Gunter did it for him. I see it is time to get supper as well.

Of course, we are really anxious and excited about seeing you. I can't get Aldene to settle down too much these days. Tell Mother not to wear herself out getting ready for us—I could not care less about the house—I just want her well when we get there!

Much love to you all.
Mother, Daddy and Aldene

* * * * *

Arriving in Minneapolis in July 1968, Eleanor landed in what seemed the strangest time warp she could remember of any furlough back to the States. The last five years of their lives were so consumed with living, and escaping, and moving, and readjusting, that the headlines of racial riots and the conflict in Vietnam seemed distant. They were used to catching up for lost time with family and friends. However, rather than subtle changes in the American culture during Eisenhower's administration, it seemed during the Johnson administration that the norms of society fell off a cliff! Fashions just beginning to trend in 1963 of miniskirts, and longhaired hippies, were in full swing with mod geometric looks mixed in with velvet and ruffles echoing the early 19th-century; or simple peasant dresses for women, and blue jeans with shirts-optional for men. Classic designers and conservative tones of beige and black were replaced with flamboyant psychedelic patterns screaming out colors. Although many of these fashions came from Europe, it seemed odd to see them manifested in America.

And music followed with its own expression of the times. Rock and roll took on a harder edge with acid rock stars Jimi Hendrix and Janis Joplin, and bands such as the Doors and Jefferson Starship. Also emerging were the messengers of folk music, singing ballads questioning the establishment. The Beatles traded in their clean-cut look, and songs of "I Want to Hold your Hand," for mod fashions and drug-in-spired songs of "Lucy in the Sky with Diamonds," taking their fans along for the ride through the last half of the turbulent 1960s.

President Johnson pushed ahead leading the country in civil rights, and sending American troops into a war that wasn't technically a war until it was legislated into one. After that, troops escalated despite anti-war protests raging across the United States, causing people to forget Johnson's efforts of his "Great Society" with social programs including Medicare. The country was also in mourning over the assassinations of Martin Luther King, Jr. in April and Robert F. Kennedy in June.

However, one thing remained familiar to Melvin and Eleanor—their miracle house on the corner of 106th and Russell in Bloomington. The grey-blue shake-sided rambler with the white-shuttered windows stood solid and welcoming. Richard pulled up in front of the three-bedroom house with his 1968 VW "Bug" that Eva Larson helped him purchase. Living with his folks would mean an extra car for Eleanor when Melvin was on the road. Once they finished cleaning up after their previous tenants, they unpacked their belongings from Brussels, and picked up Gigi at the airport. Ahead of Melvin and Eleanor was a yearlong schedule of visiting family, friends, and churches.

Aldene started eighth grade and immediately felt out of place. Tightly formed cliques of girls barricaded her from fitting in. When Aldene did join in conversation at lunch, her casual remarks about Paris and other European cities were misconstrued as uppity. She soon had a reputation for being a snoot. Lonely for her international classmates, Aldene also realized ISB was a year ahead of her public school in Minnesota. Then there were the regular "discussions" with the French language teacher.

Back at home, her parents would try to console her, "Well, Aldene, you have so many more experiences than they do and it probably intimidates them," Melvin said over a fried chicken dinner with mashed potatoes and gravy.

"I don't understand. It's not like I'm trying to brag." Aldene spooned up another bite of potatoes. "And that French teacher makes it impossible for me to get good grades!"

"What do you mean?" Eleanor's eyebrows lifted at the information.

Despite attending an English-speaking school, Aldene's immersion into the French culture from shopping and traveling enabled her to speak and write French fluently.

"My American teacher went to Paris to learn French," Aldene began to lay out her case, "so for example, in Belgium French the number for 95 is *nonante cinq*."

Her parents nodded their heads in agreement and their daughter continued, "In France it is *quatre vingt quinze* meaning—four times two, plus fifteen."

"Did you explain your background?" Melvin asked the logical question.

"Yes, I told her, 'I've just lived in Brussels and there they say *nonante cinq*,'" Aldene shrugged her shoulders.

"Then she says, 'No, that is incorrect.' The next day it is something else. She said she won't pass me on the class."

Melvin chuckled, "Your teacher maybe thought 'smarty.'"

"She probably does think I'm a smarty-pants," Aldene joined in the laugh.

Later that evening, Melvin and Eleanor decided he should go to the school to explain the situation. After that, Aldene's future of passing 8th-grade French looked promising. Meanwhile, Eleanor went to her knees talking to the Lord about Aldene's social life in America. Eventually, one girl befriended her at school, as did one girl at their church. Although Aldene was grateful for these friendships, she longed for her true home: Brussels.

* * * * *

In May of 1969, Melvin and Eleanor watched Richard received his college diploma from North Central Bible College. The previous year, Richard earned his private pilot license and now pursued his goal of earning his commercial pilot's license with the intention of being a missionary pilot.

"Just think," Melvin leaned over to whisper in his wife's ear, "it was thirty years ago for us."

Eleanor returned a thought, "and Richard worked part-time at the Sears Catalog Order desk like you did."

At one point, their son worked as a janitor at First National Bank, in downtown Minneapolis, with the glowing temperature ball atop the building. He had also worked and lived at Enger Funeral Home until moving into the house on Russell Avenue.

"Yes, the 'Earn while you Learn' is still the norm for a lot of students." Melvin thought back to his days in the office, in the newly purchased building on 910 Elliot Avenue in Minneapolis, and how many buildings North Central had added since then.

* * * * *

After Richard Nixon was inaugurated as President in January 1969, the country torn-apart on other issues, came together with pride for the July 20th landing on the moon. As if a wish for America, the Sea of Tranquility was chosen for the Apollo 11 mission. On a hot summer night in Bloomington, Melvin and Eleanor sat hushed, in front of the TV, with Richard and Aldene. Neil Armstrong stepped down the ladder of the Eagle lunar modular in his white space suite. His voice crackled from the moon to earth, "That's one small step for man, one giant leap for mankind."

* * * * *

That fall, Richard opened the envelope from his father, postmarked from North Dakota, and began reading the one-page typed letter:

Dear Richard,

I thought I should write you, and give you my schedule in North Dakota, so you can contact me when you may wish. It is so easy to locate the pastor of the A. of God church that I won't give their names.

I hope to drive to Mpls on the 20th from Mott for my service on the 21st, evening, at the Tabernacle. I am supposed to be at Little Falls for the morning service on the 21st, but as the pastor has resigned and they are trying out new applicants, it seems unsure that I will be there. If I am to go there anyway, I would drive direct to Little Falls from Mott and then to Mpls on that Sunday afternoon.

We had a good service last night, but the returns were slim. You will have to pray with me that I will be able to get what finances are necessary—and in time to go ahead with our plans to leave for Europe. The Lord has the money some place for us.

I have to say again how sorry I am that I had to leave all that work with you to finish up at the house. But the phone call last evening relieved me somewhat to know that you got along so well. I think you did a much faster job organizing the garage than I could have done, and getting rid of that trash. I don't know what is best for the goods I still have to mail by post. If you could get several big cardboard boxes to put the things into and take them over to the folk's garage (if they don't mind and if there is room), maybe that is the best.

But whatever you do from here on in, be sure to put the necessary hours into your flying and the study of the books.

That is the most important and most pressing for you now. When I get back, I will get someone to repair the gutters on the house. Thank everyone there, especially Gram, for all the work done on the house in cleaning it up. God bless you good and be with you. The Health Certificate for Gigi should be stamped. Please send me the office and address where I can mail it, to have it stamped. This should make it official for Belgium.

LOVE, Daddy

Chapter Thirty-Eight

Continental

Walking into their apartment in Brussels, Eleanor was pleasantly surprised. In contrast to coming back to Congo from furlough, everything was just as she had left it. Their barrels and trunk were due in Antwerp on Friday, September 26, 1969. Next week would be busy unpacking everything without Melvin there to help. A sudden pang of loneliness filled her. She had left without her husband, and now she had returned without him. A smile crossed her face at the memory of those last few days before she flew back to Belgium with Aldene. As Eleanor put it in a letter to her mother: *The whole thing was we just kept on living too long in the sense of keeping house and engagements.*

Consequently, they got at the packing way too late. She kept surprising Melvin by coming out to the garage with more things for the barrels. His running comment was, "Where did that come from?"

Then there was Gigi. She did end up paying for her way with a brood of nine pups, but with all the paperwork, her flight back to Belgium was not until October. Eleanor hoped the dog hadn't eaten the mailman at her parent's house. Somehow, her folks always ended up with parrots—or a poodle.

As Eleanor made her way back to the office on Avenue du Derby, she wished again for the hundredth time that her dad and mother would make the trip across the Atlantic to visit her. Maybe if she wrote to them about the round-trip flights on Sabena during the winter that could be found at three hundred dollars. Although she felt closer to her folks than when they lived in Congo, it still was hard to be separated for such long periods of time. Eleanor wanted them to see what their life looked like in Europe—the people they worked with, the apartment, and office.

Already working in the office, Virginia Sasscer greeted Eleanor in her blended accent of Eastern Seaboard and southern drawl. From time to time, Aldene stayed with Aunt Ginny if her folks traveled while she was in school. Aldene and Donna Sundell, fellow ISB classmate and missionary kid, couldn't resist teaming up to take advantage of her sweet disposition.

Eventually Aunt Ginny would put her foot down, "Aldene!" she'd quip, "you behave yourself now, ya' hear?"

After going over orders and shipments of books and literature, Eleanor turned to other matters that Melvin usually took care of, while muttering to herself, "I don't like making these decisions by myself!"

Looking at her watch, Eleanor realized she better go shopping for the next gathering with the ladies from the Bible study at her home. Although she didn't have much of a kitchen to work with, she enjoyed making the table look special with cheese fondue, bread from the bakery, assorted chocolates, and of course tapered candles—her signature trademark at meals, even in the Congo. She could already hear Aldene moan about the dishes. Usually, Melvin helped

Aldene with this chore when she had a ladies engagement at their apartment.

Pushing another pang of loneliness away, Eleanor made her way down the sidewalk past waffle vendors and stands selling frites in a paper cone swathed in ketchup. It was a meal in itself with the hearty-sized potato fries deep-fried once, cooled and deep-fried a second time. She still had a lot to do, but Claudia would come to help clean the wood floors tomorrow. Although they couldn't afford to send out for food or laundry, at least they could hire a part-time housekeeper for ironing and other chores to free up more time for other things.

After coming back from furlough, Eleanor thought the English Bible studies would end once the ladies moved back to their home countries after living in Brussels for several years. However, that was not the case. As the women returned, they told the ladies coming over about the study group, and the group continued.

* * * * *

A few weeks later Gigi arrived.

"What happened to her?" Aldene was appalled at the sight of her dog.

"Maybe she had fleas and Richard had to cut her fur down like that," Eleanor offered.

"But she was looking so nice before we left," Aldene fumed, "now she looks naked!"

"Oh, Aldene," Eleanor countered, "it won't be long and she will have her full coat back."

"I hope so with winter coming."

After a long walk in the park, mother and daughter brought travel-worn Gigi back to the apartment.

"Here you go Gigi," Aldene handed the poodle a favorite pink baby toy and Gigi seemed happy to have it.

That night Aldene slept in her bed, and Gigi in the other twin bed. As the ninth-grader closed her eyes, she sighed with contentment knowing her roommate was back in Brussels where they both belonged. Not only that, she was joining the equestrian club with her friends who understood what living abroad was all about.

* * * * *

Finally, it was Melvin's turn to cross the Atlantic by plane. Once back in Brussels, Melvin would have a lot of loose ends to tie up from his furlough. But for now, he only had one thought on his mind. When Melvin walked from the plane into the arms of his wife and his daughter, wet tears filled his eyes. It was the longest separation they had ever known.

"I felt like you were at boarding school." Eleanor couldn't seem to let go of her husband as they collected his luggage and drove to their apartment. She made his favorite meal and lit tapered candles perfectly arranged on the table.

"Best meal I've had in a long time," Melvin beamed at his wife through his newly acquired black horn-rimmed glasses, "You look good, you cook good. I think I'll keep you my little groat."

Aldene laughed at her father's obvious affection for her mother. No matter how many times she heard the story of her parents meeting in college it still made her feel the inspiration of their romantic adventure of following God together.

That night, snuggling in bed together, the married couple both agreed they never wanted to be apart like that again. Their eyes and hearts met. Melvin turned off the lamp on the side table next to the bed before kissing his bride as long as any kiss he could ever remember.

* * * * *

In the middle of November, Melvin met with the faculty at the newly acquired school building on 1, Avenue des Erables in the Rhode-Saint-Genese district ten kilometers south of Brussels. The district lay west of the town of Waterloo where in 1815, England and Prussia defeated Napoleon, with Belgians fighting on both sides.

Rather than taking the congested highway running along the western border of Forest de Soignes, Melvin enjoyed driving his tan 1969 Opel Commodore automatic through the forty-four squared kilometer forest of former hunting grounds for dukes. Echoes from medieval times left only a few monasteries holding secrets of the past within their fourteenth to eighteenth century walls. Squirrels and birds flitted from beech trees that turned amber before their leaves fell on pathways for walking, cycling, and riding horses. At one time oaks were prominent throughout the forest until Napoleon gave the orders to harvest them for his fleet.

* * * * *

Meanwhile, Eleanor made plans to have the faculty and students over to their apartment Friday night. Finishing another letter to her mother, she included a paragraph about the upcoming dinner:

I am going this afternoon with the young fellow from Egypt (a doctor) who is here in school this year. He is going to fix us an Egyptian meal this Friday and I'm going to take him to a

Spanish store today to see if we can get some Okra. I don't even know what it is, but I guess people who live in the south do. These dinners create a little interest and give the pupils a chance to see how others live and eat. We will be doing this with the people from the different countries throughout the year. We have an interesting bunch of kids.

That Friday night, at the ethnic dinner party, excitement filled the Jorgenson's apartment as teachers, and the twelve students from six different countries, chatted about the new building, a three-story white chateau southeast of Brussels. It was a classic rectangular box with five dormer windows jutting out of the dark roof. The second-floor bedroom windows were dressed with shutters as well as the door of the penthouse to its small wrought iron balcony. The cozy eight hundred square foot apartment was situated on the far left end, if viewed from the hectare of open land, a generous two acres of grass. The main floor had seven floor-to-ceiling windows graced with shutters, letting in light through diamond panes of glass to spacious rooms for dining, classrooms, and a former ballroom used for an auditorium. Opposite the penthouse was an attached one-story structure that swung out diagonally toward the house with several white pillars, which served as an enclosed grill and patio. The back of the chateau sat close to Avenue des Erables with a white picket fence that ran from the entrance and exit of the cobblestone pass-through drive. Numerous cars parked on either side of the cobblestone street. Nestled between the attached two-door garage and one-story room, stood a portico supported by twin white pillars sheltering the main entrance.

"Why did you change the name to Continental Bible College?" one of the male students at the dinner party asked Melvin.

"Well, with the new location in Brussels I thought about what an international city it is, where all the crossroads of the continent of Europe have converged on many levels throughout history. In light of this, I felt the Bible School should reflect the broad spectrum of attracting students from all over the world, and also sending them out as globally-minded servants for the kingdom of heaven."

Then the director of the school added with a chuckle, "Besides all that, I just like the sound of the word Continental."

One of the female students, Jeri Sue Hirmer, an American from California, was talking with Eleanor, "Is it true that you will be living at the college?"

"Yes," Eleanor replied. "We will keep this apartment, but we saw the need for interaction with the students on a daily basis for a while."

"Where will you live?" asked a wife of one of the students from Iran. As a mother of two young children, she welcomed the company of a seasoned wife and mother at the school.

"On the second floor, in the small penthouse. It's the original master suite when the chateau was privately owned." Then Eleanor added, "And our son, Richard, will be coming through the MAPS program to help with the Bible School. He will be living in one of the rooms with the dormer windows, formerly used for the servants."

"What is the MAPS program?" another student asked.

"Missionary and Placement Service. It's a program for short-term missions through the AG church, to assist missionaries around the world, and give people an opportunity to serve without making a permanent career change." Eleanor explained, while sampling the dish made with okra, thinking it wasn't bad with the right spices. "After Brussels he may, Lord willing, go to Congo to work in the same area we did."Eleanor noticed Sobhi Malek walking by, "Thank you for cooking this delicious meal, Sobhi!"

Aldene kept Gigi in her bedroom for the night, visiting her between mixing in with the students.

"Just think, Gigi, at the college you will have a big yard to run and play in."

Gigi wiggled and pulled back her lips into a doggy smile. However, the charcoal standard poodle could be intimidating to people not used to owning large dogs. She also had a jealousy issue with wiener dogs. It all started when as a family they took Gigi out for a walk one day, and paid too much attention to the neighbor lady's dachshund. After that, Gigi went crazy with envy whenever she saw the little brown dog. One time Melvin left the apartment with the poodle for a walk. When the doors of the elevator opened there stood the neighbor lady with her dachshund on a leash.

Gigi pounced at the opportunity to attack her nemesis. "Wroof!"

Her dangling leash snapped taut, pulling Melvin off his feet to the floor. Thud. His glasses slid down his nose. His flat ascot cap tilted over his eyes.

"Bonjour, Madame," was all the director of Continental Bible College could think to say, as the woman desperately clutched her precious pet into her arms away from the black invader. Melvin gathered himself, arranging his glasses and hat and strode out of the building with Gigi.

* * * * *

Before Melvin, Eleanor, Aldene, and Gigi merged into school life, they settled into the small but comfortable penthouse. It consisted of two bedrooms, one generous bathroom, with a living room and pocket-sized kitchen.

"If we could just live in the bathroom!" exclaimed Eleanor, "It is one of the prettiest ones I have seen—so unusual for Brussels."

"We're just like the Belgian king," remarked Melvin, "having a city home and a country home!"

Each day for the students started with prayer in the chapel at 6:30 a.m., with the morning sun streaming through the diamond-paned windows illuminating the wooden-beamed room with rounded doors. Then, after breakfast, eight male and four female students sat in classes along with Pastor David's wife, Janet. She would squeeze in a class when she could, with two young children to care for. Her husband had temporarily left his church in Iran to enrich his ministry. Originally a two-year program at Andrimont, the curriculum expanded to a four-year program under Melvin's direction. Basic Division ran for two years, with two sixteen-week semesters per school year, taught in French and English. The Advanced Division, taught only in English, consisted of eight four-week terms, with two classes per term. Implementing this method, the school benefited from the services of many qualified teachers who were limited to spending only one month at the college.

Melvin appreciated working with the faculty in developing the Basic and Advanced Divisions, and deciding how to split up the responsibilities of running Continental Bible College, or CBC. John Garlock was Dean; Fred Cottriel, Business Director; Paul Sundell, Director of Spiritual Life; and Alfred Amitie, Public Relations Director.

In addition to his duties as director and teacher, Melvin also led chapel services three times a week. Providing the students opportunities to train for their life in the ministry, he soon had Victor, a Belgian, playing the accordion and Jeri Sue, playing the piano.

"Why don't you say a few words before you play today," Melvin encouraged Jeri Sue.

Before taking her place at the piano, she softly spoke from behind the wooden pulpit. Her brunette bangs and bouffant hair, ratted and combed smooth over the crown, were separated by a silk headband tied at the nape of her closely cropped hair.

"I thank God for having brought me here to study the Bible. In order to inspire others as newborn babes in the family of God, to desire the sincere milk of the word, we have to know by personal experience how to use the word as spiritual food. I want to continue to search the depths of the Words of Truth this coming year at CBC."

After a time of worship, Melvin asked several of the students to share.

Sobhi Malek quickly volunteered. In an animated voice, with upraised hands and a contagious smile he burst with enthusiasm,

'You are crazy! You'd better think about that before going any further.' That was the reaction of some of my friends when I told them I was going to leave my prosperous pharmacy to follow God's call in full-time service. Along the way, Satan came to me in that same manner. But every time, I experienced the Lord's victory and blessings. God is good and I can see the harvest waiting to be reaped by faithful workers who have left all for His sake."

"One more volunteer for today?" Melvin coaxed, "I know this can be intimidating; I had my times of nervousness as a student at North Central."

Lili raised her hand and Melvin welcomed her to the podium. In broken French she began, "After having worked for ten years as an evangelist in Finland, God called me to serve Him in Belgium. I am attending Bible School to study the word of God in French language. Even though French is difficult for me, the Spirit of God helps me to learn and understand. I am far from Finland, but nearer to God because I obeyed His call. Glory to His Holy Name!"

During the noontime meal, prepared by Mrs. Amitie, Eleanor sat by several students asking them what brought them to CBC.

Bernard from France spoke with conviction, "Having felt the call of the Lord on my life, and with the help of my pastor, I realized that, in spite of a knowledge of the Bible and God, I needed further Bible training. I am very glad that I have come to Continental where I have found students and teachers with a single aim: To serve the Master effectively."

Bridgette, also from France, said, "God led me to Bible school in a very special way. The Holy Spirit strengthened me and encouraged me to dedicate my life to Him. I am very happy here and not at all homesick although far removed from my relatives, because here I have found a wonderful family, united in the love of our Lord."

Guy Guilbert offered, "I am happy to be here at Continental because of the friendly atmosphere and the possibility to have work here for the Lord. I believe the opportunity to give oneself to study is a good thing that comes from God, on condition that we remain humble. Knowledge of the Word of God is necessary for a spiritual life and in the service of God."

After the students filtered out of the dining room, Eleanor found herself engaged in conversation with Jeri Sue, who was on work duty after the meal.

"I find the many ethnic backgrounds, and different languages intriguing," she told Eleanor, "And at the same time, I'm finding it hard to work on using my French when everyone else wants to practice English with me."

Eleanor nodded her head in sympathy, "But it's so rewarding when a person can finally make sense of it and converse with people of another culture."

Then she added, "I enjoy all the different nationalities so much, but the thing of it is, some of them are going to fall in love with each other. And my concern is the challenge it can be for mixed marriages, because it's very hard to mix cultures and get along."

"That's an interesting observation, Mrs. Jorgenson." Jeri Sue diverted her eyes to the table she was washing down, and Eleanor bid her good-bye as she left the dining hall.

* * * * *

Going out to local churches in Belgium on Sundays was also part of the training experience for music and preaching.

At one church in Brussels, Victor stood with his hands on either side of his squeezebox while speaking in French, "It is at a place such as Continental Bible College where God's servants can receive spiritual guidance and intellectual preparation for God's work. Do you have a call to the Lord's work? Do you need further training? Then ask God if it is not His will for you to attend Bible School."

Pressing his hands together and pulling them apart, music sprang to life from the accordion, filling the church.

* * * * *

Often Aldene would sit on the back steps with some of the students and talk. She also was able to ride with them in the vans to go to church functions or activities, listening to their conversations as the van bumped along cobblestone roads throughout Brussels.

"Didn't you attend out at Andrimont?" she asked Roland.

"Yes, that's right," he broke into a smile. "When I think of how God has led me so far, I can only thank Him for His faithfulness. I hope others can have this same experience to better understand the depths of God's word and to have a fruitful ministry."

Picking up on the theme of reading the Bible, Nicole commented, "Whoever keeps God's word in his or her heart, possesses the most precious treasure. I have learned two important needs here: To know the word of God and to live in close communion with Him. I believe that in practicing this we can effectively spread the word of God for the winning of many souls."

Then she added with passion lit in her eyes and voice, "My motto is: To know Him better is to serve Him better."

* * * * *

Finding her place at Continental, Eleanor tutored students in English and helped to develop the missions program. She also planned dinners at the college for different functions, recruiting her reluctant daughter to set tables and help in the kitchen. Aldene would try to get out as quickly as she could to make more time for her friends, placing plates, napkins, flatware, and cups around the tables like a racecar driver.

Beyond the annoying occasional chore, it felt impressive for Aldene to ride up to the white pillars under the portico with her friends imagining the chateau was her entire home. One of her friends, Nicki, whose Italian father was head of Fiat had a chauffeur who drove Nicki to school, often stopping at Continental to pick up Aldene along the way. Other times, Aldene might ride with her Belgian friend, Martine, whose father held a high position with Schlitz Beer.

Aldene also learned from Martine that during World War II her father headed up the French underground. Rounding out her social life, after school, Aldene met up with Jennifer and Reagan for riding club, changing into her English riding outfit before riding the trails in Forest de Soignes. Now she could call herself a true "equestrienne."

* * * * *

That winter, Richard arrived in Brussels and immediately set to work at painting, cleaning the parquet floors, and organizing the office on Avenue du Derby. In between all of this activity, he fired off letters in January and February to Gram and Grandpa Groat:

You remember I told you of an American boy who was on dope? He was sent to Teen Challenge in New York some weeks ago now. I talked to his mother yesterday in church and she has some good news. He is much improving and seems to be coming out of it quite well. His aunt, who is not a Christian, has been visiting him and has marveled at his recovery. This has been a testimony to her and her letters are full of questions now on the Lord. The mother is a spirit-filled woman and received it in our living room.

Bob Watters will be here for one week of meetings and now the pastors are all over at the Bible School working on advertisement and so on. Mom was preparing coffee for the lot, about fifty in all. They have rented a large hall downtown. It holds four thousand I think. Should have good results.

Went to Paris about a month ago and got some flying in, through a friend, but other than that I've not been too happy about that. I'm here for a reason even if it is just to learn

French better. It is a more complicated language than most think; you can even ask a real Frenchman on that one.

Gigi is fine and keeps everyone at the school on their heels. She doesn't want to be locked up anyplace, so she just has the run of things as per usual.

After settling in at Continental, Richard joined students Bridgette and Bernard, in working on a yearbook for the college. One of the editorial staff's ideas was to include a short paragraph from each of the twelve students next to their picture. Daniel, on his way to work duty outside, handed Richard the poem he composed for the yearbook:

YES. . .How quickly time passes, And. . .what wonderful moments, Times of rich blessings, Times of real training, Times of profitable and enticing studies. YES! The moments spent at CBC are well worthwhile!

* * * * *

In the beginning of April, Richard got another letter off to Gram and Grandpa Groat, thanking them for sending an electric blanket and telling of his all-expense-paid, weeklong skiing trip during Easter vacation. A friend of Eleanor's wanted a companion to travel with her eighteen year-old to Switzerland for a holiday.

The folks went to London for the Holidays and also had a very good time. They needed the rest. They also did a bit of clothes shopping, as things are much cheaper there. Aldene got a rose Midi coat, a long scarf, and a broad-brimmed hat. It is a sharp outfit and looks very mod. She knows exactly what she wants, you know. Dad got a raincoat, a sport coat, and two hats. Mom got a cashmere sweater, and a dress, so their trip was well worth the while.

He then ended by scribbling about the main events in town:

Bob Watters comes sometime this month for a series of meetings, so all are busy with advertisements etc. The Billy Graham Crusade is on at the moment all over Europe. It is on closed circuit TV, and flashed on large theater screens all over Europe, seems to have good results for Belgium, with crowds up to three thousand.

* * * * *

That same month, Eleanor hastily sat down to write her parents.

April 22, 1970

Dear Mother and Dad,

You have been on my mind so much lately. It has been so long since we have heard from you. Rich says it has been a month and he keeps saying "we should call them." You know him. I told Rich that I reconciled myself by thinking that spring has finally come to Minnesota and that you are both busy in the yard, and too tired to write.

We haven't had much spring here. It has been rainy and cold thus far. We have had a couple of nice days—but that is all. We keep so busy between the office and the school. We are swamped with work. Rich has been so much help to us. Don't know how we could have managed without him. He does so many things for Mel—such as in the offices—waiting in lines, etc., things that have to be done, but take so much time. Now he has been going to the print shops for advertising etc. for the Watters meeting, the school, and now the youth camp.

Bob Watters comes in tomorrow. We have rented a concert grand Steinway for him and a large Hammond Organ. We do not have anyone to play the organ for the song service. I suggested that they send you the money to come here, Mother, and you could play. Richard will be playing for the song services. He has the songs that are on the song sheet so he has to work with them. He says he won't play, unless he can play them without the music! This afternoon he is out with the students handing out bills for the Watters meetings.

Aldene is over at the apartment having her piano lesson. She always comes here to the office from school.

Bob Watters just called from Holland and said that he was on his way here so I have to get busy and get some things started. Never a dull moment. Will write you again soon. I do hope everything is ok at home.

Tomorrow we are having a day of fasting and prayer for the Watters campaign.

Do write, if only a note. You are always in our thoughts and prayers.

Much love to you all,
Eleanor & family

Toward the end of the school year, Richard handed his father a copy of the marbled-sage-covered 1970 yearbook, "Here, Dad, fresh off the assembly line."

It was only twenty-six pages of glossy paper between cardstock, bound by two staples. But captured on those pages of black and white photos, hand drawings, and typewriter font in French and English, was a story of changed lives impacting the world around them through the power of God.

Melvin turned past the photo of the chateau overlooking the open field of grass, to the dedication page with a five by seven inch photo of Charles E. Greenaway wearing horn-rimmed glasses and a business suit. Below the picture Melvin read:

This first issue of THE CONTINENTAL is affectionately dedicated to the one man who has done the most in bringing the college into existence. It was largely due to his vision and foresight of what such a school could do for the countries under his supervisor that brought about the opening of the college in October 1969. The newly acquired property in Brussels was a means of changing his dreams into reality.

His wife, Mary, has worked together with him all along the way. It was she to who God gave a vision of what the future property would be like. With her inspiration and prayerful encouragement his load was made lighter and easier to bear.

Looking over the pages of the student's photos and their brief personal thoughts about their time at CBC, Melvin read aloud the comments of Stephen from Ukraine:

"I thank the Lord for leading me to this School that I might study His Word. It is a source of life and a power of God. Even though I am far from home, my Savior strengthens me. Glory to His Name!"

After that were photos of the faculty's wives thanking them for *"teaching, menu-planning, cooking to satisfy hungry students, and many hidden tasks."* Opposite the Curriculum page, listing twenty-four courses in the Advanced Division, there were two photos of several students working on the inaugural issue of the *Continental* including Richard bent over a desk and paper. Melvin noticed a picture of himself with the caption: *"Faculty adviser gave valued help."*

On the last page, editors Bridget and Bernard had composed sentiments of the school year, typed in French and English:

A Final Thought. . .Meditation and personal prayer maintain the spiritual life of the school.

The training offered by CBC is one of the intellectual as well as of spiritual value for young people or whoever wishes to serve God.

Aside from scholastic studies, weekend visits to churches in Belgium and sometimes in other countries, give the students practical experience in speaking, testimony and song. The organization of evangelistic campaigns, distribution of tracts, house-to-house calls, and other activities brings joy to us in doing and reaping for our Divine Master.

We had the pleasure of participating in two recent crusades: Bob Watters of the American Assemblies of God and Billy Graham's EURO 70.

CBC has about one aim: to mold young men and women who are entirely dedicated to God's Work. May God continue to pour out His Spirit abundantly and keep His hand on this work. Au Revoir. . . à l anée prochaine! Goodbye. . . 'til next year!

Chapter Thirty-Nine

The Active Missionary Wife

❧

After the school year at Continental ended, Richard made plans to fill in for Lillian Hogan during her furlough. Before leaving for Congo, Richard played the piano during the wedding ceremony of Sobhi Malek and Jeri Sue Hirmer. The couple planned on a second wedding in Egypt. They also joined the faculty for the 1970–71 school year with Sobhi teaching Old Testament, Doctrine, and Hebrew in the English section, and Jeri Sue teaching English and Christian Education in the French section. In addition to their teaching duties, the Maleks also served as resident staff members at the college.

That year enrollment increased with six students in the Advanced Division and eighteen students in the Basic Division. To accommodate this influx, a single men's residence was rented requiring buses to shuttle the boys in the mornings and evenings.

With students from fourteen countries, speaking twenty-five languages, their discussions were always interesting, "So you are Arabic?"

Guy and Alida Hamelle, both Belgian, listened intently as Sobhi spoke in French and then translated into English for other students.

"No, no, no. I am Egyptian, but I speak Arabic."

"What's the difference?"

Sobhi smiled and gave a sigh that translated: "here we go again."

Pierre Appokya from Congo spoke in French, "Monsieur Malek, do you come from a long line of pharaohs?"

The group broke into laughter as Sobhi replied with a grin, "Yes, something like that."

"Mbote ndeko," Aldene was passing by and couldn't resist speaking Lingala to Pierre, "Sango nini?"

"Sene mingi, many greetings little sister," his white smile lit up his brown face with joy.

That year the faculty, staff, and scope of activities increased as well. The CBC choir, directed by Frits Scheffer, rehearsed songs in both English and French in preparation for touring and recording a long play record. In addition to the large events of open-air evangelism on the Belgian coast of Oostende, along the North Sea, and the Harold Herman campaign in Paris, some of the students organized an evangelistic campaign in and around Brussels where a hundred Arabic-speaking people heard the witness of Arabic-speaking students. Literature distribution was effectively used to invite people to a Brussels church for the campaign for Arabic people. After each meeting, refreshments were served while students counseled newcomers, with several accepting Christ this way.

A highlight of the school year was the visit of Charles Greenaway, who took time to speak with the students personally as well as publicly.

"The key to the heart of Europe is college-trained preachers bearing the message of Pentecostal faith and experience. We, as a Board of Regents, and faculty, are interested in theological training, but more than that, we are interested in the training of men and women, who will be leaders, who can administrate, coordinate the work of God, inspire others, and who can bring revival into fruition so that this revival will continue."

Charles also asked Eleanor to write a paper, "The role of a missionary wife is crucial to the work of God. Yet, there are no books or information for this practical aspect of ministry. As faculty advisor to the missions program could you glean from your experiences to pass on to other women?"

The request gave Eleanor pause to reflect as the wife of a missionary since they first crossed the Atlantic in 1950 with the final words left them at the harbor in New York City, "Well, I guess you are on your own now."

Finding a few hours to start on the essay, Eleanor sat before her typewriter secluded in their apartment on Avenue d'Italie across from the office. She thought how the title, "The Role of an Active Missionary Wife" could be expanded to read: "The Joy of an Active Missionary Wife." After that, her fingers clicked the keys on her electric typewriter with inspiration.

To me, the role of a missionary wife has been one full of joy, activity, and challenge.

The very first role of the missionary wife is setting up a home in a new world and culture. Everything about you is strange. First of all, our new home must be made to feel that it is "our home." Certainly, the first responsibility of a wife and mother is her home and family. After this must come language study. This is a must, for how can one communicate

*without learning the language? It is certainly impossible to have
a spiritual ministry.*

Next, Eleanor wrote about the responsibility of teaching
the children, and the balance of ministry. She gave an
example of trying to teach Richard only to be interrupted by
a woman whose baby had been severely burned.

*"What was I to do? Tell them that I was teaching my son
and that they should wait until I had finished, or find help
elsewhere—but there was no elsewhere! No, I couldn't do that.
Did not so many of the ministries of Jesus come about because
he was interrupted? When I returned, Richard was found up
in a tree playing with his pet monkey.*

*As I look over our twenty-one years of missionary life, I
believe there has been hardly a day that our schedule was not
interrupted because someone had a need. What a privilege—
just to know that God could use us in some way to help others.
Truly missionary work is a passion, not a profession. We must
have a heart of love—a heart that can feel the needs of others.
I like the way Lillian Dickson, missionary to China, puts
it, "I don't want to be a missionary's wife—I want to be a
missionary wife." There is a great difference between the two.
We must make ourselves available. It doesn't take very long for
people to recognize whether or not we are available—whether or
not we have a concern for them and their needs.*

*It is my strong conviction that husband and wife should
work together as a team. I feel that a wife should carry the
burden, along with her husband. The needs of the field are
her burden as well as his. Together they should pray and seek
God's help and guidance. Their joint prayers can move the hand
of God. Together they can claim the promise "Where two or
three agree on any one thing." Angeline Tucker writes in her*

book, "He is in Heaven," that at the time of their marriage, they were no longer two individuals doing the same type of work—they were a team.

To be an active missionary wife one must have an active prayer life. In looking back over the years to the many answers of prayer I was especially reminded of an incident, which took place in Congo.

Eleanor went on to describe the time everyone on the mission spent the day in prayer at the church while Melvin drove a young woman in labor 160 km over dirt roads to a hospital. That morning, Eleanor had been asked to check on the woman who had been in labor three days. When she entered the hut where the lifeless woman lay, a strong thought had told her that it was no use to pray. But Eleanor ignored this voice and prayed with the woman before she was transported to the hospital. The deceased child was removed surgically, but the woman recovered and went on to have more children.

After that, Eleanor mentioned Maria, Hudson Taylor's wife:

While missionaries in China, Hudson so learned to value her judgment and prayerfulness that he never took a step without consulting her. She did not obtrude but was humble, retiring almost to shyness. She was admired by her skill in the language and had a way of getting close to the Chinese.

After explaining the scope of their ministry in Congo, Eleanor described the important aspect of hospitality by opening their home to passing missionaries from many backgrounds. Then Eleanor included a paragraph about relying on God for strength during their personal medical emergencies. She briefly lifted her fingers off the keyboard. With all the times they had been sick and the challenges of daily life it was a wonder they got anything done.

Eleanor concluded her paper:

Now that we are living in Brussels in an entirely different culture, we find that life is still full of activity. Just at this very moment—another pleasant interruption, a missionary on his way to Africa is at the airport—has the afternoon free and wants someone to help him find an anniversary gift for his wife. My plans had been to get this paper finished!

* * * * *

Winter passed and soon it was the end of another school year at Continental. Another yearbook went to press, and Melvin worked on another report to send out about the college. Instead of simply listing curriculum subjects and ministry highlights, he decided the driving force were the students themselves. As their lives changed, they themselves became an agent of change for good in the world around them.

Continental receives students from many different countries, and when testimony time rolls around, many varied experiences unfold.

Take Karl-Erik for an example. When he is at his little island home in the cold expanse of the Baltic Sea, he is closer to the shores of communist Russia than to his capital city of Copenhagen. His fine Christian parents own a hostel on the island. And while Karl-Erick has had many opportunities for hard and responsible work, he has had little occasion in which to seriously study the Word. He is getting that now at Continental.

Or, take Abraham and Sarah Lui, a promising Chinese couple from Taiwan. They originally made their way to Spain with the intention of pursing his doctoral studies, but their money gave out. At the same time they met God, and Abraham's interest was immediately drawn to attending a Bible college in order to prepare for the ministry. When they sought the Lord for His divine direction, a way, through interested parties, was made for them to come to Continental. After they finish their studies, they will return to Taiwan to carry on a ministry there. When China is opened to the Gospel, they want to be ready to return.

Karel Schubert from Indonesia came to us from our Holland Bible School to continue his studies toward a degree in theology. Although he does not have sufficient funds to take him through school, he was accepted as a student because of his fine capabilities, his testimony and consecration. Karel tells of his reasons for coming to Continental: "The Lord called me to help in Indonesia with translation for books; to help in the Bible School; and to pioneer works in the villages."

As soon as he finished his studies of leadership and Bible, he will return to Indonesia to fulfill the call of the Lord on his life. He often testifies of the burden he has for his homeland, and of his desire to go back there with the message. His worth is proven by the fact that the student body has chosen him to head the missionary program of the college.

I can't use the correct name of the next student I want to write about. So let's give him a Biblical name for our purpose—Paul. I can't even tell you what country he comes from, as this could be an obstacle for his returning there. His country does not admit missionaries, nor does it condone the teaching of Christianity even by its own citizens. Paul had come from his country, arriving in Germany, seeking his own way through life by traveling, as so many youth are doing today. While there, God got a hold of his heart, and his life was completely changed. Because of this, and his unique situation and possibilities, our missionaries and workers encouraged him to apply for entrance to Continental.

Remaining in Europe however, would be difficult for him, as his passport was to expire within a couple of weeks. He tried to have his embassy in Paris grant an extension, but France could not allow this because of his passport expiring within such a short period of time.

Finally, with only two days left on his passport, he got on a train for another European country, with the hope that he would be able to get across the border. Faculty and students were praying earnestly that God would make it possible for him to continue at Continental.

Paul was successful in crossing the border without difficulty, but it was after he entered his embassy that he began to have his problems. After the official listened to Paul's story, he said he was sorry but it would be absolutely impossible for him to grant an extension to his passport. He would give Paul several days, and during this time he would have to get back home.

While Paul was trying to persuade him to reconsider, a door opened behind the official, and a man stepped into the open doorway.

With a surprised look on his face, he said, "Paul, what are you doing here?"

Paul immediately recognized him as a neighbor and friend from back home. After receiving a quick explanation, the friend said, "I believe I can help you out all right. I will give you a one-year extension."

Chapter Forty

Growing Pains

E leanor opened the teal-green Visitors Book she had bought in 1965. Looking over the rectangle pages filled with signatures, addresses, and space for comments, she ran her right hand over the page marked with her mother's visit dated July 25, 1971. She read her mother's comments written across the entire width of the vanilla-hued page.

I am so happy that I was privileged to visit you in your home in Brussels. To me it was a dream come true. Thank you for all the nice things you did for me, and for the family trip we had together. God bless you and keep you. Mother G.

Underneath the entry, her sister, Lorraine, and her family had included their address in Mound, Minnesota. Doug, her husband, drew a little picture of himself with glasses and the words printed THANK YOU! in the comment box.

Then her fingers passed down over Phil, Edith, Philip Jr., David, Elizabeth, and Ruth who stayed with them a few days on the 28th.

Wonderful to meet again after six years & talk of Congo as friends, having fellowship. The Lord Bless you.

Congo. . . memories and emotions ran through Eleanor as she turned the page over to look at the backside to find Angeline Tucker's entry on May 23 and her daughter, Carol Lynne. Their address was still in Springfield, MO, but Angeline was making plans to return to Congo. A church in memory of her late husband Jay, was being built in Paulis, or Isiro as it was called after Mobutu changed the name of the country to Zaire. In fact, Richard worked on the roof of the structure before going to Andudu to work on clearing land for an airstrip. Because of his fluency in Lingala, his primary duties would be teaching classes at the Bible School. Eleanor couldn't imagine what it must have felt like to be there again. To be on the mission station in Andudu with the African Christians. She wiped a tear away. The talking drums of Congo never stopped beating in her heart. However, they sometimes were drowned out by everything going on in Brussels. It was such a different life here. Yet, her love for Congo and its people never diminished.

"I wonder if I'll ever go back again," she said to no one as she closed the book and put it away until their next guests arrived on the 31st.

Then it was another string of guests with Bob Watters coming again in August. The accomplished concert pianist had a way of connecting with people using music and words. Sharing between musical pieces of classical and inspirational genre, he delivered the Good News of God sending his Son for each person in the auditorium so they might have an abundant life. At the end of the evening, an offer to come forward for prayer was given, with as many as two hundred and fifty people responding, and many experiencing physical healings.

* * * * *

Meanwhile at the home front, promising Aldene they would go school-clothes shopping before she entered eleventh grade, mother and daughter set out for the downtown district. Planning to make a day of it, they stopped at a favorite café for lunch. Often times they brought Gigi with them, as other dog owners did, tying the leash to a dog hook available in stores and restaurants.

After a delightful day they returned to the apartment to find a monkey in a small cage waiting for them.

"Richard is home," Eleanor dryly stated.

"Oh, he is so cute!"

Aldene gathered the little creature into her arms and they bonded. Gigi sniffed and watched, not sure what to make of the thing. Losing interest, she went to her food bowl and then lay down by Aldene's room.

Later that night, while eating a special dinner Eleanor had cooked for her returning son, Aldene was all questions for her big brother, "Where did you find the monkey and how did you get it on the plane?"

"Well," Richard leaned back on the padded dining-room chair to tell the story, "I was in Andudu filling in for Aunt Lilli and on one of the bush treks I found the monkey at a village. I made an offer and took it back with me to the mission station. When it came time to fly here I gave the monkey a minute amount of Phenobarbital I got from the clinic and placed him in my carry-on."

"How long did he sleep?" Aldene wondered.

"He woke up in the taxi cab on the way from the airport to the apartment."

Then he finished with a laugh, "The cab driver kept looking in the back seat, trying to find out where the small chirping noise was coming from." Aldene and Melvin joined in the laughter. However, Eleanor wasn't too sure about this monkey business in a Brussels apartment.

Before Richard left for the States to find a job, he and Aldene named the red tail monkey Francois and set up the cage on the balcony off the kitchen. Sometimes Aldene would put a little leash around Francois and they would go out walking. Wide-eyed Belgians openly stared at the monkey sitting on Aldene's back with his legs in the front. When he wasn't hanging onto her ears, he was picking through her hair. One day Aldene noticed there was one Belgian lady who didn't live far from their apartment who didn't seem at all surprised about the unusual pet. She drove a large American luxury-type car, with a cheetah, wearing a studded collar, riding in the passenger seat. So, that's how it was. The fancy lady driving on Avenue du Derby and Aldene strolling along with her monkey.

But eventually Francois wore out his welcome.

"Aldene, I have put up with a lot of pets, but this is too much."

"Please, Mom, let me keep him," Aldene pleaded, "I'll keep a better eye on him."

"No, I can't have some monkey tearing the wallpaper off our entryway." Eleanor held firm, "He will have to go to the pet store."

Eleanor lost no time in escorting the red-tailed primate to the pet store and the surprised owner selected a special spot for displaying Francois. From then on, every time Aldene would go visit the monkey in the store, he would hear her coming down the sidewalk and start jumping up and down. Opening the cage, Aldene let Francois cuddle up to her for a few minutes while they both cooed in monkey talk, "oo-oo-oo" and then they would play. When it was time for her to leave she would have to pry his fingers off her in order to get him back in the cage amongst his protesting of monkey screeches, "ee-ee-ee!" One day Aldene went to see Francois and he was gone.

"I hope you have a happy life Francois," she whispered on the way home, "I'll never forget you."

* * * * *

That fall after Aldene had started back at ISB, Eleanor heard the door to the apartment open and close. Gigi's ears perked up and she sprang into action to greet her favorite person. At seventeen, Aldene's willowy frame stood taller than Eleanor. Her long smooth black hair fell down the length of her back. Parted down the middle, it framed her large almond eyes. A long-sleeved sweater top, over flared jeans with a soft, wide leather belt cinched together by leather ties accented her slim waistline.

"How was school Aldene?" Eleanor asked from the kitchen, while preparing dinner.

"Other than almost getting hit in the head with an eraser, it was fine."

Eleanor's eyebrows lifted, "What happened?"

"Oh, Mary Ann and I were talking in French class and I noticed out of the corner of my eye that Madam G picked up the eraser. I ducked and it hit Mary Ann."

Aldene said with expression, "And Mary Ann said 'Ow! What did you do that for?' and Madam G said, 'I wasn't aiming for you.'"

"Oh, dear."

"That's nothing. The last time she got mad at Mary Ann, she took her purse, opened the window and chucked it out. So between class Mary Ann and I were down there looking for her stuff."

Aldene leaned her hip against the kitchen counter and crossed her arms, "If you ask me, she should have retired ten years ago."

For the most part, Aldene felt the teachers at ISB were decent and friendly enough to their students. And the class size of fifteen students at most, was small enough that everybody knew each other, and the teachers. Aldene also enjoyed taking a train with one of her classmates, and within an hour they would be in a different culture, seeing or doing different things. She might go skiing with a friend or, if no one was available, she could hop on a tram and within an hour and twenty minutes, be at the ocean, spending the afternoon at the beach with a book. It was the only time she was content to read. Just the opposite of Rich, who could lie on his stomach on his bed and listen to classical music records all afternoon, Aldene had to be on the go.

When it came to piano lessons her Mom would quip the old adage, "You can lead a horse to water but you can't make it drink."

Not that Aldene couldn't muster up the ability to play, she just didn't have the patience to sit and practice. For a while, a piano teacher came up from Paris on the train once a week to teach a handful of students. After working with Aldene, she said something in French, threw her hands up and quit. So then her parents approached one of the CBC students, Benny Gunter, to try his hand at teaching Aldene piano. After a few times, he threw his hands up and quit. After that, Melvin and Eleanor decided to spend their time and effort on a different front.

Aldene also went through math tutors as she did piano teachers. She would say that's when her dad started losing his hair. Next in line was a classmate's dad who was a physicist.

Sitting across from Aldene at his dining room table, Martine's father stared at her with puzzlement. "Aldene, math is so easy. It's just formula. Learn the formula and everything just falls into place."

"Oh, yeah? What's the formula?"

* * * * *

One night after Melvin proofread Aldene's essay for school, he noticed her hazel eyes drooping as much as her shoulders, "Why don't you head to bed and get a good night's sleep."

"But my paper is due tomorrow," Aldene pointed out.

"I'll type it up at the office, after I take Gigi for her evening walk."

"Thanks, Daddy."

Around ten o'clock Melvin walked across the street to the office to retype it.

The next morning Aldene looked over the neatly typed paper before tucking it into her school folder.

"Aldene," Eleanor called to her daughter as she walked down the hallway toward the kitchen and entryway, dressed for the day, "I'm leaving; I'll either be at the office or the Bible School today. Now when Claudia comes I want her to work on the parquet floors, and you can do the ironing."

Aldene gave a verbal yes, but in her heart she thought about her friends going downtown. When Claudia arrived a few minutes later, Aldene said, "Mom, wants you to iron."

The she ran out the door for school.

Later on when Eleanor came home, she found Aldene working on her homework. "Did Claudia work on the floor?"

Looking around at the parquet floors, Eleanor asked, "Did you tell her to work on the floor?"

Aldene looked up from her homework, "She ironed."

"But I told you to iron."

"I wanted to go downtown with my friends after school."

When Melvin came home for dinner, Eleanor informed him of their daughter's infraction. Next thing Aldene knew, her father stood at the doorway of her bedroom, "May I come in?"

Then came a discussion of what she did and why it was wrong. After that, they read a scripture verse and prayed. The whole time Aldene thought, just hit me. Just hit me and let me out of here!

"And you will have to be grounded this weekend, "Melvin concluded.

He looked his daughter over. He knew she was sometimes defiant, quick to stiffen her back, since she was a little girl. Yet something inside him told him she would make it, as long as he was careful in how he disciplined her.

Before he left her room he turned around, "You're a good kid, Aldene."

Aldene held her tongue, wondering, *then why did we go through all of this?*

That weekend with nothing to do, Aldene cleaned her room and organized her wardrobe closet. She did have to admit her folks bought her nice clothes. But there were rules of modesty. When the mini skirt first came out, her parents wouldn't let her out of the house with something so short. Improvising, after leaving the apartment, Aldene would hitch up her skirt by rolling the top so it looked like she had a tire around her belt. Then, before she got home, would pull it all down.

After a few skirt adjustments Eleanor commented, "Why is it so wrinkly up here?"

With a shrug of her shoulders Aldene coolly replied, "I don't know. Not a clue."

"Aldene, please take better care of your clothes," Eleanor sighed. It wasn't easy for them budget-wise to have Aldene at the International School. Most of the children's parents had plenty of money for a high-end fashionable wardrobe. Not wanting her to feel inferior because she was a missionary kid, Melvin and Eleanor cut other items out of their family budget so Aldene could have a few nice things to wear to school.

One day Aldene announced, "They're having a prom at school in the spring."

Besides modesty in clothing, dancing was another matter on which her folks were strict, but she gave it a try anyway.

"Aldene, you can't go." Eleanor flatly stated.

"But why?"

"You know why. It's a dance, and what will people think if the daughter of the director of the Bible School is at a dance," Eleanor didn't bother to add that a few select people purposely kept an eye on Melvin and his family, so they could make things hard for him. It was a lot of pressure, added to the pressures of running the Bible School, and overseeing other ministries.

"With Daddy being the representative for the Belgian field we have to have higher standards, set the example."

"Well, I'm not robbing a bank or something like that."

Aldene's face knotted up and she went to her room to stew. She couldn't figure out why it was such a big deal, and if people were supposedly watching her, they were spending their time on the wrong things. Growing older, she started noticing that, although most missionaries working in Europe were there to serve the Lord and the people, some were there to serve themselves. It seemed there was more of a pecking order in Europe, in contrast to Africa where people had to pull together to survive. There was not much time in Congo for political maneuvering and positioning one's self for moving up the ladder.

* * * * *

A few weeks later, Aldene decided to attend one of the school dances. It was a low-key affair, nothing like the prom, but she wanted to be like the rest of the kids. What was the harm?

It was held in the gymnasium of the new high school building that had been built when Aldene was in America during her eighth grade. On the property nearby there was also the Protestant Church building, where the Protestants were holding a service. Aldene was dancing away with Stu, a classmate with hair down to his shoulders, sporting a loose-fitting shirt tucked into a belted pair of jeans. As Aldene glanced over his shoulder she gasped. Someone was standing at the door of the gymnasium.

"My dad's here."

Knowing the situation Stu asked, "What are you going to do?"

"Well, finish the dance 'cause I know I'm leaving."

After the two teenagers finished the dance, Aldene walked with her father to the car, and they drove home in silence. When they got to the apartment, Melvin acted like nothing had happened and life went on as usual.

After several days of this, Aldene's curiosity was eating her up inside. She just had to ask him, "Why didn't you punish me?"

Melvin looked at her and softly said, "I humiliated you in front of your friends and that was enough."

Aldene's frosted heart melted.

* * * * *

After the dance incident, Eleanor approached her daughter on a Saturday afternoon, "Aldene, we've decided to let you go to the spring prom. In fact, one of students at the Bible School, she's the Italian gal, is a seamstress."

"Let's go shopping for material!"

And out they went, mother and daughter, both surviving the growing pains of life and relationships.

The night of the prom Melvin took several pictures of his daughter wearing her special-occasion dress after Eleanor finished primping this and arranging that. Both parents beamed as Aldene turned around in her satin light-blue formal-length gown, with an empire waist accented by full-length white gloves. Her dark long hair was elegantly pulled up high in the back with long braids cascading down her graceful neck.

When Aldene's date arrived, Melvin took another picture noticing that the young man, decked out in a formal suit and tie, towered over Aldene.

After the flash went off, he instructed his daughter with a chuckle, "Well, keep looking up tonight."

Aldene almost died of embarrassment, turning fifteen shades of red. She grabbed her purse and shawl and scurried out of the apartment with her lanky-framed date following her.

* * * * *

In the midst of these family affairs, Continental Bible School had its own share of growing pains. From the start, space was limited. As the student population kept growing there was a need for more classrooms. At first, they were using space at the nearby International Correspondence Institute building, which offered correspondence courses of Evangelization, Christian Development, Lay Workers' Training, and Bible College Study for Belgium, and over seventy-five other countries. Then they rented classrooms at a hotel. In light of this space issue, Melvin began searching for another property.

After weeks of driving around the area and making inquiries, he came across Chateau Rattendaal on Chausée de Waterloo, two kilometers west of their current location. Rich in history, Rattendaal was more of a castle than a chateau during its former days of glory in the twelfth century. Surviving many wars, including World War II when German forces commandeered it, the property now sat empty waiting for its next inhabitants. As Melvin walked around the grounds adjacent to a pasture with grazing ponies, it seemed adequate for additional buildings. He felt a connection to the property and asked the Lord to guide and direct him if this should be the future home of Continental Bible College. After applying to the home office in Springfield for funds to purchase Rattendaal, Melvin waited for a reply.

When an answer finally came back, addressed to his office on Avenue du Derby, he read over the letter with disappointment. His proposal had been denied. Melvin adjusted his glasses and quietly folded up the letter and reinserted it in the envelope with the Springfield postmark. He stared at the wall across from where he sat at his desk with the tall credenza behind him. On top of the credenza stood a display of flags fanned out from nations all over the world securely stuck into a half-moon shaped stand.

And then, he did what he always did. He prayed, "Lord, your timing and plans are different than mine. Not my will but thine be done."

Melvin knew from experience that he needed to open the file cabinet in his heart marked "TRUST" and slip Rattendaal into that cabinet drawer and close it.

Leaving the property into the Lord's hands, he reached for another of the many hats he wore and set to work on something else. Besides Director of CBC, and overseeing VIDA with annual book fairs, he was on the committee of Pentecostal European Conference, or PEK, as it was known in Europe, a major conference every three years.

In addition to this, he was renting out a vacant chapel near the office, for one winter to hold services for English-speaking people. Both Melvin and Eleanor continued to be amazed at the spiritual hunger of the English-speaking population in the city of Brussels. Needing assistance, Brother Cantelon came from the States for a season to help Melvin. Light blue four by five inch cards were passed out by teams of CBC students, inviting English speakers to the Boondael Chapel for a Bible Discussion Hour and Morning Worship service featuring sacred music and singing with special speakers from various countries. Below the times of the services it read:

Topics will include such themes as: <<Current events in the light of Bible prophecy>>, <<Health and healing through prayer>>, <<The meaning of the charismatic renewal>>.

Along with others, Melvin and Eleanor began to pray and strategize for an International English-Speaking Church in Brussels.

* * * * *

In the spring of 1973, Melvin and Eleanor found themselves swirling in changes. They watched their daughter graduate from ISB. Rather than join them on their next furlough, Aldene planned on remaining in Brussels and working, while staying at the apartment with Gigi.

There was also a graduation ceremony at CBC. As director of the college, Melvin handed out diplomas along with other faculty. That past year he taught Introduction to Missions, Contemporary Mission Frontiers, and Preaching from the Prophets, while serving as the liaison representative of the American Assemblies of God in Europe. Meanwhile, Eleanor coordinated the mission programs of the school, in addition to teaching Introduction to Missions, and English I and II, while juggling duties at the office and women's Bible studies.

At the reception of dessert and coffee following the ceremony, Melvin and Eleanor made a point to talk with as many graduates and faculty members as possible.

"Merci, thank you for everything," Briditte Proveda, a fourth-year graduate from the Advanced Division said with tears, "you have taught me more than academics."

"What are your plans during furlough?" asked Jacques Roffidal, a second-year student from France, interested in chaplain work with military forces.

"Besides itineration and visiting family, we may possibly travel to South America to assist with Guy and Alida Hamelle," Melvin replied.

Eleanor finished the reply, "They were students here right before you came."

"Oh, yes," Jacques nodded his head, "I remember praying for them and Guadalupe."

After most of the students bid their farewells, Melvin and Eleanor had a few minutes with Sobhi and Jeri Sue Malek.

"So, after three years teaching at CBC, you are making plans to pioneer the Assemblies of God mission in Tunisia," Melvin stated warmly.

"Your French degree from America really got a workout this year," Eleanor said, while Melvin and Sobhi began discussing the logistics of moving a family to another country.

"Yes, it did!" Jeri Sue exclaimed. "It seems like the time has flown since we first met and ate the Egyptian meal at your apartment. Eleanor, one of the things I hope to imitate in Tunisia is your gift of hospitality."

"Why, thank you, I appreciate that." Then Eleanor added, "I have to laugh when I think back to my opinion on mixed-culture marriages, not knowing you and Sobhi had eyes for each other. You make a lovely couple."

"We are happy together, but you were right about the challenges of mixing cultures. It is only by God's grace that we can overcome our differences walking in a spirit of forgiveness and love."

Chapter Forty-One

Salle Regina

❧

Tuesday, November 5, 1974 Brussels, Belgium
Dear Mother, Richard & Aldene,

Just a quick note. Had planned to write you yesterday but didn't get it done. Hope you get this at least by Saturday. Mail seems to be a bit slower these days.

Had a good flight over. A "gentleman" met me and gave me a bouquet of long-stemmed red roses. Gigi gave a royal welcome. When we got home, I found that Melvin painted the living room and Aldene's bedroom. It all looked so nice and fresh. I still haven't gotten adjusted time-wise but it will come.

Daddy and I moved the living room around again and we like it this way. Put the piano on the entryway wall and put the Spanish davenport where we had the piano. The TV is in the corner. It looks real cozy. That will be used most of the time and will keep the living room in order—and protected. I taught my English class yesterday. Today we met Jeri Sue and Sobhi at the airport. Sobhi leaves on Thursday morning for Tunisia where he hopes to get a visa and also look for a house. Jeri will stay in Brussels with the two children. They both look like Sobhi. Will have them over tomorrow night for dinner.

Got my hair fixed and cut today so feel better. Had a good talk with Aunt Grace while waiting in N.Y.

You are always in our thoughts and prayers. So hope everything is going along ok. Will write in more detail later—just wanted to let you know that I'm here and getting adjusted again. Have so much work in the office and must get at it soon.

Just came from the bank and find the dollar is still going down. Makes us sick but nothing to do about it. Just tighten our belts I guess.

Please try to write often. We are always so anxious to hear. We love you.

Eleanor & Melvin, Mother & Daddy Special love from Daddy—he says.

E leanor sealed the letter and set it aside on the table in the office on Avenue du Derby to take to the post office later, "Should we head over to the apartment for dinner?"

Feeling the tension of wanting to care for her mother after her father died in October at age seventy-nine, and not wanting to be separated too long from Melvin, Eleanor had returned to Brussels as soon as she felt her mother could be without her. Knowing both Richard and Aldene were in Minneapolis helped to ease her anxiety.

"I suppose so," Melvin returned, "Gigi is no doubt waiting for a walk."

The empty nesters walked across the street and took the elevator to the third floor.

After Melvin walked the dog, and Eleanor prepared dinner, they sat down at the dining room table adorned with white tapered candles warmly glowing.

"My, what a furlough it was in America, with the Watergate scandal and President Nixon resigning," Eleanor began the conversation after Melvin gave thanks for the food and safe return of his wife.

"It hardly seems possible to have a president in office that wasn't elected, but Gerald Ford seems like a decent fellow."

After a few bites, Eleanor smiled at her husband, "Thanks again for making the apartment look so nice for me."

"I had to do something while you were gone. I missed you terribly."

"And I, you."

After a few more bites, "Were you able to clear up that mess with the cars?"

"Yes," Melvin replied, "once I explained that the red Opel Commodore was our personal car and the other one was the missionary car for everyone's use, the dust settled."

Before Aldene had left for her visit to the States, she drove the family car quite a bit causing angst with a few people that misunderstood the situation.

"Well, I'm glad she had the chance to use the Opel to tour Europe with her girlfriends during our absence."

"Yes, I am too. Although it was quite a surprise to learn about it from a postcard sent from Paris," laughed Eleanor.

Then she grew serious, "The thing of it is, I think she should do some of these things while she's still single, because she might be serious about that one boyfriend of hers in Minnesota."

"The one she met on a blind date, during her summer visit before her senior year at ISB?"

"Yes, Todd, that's the one."

That night Melvin and Eleanor sat talking as late as they could hold their eyes open. A wider door of opportunity opened before them to work with the French-speaking church. During his last furlough, Melvin discussed with the board in Springfield, his transition from Director of CBC to pioneering a church plant in Brussels. Details, such as a funding-project number needed to be arranged. Melvin also had a desire to work with the Belgian pastors more in encouraging and mentoring. Eleanor shared the same vision, with a burden to start French speaking Bible studies among the women.

The Board had given their blessing for the move into full-time ministry with the French-speaking Belgians with one request: oversee the transition of CBC through the purchase of a larger property, and any renovations immediately needed.

So Melvin started another search for a new home for CBC. There was a hotel close to a beautiful park that would adequately satisfy the needs of classroom, housing, and dining. And yet, Chateau de Rattendaal kept coming to his mind. However, he heard that it had been sold.

"Just for kicks let's go take a drive past the chateau," Melvin invited his wife.

After driving up and down and around the area two kilometers east of the Bible College's current location Melvin realized he had a problem, "Where is that property?"

"Things look so different," Eleanor had only been out to the property a few times.

"The trees and shrubbery have grown."

They came to a landscaped island in the middle of the road with enough room for Melvin to pull their Opel off to the side. Then he reached for Eleanor's hand, "Let's pray."

Eleanor gave his hand a little squeeze that said yes, and amen. Then she listened to her husband thank the Lord for his divine timing and guidance for CBC.

Melvin finished with, "Show us where the chateau is, Lord, so we can know if this is your will."

Melvin started the car, turned around the tiny island in the road and drove right to the property.

"That's it! That's it!" Eleanor exclaimed.

The couple got out of their car and began walking around the property. Melvin saw a neighbor outside and strolled over for a chat. "Do you know anything about this property?"

"Sure I do," said the man, "the owners were going to make some fancy resort club out of it. But it never happened."

On the way home, Melvin and Eleanor couldn't help wondering what would happen next. They let as many people know as possible to keep praying about the situation.

* * * * *

In the midst of this, Melvin and Eleanor made plans to rent Salle Regina for a French-speaking church plant. In 1976, they signed a four-year contract for the hall. They also asked the small French-speaking church they had been a part of and Pastor Ametie, who took over for Pastor Knops, to join them as they began regular Sunday services.

Fliers were printed with the location and picture of the nearby landmark, a broad stone tower accented with a turret, all enveloped in vines. If a person could find Porte de Hall, they would be able to find Regina Hall, which was the same hall they had rented for the David Wilkerson meetings, only now it was completely renovated.

Inside the flier were the times of the services and beliefs of the Assemblies of God with supporting scripture references. Also included was a list of activities: choir, orchestra, children's and youth clubs, literature distribution, and visiting the sick. Practically the whole day was planned for facilitating the various groups, in addition to adult classes. The fliers could also be used for literature distribution with significant scriptures listed on the back of the white tri-fold brochure for spiritual guidance.

However, the new church plant had a few challenges. On Saturday nights, the hall was used for drinking and dances, leaving the auditorium in disarray for services. A team of men volunteered to come several hours before the service to properly clean before the first service started at 9:30 a.m. After several weeks, it became apparent that the piano stored in a locked room was being "borrowed" by the Saturday night crowd for their barroom songs and dances.

But this was minor compared to the spiritual battle. After ten years of living amongst the Belgians, Melvin and Eleanor discovered an appreciable amount of information about the people they had come to serve. There was a spiritual darkness that Melvin and Eleanor could sense as they prayed and fasted for Belgium. Often, they felt that the resistance to the living gospel of Jesus Christ was greater in this European country than it was in Congo.

In a conversation with a Belgian CBC student Eleanor admitted, "In building trust with the Belgian people, it seems that we take a few steps forward and then a few steps back."

Often when conducting follow-up after evangelistic campaigns or other types of meetings, those who had come forward for prayer were not willing to give their names and contact information.

"Let me explain it this way," the student offered.

"When a Belgian goes home at the end of the day, they lock, double-lock the door and wonder who is at the door: friend or foe? They will not open it to anyone because of what happened during the world wars."

He continued, "In many families, a brother or uncle could come to the door, and be the enemy to drag you and your family out of the house."

However, the modern-day wars were only the tip of the iceberg of political and spiritual turmoil that led to bloodshed on this land of French- and Flemish-speaking people. Before the time of Julius Caesar, a sub-tribe of the Celts known as the Belgae lived in what is now modern-day Belgium, until they were conquered by the Roman Empire. From then on, it was a military tug of war until modern times.

As the Roman Empire diminished, the Franks, a Germanic dynasty led by Claudine rose to power and took control of Tournai, the first established city of modern-day Belgium, located near Liège. One of Claudine's great-grandsons, Clovis, born in Tournai during the first century, became a leader and converted to Christianity. Influenced by Irish and Scottish Celtic monks, Christianity spread, and with it came the building of monasteries. Years later, a different Frankish dynasty in Belgium emerged when a son was born, Charlemagne, who was crowned emperor in eight hundred by the Pope of the Catholic Church.

During the Middle Ages, Charlemagne's empire encompassed the lands around Belgium including the Netherlands, Austria, northern Italy, western Germany and almost all of France. After his death, the divided empire created an opportunity for the Vikings to swoop down from Scandinavia to vandalize towns. This led to the Belgian people seeking refuge with wealthy landowners, who began building castles and fortifications around the towns. At the turn of the century, after the Norseman invasions subsided, there was a period of growth of manufacturing of goods including fabric sought out by all of Europe for its fine qualities.

Next, came the Dukes of Burgundy, France, who ruled during the 1400s until they married into the Hapsburg family through the marriage of Mary of Burgundy to Maximilian of Austria. Eventually the Hapsburg family produced an heir, Charles V, born and raised in Belgium, who became the Holy Roman Emperor and King of Spain. Charles accumulated the Burgundy lands, the Spanish colonies in the world, and Belgium became part of the Low Countries, also called the Spanish Lowlands. It was also during this time that a new branch of Christianity emerged under the influence of Martin Luther, and the Protestant Reformation spread to Belgium. As a Catholic, Charles took an intellectual approach to battle Protestantism involving himself in the Counter Reformation.

And yet, it was during this time, in 1533, that English scholar William Tyndale, who had completed an English translation of the New Testament from Greek and printed it in Worms, Germany, was seized in Antwerp and held in a castle in Vilvoorde, near Brussels. Requesting his translation books, Tyndale continued working on the Old Testament from Hebrew into English by candlelight in his prison cell. In 1536, Tyndale was found guilty of heresy and executed. He was strangled to death, and then burned at the stake.

Legend has it that Tyndale regained conscious uttering his last words as flames surrounded him, "Lord! Open the King of England's eyes!"

Several years later, the King of England authorized the publishing of English Bibles.

However, when Charles's son, Phillip, became King of Spain in 1555, Phillip took a militant approach to religion and a bloody religious cleansing was unleashed on Belgium, prompting a mass exodus of Belgian Protestants to Holland.

Sadly, domination of the Belgians continued. This time from France, which, under pressure from European countries, relinquished Belgium to Austria until 1790 when the Belgians declared their independence. Nonetheless, the tiny country would have to wait for freedom until Napoleon was defeated in the battle of Waterloo by the English and Prussians in 1815. Outraged by Great Britain putting them under control of the Dutch, the Belgians protested, knowing their time to be their own independent country was within grasp. Europe finally acknowledged Belgium in 1831, and the "cockfight arena of Europe" was at rest and peace, until the Great War began in 1914 and the tug of war continued.

Ironically, it was during that span of freedom that Belgium locked its grip on Congo through the appetite of King Leopold II for colonization, and kept governmental control through two World Wars, until 1960. The oppressed had become the oppressor, as often happens.

All these layers of history branded the souls of the Belgians in an enigmatic mixture of cultural worldviews that was a challenge for outsiders to decode. Intricately woven through this political history, was a syncretism of Celtic and Roman paganism. This belief system of polytheism included various superstitious rituals based on animism, druid-influenced witchcraft, and Roman mythology. The god of commerce, Mercury, was especially appealing to the Belgae. Many of these religious practices were passed on through oral traditions, despite the enormous influence of Christianity. Belgium also had many adherents to forms of enlightenment, secularism, and other world religions.

Although the majority of Belgians would consider themselves Catholics, the church had little impact on their lives anymore. With self-reliance as the backbone of their identity, there wasn't much of a need for God, except for ceremonial purposes. Nonetheless, there was pride in the history of Belgian Catholics, inspired by their faith to become missionaries. Notable among these were Father Hennepin, who explored the Mississippi River, naming Saint Anthony Falls in Minnesota; and Father Damien, who died of leprosy while serving on the Hawaiian Island of Molokai, a colony for lepers.

* * * * *

At the office on Avenue du Derby, Melvin read over their latest update before making enough copies to send across the Atlantic Ocean. Short, and to the point, it was only one page with photos of the new home of CBC and the owner and officials involved in the transfer of the property.

NEWS FROM The Jorgensons Assemblies of God Missionaries in Europe

With a stroke of the pen, this beautiful structure and land became the property of the Assemblies of God. It was in 1971 that I first found the beautiful Chateau de Rattendaal. A permanent home for Continental Bible College, Brussels, Belgium, was needed, and this centuries-old property with its seven and a half acres, would prove to meet present and future needs. Its picturesque lake and island would add to its beauty and atmosphere for study and meditation.

However, it wasn't until 1976 when the need became acute, that the home committee decided it was time to act. I found the property to be still available and immediate steps were taken for its purchase. Renovation began last October and final steps are now being taken to complete the task by September 15. The next phase is the erection of a chapel, for which plans are already drawn.

Pray with us for the work here, as we leave for the States on furlough. We arrive the last part of August. We will be visiting churches and hope you will be among those we see. Our heartfelt thanks for your prayers and support during another term of service for the Master.

* * * * *

As Melvin prepared to leave Brussels for the States, he wrote out his thoughts concerning the church plant at Salle Regina. Wanting to communicate to the churches in America, he prepared a slice of ministry from his full plate as representative of the AG USA in Belgium that he could share from the pulpit or make available through printed matter.

Report by Melvin Jorgenson

Salle Regina is a magical word in Brussels. At least that is what many people say. Something wonderful has happened to them there, and they carry this sentiment with them.

Salle Regina is an auditorium. It seats four hundred. It is new. It is beautiful. Upon viewing it for the first time, my wife exclaimed, "Just see what the Lord has prepared for us." It had once been an old hall, unkempt and gloomy, but a fire finished all that, and a new one was built in its place—Salle Regina.

It is located at the heart of Brussels, its doors open to the many who pass by. Those who enter are the ones who call it a "place of magic." This, of course, is not so, as no magician performs there. But it is true that many have experienced a magical change in their lives, a change that can hardly be explained or expressed. What has occurred is that they have found in Jesus the source of all joy and goodness.

During the past months souls have been saved, bodies healed. More than twenty have received water baptism within the last few weeks.

Special meetings are scheduled every week. Gifted speakers bring the Word. Consecrated musical groups have been engaged to attract the people—and they come! Christian films have also been used.

An excellent youth choir has been formed and has been recorded on cassette (do you want a copy—without charge?). And an orchestra has been organized, which has been a constant blessing in the services. An active children's program is in operation.

Brussels is the capital city of Belgium, a land of strife over the past centuries. Its history has been one of struggle for survival. Brussels, the largest city, has suffered along with the rest of the country, and it has become the center of all big-city evils. Salle Regina is located in an area permeated with sorcery and witchcraft. Some who have been caught in the web have been delivered.

A young Christian nurse, Evangeline, was led to speak to a lady held by sorcery. She became aware of the lady's difficulty during her routine duties at the hospital. The lady spoke to her of a great fear that possessed her, and of a continual quivering and nervousness that centered in her breast. At times this literally, physically shook her until she was unable to bear it. She related how a man had offered her a small, square box, explaining that she would be completely delivered if she would place it on the mantle in her home. She gladly accepted the offer, even though she had to pay the man four hundred dollars.

Following instructions, she was perfectly well for a period of time, but then the same strange malady took hold of her. Frantic with fear, she had contacted the man again. He would provide her with another box that would once again remover her ailment, but she would have to pay him another four hundred dollars.

"But I have no money," she tearfully complained to Evangeline, "and I don't know what to do. I live in continual fear, and this shaking in my breast is more than I can bare."

Evangeline said, "I know Someone Who can heal you completely, and He won't charge you anything."

Anxiously, the lady asked for the name, and Evangeline said, "His name is Jesus."

Disappointed, she replied, "But I am an atheist."

"That's all right, Madam, but I will pray for you every day this week."

This show of concern caused the lady to weep profusely, and Evangeline went on to tell her of the meetings being held in Salle Regina. The next Sunday she was there, and came forward for prayer. Pray with us for her complete deliverance.

More testimonies could be given. One big plus is the influence this evangelistic effort has had on other churches in Belgium. Special meetings are being scheduled by them, and great things are expected from God.

We have joined forces with a tiny, local church in this new evangelistic thrust, and its few members are working with zeal and consecration. Only three or four very small Pentecostal churches exist in Brussels. God will be honored by a large well-established church that can witness effectively to this cosmopolitan area.

Working with the pastor and myself, are a young Frenchman and his American wife. A young Belgian lady directs the music with real ability. Faye Clark, missionary, directs the children's work in the Sunday school and through several Bible Clubs.

This is one of the most productive opportunities we have ever had in Brussels. Strangers are present at every service, and at times as many as twenty come forward for prayer and salvation.

Offerings are needed to continue this ministry at the heart of Brussels. A church is being established, but until it can carry on alone, your help is vital. Offerings should be sent to the division of foreign Missions labeled:

Evangelistic Effort, Brussels   *Melvin E. Jorgenson*

* * * * *

When Todd asked Aldene to marry him her reply was, "I'm not sure." They had met on a blind date when Aldene traveled to the States the summer before her senior year of high school. Uncertainty swirling inside her, she hopped on a plane and went home to Brussels. Lying in bed at night watching the tram lights flicker, while Gigi slept in the other twin bed, Aldene thought about her future. She was in love with Todd, but she felt uncomfortable in the States and had few friends there.

After six weeks in Brussels Aldene told her parents her decision, "I think I will always call Brussels my home, but it's time I carve out a new life. And I want it to be with Todd."

Aldene took one last look at the framed painting of the horse Great Tarzan, before wrapping it in newspaper for packing. Dottie, an artist friend of her mother's, created the painting from a photograph Aldene had taken of his chestnut-brown head with butterscotch mane peering over a stable door with soft intelligent brown eyes. Great Tarzan, a Morgan, had been her favorite of all the horses she ever rode since starting riding club.

After a few years of riding with the club near her school, Aldene joined another riding group just outside the large forest with her friend Jennifer Morgandorf and they progressed to jumping. Every time Aldene returned to the stable with the dappled gray mare she used for jumping, she would walk by the large chestnut Morgan to check on him. Standing seventeen to eighteen hands, Aldene couldn't help admire such a high-quality horse.

One day the owner told her, "I don't have enough time to get Great Tarzan out as much as I should. He really should get more exercise."

And then, to Aldene's surprise he offered, "You're welcome to take him out whenever you find him in his stall."

After wrapping the painting, Aldene carefully packed her riding gear of pants, blouse, and burgundy ties with horse heads on it and her navy blue jacket. Then she folded her black riding gloves and slipped them in the riding hat, reached for her crop and tucked them neatly in her suitcase. She would always treasure the opportunity she had to join the riding club. She might have been a "poor missionary kid" in some people's eyes, but she had never felt deprived, in fact, she felt rich in many ways.

On July 2, 1977, a month before Aldene turned twenty-three, she walked down the aisle of a church on Portland Avenue in Minneapolis, on the arm of her father toward her future. Todd stood near the altar waiting for his bride, while Grandma Groat played the piano.

After the ceremony, Aldene mingled with their wedding guests at the reception, passing out netted sachets filled with candy-covered almonds from Belgium. Walking between tables with a wicker basket on her arm, a woman commented on her veil.

"Is that Belgium lace?"

"Yes, I wanted to splurge on the veil rather than the dress, so I just bought the dress here. If I ever do have a daughter that gets married, she can use the veil easier than my dress."

A few days later, Aldene signed the Guest Book at the apartment on Avenue d'Italie:

7/7/77, Mr. and Mrs. T.C. Birkeland, Nicollet Ave So, Bloomington, Minnesota Thank you for the beautiful honeymoon!

And off the young couple went on a tour through Europe with Melvin and Eleanor's 1977 red BMW, revisiting Aldene's travels with her girlfriends and with her parents.

Only this time, Melvin and Eleanor knew about it before Aldene sent them a postcard: "Put the car on the train through Locarno Pass, Switzerland. Thanks for letting us use your car while you are in America."

The following April Aldene delivered Sonja, a beautiful baby girl with dark hair and eyes. Richard married Lynae Eliason in December. A year later at age thirty-four, Richard held his firstborn, Chad Richard, in his arms. It was also during this time that Aldene's faithful "roommate," Gigi, died while sleeping in the doorway to their bedroom.

＊ ＊ ＊ ＊ ＊

In the midst of family happenings, Melvin and Eleanor continued to visit churches in America, sharing their vision of pioneering a church amongst French-speaking Belgians, and building a chapel at CBC. While speaking at a church in Grafton, North Dakota, for the Sunday morning service, Melvin remembered what happened to him in Subotica, Yugoslavia. Later, while in the car, driving to the next town on their itinerary, he relayed the experience to Eleanor.

Several months prior to coming to the States, Melvin was scheduled to speak at a conference in Yugoslavia. On the flight from Brussels to Belgrade Melvin knew the pastor of the large and thriving church in Subotica would be at the airport to meet him so he lay back in the seat, relaxed, and enjoyed the couple of hours of rest.

When the plane landed in Belgrade, Melvin went through the customary passport control and into the passenger area where he was to meet the pastor. Melvin was not surprised that the pastor was not there, assuming the pastor might be a little late driving 150 kilometers from Subotica. However, the minutes ticked by until his watched showed a half hour had passed and still no sign of the pastor.

As the main speaker for the conference, Melvin was scheduled to speak at 8:30 the next morning. Anxiety filled Melvin as the crowd in the passenger area thinned out. He was still recovering from a recent illness and felt its lingering effects on his body. Friends had urged him not to go, but Melvin felt it was the Lord's will not to miss this opportunity to minister to the people of Yugoslavia. Not being able to speak the language made him feel like he had "straw in his pockets" like his first day arriving at North Central College. He didn't have a map or know the first thing about getting around in Belgrade. There were no signs in English or French. In his weakened condition he did not have the will or the power to make himself understood.

His mind began to race, *what will I do? How will I find my way to Subotica? I must be there by 8:30 in the morning and it is now early evening.*

Melvin decided he could at least take the bus to the terminal in the city. As the bus bumped along unfamiliar roads Melvin mulled the question over in his mind, *what will I do when I reach the terminal?*

As the bus halted, Melvin felt dismayed at the large number of people there. Surely at least a thousand would-be travelers were milling about as dozens of buses came and went. All seemed in turmoil and confusion. Melvin preferred to stay in the shelter of the bus. He felt sick and lost. But he had to get off, no matter what might follow.

And then it happened. Going down the steps of the bus, his eyes were drawn to one man looking at him and smiling. Melvin smiled back weakly, not sure if the stranger meant the friendly smile or not. Melvin tightened his grip on his suitcase and continued to make his way down into the crowd while the stranger waited for him. Melvin managed another smile directed at the stranger in spite of the problem confronting him.

Without saying a word, the stranger motioned for Melvin to follow him. When Melvin drew close to the man, he assessed that the man was of average height, and his dress was no different than the other people mingling about in the terminal.

Now Melvin had to make a decision. Should he follow this stranger or seek out help elsewhere? He went over his list of options. He had none. The stranger motioned with his hand for Melvin to follow him. So like a lost puppy Melvin walked behind him some distance through the crowd making sure he kept close to him until they entered a building full of ticket windows.

Now what? Thought Melvin, feeling overwhelmed.

But the man just smiled and walked up to a ticket window. He purchased a ticket and came back to Melvin and gave him the ticket. He then motioned with his hand for Melvin to follow him. They walked down a hallway that led to a door to the outside loading area. Buses were coming and going. Puffing exhaust and shifting gears, the long tin cans with wheels lined up one beside the other to discharge and receive passengers.

Once more, the man motioned to Melvin, indicating he should wait for his bus at the empty stall before him. Melvin looked down at his ticket and saw it was for Subotica. Suddenly Melvin thought to offer the man money for the ticket and his help, but the stranger refused waving his hand in front of him. Then the stranger left, and Melvin stood alone waiting for the bus.

And he waited. Five minutes. Ten minutes. Fifteen minutes. Twenty minutes.

No bus was coming to his stall. Melvin felt his stomach churning. Suddenly from somewhere in the crowd the man appeared again, smiling as before. He reassured Melvin to keep waiting. Again with no words, and then he disappeared again.

At that moment, a bus pulled into the parking place before Melvin and he climbed into the bus. He showed the conductor his ticket and took a seat, totally at ease for the rest of the trip. That night, Melvin slept peacefully in a hotel next to the bus terminal in Subotica. Early the next morning, the pastor stopped by the hotel to see if by chance Melvin had arrived. That's when Melvin found out the pastor had made the trip to the airport to pick him up. However, when he inquired at the desk he was told the plane had arrived, and Melvin was not on it so he left, wondering what to do about his conference meetings at his church the following day.

After Melvin finished his story, he said to his wife, "I have no idea who this man was, or how he knew I needed help, not to mention knowing where I was going! I have to conclude it was nothing short of an angelic escort."

Hanging onto every word of the story, Eleanor couldn't help wonder, "Why do you think several months have passed until all of a sudden, you think of your encounter with the stranger?"

"I don't understand why something like this would be clouded from my mind except that in God's divine wisdom He mellowed and nurtured the truth in my heart that He cares for His own, no matter where we may be. He will make a way for us where there is no way."

* * * * *

Melvin carried this seed of faith in his heart, back to Brussels, that God can make a way as he faced a waiting dilemma. The next phase for the erection of the chapel had been on the drawing board waiting for funds. Now Melvin found the project blocked by city ordinances. Apparently, they would not be allowed to add any buildings onto the property. But Melvin kept at it, visiting three different official's offices.

Finally, at the last one he got somewhere, "Well, you are not allowed to build, but you can attach all you want to the existing building."

An attached walkway between the chateau and future chapel was designed, and construction completed, including housing for students!

Chapter Forty-Two

The Burden and the Advance

❧

A s Melvin and Eleanor began their march through the 1980s and Jimmy Carter lost his second term to Ronald Reagan in the US presidential election, an invitation came from former CBC students, Guy and Alida Hamelle, to come to Guadeloupe. The French Missions had offered to pay for their round-trip tickets.

Meanwhile, spring and summer were filled with many activities to distant and interesting places. Iceland was the first stop, where Melvin represented Belgium in the working committee of PEK (Pentecostal European Conference) held every three years. Pentecostal leaders from most European countries were there to plan for the Europe-wide PEK Conference scheduled for Stuttgart, Germany in July 1984. Evening services were open to the public, reaching out with the message of hope to the surrounding community.

Working on the itinerary for the Guadeloupe trip, Melvin coordinated the travel dates for a stopover in Miami, Florida. This would give him an opportunity to attend a literature conference and meet with Bob Hoskins, his stateside VIDA liaison. With the church plant in Brussels holding services at Salle Regina, and the needs of many Pentecostal churches in Belgium and Europe, Melvin planned on turning over all his translations in French to VIDA, and concentrate on distribution and book fairs.

Eleanor decided to attend the conference as well, with a little side trip. When one of the past participants of the English-speaking women's Bible studies in Brussels found out Eleanor was passing through Florida, she lost no time in arranging tickets for Eleanor to come visit her for several days.

"Eleanor, I can't believe you are here in my home in Longwood, Florida," Cathy smiled, helping Eleanor stow her luggage in the guest room of her home on the golf course lined with palm trees. Hung on the walls of the smartly decorated living room were many of Cathy's paintings.

"It's so good to see you Cathy." Eleanor beamed back at her friend, "It has been a long time since Brussels."

"Yes, and to think I didn't like you at first," Cathy laughed at the memory of finding faith through a Bible study she didn't know why she was attending. After several weeks, she had invited Eleanor to her home and prayed for the first time, calling upon the name of Jesus.

"And now I want my golfing friends to find Jesus like I did. I've told them that when they come for the luncheon today you will share about your experience of escaping from Congo. After that just share as the Lord leads you."

It warmed Eleanor's heart to see the marked changes in Cathy and her husband who found Christ through Full Gospel Men's Business Meetings.

Before he left for the day, Cathy's husband waved and smiled, "Well, you ladies have a Holy Ghost meeting!"

After meeting at the Miami airport, Melvin and Eleanor flew southeast, past Puerto Rico, following an arc of islands tumbling down to South America known as the Lesser Antilles. Guadeloupe consisted of five islands with the capital, Basse-Terre, situated on the west shore of the larger two islands linked together by a bridge over a three kilometer sea passage. An overseas region of France, Christopher Columbus named the island Santa Marie de Guadeloupe in 1493 after the Virgin Mary. Later in 1674, the island was annexed to France after wiping out the Carib Amerindians. The lucrative sugar trade during the seventeenth century made Guadeloupe enticing enough to fight back and forth with Britain many times. Eventually, slavery was abolished on the island in 1848, but not without a struggle.

Melvin and Eleanor stepped off the plane, into a climate with plenty of sunshine, and average temperature ranging from the 70s to 80s. After greeting Guy and Alida, and their children, the Jorgensons explored their tropical surroundings. For a little sightseeing on the more populated east island, Grande-Terre, where the sugar cane was grown, Guy took Melvin to Pointe des Chateaux. The southeastern peninsula stuck out into the azure waters like the elongated tip of a butterfly wing.

"As I wrote you, the official language is French," Guy explained, "but Antillean Creole is spoken as well."

That night, over a Creole dinner on the veranda of Guy and Alida's home, everyone chattered, catching up on life.

"I must admit," Alida said, "all the theory of missionary life has gone out the window with the trade winds. The reality of daily life on an island without easy access to the necessities of life and the culture of Europe has been an adjustment."

"Yes, there is good and bad to both sides of the equation," Melvin said, "no matter where you live."

Eleanor agreed, adding contrasting examples of living on a simple mission station in Congo to the sophisticated city of Brussels. Guy and Alida soaked up the words of seasoned veterans of the mission field, asking questions about practical living and spiritual work amongst the locals. No strangers to raising children on the mission field, Melvin and Eleanor were able to lend a listening ear and offer sage advice on the topic.

Over the next several weeks, the Jorgensons worked alongside the Hamelles. Melvin gave a seminar on Christian living and preached on Sundays, all in French.

At the end of their time, it was hard for Melvin and Eleanor to say goodbye.

"Our hearts are melded with you and the work here in Guadalupe," Melvin said to Guy and Alida at the tiny airport in Basse-Terre.

Later on the plane he confided to Eleanor, "How satisfying it was to work with former CBC students and see firsthand what they are doing."

"Yes," Eleanor mused, "it was an encouragement to see their gift of caring for people and nurturing the church."

Melvin jotted down a few notes for an upcoming newsletter:

We stayed with missionary family from Belgium, Guy and Alida Hamelle. The seminar and nineteen days of meetings were of great blessing, with souls saved, filled with the Spirit, and bodies healed. The cooks kept everyone happy with the fine meals they prepared during the seminar. This growing mission field in Guadeloupe has nearly two thousand believers that worship in the fifteen Pentecostal churches.

* * * * *

The Jorgensons arrived back in Brussels in time to speak at the five-day Chinese camp with Pastors Abraham Liu and John Cheng.

As field director of Belgium, Melvin worked alongside the pastors of Belgium. One couple, Guy Guilbert, French, and his wife Lina, Finnish, who did their courtship in Swedish, had a church in Mons. Their dream was to have a youth retreat. Eventually, they purchased an old place out in the country that had a swimming pool. Mentoring the couple through the process, Melvin started thinking about an idea to help many more of the young pastors to get started, prompting him to initiate a revolving loan fund.

As money came from the States, instead of just giving it to the pastors for a church, Melvin put it in a fund. Then the new churches could use the money and pay it back, which helped the churches see their responsibility. Melvin would set up a reasonable payment plan per month without interest. After it was paid back, Melvin would help another church. Over the years, as a testament to God's faithfulness and the integrity of the churches, every payment was made, and on time!

In addition to the revolving loan fund, Melvin also gave quite a bit of stability to the pastors as a mentor.

* * * * *

Wanting to shore up all aspects of work in Europe, Melvin frequently sent out "prayer bulletins."

When Praying for Belgium - read these items first by M.J.
Prayer requests are a vital part of missionary ministry.
Come with me to the industrial city of Charleroi, where a
new fine church has been constructed with three hundred seats

in a most advantageous location across the avenue from the huge regional exposition hall. Continue with me to an area populated by Polish refugees from the last World War, where a beautiful church has been established among them with a fine congregation. Then there is James Barnard, and his wife, who head the evangelistic program among service members with meetings Sundays and during the week. Most people have heard of SHAPE—Supreme Headquarters of Allied Powers in Europe—located near the city of Mons. This plays an important part in the defense of Europe and the Western world, and is a center drawing many of our enlisted American youth. Many are saved through these meetings, and Christian lives are strengthened to meet the enemy forces of their souls. In addition to this, is a pioneer work started among the Belgians at a town near Mons, and also in the Flemish provinces, Bruges, a beautiful and quaint Burgundian city with a population of 100,000. The pastor is thrilled with the results and welcomes the prayers of others in keeping the guiding Spirit of the Lord upon the work.

The Brussels Evangelistic Center is looking for facilities to continue its evangelistic ministry in the capitol city of Belgium, home of NATO headquarters and the Common Market Community. Meetings have been held for four years in an auditorium that has served well to this time, but more suitable facilities are now urgently needed. Campaigns have been held in the past, with American and European evangelists and musicians with a large number of people saved. Others have been healed and baptized in the Holy Spirit. Two buildings have been found both of which could possibly serve the work well. The Lord's guidance is desired, and His help is needed in meeting the financial obligations. Being the only Assemblies of God church in Brussels, a city of one million people, lends importance and urgency to the work.

Ladies weekly prayer meetings and Bible studies have been conducted by Eleanor Jorgenson for many years. They have proven to be of immense help and blessing to many who find themselves estranged and lost in a foreign land. The two weekly studies are offered in both the French and English languages. Many families, having moved back to the States, testify to the vital and refreshing help received from these studies and times of prayer during their stay in Belgium, saying they never would have made it without such gatherings.

A visit to our Teen Challenge coffee bar in downtown Brussels would do much to stir the heart to prayer. But, already knowing the drastic situations workers meet in this type of ministry, such a visit is not necessary. The sad, hopeless condition of many young people has been turned around by the saving, healing message given through this program. Jean Marc, Joseph and Per will be encouraged to know you are praying for them as they reach out to these lost young people.

ICI students located in every province of Belgium are another subject of prayer. They are found in all walks of life, among college students, church members, drug addicts, prisoners, and of all ages. They seek help and prayer to solve personal problems they themselves have often woven, and family problems that seem to have no solution. Missionary Gail Winters, a former colleague of ours in Congo, is in close contact with these people, reviewing their lessons, corresponding with them, and sometimes being able to deal with them in person.

Melvin wrapped up his prayer letter with mentioning the new venture of a music program working with various musical groups, and that VIDA publications had recently begun publishing Christian literature in the French language, already offering more than twenty-five titles through the Brussels office with MAPS worker of six years, Penny Klein

Urban, at the helm. From Wisconsin, Penny came to Brussels for a two-year commitment, but it was stretching far past that as she dedicated herself to working in the office, wrapping and shipping out thousands of copies of *The Cross and the Switch Blade*. And after Virginia began working for CBC in 1975, Penny became a welcomed blessing to the Jorgensons.

It seemed Melvin had barely sent off the prayer bulletin and it was time for a newsletter highlighting the impact of the printed word. Only time in eternity would show the outcome of publishing and distribution of literature for God's kingdom.

NEWS FROM *The Jorgensons*

The 1981 International Book Fair of Brussels is now history. Stands, large and small, are dismantled. Furnishings have been hauled away. Lights in the two immense halls are turned out. Over three hundred thousand visitors have returned to their places, and the personnel of 1050 publishing houses to their offices and shops. We who represent VIDA (LIFE Publishers of Miami) are among them.

Located across the aisle from the huge USSR display and among the large commercial enterprises, contacts were made for the spread of Gospel literature. Immediate results were seen through witness and distribution of tracts and brochures.

Of all the literature given or sold, most of it was to young people. Schools arranged for students to attend, requiring each one to prepare a report. A result was that much of our literature was taken to be presented before large classes. Pray that this special ten-day ministry will continue to bear fruit in the days ahead.

I have published well-known books for many years in the French language, realizing the great need for gospel literature in that language. Among these are "The Cross and the Switchblade" by David Wilkerson (more than one hundred and fifty thousand copies sold), "Knowing the Doctrines of the Bible" by Myer Pearlman (used in all of our own and other Bible Schools around the world), "The Church on March" and "A Guide to Church Planting" by Melvin Hodges, as well as a book on tithing by myself (which has been translated into different African languages). The Adult Teachers quarterly from Springfield, translated and published in French for almost thirty years, was my responsibility for a number of years.

When VIDA, the largest AG foreign publishing house, entered the French language areas, I turned over to them all that I was doing. I continued, however, to work with them in distribution, which is growing rapidly week by week. We are pleased that within a year's time they have placed forty new titles on the market plus three different study Bibles. And new titles keep arriving. Impressive!

————+++————

We are still looking for a building to house THE BRUSSELS EVANGELISTIC CENTER. The owner of the building we had recently located decided not to sell. Pray with us for this desperate need.

————+++————

Melvin and Eleanor Jorgenson

* * * * *

Looking for a permanent place for a church home was no easy task. Discussion circled around options of either building a new building from the ground up or renovating an old movie theater. Because space was limited in the heart of the city, with buildings built wall-to-wall, a new building meant a location on the outskirts of Brussels. But that would create transportation problems as most people didn't have cars and neither did the young people, a prime component of their outreach. The scales began to tip toward finding a place close to public transportation.

The only thing Melvin knew for certain was the Lord directing him that at some time in the future, the total responsibility of the church would be turned over to a national pastor.

Then one day, someone mentioned an old warehouse building for sale on Avenue Van Volxem. Located one block south of Gare du Midi train station, a hub for public transportation of bus and tram, even people in the suburbs would be able to come in by train. It was an older building that had been built on top of another building. In fact, it was so old that the ground floor would have to be gutted, including excavating the foundation. However, the second floor and its street-front apartment could be easily renovated for a temporary auditorium and lodging for MAPS volunteers. And looking toward the future, a pastor's residence!

At seven kilometers from the Jorgenson's apartment, it was only a fifteen-minute drive to the property. After Melvin pulled out the oversized skeleton key from his coat pocket, he inserted it into the keyhole large enough for spying through. The door creaked opened and Melvin and Eleanor walked through the large, green, double doors.

* * * * *

LAST-MINUTE NEWS FLASH!

From the Jorgensons   *Brussels, October 1982*

We have been waiting a long time to be able to send you this thrilling news. Not waiting, but working, searching, praying—over a period of several years—and here it is:

*A building has been found for the BRUSSELS EVANGELISTIC CENTER!

A sanctuary seating close to four hundred, Sunday School rooms, a prayer room, office space, a fellowship hall, two apartments, and fronting a broad boulevard lined with tall, beautiful trees—all this in what the Lord is making possible.

The first papers for this property have been signed, and the final ones must be completed before the end of this year. The present slow market in the sale of larger buildings helped us bring the original price down to half. HOWEVER, $20,000 is still needed to complete the purchase by the end of December, and $40,000 is needed for renovation, $60,000 total. Not a drastic sum for a building of this worth.

However, even the amount due by the end of December is a great mountain before us. We have no one else to look to but you for help in providing the remaining amount needed for this missionary endeavor in the Capitol of Europe. We have been amazed and pleased by what the local Christians have given, but all their resources are entirely exhausted.

Your immediate sharing will help us move into this location for services by next summer or fall. Please pray over this matter, and send your offering (tax-deductible) to: Assemblies of God, Melvin Jorgenson, Division of Foreign Missions, 1445

Boonville, Springfield, MO 65802. Marked designated for: Brussels Evangelistic Center, Project number 684, class 40.

MAPS (Mobilization And Placement Service) volunteers are needed, skilled and unskilled, singly or in groups, to help renovate the interior of the building. Contact the MAPS office right away at the Springfield address above, and write me of your desire to work with us—a week, a month, or more. Lodging will be provided. An experienced construction super-visor is urgently needed.

God bless you as your share the burden—and advance—with us!

* * * * *

Not wanting to sign another contract for renting Salle Regina, they bid the hall farewell and held services back at the small church on 11, Rue Joseph Claes, only one hundred meters from Gare du Midi. And then a stream of MAPS vol-unteers came like an ant colony to a picnic! Groups arrived from the west coast, the Midwest, and the east coast with quite a few from Florida. Each group would stay an average of two weeks, and consisted of plumbers, electricians, car-penters, and laborers. One carpenter specialized in making doors. Another couple from Hibbing, Minnesota stayed for a year. The husband crafted a built-in corner booknook for selling books and literature situated near the entryway. His wife, an artist, painted a scene depicting Noah and the Ark in the children's room. A rainbow curved over the cluster of animals with skillfully created details including a charming smile on every face.

In addition to major renovations on the first floor, fin-ishing off the second floor became a top priority in order for the fellowship hall to serve as a temporary sanctuary.

Melvin stopped by the worksite as often as he could between his other duties. The rumble and sound of the Caterpillar roared in his ears as it dug down to the foundations of the pre-WWI era building.

"H-m-m-m, no pot of gold," he mused to himself, "I guess we'll have to get the building funds some other way."

Later he discussed the building plans with Pastor Amitie and Eleanor.

"It's an old, old city with cold cathedrals, so central heating is a must at the church," Melvin started out, "also separate bathrooms."

"Why put in separate bathrooms?" Pastor Amitie couldn't understand why the church needed two bathrooms.

In Belgium, bathrooms weren't separated with walls like they are in America. Furthermore, when Melvin and Eleanor went into public restrooms in restaurants they might see the feet and head of the person in the stall. When they had first arrived in Belgium in the 1950s men's urinals were common in the middle of the boulevards running down the center of city streets. In fact, it was not unusual to walk into a public place and find the facilities for personal business were simply a hole in the floor with raised bricks for a person's feet.

Melvin and Eleanor gently persisted in installing private-type bathrooms, even adding wee little toddler accommodations in the children's area.

Renovations continued, and MAPS workers kept working, while Belgian ladies prepared meals for volunteers of meat and potatoes in the old kitchen tucked in the basement. Exceptional cooks, Belgians usually started a meal with homemade soup or salad, with a loaf of 'la baguette,' bread from the local bakery. Besides sumptuous meals, many fond memories were made in that kitchen.

Eventually, the second-floor fellowship hall, with classrooms and bathrooms, was completed. Now they could start using the open room for a sanctuary during phase two of renovating the first floor.

Before each group of MAPS volunteers left Brussels, there was an after-church gathering of appreciation for them with coffee and refreshments. Often, the Belgian people would openly weep, saying, "When would we ever give up our vacation and spend our own money to help someone else?"

* * * * *

August 1985

Dear friends - partners in the Lord's work, for a long time we have been surrounded by, bricks planks tools of all sorts mortar boards hammers cement drywall planes plaster panels trowels drills, etc., etc., etc., and the many problems involved in putting all of this together.

But things are taking shape now, and the sanctuary of the BRUSSELS EVANGELISTIC CENTER CHURCH will soon be completed. We are looking forward to having our first services in the sanctuary in early fall.

THIS MEANS that the entryway, restrooms, nursery, literature corner, and sound and light control room will be ready for use. The public address system will be installed, the carpet laid, and the pews in place.

THIS MEANS that we can soon begin citywide evangelistic meetings, reaching out to the French-speaking people of this strategic city. Brussels, Capital of Europe, is headquarters for political SHAPE, military NATO, and the ever-growing Common Market countries of Europe.

THIS MEANS reaching Brussels and Belgium with the Gospel can be the means of reaching many other areas of Europe.

PRAY WITH US that the message of Truth and of Salvation may be preached in the power and fullness of the Holy Spirit.

THANK YOU for your prayer and financial support. Your continued sharing as partners is still needed—to complete the space reserved for "La Fraternite", the youth of this city.

God bless you!

Melvin & Eleanor Jorgenson

* * * * *

By 1986, the sanctuary seating three hundred and fifty was nearing completion. The entrance off 194, Avenue Van Volxem, Forest, Belgium Zip Code: 1190 had two sets of doors to guard against the cold. From there, a marble-floor hallway led to a set of double doors opening to the sanctuary. Inside, the sanctuary consisted of white walls with a dropped ceiling, dotted with clear panels covering fluorescent lights. Brick-type stones served as a baseboard for the new tile floor. A center aisle with wooden pews on either side led to the speaking platform with a wooden pulpit flanked by open space for musicians and vocalists. A baptismal area installed directly behind the platform and pulpit featured a white dove painted gracefully over a light-blue background. Steps cascaded from each side of the platform creating natural risers for the choir.

The custom-made pews were a gift from the Pentecostal churches of Sweden. Through attending meetings in Sweden, Melvin met furniture makers that were members of a church. Before Melvin could raise the funds to pay for the pews, they were fabricated and delivered! A Swedish pastor who often came to Belgium for meetings had made the arrangements.

Accenting the two long walls of the sanctuary were six stained-glass windows. Three on each wall, each one depicted a different scene from the Bible, using imagery such as grapes, wheat, and people. The stained-glass artist, a young woman, had become part of the church through attending meetings at Salle Regina. Like many who had come through word of mouth, personal invitation, advertising and door-to-door literature, she came out of curiosity and left as a believer in Christ.

The final crown jewel was the light-up cross on the outside of the building near the front entrance. Melvin went to the factory to check on the progress of the white, with blue-trim cross before its installation. As at previous churches in the past, an annual safety check would be conducted.

In the midst of the building project, Melvin and Eleanor made a short trip back to the States to continue raising funds for the Belgian church and other ministry initiatives. Scheduling their trip during the summer months allowed Melvin and Eleanor to spend time with their grandchildren at Lake Geneva Bible Camp. With living in Belgium, it seemed the children grew older quickly. Richard's Chad and Rachel, in third and first grade, and Aldene's Sonja and Chris, in fourth and second grade, kept things lively around the camp, creating memories for Melvin and Eleanor to take back with them to Europe to savor in the coming months.

* * * * *

Another highlight for them that year was the October book fair. Fabiola, Queen of Belgium attended the 1986 International Religious Book Fair in Tournai. Born in

Madrid, she was a Spanish Princess from a family of seven children, fluent in many languages and a devout Catholic. Before marrying King Baudouin in 1960, she had trained in nursing and worked in a hospital in Madrid. Queen Fabiola was known for her concern for social and health issues.

Walking along the rows of bookstands, she paused at the stand before VIDA. With keen interest Melvin noticed the table next to them offered her a Bible.

"No thank you," the queen politely replied, "I don't need that, I have a Bible."

Melvin thought through their inventory and selected a French book, *The Incomparable Christ.* "Here's a book that might interest you," he held out the book, while speaking in French.

And the queen took the book, "Well, thank you, I don't have that book."

Also working at the VIDA table, Eleanor watched Melvin's interaction with the queen as they conversed for several minutes.

"I've never seen a real queen up close before," Eleanor exclaimed as she watched royalty gracefully pass from table to table.

* * * * *

Of all the things Melvin did, nothing gave him as much satisfaction as building the church spiritually and physically. Both pieces worked in tandem as spiritually growing people were actively serving the Lord.

Sometimes Melvin and Eleanor would introduce new ideas to the church, such as breakfast before the Easter service. Knowing that chocolate for breakfast was part of the

Belgian culture Eleanor planned a menu of French chocolate croissants, and coffee and fruit.

One year for Easter, peep-peep-peep sounds were coming from the Fellowship Hall. One of the young people at church, Nicole, had brought in baby chicks and placed them in the fireplace in the corner of the second floor fellowship hall!

Wanting to build community through hospitality, the Jorgensons designed a well-appointed kitchen to serve the fellowship hall events. One of the ladies that came from Florida had purchased a commercial-grade dishwasher. And after that, Eleanor said to the women of the church, "Okay, now let's furnish the kitchen."

They set a goal of purchasing quality dishes for one hundred people. Gradually, pure white Villroy Boc dishes from Luxembourg began to fill the cupboards and silver wear was organized in the drawers. And then the women bought pots and pans. Over time, the Fellowship Hall became a blessing to other churches that didn't have a gathering place like that and churches would ask to use the hall for a wedding or other special occasions.

To keep their flock mission-minded and extend a warm welcome to all the different nationalities coming into the church, an annual international dinner was held. Everyone made a dish to represent their country: Polish, Spanish, Italian, and Congolese, and a few other nationalities made for a melting pot of people speaking French under the umbrella of faith in Christ.

* * * * *

One of the spiritual challenges Melvin and Eleanor encountered in the Pentecostal churches of Belgium, and other parts of Europe was in supporting the pastors financially. Pastors in Belgium had to rush home from work to church and pick up their Bible and not have the time to prepare for a sermon or other work needed at the church with their flock. After noticing there was no teaching on tithing and giving, Melvin wrote an eighteen-page booklet on the subject entitled, *Etude Sur La Pratique De La Dime: Le secret d'une vie d'abondance.*

When discussing the principal of investing in God's kingdom Melvin and Eleanor heard comments such as, "Well, when we were Catholics we were forced to give so now that we are saved we don't have to give." And also, "The priests came and told us what to tithe and now we are free from that."

This was one of the reasons Melvin started the revolving loan fund for pastors. Initially, most of the money for their churches came from America. However, over time, the Belgian people discovered the joy of giving. Instead of a heavy burden, tithing and gifts of generosity were seen as a blessing, bringing an abundance of freedom for the giver.

* * * * *

As the date of the dedication service approached, Pastor Amitie and the church prepared to pass the baton of leadership of Brussels Evangelistic Center Church to national pastors Guy and Alida Hamelle. Also during this time, Eleanor's mother, Hazel Groat, passed on to her eternal reward on January 7, 1988 at the age of ninety-three.

Added to significant changes of church and family, were the political events concerning Europe. Cracks were forming in the Iron Curtain as President Reagan turned over the Oval Office to Vice-President George Bush. In September 1989, Hungary took down the barriers on its border to Austria.

Meanwhile, in southern East Germany, thousands of citizens joined the weekly Monday night prayer group at the Saint Nicholas Church in the city of Leipzig. This silent protest turned into a growing demonstration with each passing week until by Monday, November 4, 1989, the group reached a half million, with one million East Berliners joining the movement.

And then, the Berlin Wall came down. That symbolic event lit the fuse to the collapse of communism in the eastern bloc and eventually the fragmentation of the Soviet Union.

* * * * *

On November 17, 1989, Melvin and Eleanor drove fifteen minutes to the church for the dedication service to meet special guests and longtime friends, Norm and Norma Correll. Also attending were many former CBC students. One of them, Jacques Dernelle, had become the president of the French pastors. Attending the college at almost eighteen years old, he was the youngest student Melvin ever allowed to register for classes. He also became one of the professors at CBC.

Right before the service began, a middle-aged man and his teenage son walked into the first floor auditorium, "Hi Mom, Hi Dad!"

Melvin and Eleanor's mouth dropped open at the sight of their son, Richard, and grandson, Chad.

"We just got in on Air France via Paris, so we hurried over to the apartment, changed and caught a taxi over," Richard beamed, happy as most boys are to spring a surprise on their parents.

Large sprays of flowers in white vases flanked the wooden podium while musicians and vocalists led the congregation in worship and thanksgiving to God's faithfulness in bringing about this flock of believers. It provided a gathering place where a community of saints could express their gifts and talents for the blessings of others in the city of Brussels, Belgium, known as the Capital and Crossroads of Europe.

The total property of seven and a half acres included a two-story church, with a furnished one-bedroom apartment and an adjacent townhome for the pastor's residence.

After a time of singing and prayer, Brother Norm preached a powerful message to a crowded sanctuary, followed by Pastor Amitie. The day after the dedication service came the passing of the torch of Centre Evangelique on Avenue van Volxem to Pastors Guy and Alida Hamelle.

Chapter Forty-Three

Puissance!

One day Melvin came home from a board meeting at the French-speaking Belgian church, "Well, Eleanor, you made it in today."

He slipped off his coat and set his brief case aside before giving his wife a peck on the cheek.

"They even consented that you would be able to go up front and pray with people."

"Oh, really?" Eleanor lifted her eyebrows in surprise. She searched her husband's face for clues of information.

"Well, I didn't talk up for you, they suggested it."

Eleanor smiled, "It was probably some of the wives from the ladies Bible study that suggested it to their husbands."

"Well, either way, you're in finally, so congratulations."

Eleanor rejoiced, "Hallelujah! The Lord has broken down the glass ceiling for women to minister in the French-speaking church!"

She knew that, by the grace of God, once she pioneered the way, other women would follow. The scripture foretold thousands of years ago in the book of Joel and then repeated by Peter after the initial outpouring of the Holy Spirit on Pentecost leaped from the pages of the Bible.

"And it shall come to pass afterward, that I will pour out my spirit upon all flesh; and your sons and your daughters shall prophesy, your old men dream dreams, your young men shall see visions: And also upon the servants and upon the handmaids in those days will I pour out my spirit." (Joel 2: 28, 29; Acts 2: 17, 18) KJV

When Eleanor came to Brussels in 1964, she had it in her heart to work with the French-speaking ladies. However, after awhile there she discovered that it was not an easy thing to do, because women were not accepted in ministry.

Once, on a ministry trip with Belgian pastors, one of them dropped his jaw at the sight of a woman involved in public ministry, "Look, that's a woman and she's praying for that person!"

Melvin would try to explain to the pastors how the Holy Spirit came for the equipping of the saints to do the work of the Lord. However, the pastors felt women were supposed to be quiet in the church. Technically, men weren't supposed to pray for others in church unless they were a pastor or a deacon. A female pastor or deaconess was unthinkable.

Nonetheless, prodded by a desire to see the French-speaking women come alive spiritually, Eleanor asked permission from some of the Belgian pastors to have a Bible study in the church. The request was denied, so Eleanor opened her home for a Bible study.

When she first invited the ladies to her home they said, "Oh, no, we wouldn't want to intrude."

"You aren't intruding," Eleanor sweetly countered, "I'm inviting you!"

At the first meeting there were eight women including Eleanor. The newcomers were unfamiliar with a women's Bible study or praying together. It was a new experience for them opening up to share about their spiritual needs or their family needs or whatever life brought to a person. Eleanor thought how wonderful it was to watch the women begin to feel comfortable with praying for each other.

"Thank you, Lord, for this home that was opened up."

"Yes, Lord thank you," another woman added, "it has been a refuge."

Eventually, Eleanor was allowed to have the study at the church and the group grew to an average of twenty or thirty women coming every week.

* * * *

Melvin sat at his desk in his office on Avenue du Derby tossing around ideas for the upcoming conference in March 1991. It would be a Wednesday night through Friday afternoon retreat for missionaries and their families from the Benelux group of Belgium, Holland, and Luxembourg. The location for this year's missionary retreat was Castel de Pont-a-Lesse in the historic town of Dinant. Seventy kilometers southeast of Brussels, and less than twenty miles north of France, Dinant offered dramatic views of the River Meuse overshadowed by the formidable Gothic-style Collegiate Church of Notre-Dame, with the Citadel rising above in the background perched on a stone cliff accessible by four hundred and eight steps.

Castle de Pont-a-Lesse was a renovated stately three-story home with a stone and stucco exterior accented with turrets. Just east of the river, the castle-like structure situated on a rocky bluff overlooking forested hills would be spacious enough for lodging, dining, and the meetings. Of special interest to first time tourists was the statue of the saxophone in the city square in honor of its inventor, Adolphe Sax, born in Dinant in 1814.

On a pad of paper, Melvin began jotting down the basic outline for the conference programs including the schedule of meals and meetings. Then he listed all the international ministries located in Brussels: Continental Bible College, International Media Ministries, International Correspondence Institute, church planting, literature, radio, Teen Challenge, and University Ministries.

Because the three countries were known as the Benelux group since 1944, which was the forerunner to the European Union, the official title of the conference would be the Benelux Retreat. But what would they select for the theme of the retreat?

He knew the Assemblies of God were calling the 1990's the "Decade of Harvest" and that their theme for 1991 was "Lord Send Me." But how would they accomplish this except by the power of the Holy Spirit? And how would they be able to tap into this power except through prayer?

Melvin also knew their main speaker, G. Raymond Carlson, elected as General Superintendent for the Assemblies of God in 1985, was challenging everyone who considered themselves part of the AG family to pray and believe God for five thousand new churches during the Decade of Harvest. Brother Carlson also set goals of twenty thousand new ministers to reach five million people whom he referred to as "unchurched."

As the weeks went by Melvin continued to pray and plan with the other people on the planning committee for the retreat. Gradually a theme for the retreat emerged based on the song, *Lord, Send the Power*, composed by Charles D. Tillman.

The first two verses recounted the story of the first Pentecost with a repeating chorus of *"O Lord, send the pow'r just now."*

However, it was the third verse, written by Gwen Jones that struck at Melvin's heart:

As we go forth to the harvest, Face the overwhelming need, in our own strength we will falter. . .

Yes, thought Melvin, while working at his office, there are so many needs and so many people to reach that it can become overwhelming. How often he and Eleanor felt this way and so did other workers in God's field of harvest, if they were honest enough to admit it.

Melvin's eyes found the last phrase of the verse and read it aloud: "For the Spirit now we plead."

Then he began singing the chorus in his baritone voice, letting it fill the office and his heart, "O Lord, send the pow'r just now, O Lord, send the pow'r just now!"

* * * * *

A few months later, at the retreat held at the beautiful Castle de Pont-a-Lesse, Melvin asked everyone in the meeting room to pull out the pink-colored insert in their program to join him in singing *Lord, Send the Power*.

Before introducing Brother Carlson as this year's spiritual enrichment speaker, Melvin called their attention to the scripture printed on the inside of the peach-colored program, "I want to encourage all of us to reflect on the words from Isaiah, Chapter forty, verses 28-31, during our time together and afterward when we all depart to our homes and the daily needs of ministry."

After the sound of papers shuffling he continued, "At almost seventy-three years old, I can look back over fifty years of ministry since my first church in Jackson, Minnesota, and see, 'that the everlasting God, the Lord, the Creator of the ends of the earth, fainteth not, neither is weary. . .He giveth power to the faint; and to them that have no might he increaseth strength.'"

Melvin looked over the group of men and women who were looking to the Lord for refreshment this weekend and kept reading, "Even the youths shall faint and be weary, and the young men shall utterly fail. . ."

Sitting in the crowd of missionaries, Eleanor began to mouth the words her husband was reading from the book of Isaiah, "But they that wait upon the Lord shall renew their strength; they shall mount up with wings as eagles; they shall run, and not be weary; and they shall walk, and not faint."

Eleanor thought to herself how through the years she had grown weary many times, beaten down by the workload and pressures of the ministry, not to mention the resistance of darkness she felt at times. Nonetheless, as she leaned on the Lord and looked to Him, He had been faithful to renew her strength. A tear of gratitude slipped from her eyes. She might look older on the outside, but on the inside, she was still young, soaring high for the Lord. There was much to look forward to in the Decade of Harvest.

After Melvin introduced Brother Carlson by adding he was also president in 1962 of his alma matter, North Central College, Melvin sat down off to the side of the speaker podium.

After his introductory remarks, Brother Carlson highlighted the theme of the Benelux Retreat, "Christian living and Christian service are so interwoven we cannot separate them. The power of the Spirit makes both possible. We cannot please God without it. We cannot reach our world without it. The power of the Holy Spirit has divine dimension, for it is a spiritual power."

Brother Carlson paused a moment to scan his audience, "I need that power. You need that power. Why? The Holy Spirit provides power for living. It is the secret of effective Christian service."

Then he listed in a rhythmic preaching voice: "By the power of the Holy Spirit we are enabled to live holy lives. By the power of the Holy Spirit we have understanding of the Word of God. By His power the Holy Spirit effectively intercedes through us. By the Holy Spirit's power we are enabled to speak to others about faith in Christ."

* * * * *

The following year, back in Minnesota, Melvin and Eleanor celebrated their fiftieth wedding anniversary at the "Tab," the church they were married in, with their family and friends. The previous November, they had bought and moved into a townhouse in Burnsville after selling their miracle house they had rented out for many years. Their plan for the future was to have dual residence in Minnesota and Belgium.

After returning to Brussels the end of August, Melvin and Eleanor were interviewed for an article in *PUISSANCE*, or POWER, the bimonthly magazine of the Assemblies of God of Belgium inspired by the occasion of their fiftieth wedding anniversary. Translated from French to English, the composition for the 1993 issue of *POWER* began with stating that the Jorgensons were "well-known and loved in the Pentecostal churches in Belgium. They have lived together for more than fifty years in love and companionship."

Besides featuring black and white photos, one of their wedding day, and one from their Golden Anniversary, the article covered an overview of their years of ministry. Then the essay ended with, "They have always served the Lord with much discretion and abnegation. May they find here the homage and deep respect and our sincere fraternal affection."

* * * * *

It was during this time that Eleanor thought, wouldn't it be nice to have a women's retreat, "That way I could invite not only the women in Brussels, but other women from French-speaking churches."

After discussing the matter with Melvin, and praying about it, Eleanor happened to mention the idea one day while riding in the pastor's car with his wife and daughter.

"Well, it's okay, you can have the retreat, but I'll go there and be the speaker."

Eleanor's heart sank until the pastor's daughter blurted out, "Dad, what do you know about talking to women?"

"Oh, well," the pastor conceded, "since it is Sister Jorgenson, I have confidence in her, and because it's her that will lead it, I will put my okay on it."

The retreat was organized and held in Liège, seventy kilometers east of Brussels. Afterward, the enthusiasm of the women caused a desire for future retreats. However, there was still resistance to women in ministry. When Eleanor tried to get Bible studies going in the other French-speaking churches, the pastors came to the office on Avenue du Derby to talk about it. They said their wives were too busy to take on any extra activity. Still, the seeds were planted, and over time, Eleanor heard that one pastor did have his wife teach a study at his church.

Encouraged by the response of the women to the work of the Holy Spirit during a weekend set apart for spiritual enrichment, Eleanor began making plans for another one in the fall. As the time of the retreat grew close, she felt a stirring inside her to communicate with her sisters in Christ in America about the retreat.

Dear friends in Women's Ministries, 29 August 1994

This is the first time in my missionary career that I have personally written a letter to you. Previous letters have always concerned our work as a whole.

However, I feel impressed by the Holy Spirit to write asking you to pray for our French Women's Retreat to be held September 23, 24 and 25. It is to be held at a government retreat center one hundred kilometers from Brussels.

For almost twenty years I have held Bible Studies and prayer meetings among English speaking ladies. At the beginning, these meetings were attended mostly by ladies of the Guild of the American Protestant Church in Brussels. For the most part, these ladies knew nothing of the saving grace of Jesus. Through the years, many of these ladies found Jesus as their Savior and many were filled with the Holy Spirit.

I might add that on several occasions whole families found the Lord because of the wife's personal experience in Christ. Even now, with the passing of many years since seeing them, especially at Christmas time, I receive letters and greetings from them.

During those years, my heart was always burdened for the French-speaking ladies of Belgium. I sensed in my spirit their spiritual bondage, and meetings among them were made possible when I opened our home for Bible Studies and Prayer.

The first prayer and Bible Study consisted of eight ladies. They did not know how to pray; they could not find the passages of scripture to read. It was beautiful to see how they began to grow in the Lord, how the Holy Spirit taught them to pray. Eventually they began sharing their individual needs. This in itself was a miracle, as the Belgians are a very closed people. We then began to deal with and pray for the needs of each other.

Our group began to grow; we needed a bigger place in order to reach out to others. After praying about this need, I felt led to contact the board of our French-speaking church, asking them to allow our ladies meetings in the fellowship hall. My request was granted.

You must understand, women in Belgium have had no prominence in the churches. Women are not allowed to teach or preach. They cannot have a ministry as such. So, for some years I prayed and worked for an opening to have a ministry among them. We now have forty-five to fifty ladies in our group.

The next step taken was to impress on them and the pastors the blessings a Ladies Retreat could bring to them. The result was our first Ladies Retreat held in September 1993. The presence of the Lord was so very real to all. Lives were touched and changed by the moving power of the Holy Spirit in the meetings. The Sunday morning service was especially blessed when it seemed the whole room was surcharged and electrified by His presence.

These were some of the comments expressed to me: "I have never experienced anything like this before"; "I came having suffered with a painful physical disorder, but since last night I have had no pain and I am leaving healed"; and "I am glad I didn't miss out on these meetings!"

The main purpose of my letter is to ask you, the Women's Ministries, to pray for us as we have our second retreat. We long to see a real move of the Holy Spirit among us again, reaching into every part of the church.

I am praying the Lord *to baptize these ladies with His Holy Spirit, *that these women will become "Women of Freedom," *that they will no longer be in bondage, *but be free to walk a new life in Him, *serving Him faithfully.

"BECOMING A WOMAN OF FREEDOM" is the theme of our Retreat.

"If the Son, therefore, shall make you free, ye shall be free indeed." (John 8:36)

Thank you for your prayers in our behalf!

In Christian love,
(Mrs.) Eleanor Jorgenson

The following year Eleanor sent out another letter to her friends in the Women's Ministries thanking them for interceding:

We felt the prayers as we were blessed by the mighty and precious Presence of the Holy Spirit. The ladies left the Retreat in an atmosphere of praise and worship. In fact, they composed a song at the close of the retreat based on our theme, "Becoming a Woman of Freedom." On the way home, the chartered bus was filled with the singing of this song. I will translate it for you from French.

"Come to the Retreat and you will be fortified—liberated from your sorrows and your worries, because God is here. We have received much, but above all, God blessed, and now we are different, ready to begin anew. We are transformed, fortified, liberated, blessed, liberated and blessed by Jesus."

Now they are looking forward with great anticipation to our next Retreat, September 29, 30, and October 1. We are *expecting new ladies to join us in answer to invitations that have been sent out.*

Now may I ask you once again, to pray for, and with, us for this coming Retreat? My prayer is that many lives will be changed and enriched, and that the ladies will return home to be a blessing in their homes, their families and their church. May God grant it to be so—this could be the start of a revival for which we are longing. The theme of this year's Retreat is "Becoming a Woman of Purpose."

Lill Sundberg Anderson will be with me again. The ladies so enjoyed her anointed singing and heart-felt sharing. I will be speaking on Saturday and Sunday. I feel so much my need of your prayers, for it is by the anointing of the Holy Spirit that the retreat will be a success.

After closing with, "Again, thank you for remembering us!" Eleanor chose a photograph taken at the previous retreat of Lill, herself, and Alida Hamelle to tuck into the left-hand corner of her letter.

* * * * *

That September, as Eleanor arrived at the government retreat center for her fourth women's retreat she felt a heavy burden, which intensified after the evening service. All night long, she wrestled with this burden.

The next morning during the first service, she opened her Bible to Ephesians 6:12 and read, "For we wrestle not against flesh and blood, but against principalities, against powers, against the rulers of the darkness of this world, against spiritual wickedness in high places."

Then Eleanor recounted one of her many experiences while serving as missionaries in Congo, now Zaire. While giving this testimony of God's deliverance, a woman named Marie, from one of their new church planting efforts, left the room. Later she told the pastor's wife who had invited her that she was sorry she had come, and that she would never return to another retreat. Of course, the pastor's wife was greatly disturbed. That afternoon, Eleanor and the pastor's wife prayed fervently.

In the evening, the meeting opened with singing, "We've got the power in the Name of Jesus. . . ."As Alida Hamelle was leading the women in worship, Eleanor noticed Marie, the guest invited by the pastor's wife, stiffen out like a board in her chair. Then to the shock of Eleanor and the rest of the women in the room, the chair began to dance across the room! Eleanor knew this kind of activity could ruin the women's ministry for years to come. But she also knew the Lord was with her. Inside she prayed, *Lord, you have to help me with this or there will no open doors for ladies ministries in Belgium.*

Fear changed to courage. Eleanor instructed several women to hold down the chair while she and a few others began to pray over Marie. Following examples in scripture, Eleanor rebuked the manifesting evil spirit using the Name of Jesus.

The chair kept bouncing, so Eleanor tried a different approach. In a calm, direct voice she said, "Marie, repeat the Name of Jesus and thank Him for the blood that He has shed for you."

A voice came from the woman: *Leave me alone.*

Undeterred, the others continued to pray.

Then Marie opened her lips again, "Jesus, I thank you for the blood that was shed for me."

Immediately a change came over her whole being reflecting peace and tranquility.

The small group around the chair prayed with Marie for a while, letting the Holy Spirit minister to her. It was close to midnight when she went to her room in victory.

Eleanor was overjoyed, and ready for a good night's sleep, when a woman walked over to the pastor's wife to complain, "Why did you bring Marie? She is ruining our retreat!"

The pastor's wife didn't know what to say to the comments.

However, later that night while in her room, the offended woman donned her housecoat and walked to the dining room where a few ladies gathered around the table discussing the events of the evening.

"I just came out to say that I am sorry for my outburst earlier against Marie," then she sat down and told her story, "When I got to my room the Holy Spirit began to deal with me. I've been a Christian for many years and I have never seen anything like deliverance. But the Holy Spirit reminded me, 'Have you forgotten that fifteen years ago you were in darkness just like Marie? You were delivered, but you have been sitting in your cocoon enjoying a life I have given you, and forgetting others who are in need.'"

Then she looked directly at the pastor's wife who invited Marie, "I am sorry, will you forgive me for the things I said?"

The next morning, the Sunday service was a joyful time as Marie thanked everyone for their prayers and friendship, "I have two daughters at home who have been practicing witchcraft. But now that I am free through the Name of Jesus and His shed blood, I want that for them as well."

Eleanor quickly suggested, "Let's lay hands on Marie and pray that she will become strong in the Lord and be used as a real witness in this newly planted church."

After they finished praying Eleanor instructed, "As you all leave this retreat I want to remind you that although you have been made aware of the spiritual darkness we must fight, remember that there is a *puissance*—a *power* greater, that God is greater than he that is in the world, as it says in 1 John, Chapter 4:4."

Chapter Forty-Four

Back to Congo

⊛

After the Ladies Retreat, Melvin and Eleanor turned their thoughts toward Congo.

Congo. It called to them. And now—they were going back.

On December 2, 1995, Melvin sent a request marked <u>URGENT</u> from their townhome in Burnsville, Minnesota, to the director of Eurasia Field, AG in Springfield, MO.

We have been invited by the Zaire field to attend the Zaire Celebration of seventy-five years of missionary work in that field. It begins 15 February.

I am asking if funds for my wife and myself to attend would be available from my Class 00 account.

The amount would be about four thousand dollars and could be transferred to our Credit Union account.

I will then take the final steps to find out if all is clear for us to go.

God bless, and best regards, Mel Jorgenson

Once the transfer was made, Melvin could contact their agent with Daytons' Travel Service at the Southdale Shopping Mall, to confirm their flights to Nairobi via Amsterdam. Next on his list—apply for the needed visas for Kenya and Zaire. Leaning back in his chair in his office, located in the front of their blue-gray townhome, he stared out the window toward the quiet dead-end street. In his mind, he ticked off the list of inoculations and several necessary tropical items they would need such as anti-malaria drugs, and bottles of iodine and chlorine tablets. Maybe they should bring a water purifier. Without the official "yellow fever" immunization card, they would not be able to obtain a visa to either Kenya or Zaire.

Despite all the myriad of details needed to attend the celebration, anticipation grew with every day. Would he really be setting foot in his beloved Congo again? As if it were yesterday, Melvin remembered the vision God had given him at the tender age of thirteen, of a map of Africa that closed-in on a region with a mighty river snaking from the west coast above and below the equator spreading its tentacles eastward from where it began.

Everyday Melvin and Eleanor's thoughts and discussions revolved around the people they would see in Congo, the places they would see, and the foods they longed to savor again.

On January 30, 1996, Melvin sent a fax to Larry Walker in Nairobi, Kenya.

We are to arrive in Nairobi on KLM Fight 563 at 9:55 AM, Tuesday, 06 February. We are to leave Nairobi on an AIM flight the morning of Friday, 09 February.

Our son, Richard arrives in Nairobi on AF 476 on Tuesday, 13 February at 9:00 AM. He leaves for Zaire on Friday, 16 February.

Would you please confirm our UTALI HOTEL reservations for the 3 nights we are there; and our flights into Zaire.

We are so thankful that Nancy V. told us you would meet us at the airport and confirm arrangements she has made. We appreciate greatly your willingness to do so in your busy schedule. Best regards - and God bless!

* * * * *

Upon arriving in Isiro, formerly Paulis, Melvin and Eleanor were struck by the extremely difficult living conditions still existing, as in the early days when they had first come to Congo, and then after Independence in 1960. They also noticed a complete breakdown and disappearance of banking facilities, which made obtaining local currency for daily living very difficult. Although uncomfortable for traveling and crippling many vehicles, as a colony of Belgium, the roads had been maintained with connecting bridges over the web of rivers. Now, however, impassable roads made travel by small plane imperative.

And yet, there was a sense of place, of belonging, that hit to their very core. The smells. The sounds. Even the red dust of Congo that clung to everything and everyone greeted their senses like a forgotten friend.

Melvin and Eleanor stayed with two missionary nurses both with the same first names, "I will call you the Nancy's," teased Melvin during introductions.

"Very well, Brother Jorgenson," one of the Nancy's replied, "it's best to keep things simple. I assume Larry met you in Nairobi and your stay went well there?"

"Oh, yes, it helps tremendously with the jet lag."

The other Nancy added, "It's an honor to have you both stay in our humble guest house for as long you like!"

The two women rented a property from Mario, the man who used to deliver fresh vegetables to Andudu and the other mission stations from farms in the Kivu Goma area. The property also included a separate guesthouse of two rooms separated by a bathroom. It was an ideal set up with Melvin and Eleanor in one room, and the other room reserved for Richard.

Eleanor bubbled over to her husband, "It's like old times with the girls, Lillian and Gail."

Joining the Nancy's for dinner, the Jorgensons sat down to a table of familiar African food of bush meat, boiled manioc leaves, and rice flavored with pili pili. That night, as Melvin and Eleanor lay their heads on their pillows, a delightful sense of enjoying all things Congo came over them while the night sounds of Africa gently rocked them to sleep.

* * * * *

The next day, Melvin and Eleanor went to the open market and stores in downtown Isiro and began practicing their Bangala.

"There's nothing quite like African peanuts," Melvin exclaimed after purchasing some and cracking their shells for a quick snack.

"Yes, we have to make sure we bring some peanuts home for Aldene," then Eleanor added with a note of sadness, "I sure wish she could be here with us."

"Yes, it would have been the frosting on the cake of this experience," Melvin agreed.

Walking through the stands of produce and handmade items, it seemed their Bangala was as worn out as the surrounding buildings, but by the end of the day words and phrases clicked together in flowing syntax.

"You're getting it, Bwana!" Eleanor laughed quoting the locals when Melvin first attempted to preach in Bangala in the early days.

"Yes, it is coming back, but I may need to preach in French during the conference."

Spotting a pith helmet Melvin tried it on for size, "What do you think?"

"It's large enough to do the job that's for sure," Eleanor smiled at the extra-wide brim casting shade on her husband's face.

* * * * * *

That Sunday, Melvin and Eleanor joyfully attended one of the local churches in Isiro. They were pleased to find how the Bangala language came back to them as they readily communicated with the Congolese.

"Bwana and Madame Jorgenson," an older woman with wisdom shining in her eyes, reached for them both with tears streaming down her face.

"Sister Sarah Anabote!" Melvin and Eleanor embraced their dear friend, now an ordained minister, and all three rattled questions and answers in Bangala.

"Please stop by the Nancy girls' house after service, I have something for you," Eleanor said, delighted she remembered to pack the blue dress she had purchased for her friend, knowing that Anabote preferred to wear a dress rather than an African dhoti.

Another treat for them was their time of fellowship with Pastor Simona Karada. After a tearful greeting he said, "Thank you, Bwana Jorgenson, for your faithfulness to me and the other pastors in training us at the Bible School at Andudu with word and example."

Pastor Simona had become the first national pastor to take over Jay and Angeline Tucker's church plant in Isiro.

Before the anniversary celebration began on Thursday, Phil and Edith Cochrane arrived in Isiro, along with Gail Winters, and her cousin Wil, and his son Tom. That night, familiar faces gathered around the table at the home of missionaries Pat and Suzanne. Although it was a joyful occasion, it was also a sacred time of reflection of the darker days of their evacuation.

"To see Sarah Anabote again, oh my, what a jewel she is!" Gail declared.

Then she explained to her cousin and his son, "She is the one who said to Lillian and me during the upheaval in 1964, 'I will not leave you. If you die, I'll die with you.' She suffered a beating and imprisonment when she refused to go home."

"She has been a woman of godly strength ever since she became a believer, and refused to cook the Paramount Chief's beer for him," Eleanor added.

Being with Gail and the Cochranes brought back many vivid memories of the days of rebel uprising, when they were captives until finally making their escape. It was one thing to meet up with their former colleagues as they passed through Brussels, and an entirely different thing to meet in the former town of Paulis.

"Have you gone by the print shop and Tucker's old house yet?" Phil asked.

"Yes, we did manage to get across town while shopping," Melvin replied, "and we'll probably go again when Richard arrives."

Then he added, "Although with a shudder I could picture him sitting in jail after walking through town with a gun at his back!"

"You know I've been by our old apartment and Tucker's house many times with coming back to work here after the evacuation," said Gail, "and it's always a double-edged feeling of eeriness and thankfulness."

Both Edith and Phil agreed that seeing the buildings after returning for another term of missionary work had brought back strong feelings of danger and of deliverance. From an inner place in her soul, Eleanor quoted Psalm 41, verses one and two, the scripture given to Edith from the Lord during their 1964 evacuation, "Blessed is he who considers the poor: the Lord will deliver him in time of trouble."

In her British accent, Edith robustly joined her sister in Christ, "The Lord will preserve him, and keep him alive; and he shall be blessed upon the earth; and thou wilt not deliver him unto the will of his enemies."

"For there shall be no loss of any man's life among you, save that of the ship," Melvin added the verse from the Book of Acts he had received the same day during their escape from Congo.

Then Melvin added with passion: "We are reminded once again of the goodness and faithfulness of the Lord!"

* * * * *

By midweek, Isiro's population swelled as people came from every direction and from great distances, most on foot, others by bicycle, spending as much as two weeks on the road. One group walking five 500 km from Kisangani on the Zaire River was robbed on the way, with even their shirts on their backs taken. But they continued their journey not letting the incident keep them from the blessings that lay ahead. The number attending by count was over thirteen thousand, which exceeded all expectations.

To kick-start the event, a parade of church members in the area of the AG Gombari Mission made its way past dignitaries toward the town square. Leading the procession, several people carried large white banners with blue print that read *Les Assemblées de Dieu* emblazoned on an arch over *Au Zaire* and the insignia of the AG church in Africa. Below the insignia was inscribed the seventy-five year span of *1921–1996*. Watching and listening, Melvin and Eleanor sat under one of the many mafikas constructed for shade. Various groups of Congolese marched past them with vibrant banners representing their choir, Bible School, elementary and high school, and medical workers. It warmed Melvin and Eleanor's hearts to see the names of the mission stations such as Betongwe, Gombari, and Andudu proudly swaying in the breeze. Memories sprang back to life in their minds, mingled with the music of Congo.

Between the participants singing, marching, and dancing, were bands and orchestras of African instruments. A kaleidoscope of colorful clothing and headgear swirled together with the cacophony of sounds from stringed instruments from Biodi, one of which was the size of a coffee table, wheeled the 130-mile distance to Isiro. Drums were beating; one of them a Makalima, sounding the call to joyful worship. Wooden wind instruments made by the pygmies augmented all of these African sounds. To see this group of Christian believers and Bible students trained to minister to their own people was a touching scene for many missionaries of the early days. Trailing the end of the pageant were several Speed the Light-sponsored vehicles painted with simple AG emblems.

After the hour-long parade melted into the crowd of spectators, the event concluded with a powerful Pentecostal sermon by the Superintendent of the Assemblies of God in

America, Brother Thomas Trask, who was also the keynote speaker for the conference. This opening meeting and other main meetings were held in the open air under a great brush arbor erected for the occasion near the town square.

During the rest of the conference, speakers brought stirring messages that led people to wholehearted consecration. Thursday through Saturday, former missionaries of Congo including Melvin, Gail, and Phil spoke in one of the eight churches in the Isiro area. Choirs from Betongwe, Andudu, and other mission stations rotated for the meetings as well. Men, young and old, and women clustered with children, some with nursing babies, sat on either side of the churches on wooden benches or hand-carried stools. Offerings lasted an hour as each person danced their way up to the basket, dropping in a Congo franc, and then danced their way back to the bench, while the crowd sang and rejoiced.

During one of the main sessions, forty candidates were ordained to the ministry, including two women, and another forty more received licenses. The men clad in trousers, white shirts, and ties for the special occasion, stood proudly with their two sisters in the ministry for a photograph.

Between meetings, many people approached Melvin and Eleanor, "Do you remember me?"

For the most part, they didn't, so much time had passed since the Congolese were children at the mission stations attending school or church services. Many told Melvin and Eleanor of events that took place during their former ministry among them that caused both parties to smile and weep.

One woman, in an African dhoti, came up to Eleanor, "You don't remember me, but I was this high when you taught me to read and write at school." She lifted her hand to her waist.

Then her smile faded, "My mother is dying. Would you come and see her?"

Eleanor walked a short distance to the windowless hut. Inside it was dark, with an earthy scent of banana leaves covering the dirt floor.

Eleanor waited for her eyes to adjust to the dimness, but she could barely see the frail woman lying on the leaves who spoke in a whisper, "I remember when my daughter was born and you came to see me and you brought me clothes for her."

Eleanor gently spoke with the woman and offered to pray with her. What an honor it felt to Eleanor to be with this precious soul.

Meeting several pastors, deaconesses and workers who still remained of that period, and now retired, was a moving experience for all involved. A few young men slowly led an elderly man to Melvin and Eleanor.

"He wanted to come to the conference so he got on a kinga," explained one young man, "and we pushed him on the bicycle for many days through the jungle."

"Sene mingi, many greetings, Bwana Jorgenson," the old man's skin crinkled around his eyes and mouth as he smiled, "Do you remember your old student who you trained to help with the Bible School?"

Melvin's breath caught, "Komobondry?"

"Yes, it has been a long time. We have both changed on the outside, but inside the Spirit is strong like the wings of an eagle is it not?"

As another woman approached, Eleanor heard the woman tell her adult children, "This is the missionary that refused to believe the lie from the enemy that it was too late to pray for me when she came into the hut when I was a student at the Bible School."

Eleanor's mouth dropped open, recalling the vivid image of this woman lying on the floor of the hut dying from a full term miscarriage, with blood oozing from her mouth. Pastor Simona Karada had come in after her and heard the same lie that it was too late to pray for the young woman with eyes set like death. However, they both ignored the voice, sending for help and organizing a day of prayer. Melvin had spent the day driving her to the hospital, where the stillborn child was surgically removed. Now, here she was standing before Eleanor.

"Oh, my eyes, what a glorious thing to see you again," Eleanor rejoiced, "and look at your grown children. What a Savior we serve!"

* * * * *

On the last evening of the conference, a communion service was held in the J.W. Tucker Memorial Church, a benediction for the people as they prepared to make the long, long trek back to their homes. The W-shaped roof that Richard had worked on during his time as a MAPS volunteer stretched over the cavernous auditorium. Once the inside of the church filled, the overflow crowd spilled out onto the surrounding grass, sitting on stumps and stools.

Silent thoughts stirred within the congregation of Jay Tucker's life and his pioneering work in Paulis with his wife Angeline, who returned to Congo after his death. With her passing onto glory in 1976, Angeline and Jay were present with the Lord and death had lost its sting for them.

As the whole congregation joined in one voice of worship to their Lord, with harmonies perfectly blending, the six thousand believers both inside and outside the church sensed a sweet presence of the Holy Spirit.

Nzambe tika ete bato nse
Basanjola nkombo na Yo
Bosanjola na esengo
Boya na Ye kosepla

However, when it came time to serve communion, doubts arose concerning the quantity of the small cups and communion juice. The attendance of such a large group was beyond expectations. Only a limited amount of grape juice had been purchased for the occasion. As the cups were passed out, they returned empty and more juice was poured in the cups. The servers wondered amongst themselves, would there be enough juice? Cups kept returning, and the juice poured until all six thousand had been served. And then the juice ran out.

No one stirred for quite a long time at the conclusion of the service, basking in the presence of the Lord. Finally, Melvin and Eleanor made their way back to their guesthouse. Tomorrow, weather permitting, they and Richard were flying to Andudu for the day.

Chapter Forty-Five

Return to Andudu

W aiting at the small airport in Isiro for the downpour of rain to stop, the passengers waited for their flight to Andudu. Because the plane could only carry five extra people, Edith had graciously given up her seat to Gail. Making small talk, the Jorgenson three, Gail, and Phil sputtered out thoughts bursting with joy. Everyone agreed that the conference was beyond expectations and the experience breathtaking!

Melvin summed up his thoughts, "Viewing the progress of the work under the leadership of national pastors and missionaries was overwhelming!"

"I will have to say, to see those pygmies in the parade was a highlight to me," exclaimed Gail, "And also to see the large numbers that came to the conference. In the early years, we had almost despaired at the slow growth of the church. The missions committee had, in fact, three times considered withdrawing missionaries and turning the work over to neighboring missions."

"Yes, it can be disheartening to be a trailblazer at times," agreed Melvin.

"But the thing of it is, we just need to do our part as unto the Lord," Eleanor stated, "and leave the rest to the Holy Spirit's timing."

Taking off from Isiro, the red-striped MAF Cessna 206 flew over elephant grass. Glancing from the pilot and the panel of navigation instruments to the waving grasslands below, Richard commented above the buzz of the Cessna's engine, "That's some mighty fine hunting country."

Melvin and Phil agreed, while Eleanor and Gail exchanged smiles, knowing how much Richard enjoyed his former hunting days, as a young man.

Soon the grasslands disappeared, swallowed up by solid jungle.

"Just think of the monkeys and chimps down there," Richard mused.

"Yes, and the snakes!" Eleanor laughed, "I'm glad we're flying rather than walking."

The flight, less than one hour, passed quickly with memories dancing in and out between spurts of conversation. Flashes of their final evacuation and the drive out through the valley of the shadow of death flickered of horrific bloodshed and the final lifting of the white pole at the border.

Then suddenly Richard's eyes caught the thread of land carved out of the Ituri Rain Forest, "There's the airstrip for Andudu!"

Melvin and Eleanor gazed at their son's handiwork from his MAPS volunteer trip in 1972. With the help of Bomo, their former cook, a sight was selected on the land that could accommodate a two thousand foot airstrip. After pacing it off, a five-foot swath was cleared down the middle the entire length of the airstrip with plans to clear on either side. In the mornings, Richard would discuss the goals of the day with the work crew before teaching classes in Bangala at the Bible School, and then join in the project in the afternoon.

"I'm glad you put that in Richard," Melvin said as the sliver of cleared land became larger, "It's certainly coming in handy today."

"I can't take the credit," Richard explained, "I simply engineered it, and others finished it. The plane made its final circle of approach and descended for the landing."

Beep-beep-beep-beep sounded the plane's stall warning system just before the plane kissed the runway. After a few bumps on the airstrip, maintained by hoe and machete, the Cessna rolled to a stop and a sea of smiling brown faces closed in shouting, "Mbote Bwana! Mbote Madamo!"

"We've come home," Melvin softly spoke to his wife in his baritone voice.

"Yes, dear, indeed we have," Eleanor stepped down the narrow collapsible ramp from the plane to the red earth of Andudu.

Immediately they were informed that the pastor's mother had passed away thirty minutes ago. Adjusting to the circumstances, the group of five went to pay their respects at the mafika where the body lay on banana leaves. Mourners waved palm fronds over the deceased woman to keep the flies away. A small prayer service spontaneously started with singing.

Then Melvin and Gail each said a few words before ending with prayer. Listening to Aunt Gail, Richard was amazed at her grip of the Lingala language as she stood before the people in her simple pink dress. The elderly woman's long gray hair, twisted into a bun, blew loose strands in the wind as she spoke with passion, reminding the deceased loved ones of the promises of eternal life for the believers of Christ.

Melvin cleared his throat and spoke next, with the sounds of chopping in the background as men built a fresh coffin for the burial. For Eleanor it was like the years melted away, and she thought how odd it seemed to think she hadn't been here since 1964.

Turning from the cluster of mourners, Melvin and Eleanor scanned the grounds of the mission station as they walked along a bare red path toward the church, Bible School, and housing. Tucked beyond those buildings near the overgrown spur road of the Cape-to-Cairo highway, stood the two mission houses.

Sounds of katydid sirens, adults and children, and chickens scurrying out of the way, played on the wind and in their ears. African heat bore down on the vegetation of palm trees and fruit trees hiding winged creatures, critters with tails, and mamba snakes slithering about for a meal.

Many of the people from the station were still in Isiro for the convention. Walking the distance of one hundred kilometers from Isiro to Andudu, they wouldn't be home for several more days.

"Well, this is where I spent most of my time as Director of the Bible School," Melvin walked into the building, still filled with homemade mahogany desks, and black-painted chalkboards.

"Remember, I made the first one and the students made the rest?"

"Yes," Eleanor nodded her head. "What did they say the enrollment was at?"

"It's grown to one hundred and thirty-five students, giving great impetus to the ministry among the churches. Just to think, Eleanor, students of our day have gone on to productive ministries as pastors, teachers, field superintendents, and leaders in other areas of work."

"It's a wonder we got anything done here," reflected Eleanor, "with all the challenges of daily life and health concerns."

"We did get sick a lot, more than I care to remember, but the Lord saw us through."

"Yes, He did."

Walking over to the student housing with Eleanor at his side, Melvin thought of the generous man from Detroit Lakes who had sent a sizeable offering for the construction of living quarters for the students. Not only that, but when in the States on itineration among the churches, they would stop at the man's store that he operated with his wife. Although always busy, the storeowner would invariably take time to visit, or invite the Jorgensons to his home for conversation over a meal. Melvin could see that the man must have assimilated a lot of knowledge of the Congo. He asked many searching questions and drew out many verbal pictures from them.

It was true the forest provided poles and mud for the walls of their homes, and grass and leaves for the roofs, Melvin had explained to the man and his wife. But these houses were temporary at best, and required a lot of time and work, taking away from their studies, to keep livable. It would be no easy task to assemble cement blocks for the walls, and cement and sand for the foundations, and corrugated metal for roofing. But with work, patience, and the funds provided, it was entirely possible. Now, forty years later the block housing stood a little weatherworn, yet still serving the school and students. . .and the Lord.

Melvin reflected on this one example that represented many people who encouraged them as missionaries through the years, and gave to the work of the Lord.

Turning to Eleanor, he brought up the man's name and finished his thoughts with, "What we do for the Lord in this life will last through time and all the ages of eternity. What this man has done in this instance, and many more, known and unknown to us, still remains to bless and to bring glory to God."

Finally, they came to the Griffin house and their house. Richard ran his video camera panning the outside of the red brick houses. The Griffin house was swept and kept clean for visiting missionaries. It stood erect and sturdy. Unfortunately, for their house, the case was not the same.

"Look," Melvin commented, "there's Richard's corner room. Too bad the house is uninhabitable."

Richard continued to pan the camera left toward Aldene's middle room, and then his parents' corner room. For a moment in his mind's eye, Richard could see Bomo in his apron, cooking at the stove on the back kitchen porch.

All of a sudden, Melvin was struck by the green rolling hills of dense vegetation spreading out for miles, "Take a look at that beauty. All that jungle. We are right smack in the middle of the second-largest tropical rain forest in the world."

Then he added, "We had a nice view here didn't we?"

"Yes, beautiful," Richard said softly.

"You would hardly know it's the same place looking down at the spur of the Cape-to-Cairo road. I don't see how a car could even manage to go down there," observed Eleanor.

"Three miles down the road is the Nepoko River," said Melvin, "and now the bridge is out. We used to take that road to Rethy.

Just then, Phil walked into the front of the house across the cement porch, and the rest of the group followed, "I remember a lot of meals in this home together."

"Yes, those were some good times with the kids together." Eleanor glanced at the fireplace and the cement floors she had hired help to wash every day. How many times she had sanitized these floors! The curtains and furniture were gone, but the echoes of the past remained.

Someone stopped by with a chicken in a basket to sell, and Eleanor started bargaining as if she needed it for dinner. Another man strode over to Richard, showing off his knife. As Richard conversed with the national, he spoke like the locals, without a white man's accent. Even his gestures, learned as a young child, were appropriate for the expressive language. Many in the village asked about Aldene, retelling their memories of her as a child on the mission station. Gail wandered by, in-between visiting people, and peered into the house.

Before they knew it, the pilot was announcing that it was almost time to fly back to Isiro, and they began their farewells.

Sitting in the tiny cabin of the plane, Melvin and Eleanor waved to the crowd of Congolese. Brown faces and arms moved with joy of the reunion of their Bwanas and Madamos. For a moment, the talking drums of Congo whispered, *Well done, faithful servants. It wasn't how long you were here. It's that you came.*

Epilogue

The Completion of the Trailblazers

Andudu Mission Station

Having to wait nine more days for an available plane to Nairobi, Melvin and Eleanor, ministered in churches around Isiro, and visited with the many who came to see them at the home where they were staying. One pastor, Kanifi-Bafulu, handed Melvin a letter written in French.

"Brother Jorgenson, could you please ask the Christians to intercede for us in your prayers that God will help us in our Christian life," he asked, "and answer to the different cases given in this letter?"

Melvin glanced over the prayer requests noting that it was not material things the people desired, but strength for the Lord's service as a minister, or in the medical field, or as a mechanic. There were also requests for a physical healing and for grandchildren, *"that God will guard them as they grow, and stay only in His paths."*

On one of their last nights in Isiro, Melvin and Eleanor ate dinner again at Pat Suzanne's home. Seated around the table were the Nancys, and a missionary couple Ernie and Marge, all part of the North Zaire Missionary Field Fellowship. They all had comments to share with the veteran missionary couple, before Melvin and Eleanor left to go back to Minneapolis.

"The trip to Isiro is long, exhausting, and expensive, and we appreciate the time and sacrifices that you made to come."

"It was extra special to have you here, as you were one of the instruments that God used to help the church here become what it is today. Your years of sacrifice and work here have not been, and will never be, forgotten."

"Yes, I think I can speak for all of us here at the table that having our missionary predecessors here was an honor and an encouragement to us, as missionaries, and to the national brethren. Thank you for your years of service here."

* * * * *

Arriving in Minneapolis, Melvin recounted their experiences in a newsletter, while Eleanor went to get four albums worth of pictures developed. Once again sitting at his desk in his office, Melvin reflected for several minutes about their trip back to Congo before typing his thoughts on paper.

We thank the Lord for this opportunity to participate in the greatest gathering the work in upper Zaire has experienced in its long and rewarding history.

After writing several paragraphs about the conference and their day trip to Andudu, tears swelled in his eyes as he wrote the final paragraph:

We cannot forget the courage, dedication, perseverance, and faithfulness of the people of Zaire. Their happy spirit in sacrificial giving of time, effort, even of finance given from their extreme poverty, and life itself, is full proof that God is working among them. Please bring each one, known or unknown to you, before the throne of grace, prayer and supplication, remembering that. . .
   "The earnest heartfelt prayer of a righteous man makes tremendous power available." (Amplified Bible)

On March 11, 1996, Melvin sent a similar report to the director of the Eurasia Field, AG in Springfield with a P.S. that read:

Our plans are to leave for Belgium the 31st of this month. How happy we would be if we could give a similar report for Belgium! That could be a prayer request.

Melvin and Eleanor spent their last eighteen months in Brussels as missionaries, living in the church apartment overlooking Avenue Van Volxem. The quaint one-bedroom apartment included a combination kitchen-living room that held two recliner chairs, and a davenport that made into a bed.

Looking over their downsized living quarters, Melvin quipped, "Here we are above the church entrance again like in Jackson."

"Hopefully nothing will blow up!" added his wife with her charming smile, remembering their first Christmas dinner using a breadboard on their laps for their table, and the Thanksgiving meal of beans and wieners with Greenaways, after the new electric stove exploded from improper voltage connection.

"Well, either way, my little groat, we were, and are together," Melvin returned her smile addressing her as he did in college when they first met, using the term for an English coin. The moment called for a warm embrace and a kiss.

* * * * *

In one of his last newsletters from Brussels, Melvin selected a recent picture to photocopy for the bottom, left-hand corner. He studied the picture of himself and Eleanor walking along a brick sidewalk with an unwrapped fresh loaf of 'la baguette' French bread from the local bakery. He jotted down a caption: Daily bread and the Bread of Life.

Then he turned his attention to the letter:

We have returned recently to Minneapolis from Belgium to spend the Christmas Holidays with our two children, Richard and Aldene, and their families. We feel especially blessed as we remember the many Christmases when great distances have

570

separated us. The goodness of the Lord is sure to be remembered in special seasons such as this.

We also thank the Lord for the many recent victories, which we find among the youth of Belgium. Great hunger has been shown as I ministered to them, giving the Word and sharing my own Pentecostal experiences when I was their age. Many have never heard of, nor experienced Pentecost, and asked me to promise to share more with them, leading them into a Spirit-filled life.

During the Annual Ladies Retreat the end of September, the Holy Spirit ministered in a wonderful and beautiful way. Eleanor wishes to thank the many who responded to her request to pray for the retreat.

May the Joy of Christmas be with you now and through the New Year 1998.

Melvin and Eleanor Jorgenson
Assemblies of God Missionaries Belgium, Europe

In June 1999, Mr. and Mrs. Jorgenson traveled to Springfield, Missouri, to officially retire from the mission field. While at the home office, Melvin, age eighty-one, and Eleanor, age eighty, were presented with a plaque of recognition from the Assemblies of God that read:

Presented to MELVIN and ELEANOR JORGENSON

You have blazed a trail for our mission in Europe. We thank God and honor you for your 50 years of Foreign Mission Ministry Revelations 14:12 (NIV)

Division of Foreign Missions Europe Regional Office June 1999

Here is the patience of the saints: here are they that keep the commandments of God, and the faith of Jesus. (Rev. 14:12 KJV)

Bibliography for Jorgenson Project 2011-2013

E very care has been taken to give credit where credit is due, and to seek out permission when necessary. However, if there have been unintentional mistakes or failures concerning copyright holders, we apologize and will, if informed, strive to make corrections in any future edition. Compiled by Kim Halberg.

Part One: The Call

From North Central:

*Seventh Annual CATALOG of the North Central Bible Institute 1936-1937,*Published by NCBI and Minneapolis Gospel Tabernacle, 3015 Thirteenth Avenue South, Minneapolis, Minnesota, 1937. (An office worker, during my visit to North Central in 2011, made me a copy of the entire catalog, which proved to be an important source for understanding the Bible college at that time giving me a slice of their life and interesting details such as cost of tuition and the dress code. I also listened to a taped interview from 2-28-02.)

The ARCHIVE, Volume V, 1937 published by the Senior Class of North Central bible Institute, Minneapolis, Minnesota, 1937.

The ARCHIVE, Volume VI, 1938 published by the Senior Class of North Central Bible Institute, Minneapolis, Minnesota, 1938.

The ARCHIVE, Volume Seven, 1939 published by the Student Body of NCBI, NCBC. North Central Bible Institute and North Central Bible College, 901 Elliot Avenue South, Minneapolis, Minnesota, 1939.

My heartfelt appreciation to the Library at North Central. I enjoyed the ARCHIVEs 1937-1938 so much, and found them to be an invaluable source and "time machine" for the late 1930's. Do I really have to return them?

Other sources and books (thanks to my favorite Rum River Library in Anoka, MN.)

Children's History of the 20th Century, written by Simon Adams, Robin Cross, Ann Kramer, Hayden Middleton, Sally Tagholm, A DK Publishing Book, www.dk.com, 95 Madison Avenue, New York, NY 10016 1999

Allen, Tony, *the Cause of World War I (20th Century Perspectives)*. Heinemann Library, Chicago IL, 2003.

Burgan, Michael, *South Dakota (America the Beautiful. Third Series)*. Children's Press, Scholastic Inc., 557 Broadway, New York, NY 10012, 2010.

Corey, Melinda, *Chronology of 20th-Century America (Decades of American History)*. Facts On File, Inc., 132 West 31st Street, New York, NY 10001, 2006.

Heinrichs, Ann, *The Dust Bowl (We the People)*. Compass Point Books, 3109 West 50th Street, #115, Minneapolis, MN 55410, 2005.

Heinrichs, Ann, *Minnesota (America the Beautiful. Third Series)*. Children's Press, Scholastic Inc., 557 Broadway, New York, NY 10012, 2009.

Stone, Tanya Lee, *The Progressive Era and World War I (The Making of America)*. RSVP, Raintree Steck-Vaugn Publishers, P.O. Box 26015, Austin, TX 78755, 2001.

125 Years, *STAR TRIBUNE: 125 years of history in the making*. Joel R. Kramer, Publisher and President Star Tribune, Cowels Media Company, 1992.

Millet, Larry, *Twin Cities, Then and Now*. Minnesota Historical Press, 345 Kellogg Blvd., St. Paul, MN 55102, 1996.

Ziebarth, Marilyn and Ominsky, Alan, *Fort Snelling: Anchor Post of the Northwest*. Minnesota Historical Society, 1970.

Dowswell, Paul, *The Causes of World War II* (20th Century Perspectives). Heinemann Libray, Chicago IL, 2003.

Saint Anthony Falls Rediscovered. Minneapolis Riverfront Development Board, Editor, Berman, James, 1980.

Wills, Charles A., *Decades of American History: America in the 1940's*, Stonesong Press, LLC, 132 West 31st Street, New York, NY 10001, 2006.

Callan, Jim, *Decades of American History: America in the 1930's*, Stonesong Press, LLC, 132 31st Street, New York, NY 10001, 2005.

Jackson Chapter:hhttp://www.jacksonmn.com/historical. htmJackson County Pilot

Crookston Chapters:Polk County Historical Society, box 214, Crookston, MN 56716Research: Doris and Gerald Amiot Crookston Chamber of Commerce and Visitors Bureauwebsite: www.visitcrookston.com

Detroit Lakes Chapters:Gayle Lambertson Detert and familyBecker County Historical Society and city webpages http://www.visitdetroitlakes.com/relocation/historyhttp://cityweb.lakesnet.net/government/mayor/http://www.dnr.state.mn.us/lakefind/showreport.html?downum=03038100http://www.fws.gov/Midwest/detroitlakes/Environment.html

Sheboygan Chapter:Historical Research Center Sheboygan Countyhttp://www.ci.sheboygan.wi.us/historystatistics/city-maps/Kohler webpage

Minneapolis Historical, Park, and City websitesMinneapolis Park and Recreation Board, 2008, Compiled and written by David C. Smith

Lemon and Thunder Hawk Chapters:http://lemmonsd. com/history.html (petrefied.html)

Wikipedia.org for starting points of cities, history, and products

Part Two: The Course

The Jorgenson family letters were kept as close as possible to their original content and provided crucial timeline information. This treasure trove is primarily credited to Eleanor's mother, Hazel Groat for preserving them throughout the years. Without them, the vibrant soul of this story would have been diminished.

Belgium & Luxembourg (Eyewitness Travel) Ghose, Anna, managing editor. DK Publishing, 375 Hudson Street, New York, 2009, 2011.

Burgen, Michael, *Belgium,* (*Enchantment of the World. Second Series*). Children's Press, 2000.

Davis, Rebecca, *The Good News Must Go Out: Stories of God at Work in the Central Africa Republic,* (*Hidden Heroes*). Christian Focus Publication, Great Briton, 2011.

Cochrane-MacLennan, Edith M., *Who, Me Lord?.* Printed in the United States of America, 1995. Permission of direct quotations from page 97 granted by Edith Cochrane.

Edgerton, Robert B., *The Troubled Heart of Africa: A History of the Congo.* St. Martin's Press, 175 Fifth Avenue, New York, 2002.

Feinstein, Stephen, *The 1960's: From the Vietnam War to Flower Power (Decades of the 20th Century)*. Enslow Publishers, Inc., 2000.

Hochschild, Adam, *King Leopold's Ghost: A Story of Greed, Terror, and Heroism in Colonial Africa*. Houghton Mifflin Company, New York, 1998.

Joris, Lieve, translated by Stacey Knecht, *Back to the Congo*. Macmillan, New York, 1987, trans. 1992.

Kallen, Stuart A., book editor, *The 1950's (America's Decades)*. Greenhaven Press, Inc., San Diego, 2000.

Kingsolver, Barbara, *The Poisonwood Bible*. HarperCollins Publishers, Inc., New York, 1998

Tucker, Angeline, *"He is in Heaven"*. McGraw-Hill, Inc., 1965.

Willis, Terri, *Democratic Republic of the Congo (Enchantment of the World)*. Children's Press, Scholastic Inc., 2004.

Wikipedia.org for starting points of cities, countries, history, and products.

Part Three: The Completion

Jorgenson family letters, Eleanor's *Visitors Book*, Melvin and Eleanor Jorgenson Newsletters, and Melvin's reports were of critical importance to Part Three: The Completion.

Mark Elliot, *Belgium & Luxembourg* (Lonely Planet). Australia (Head Office) Locked Bag 1, Footscray, Victoria 3011, 2010

Belgium & Luxembourg (Eyewitness Travel). Ghose, Anna, managing editor. DK Publishing, 375 Hudson Street, New York, 2009, 2011.

Burgen, Michael, *Belgium, (Enchantment of the World. Second Series)*. Children's Press, 2000.

Blashfield, Jean, *Germany, (Enchantment of the World. Second Series)*. Children's Press, 2003.

Camardella, Michele L., *America in the 1980's (Decades of American History)*. Stonesong Press, LLC, Facts On File, Inc., 132 West 31st Street, New York, 2006.

Continental Bible College Yearbooks 1970-1975. 1, Avenue des Erables, 1640, Rhode-Saint-Genese, Bruxelles, Belgique. Melvin Jorgenson, faculty adviser/1970-1973 issues, Robert Carlson, faculty advisor/editor 1974 issue, Donald Smeeton 1975 issue.

Introduction to the History of Christianity. Fortress Press, Minneapolis, 1995.

Mason, Anthony, *Top 10 of Brussels, Bruges, Antwerp & Ghent (Eyewitness Travel)*. DK Publishing, 375 Hudson Street, New York, 2009, 2012.

Ochoa, George, *America in the 1990's (Decades of American History)*. Stonesong Press, LLC, Facts On File, Inc., 132 West 31st Street, New York, 2006.

Puissance, Revue bimestrielle, No 1-1993, Janvier-fevrier. Editor, Bernard Van Lesberghe, Rue des Forges 147, 1480 Clabecq, Belgigue (Belgium, Europe).

Showker, Kay, *Caribbean Ports of Call: Eastern and Southern Regions.* The Globe Pequot Press, Guilford, CT, 2004.

Wilkerson, David, *Beyond the Cross & the Switchblade.* Chosen Books, Inc., distributed by Fleming H. Revell Company, Old Tappon, New Jersey, 1974.

Wilkerson, David, with Sherrill, Elizabeth and John, *The Cross & the Switchblade (Teen Challenge 50th Anniversary Edition).* The Berkley Publishing Group, Penguin Group, 375 Hudson Street, New York, 1962 by David Wilkerson, special sales edition 2008.

Willis, Terri, *Democratic Republic of the Congo (Enchantment of the World).* Children's Press, Scholastic Inc., 2004.

Wikipedia.org for starting points of cities, countries, history, and products.

Winters, Gail, newsletter about trip to Congo/Zaire 75th Anniversary Celebration, 1996.

www.worldchallenge.org/ David Wilkerson-World Challenge, http://www.worldchallenge.org/about_david_wilkerson